# MASCULINITY

## JUDITH HALBERSTAM

Duke University Press   Durham and London   1998

© 1998 Duke University Press

All rights reserved   Printed in the United States

of America on acid-free paper ∞

Designed by Amy Ruth Buchanan

Frontispiece: Sadie Lee, *Raging Bull* (1994)

Typeset in Scala by Tseng Information Systems, Inc.

Library of Congress Cataloging-in-Publication Data

appear on the last printed page of this book.

Seventh printing, 2006

FOR GAYATRI

# CONTENTS

# ILLUSTRATIONS

There is something all too obvious about the concept "female masculinity." When people have asked me over the last few years what I am working on, I have explained quickly to them the concept of this book. Usually I can do it in one or two sentences. I will say, perhaps, "I am writing about women who feel themselves to be more masculine than feminine, and I am trying to explain why, as a culture, we seem to take so little interest in female masculinity and yet pay a considerable amount of attention to male femininity." People tend to nod and say, "Yes, of course, female masculinity," as if this is a concept they have grown up with and use every day. In actual fact, there is remarkably little written about masculinity in women, and this culture generally evinces considerable anxiety about even the prospect of manly women. I hope that this book opens discussion on masculinity for women in such a way that masculine girls and women do not have to wear their masculinity as a stigma but can infuse it with a sense of pride and indeed power. Already, lesbian counterproductions of female masculinity, from the spectacle of dykes on bikes to the outrageous performances of the drag king, are certainly taking aim at the cultural mandates against masculinity in women. This book, I hope, will eventually form just one part of a cultural onslaught on the privileged reservation of masculinity for men.

I was a masculine girl, and I am a masculine woman. For much of my life, my masculinity has been rendered shameful by public responses to my gender ambiguity. However, in the last ten years, I have been able to turn stigma into strength. This book is a result of a lengthy process of both self-examination and discussion with others. Many people have contributed both emotionally and intellectually to this book. My colleagues at UC San Diego have been supportive and encouraging of this project, and because the Literature Department at UCSD, unlike so many traditional English programs, has a serious commitment to cultural studies and interdisciplinary work, I have felt encouraged to take this project in the many nonliterary directions that it has needed to go. I have been influenced and enriched by reading the work of my UCSD colleagues Rosemary Marangoly George, Page Dubois, Michael Davidson, Shelley Streeby, Mike Murashige, Rosaura Sanchez, Ann DuCille, George Lipsitz, Steven Epstein, and Ramon Gutierrez, and especially Lisa Lowe. I benefited during the writing of this book from several UC Senate travel and research grants. I also held a postdoctoral fellowship at NYU while finishing research for *Female Masculinity*. The primary benefit of this postdoc was that it put me in conversation with the amazing group of New York–based queer scholars, including José Muñoz, Philip Brian Harper, Chris Straayer, Jill Dolan, Peggy Phelan, and others. I feel my work has really improved as a result of such close contact with other queer academics. Meeting and working with Lisa Duggan at NYU was an important influence on the course of this book. Her work on femme subjectivities and her historical research on turn-of-the-century lesbian subjectivities has greatly affected my thinking on lesbian genders.

I met another person while in New York who has become indispensable to this project and my own intellectual development: Esther Newton. In many ways, Esther Newton is my scholarly role model; she has been a mentor and a friend, and she has helped to shape this book with her many insightful and tough readings of it. I could not have foreseen the importance of a dialogue with a butch scholar from a different generation, and I have realized while writing this book that my work has been influenced by her thinking and her formulations throughout. I have also been able to learn other less tangible things from Esther about how to be in the world, about inhabiting female masculinity and about shaping an intellectual project around issues of great personal importance. I believe Esther's work provides an exemplary model of how to create subtle interactions between the personal and the theoretical; indeed, her work skillfully prevents the weight of the personal from crashing through finely meshed theoretical webs but also prevents theoretical abstractions from obscuring completely the coarse lines of personal experience. My debt to Esther, fittingly, is both personal and theoretical.

I also benefited from an extremely insightful reading of the book by Valerie Traub, whose own work is a model of historically based, careful, and rigorous scholarship. Laura Doan's research in progress on British lesbian culture in the 1920s has been extremely provocative for my work on Radclyffe Hall, and I eagerly await Doan's book. Others who have left their stamp on my thinking include transgender theorists Jacob Hale, Jay Prosser, Del Grace, and Jordy Jones. Jacob has been a demanding interlocuter, and I have learned much from our various collaborations; although Jay and I disagree over many issues within what can now be called transgender politics, I feel the greatest admiration for his work and feel fortunate to be in dialogue with him. Jordy has inspired me with his strange and wonderful artwork, and Del has proven to be a steadfast friend and continues to amaze me with his breathtaking portraits of queer lives and bodies. I have been helped and supported by the work and advice of many friends and colleagues: Henry Abelove, Juanita Diaz, Deb Amory, Ed Cohen, Barbara Cruikshank, Ann Cvetkovich, Stacey Foiles, Heather Findlay, Beth Freeman, Jane Gallop, Laura Green, Ira Livingston, David Lloyd, Martin Manalansan, Sally Munt, Geeta Patel, Saeed Rahman, Chandan Reddy, Javid Sayed, Nayan Shah, Cherry Smyth, Patti White, Kath Weston. I owe much gratitude to the drag kings in New York, who are an inspiration to me, not to mention a source of many evenings of entertainment: Mo B. Dick (Maureen Fisher), Dred (Mildred Gerestant), Shon (Shavell Lashon Sherman), Lizerace (Liz Carthaus), and especially Murray Hill (Betsey Gallagher). I would like to thank Ken Wissoker at Duke University Press for his generosity and his belief in this project and Richard Morrison for encouraging me at all the right moments and for carefully guiding the book into print.

I want to thank my pal Jenni Olson for being a great butch buddy over the past decade and for helping me learn to be more open-minded and generous in my judgments and speculations not only on gender but also on life in general. My family has also been very supportive of this project, and I must especially thank my younger sister Lucy for her affection and love in general, but also for always showing interest in, and enthusiasm for, my queer work. And, finally, I thank Gayatri Gopinath for her brilliant intellectual insights, which have completely changed this book in form and content. This book is dedicated to Gayatri, and I want to thank her here for bringing beauty and wisdom into my life.

Parts of some chapters of *Female Masculinity* were published previously in different versions. I thank those publishers for permission to reprint. Parts of chapter 1 appeared as "Techno-Homo: On Bathrooms, Butches, and Sex with Furniture," in *Processed Lives: Gender and Technology in Everyday Life*, edited by Jennifer Terry and Melodie Calvert (London: Routledge, 1997), 183–94, and as "Bathrooms, Butches, and the Aesthetics of Female Masculinity," in *Rrose Is a Rrose Is a Rrose: Gender Performance in Photography*," edited by Jennifer Blessing (New York: Guggenheim Museum Publications, 1997), 176–89. Part of chapter 4 appeared as "Lesbian Masculinity, or Even Stone Butches Get the Blues," in a special issue, "Queer Acts," edited by José Muñoz and Amanda Barrett, in *Women and Performance* 8, no. 2 (1996): 61–74, and another small section of this chapter appeared in *The Lesbian and Gay Studies Textbook*, edited by Sally Munt and Andy Metcalf (London: Cassell, 1997). A shorter version of chapter 5 appears in a special issue, "The Transgender Issue," edited by Susan Stryker, in *GLQ* 4, no. 2 (spring 1998). A small section of chapter 6 also appears in "Mackdaddy, Superfly, Rapper: Gender, Race, and Masculinity in the Drag King Scene," in a special issue, "Queer Transexions of Race, Nation, and Gender," edited by Phillip Brian Harper, Ann McClintock, José Esteban Muñoz, and Trish Rosen, in *Social Text* 15, nos. 3–4 (fall/winter 1997).

*What's the use of being a little boy if you are going to grow up to be a man?*

— *Gertrude Stein,* Everybody's Autobiography *(1937)*

# 1 AN INTRODUCTION TO FEMALE MASCULINITY

*Masculinity without Men*

## The Real Thing

What is "masculinity"? This has been probably the most common question that I have faced over the past five years while writing on the topic of female masculinity. If masculinity is not the social and cultural and indeed political expression of maleness, then what is it? I do not claim to have any definitive answer to this question, but I do have a few proposals about why masculinity must not and cannot and should not reduce down to the male body and its effects. I also venture to assert that although we seem to have a difficult time defining masculinity, as a society we have little trouble in recognizing it, and indeed we spend massive amounts of time and money ratifying and supporting the versions of masculinity that we enjoy and trust; many of these "heroic masculinities" depend absolutely on the subordination of alternative masculinities. I claim in this book that far from being an imitation of maleness, female masculinity actually affords us a glimpse of how masculinity is constructed as masculinity. In other words, female masculinities are framed as the rejected scraps of dominant masculinity in order that male masculinity may appear to be the real thing.

But what we understand as heroic masculinity has been produced by and across both male and female bodies.

This opening chapter does not simply offer a conventional theoretical introduction to the enterprise of conceptualizing masculinity without men; rather, it attempts to compile the myths and fantasies about masculinity that have ensured that masculinity and maleness are profoundly difficult to pry apart. I then offer, by way of a preliminary attempt to reimagine masculinity, numerous examples of alternative masculinities in fiction, film, and lived experience. These examples are mostly queer and female, and they show clearly how important it is to recognize alternative masculinities when and where they emerge. Throughout this introduction, I detail the many ways in which female masculinity has been blatantly ignored both in the culture at large and within academic studies of masculinity. This widespread indifference to female masculinity, I suggest, has clearly ideological motivations and has sustained the complex social structures that wed masculinity to maleness and to power and domination. I firmly believe that a sustained examination of female masculinity can make crucial interventions within gender studies, cultural studies, queer studies, and mainstream discussions of gender in general.

Masculinity in this society inevitably conjures up notions of power and legitimacy and privilege; it often symbolically refers to the power of the state and to uneven distributions of wealth. Masculinity seems to extend outward into patriarchy and inward into the family; masculinity represents the power of inheritance, the consequences of the traffic in women, and the promise of social privilege. But, obviously, many other lines of identification traverse the terrain of masculinity, dividing its power into complicated differentials of class, race, sexuality, and gender. If what we call "dominant masculinity" appears to be a naturalized relation between maleness and power, then it makes little sense to examine men for the contours of that masculinity's social construction. Masculinity, this book will claim, becomes legible as masculinity where and when it leaves the white male middle-class body. Arguments about excessive masculinity tend to focus on black bodies (male and female), latino/a bodies, or working-class bodies, and insufficient masculinity is all too often figured by Asian bodies or upper-class bodies; these stereotypical constructions of variable masculinity mark the process by which masculinity becomes dominant in the sphere of white middle-class maleness. But all too many studies that currently attempt to account for the power of white masculinity recenter this white male body by concentrating all their analytical efforts on detailing the forms and expressions of white male dominance. Numerous studies of Elvis, white male youth, white male feminism, men and marriage, and domestications of maleness amass information about a subject whom we know intimately and ad nauseam. This study professes a degree of indifference to the whiteness of the male and the masculinity of the white male and the project of naming his power: male masculinity figures in my project as a hermeneutic, and as a counterexample to the kinds of masculinity that seem most informative about gender relations and most generative of social change. This book seeks Elvis only in the female Elvis impersonator Elvis Herselvis; it searches for the political contours of masculine privilege not in men but in the lives of aristocratic European cross-dressing women in the 1920s; it describes the details of masculine difference by comparing not men and women but butch lesbians and female-to-male transsexuals; it examines masculinity's iconicity not in the male matinee idol but in a history of butches in cinema; it finds, ultimately, that the shapes and forms of modern masculinity are best showcased within female masculinity.

How else to begin a book on female masculinity but by deposing one of the most persistent of male heroes: Bond, James Bond. To illustrate my point that modern masculinity is most easily recognized as female masculinity, consider the James Bond action film, in which male masculinity very often appears as only a shadow of a more powerful and convincing alternative masculinity. In *Goldeneye* (1995), for example, Bond battles the usual array of bad guys: Commies, Nazis, mercenaries, and a superaggressive violent femme type. He puts on his usual performance of debonair action adventure hero, and he has his usual supply of gadgetry to aid him—a retractable belt, a bomb disguised as a pen, a laser weapon watch, and so on. But there's something curiously lacking in *Goldeneye*, namely, credible masculine power. Bond's boss, M, is a noticeably butch older woman who calls Bond a dinosaur and chastises him for being a misogynist and a sexist. His secretary, Miss Moneypenny, accuses him of sexual harassment, his male buddy betrays him and calls him a dupe, and ultimately women seem not to go for his charms—bad suits and lots of sexual innuendo—which seem as old and as ineffective as his gadgets.

Masculinity, in this rather actionless film, is primarily prosthetic and, in this and countless other action films, has little if anything to do with biological maleness and signifies more often as a technical special effect. In *Goldeneye* it is M who most convincingly performs masculinity, and she does so partly by exposing the sham of Bond's own performance. It is M who convinces us that sexism and misogyny are not necessarily part and parcel of masculinity, even though historically it has become difficult, if not impossible, to untangle masculinity from the oppression of women. The action adventure hero should embody an extreme version of normative masculinity, but instead we find that excessive masculinity turns into a parody or exposure of the norm. Because masculinity tends to manifest as natural gender itself, the action flick, with its emphases on prosthetic extension, actually undermines the heterosexuality of the hero even as it extends his masculinity. So, in *Goldeneye,* for example, Bond's masculinity is linked not only to a profoundly unnatural form of masculine embodiment but also to gay masculinities. In the scene in which Bond goes to pick up his newest set of gadgets, a campy and almost queeny science nerd gives Bond his brand-new accessories and demonstrates each one with great enthusiasm. It is no accident that the science nerd is called Agent Q. We might read Agent Q as a perfect model of the interpenetration of queer and dominant regimes—Q is precisely an agent, a queer subject who exposes the workings of dominant heterosexual masculinity. The gay masculinity of Agent Q and the female masculinity of M provide a remarkable representation of the absolute dependence of dominant masculinities on minority masculinities.

When you take his toys away, Bond has very little propping up his performance of masculinity. Without the slick suit, the half smile, the cigarette lighter that transforms into a laser gun, our James is a hero without the action or the adventure. The masculinity of the white male, what we might call "epic masculinity," depends absolutely, as any Bond flick demonstrates, on a vast subterranean network of secret government groups, well-funded scientists, the army, and an endless supply of both beautiful bad babes and beautiful good babes, and finally it relies heavily on an immediately recognizable "bad guy." The "bad guy" is a standard generic feature of epic masculinity narratives: think only of *Paradise Lost* and its eschatological separation between God and Devil; Satan, if you like, is the original bad guy. Which is not to say that the bad guy's masculinity bars him from the rewards of male privilege—on the contrary, bad guys may also look like winners, but they just tend to die more quickly. Indeed, there is currently a line of clothing called Bad Boy that revels in the particular power of the bad guy and reveals how quickly transgression adds up to nothing more than consumerism in the sphere of the white male. Another line of clothing that indulges in the consumer potential of male rebellion is No Fear gear. This label features advertisements with skydiving, surfing, car-racing men who show their manliness by wearing the No Fear logo and practicing death-defying stunts in their leisure time. To test how domesticated this label actually is, we have only to imagine what No Fear might mean for women. It might mean learning how to shoot a gun or working out or taking up a martial art, but it would hardly translate into skydiving. Obviously, then, No Fear is a luxury and can in no way be equated with any form of social rebellion.

There is also a long literary and cinematic history that celebrates the rebellion of the male. If James Stewart, Gregory Peck, and Fred Astaire represent a few faces of good-guy appeal, James Dean, Marlon Brando, and Robert De Niro represent the bad-guy appeal, and really it becomes quite hard to separate one group from the other. Obviously, bad-boy representations in the 1950s captured something of a white working-class rebellion against middle-class society and against particular forms of domestication, but today's rebel without a cause is tomorrow's investment banker, and male rebellion tends toward respectability as the rewards for conformity quickly come to outweigh the rewards for social rebellion. To paraphrase Gertrude Stein, what's the point of being a rebel boy if you are going to grow up to be a man? Obviously, where and when rebellion ceases to be white middle-class male rebellion (individualized and localized within the lone male or even generalized into the boy gang) and becomes class rebellion or race rebellion, a very different threat emerges.

## Tomboys

What happens when boy rebellion is located not in the testosterone-induced pout of the hooligan but in the sneer of the tomboy? Tomboyism generally describes an extended childhood period of female masculinity. If we are to believe general accounts of childhood behavior, tomboyism is quite common for girls and does not generally give rise to parental fears. Because comparable cross-identification behaviors in boys do often give rise to quite hysterical responses, we tend to believe that female gender deviance is much more tolerated than male gender deviance.[1] I am not sure that tolerance in such matters can be measured or at any rate that responses to childhood gender behaviors necessarily tell us anything concrete about the permitted parameters of adult male and female gender deviance. Tomboyism tends to be associated with a "natural" desire for the greater freedoms and mobilities enjoyed by boys. Very often it is read as a sign of independence and self-motivation, and tomboyism may even be encouraged to the extent that it remains comfortably linked to a stable sense of a girl identity. Tomboyism is punished, however, when it appears to be the sign of extreme male identification (taking a boy's name or refusing girl clothing of any type) and when it threatens to extend beyond childhood and into adolescence.[2] Teenage tomboyism presents a problem and tends to be subject to the most severe efforts to reorient. We could say that tomboyism is tolerated as long as the child remains prepubescent; as soon as puberty begins, however, the full force of gender conformity descends on the girl. Gender conformity is pressed onto all girls, not just tomboys, and this is where it becomes hard to uphold the notion that male femininity presents a greater threat to social and familial stability than female masculinity. Female adolescence represents the crisis of coming of age as a girl in a male-dominated society. If adolescence for boys represents a rite of passage (much celebrated in Western literature in the form of the bildungsroman), and an ascension to some version (however attenuated) of social power, for girls, adolescence is a lesson in restraint, punishment, and repression. It is in the context of female adolescence that the tomboy instincts of millions of girls are remodeled into compliant forms of femininity.

That any girls do emerge at the end of adolescence as masculine women is quite amazing. The growing visibility and indeed respectability of lesbian communities to some degree facilitate the emergence of masculine young women. But as even a cursory survey of popular cinema confirms, the image of the tomboy can be tolerated only within a narrative of blossoming womanhood; within such a narrative, tomboyism represents a resistance to adulthood itself rather than to adult femininity. In both the novel and film versions of the classic tomboy narrative *The Member of the Wedding*, by Carson McCullers, tomboy Frankie Addams fights a losing battle against womanhood, and the text locates womanhood or femininity as a crisis of representation that confronts the heroine with unacceptable life options. As her brother's wedding approaches, Frankie Addams pronounces herself mired in a realm of unbelonging, outside the symbolic partnership of the wedding but also alienated from belonging in almost every category that might describe her. McCullers writes: "It happened that green and crazy summer when Frankie was twelve years old. This was the summer when for a long time she had not been a member. She belonged to no club and

Figure 1. "She belonged to no club and was a member of nothing in the world." Julie Harris as Frankie Addams and Ethel Waters as Berenice in *The Member of the Wedding* (1953), directed by Fred Zinneman.

was a member of nothing in the world. Frankie was an unjoined person who hung around in doorways, and she was afraid."[3] McCullers positions Frankie on the verge of adolescence ("when Frankie was twelve years old") and in the midst of an enduring state of being "unjoined": "She belonged to no club and was a member of nothing in the world." While childhood in general may qualify as a period of "unbelonging," for the boyish girl arriving on the doorstep of womanhood, her status as "unjoined" marks her out for all manner of social violence and opprobrium. As she dawdles in the last light of childhood, Frankie Addams has become a tomboy who "hung around in doorways, and she was afraid."

As a genre, the tomboy film, as I show in chapter 6, "Looking Butch," suggests that the categories available to women for racial, gendered, and sexual identification are simply inadequate. In her novel, McCullers shows this inadequacy to be a direct result of the tyranny of language—a structure that fixes people and things in place artificially but securely. Frankie tries to change her identity by changing her name: "Why is it against the law to change your name?" she asks Berenice (107). Berenice answers: "Because things accumulate around your name," and she stresses that without names, confusion would reign and "the whole world would go crazy." But Berenice also acknowledges that the fixity conferred by names also traps people into many different identities, racial as well as gendered: "We all of us somehow caught. . . . And maybe we wants to widen and bust free. But no matter what we do we still caught" (113). Frankie thinks that naming represents the power of definition, and name changing confers the power to reimagine identity, place, relation, and even gender. "I wonder if it is against the law to change your name," says Frankie, "Or add to it. . . . Well I don't care. . . . F. Jasmine Addams" (15).

Psychoanalysis posits a crucial relationship between language and desire such that language structures desire and expresses therefore both the fullness and the futility of human desire—full because we always desire, futile because we are never satisfied. Frankie in particular understands desire and sexuality to be the most regimented forms of social conformity—we are supposed to desire only certain people and only in certain ways, but her desire does not work that way, and she finds herself torn between longing and belonging. Because she does not desire in conventional ways, Frankie seeks to avoid desire altogether. Her struggle with language, her attempts to remake herself through naming and remake the world with a new order of being, are ultimately heroic, but unsuccessful. McCullers's pessimism has to do with a sense of the overwhelming "order of things," an order that cannot be affected by the individual, and works through things as basic as language, and forces nonmembers into memberships they cannot fulfill.

My book refuses the futility long associated with the tomboy narrative and instead seizes on the opportunity to recognize and ratify differently gendered bodies and subjectivities. Moving from the nineteenth century to the present and examining diaries, court cases, novels, letters, films, performances, events, critical essays, videos, news items, and testimonies, this book argues for the production of new taxonomies, what Eve K. Sedgwick humorously called "nonce taxonomies" in *Epistemology of the Closet*, classifications of desire, physicality, and subjectivity that attempt to intervene in hegemonic processes of naming and defining. Nonce taxonomies are categories that we use daily to make sense of our worlds but that work so well that we actually fail to recognize them. In this book, I attempt to bring some of the nonce taxonomies of female masculinity into view, and I detail the histories of the suppression of these categories. Here, and in the rest of the book, I am using the topic of female masculinity to explore a queer subject position that can successfully challenge hegemonic models of gender conformity. Female masculinity is a particularly fruitful site of investigation because it has been vilified by heterosexist and feminist/womanist programs alike; unlike male femininity, which fulfills a kind of ritual function in male homosocial cultures, female masculinity is generally received by hetero- and homo-normative cultures as a pathological sign of misidentification and maladjustment, as a longing to be and to have a power that is always just out of reach. Within a lesbian context, female masculinity has been situated as the place where patriarchy goes to work on the female psyche and reproduces misogyny within femaleness. There have been to date remarkably few studies or theories about the inevitable effects of a fully articulated female masculinity on a seemingly fortified male masculinity. Sometimes female masculinity coincides with the excesses of male supremacy, and sometimes it codifies a unique form of social rebellion; often female masculinity is the sign of sexual alterity, but occasionally it marks heterosexual variation; sometimes female masculinity marks the place of pathology, and every now and then it represents the healthful alternative to what are considered the histrionics of conventional femininities.

I want to carefully produce a model of female masculinity that remarks on its multiple forms but also calls for new and self-conscious affirmations of different gender taxonomies. Such affirmations begin not by subverting masculine power or taking up a position against masculine power but by turning a blind eye to conventional masculinities and refusing to engage. Frankie Addams, for example, constitutes her rebellion not in opposition to the law but through indifference to the law: she recognizes that it may be against the law to change one's name or add to it, but she also has a simple response to such illegal activity: "Well, I don't care." I am not suggesting in this book that we follow the futile path of what Foucault calls "saying no to power," but I am asserting that power may inhere within different forms of refusal: "Well, I don't care."

## Queer Methodologies

This book deploys numerous methodologies in order to pursue the multiple forms of gender variance presented within female masculinity. On account of the interdisciplinary nature of my project, I have had to craft a methodology out of available disciplinary methods. Deploying what I would call a "queer methodology," I have used some combination of textual criticism, ethnography, historical survey, archival research, and the production of taxonomies. I call this methodology "queer" because it attempts to remain supple enough to respond to the various locations of information on female masculinity and betrays a certain disloyalty to conventional disciplinary methods. Obviously, I could have produced methodological consistency by confining myself to literary texts, but the queer methodology used here, then, typifies just one of the forms of refusal that I discussed in my last section.

Although some of the most informative work on alternative sexual communities has come in the form of ethnography, and although autobiographies and narrative histories tend to be the material that we turn to for information on sexual identities, there is nonetheless some disagreement among queer scholars about how we should collect and interpret such information on sexual identity. Indeed, some of the most bitter and long-lasting disagreements within queer studies have been about disciplinarity and methodology. Whereas some cultural studies proponents have argued that social science methods of collecting, collating, and presenting sexual data through surveys and other methods of social research tend to rediscover the sexual systems they already know rather than finding out about those they do not, social science proponents argue that cultural studies scholars do not pay enough attention to the material realities of queer life. And while there has been plenty of discussion in the academy about the need for interdisciplinary work, there has been far less support for such work in the university at large. A project such as this one, therefore, risks drawing criticism from historians for not providing a proper history, from literary critics for not focusing on literary texts, and from social scientists for not deploying the traditional tools of social science research. While I take full responsibility for all the errors I may make in my attempts to produce readings and histories and ethnography, I also recognize that this book exemplifies the problem confronted by queer studies itself: How do we forge queer methodologies while as scholars we reside in traditional departments?

At least one method of sex research that I reject in creating a queer methodology is the traditional social science project of surveying people and expecting to squeeze truth from raw data. In a review essay in the *New York Review of Books* about a series of new sex surveys, R. C. Lewontin comments on the difficulty associated with this social science approach to sexuality: "Given the social circumstances of sexual activity, there seems no way to find out what people do 'in the bedroom' except to ask them. But the answers they give cannot be put to the test of incredulity."[4] Lewontin suggests that people tend not to be truthful when it comes to reporting on their own sexual behavior (men exaggerate and women downplay, for example), and there are no ways to make allowances for personal distortion within social science methods. Furthermore, social scientists seem not to be concerned with the high levels of untruth in relation to sexuality but spend all their energy on solving methodological problems. Ultimately, Lewontin claims—and I think he has a point—social science surveys are "demonstrations of what their planners already believed they knew to be true" (25). At a time when the humanities are under severe scrutiny and attack, it is important to point to the reliance of social science methods on strategies such as narrative analysis, interpretation, and speculation. As Lewontin says in his conclusion: "How then can there be a social science? The answer surely is to be less ambitious and stop trying to make sociology into a natural science although it is, indeed, the study of natural objects" (29). This is not to say, however, that traditional social science research methods such as questionnaires are never appropriate. Indeed, there are certain questions that can be answered only by survey methods in the realm of sexuality (i.e., how many lesbians are using dental dams? What age-groups or social classes do these lesbians belong to?), but all too often surveys are used to try to gather far less factual information, and all subtlety tends to be lost.[5]

There is some irony in the apparent impossibility of applying traditional social science methods to the study of sex because as queer sociologists are all too quick to point out, many of the theoretical systems that we use to talk about sex, such as social constructionism, come from sociology. In a recent "queer" issue of *Sociological Theory*, a group of sociologists attempted to account for the currently strained relations between sociological theory and queer theory. Steven Epstein pointed out that sociology asserted that sexuality was socially constructed and indeed that "without seeking to minimize the importance of other disciplines, I would suggest that neither queer theory nor lesbian and gay studies in general could be imagined in their present forms without the contributions of sociological theory."[6] Arlene Stein and Ken Plummer continue Epstein's line of inquiry and add a critique of the present state of queer theory:

> Queer theorists . . . appreciate the extent to which the texts of literature and mass culture shape sexuality, but their weakness is that they rarely, if ever, move beyond the text. There is a dangerous tendency for the new queer theorists to ignore "real" queer life as it is materially experienced across the world, while they play with the free-floating signifiers of texts.[7]

In an effort to restore sociology to its proper place within the study of sexuality, Stein and Plummer have reinvested here in a clear and verifiable difference between the real and the textual, and they designate textual analysis as a totally insular activity with no referent, no material consequences, and no intellectual gain. But as Lewontin's review suggested, it is precisely this belief in the real and the material as separate from the represented and the textual that creates the problems of survey analysis. To be fair, Stein and Plummer are clearly not suggesting merely a quantitative approach to the study of sexuality and queer subcultures, but they do, on some level, seem to have re-created some essential divide between the truth of sexual behavior and the fiction of textual analysis.

The answer to the problem of how to study sexuality, I am trying to suggest, must lie to some extent in an interdisciplinary approach that can combine information culled from people with information culled from texts. So, whereas Cindy Patton, for example, in "Tremble Hetero Swine," remarks with dismay on the dominance of "textually based forms of queer theory," we must question whether there is a form of queer theory or sexual theory that is not textually based.[8] Isn't a sexual ethnographer studying texts? And doesn't a social historian collate evidence from texts? Sometimes the texts are oral histories, sometimes they might be interview material, sometimes they might be fiction or autobiography, but given our basic formulation of sex as "private," something that happens when other people are not around, there is no way to objectively observe "in the bedroom." Conversely, readings of texts also require historical contexts and some relation to the lived experience of subjects. The text-based methodologies err on the side of abstraction, and the sociological studies err on the side of overly rationalizing sexual behavior. Finally, although some have criticized literary or cultural studies approaches to identity construction as apolitical or ahistorical, theories that tie the history of sexuality unproblematically to economics or the movement of capital tend to produce exactly the linear narratives of rational progress and modernization that sexuality seems to resist.

A queer methodology, in a way, is a scavenger methodology that uses different methods to collect and produce information on subjects who have been deliberately or accidentally excluded from traditional studies of human behavior. The queer methodology attempts to combine methods that are often cast as being at odds with each other, and it refuses the academic compulsion toward disciplinary coherence. Although this book will be immediately recognizable as a work of cultural studies, it will not shy away from the more empirical methods associated with ethnographic research.

## Constructing Masculinities

Within cultural studies itself, masculinity has recently become a favorite topic. I want to try here to account for the growing popularity of a body of work on masculinity that evinces absolutely no interest in masculinity without men. I first noticed the unprecedented interest in masculinity in April 1994 when the DIA Center for the Performing Arts convened a group of important intellectuals to hold forth on the topic of masculinities. On the opening night of this event, one commentator wondered, "Why masculinity, why now?" Several others, male critics and scholars, gave eloquent papers about their memories of being young boys and about their relationships with their fathers. The one lesbian on the panel, a poet, read a moving poem about rape. At the end of the evening, only one panelist had commented on the limitations of a discussion of masculinity that interpreted "masculinity" as a synonym for men or maleness.[9] This lonely intervention highlighted the gap between mainstream discussions of masculinity and men and ongoing queer discussions about masculinity, which extend far beyond the male body. Indeed, in answer to the naive question that began the evening, "Why masculinities, why now?" one might state: Because masculinity in the 1990s has finally been recognized as, at least in part, a construction by female- as well as male-born people.[10]

The anthology that the conference produced provides more evidence of the thoroughgoing association that the editors have made between masculinity and maleness. The title page features a small photographic illustration of a store sign advertising clothing as "Fixings for Men." This illustration has been placed just below the title, *Constructing Masculinity*, and forces the reader to understand the construction of masculinity as the outfitting of males within culture. The introduction to the volume attempts to diversify this definition of masculinity by using Judith Butler's and Eve Sedgwick's contributions to suggest that the anthology recognizes the challenges made by gays, lesbians, and queers to the terms of gender normativity. The editors insist that masculinity is multiple and that "far from just being about men, the idea of masculinity engages, inflects, and shapes everyone."[11] The commitment to the representation of masculinity as multiple is certainly borne out in the first essay in the volume, by Eve Sedgwick, in which she proposes that masculinity may have little to do with men, and is somewhat extended by Butler's essay "Melancholy Gender." But Sedgwick also critiques the editors for having proposed a book and a conference on masculinity that remain committed to linking masculinity to maleness. Although the introduction suggests that the editors have heeded Sedgwick's call for gender diversity, the rest of the volume suggests otherwise. There are many fascinating essays in this anthology, but there are no essays specifically on female masculinity. Although gender-queer images by Loren Cameron and Cathy Opie adorn the pages of the book, the text contains no discussions of these images. The book circles around discussions of male icons such as Clint Eastwood and Steven Seagal; it addresses the complex relations between fathers and sons; it examines topics such as how science defines men and masculinity and the law. The volume concludes with an essay by Stanley Aronowitz titled "My Masculinity," an autobiographically inflected consideration of various forms of male power.

None of my analysis here is to say that this is an uninteresting anthology or that the essays are somehow wrong or misguided, but I am trying to point out that the editorial statement at the beginning of the volume is less a prologue to what follows and more of an epilogue that describes what a volume on masculinity *should* do as opposed to what the anthology does do. Even when the need for an analysis of female masculinity has been acknowledged, in other words, it seems remarkably difficult to follow through on. What is it then that, to paraphrase Eve Sedgwick's essay, makes it so difficult *not* to presume an essential relation between masculinity and men?[12]

By beginning with this examination of the *Constructing Masculinity* conference and anthology, I do not want to give the impression that the topic of female masculinities must always be related to some larger topic, some more general set of masculinities that has been, and continues to be, about men. Nor do I want to suggest that gender theory is the true origin of gender knowledges. Rather, this conference and book merely emphasize the lag between community knowledges and practices and academic discourses.[13] I believe it is both helpful and important to contextualize a discussion of female and lesbian masculinities in direct opposition to a more generalized discussion of masculinity within cultural studies that seems intent on insisting that masculinity remain the property of male bodies. The continued refusal in Western society to admit ambiguously gendered bodies into functional social relations (evidenced, for example, by our continued use of either/or bathrooms, either women or men) is, I will claim, sustained by a conservative and protectionist attitude by men in general toward masculinity. Such an attitude has been bolstered by a more general disbelief in female masculinity. I can only describe such disbelief in terms of a failure in a collective imagination: in other words, female-born people have been making convincing and powerful assaults on the coherence of male masculinity for well over a hundred years; what prevents these assaults from taking hold and accomplishing the diminution of the bonds between masculinity and men? Somehow, despite multiple images of strong women (such as bodybuilder Bev Francis or tennis player Martina Navratilova), of cross-identifying women (Radclyffe Hall or Ethel Smyth), of masculine-coded public figures (Janet Reno), of butch superstars (k. d. lang), of muscular and athletic women (Jackie Joyner-Kersee), of female-born transgendered people (Leslie Feinberg), there is still no general acceptance or even recognition of masculine women and boyish girls. This book addresses itself to this collective failure to imagine and ratify the masculinity produced by, for, and within women.

In case my concerns about the current discussions of masculinity in cultural studies sound too dismissive, I want to look in an extended way at what happens when academic discussions of male masculinity take place to the exclusion of discussions of more wide-ranging masculinities. While it may seem that I am giving an inordinate amount of attention to what is after all just one intervention into current discussions, I am using one book as representative of a whole slew of other studies of masculinity that replicate the intentions and the mistakes of this one. In an anthology called *Boys: Masculinities in Contemporary Culture,* edited by Paul Smith for a Cultural Studies series, Smith suggests that masculinity must always be thought of "in the plural" as masculinities "defined and cut through by differences and contradictions of all sorts."[14] The plurality of masculinities for Smith encompasses a dominant white masculinity that is crisscrossed by its others, gay, bisexual, black, Asian, and Latino masculinities. Although the recognition of a host of masculinities makes sense, Smith chooses to focus on dominant white masculinity to the exclusion of the other masculinities he has listed. Smith, predictably, warns the reader not to fall into the trap of simply critiquing dominant masculinity or simply celebrating minority masculinities, and then he makes the following foundational statement:

> And it may well be the case, as some influential voices often tell us, that masculinity or masculinities are in some real sense not the exclusive "property" of biologically male subjects — it's true that many female subjects lay claim to masculinity as their property. Yet in terms of cultural and political *power*, it still makes a difference when masculinity coincides with biological maleness. (4)

What is immediately noticeable to me here is the odd attribution of immense power to those "influential voices" who keep telling us that masculinity is not the property of men. There is no naming of these influential voices, and we are left supposing that "influence" has rendered the "female masculinity theorists" so powerful that names are irrelevant: these voices, one might suppose, are hegemonic. Smith goes on to plead with the reader, asking us to admit that the intersection of maleness and masculinity does "still" make a difference. His appeal here to common sense allows him to sound as if he is trying to reassert some kind of rationality to a debate that is spinning off into totally inconsequential discussions. Smith is really arguing that we must turn to dominant masculinity to begin deconstructing masculinity because it is the equation of maleness plus masculinity that adds up to social legitimacy. As I argued earlier in this chapter, however, precisely because white male masculinity has obscured all other masculinities, we have to turn away from its construction to bring other more mobile forms of masculinity to light. Smith's purpose in his reassertion of the difference that male masculinity makes is to uncover the "cultural and political *power*" of this union in order to direct our attention to the power of patriarchy. The second part of the paragraph makes this all too clear:

> Biological men — male-sexed beings — are after all, in varying degrees, the bearers of privilege and power within the systems against which

women still struggle. The privilege and power are, of course, different for different men, endlessly diversified through the markers of class, nation, race, sexual preference and so on. But I'd deny that there are any men who are entirely outside of the ambit, let's say, of power and privilege *in relation to women*. In that sense it has to be useful to our thinking to recall that masculinities are not only a function of dominant notions of masculinity and not constituted solely in resistant notions of "other" masculinities. In fact, masculinities exist inevitably in relation to what feminisms have construed as the system of patriarchy and patriarchal relations.[15]

The most noticeable feature of this paragraph is the remarkable stability of the terms "women" and "men." Smith advances here a slightly old-fashioned feminism that understands women as endlessly victimized within systems of male power. Woman, within such a model, is the name for those subjects within patriarchy who have no access to male power and who are regulated and confined by patriarchal structures. But what would Smith say to Monique Wittig's claim that lesbians are not women because they are not involved in the heterosexual matrix that produces sexual difference as a power relation? What can Smith add to Judith Butler's influential theory of "gender trouble," which suggests that "gender is a copy with no original" and that dominant sexualities and genders are in some sense imbued with a pathetic dependence on their others that puts them perpetually at risk? What would Smith say to Jacob Hale's claim that the genders we use as reference points in gender theory fall far behind community productions of alternative genderings?[16] Are butch dykes women? Are male transvestites men? How does gender variance disrupt the flow of powers presumed by patriarchy in relations between men and women? Smith, in other words, cannot take female masculinity into account because he sees it as inconsequential and secondary to much more important questions about male privilege. Again, this sounds more like a plaintive assertion that men *do* still access male power within patriarchy (don't they?), and it conveniently ignores the ways in which gender relations are scrambled where and when gender variance comes into play.

Smith's attempt to shore up male masculinity by dismissing the importance of other masculinities finds further expression in his attempt to take racialized masculinities into consideration. His introductory essay opens with a meditation on the complications of the O.J. Simpson case, and Smith wonders at the way popular discourse on the O.J. case sidesteps issues of masculinity and male domination in favor of race. When he hears a black male caller to a radio talk show link O.J.'s case to an ongoing conspiracy against black men in this country, Smith ponders: "His spluttering about the attempted genocide of black men reminded me, somehow, that another feature of the O.J. case was the way it had started with the prosecution trying to establish the relevance of O.J.'s record as a wife beater" (Smith, *Boys*, 1). Noting that the callers to the talk show did not have much to say about this leads Smith to wonder whether race can constitute a collective identity but masculinity cannot, and finally he suggests that although "it might be difficult to talk about race in this country, it is even more difficult to talk about masculinity" (1). If you are a white man, it is probably extremely difficult to talk about either race or masculinity let alone both at the same time. But, of course, race and masculinity, especially in the case of O.J., are not separable into tidy categories. Indeed, one might say that the caller's "spluttering" about conspiracies against black men constituted a far more credible race analysis in this case than Smith's articulation of the relations between race and masculinity. For Smith, masculinity in the case of O.J. constitutes a flow of domination that comes up against his blackness as a flow of subordination. There is no discussion here of the injustices of the legal system, the role of class and money in the trial, or the complicated history of relations between black men and white women. Smith uses O.J. as shorthand for a model that is supposed to suggest power and disempowerment in the same location.

I am taking so much time and effort to discount Smith's introduction to *Boys* because there is a casualness to his essay that both indicates his lack of any real investment in the project of alternative masculinities and suggests an unwillingness to think through the messy identifications that make up contemporary power relations around gender, race, and class. The book that Smith introduces also proves to have nothing much to offer to new discussions of masculinity, and we quickly find ourselves, from the opening essay on, in the familiar territory of men, boys, and their fathers. The first essay, for example, by Fred Pfeil, "A Buffalo, New York Story," tells a pitiful tale about father-son relations in the 1950s. In one memorable moment from the memoir, he (Fred) and Dad have cozied up on the couch to watch *Bonanza* while Mom and Sis are doing the dishes in the kitchen. Boy asks Dad "why bad guys were always so stupid," and Dad laughs and explains "because they were bad" (10). The story goes on to detail the innocent young boy's first brushes with his male relatives' racism and his own painful struggle with car sickness. Besides taking apart the dynamics of fathers and sons cozying up together to watch *Bonanza,* there most certainly are a multitude of important things to say about men and masculinity in patriarchy, but Smith and some of his contributors choose not to say them. We could be producing ethnographies on the aggressive and indeed protofascist masculinities produced by male sports fans.[17] Much work still remains to be done on the socialization (or lack thereof) of young men in high schools, on (particularly rich white male) domestic abusers, on the new sexism embodied by "sensitive men," on the men who participate in the traffic in mail-order brides and sex tourism (including a study of privileged white gay masculinity). But studies in male masculinity are predictably not so interested in taking apart the patriarchal bonds between white maleness and privilege; they are much more concerned to detail the fragilities of male socialization, the pains of manhood, and the fear of female empowerment.[18]

Because I have criticized Smith for his apparent lack of investment in the project of producing alternative masculinities, let me take a moment to make my own investments clear. Although I make my own masculinity the topic of my last chapter, it seems important to state that this book is an attempt to make my own female masculinity plausible, credible, and real. For a large part of my life, I have been stigmatized by a masculinity that marked me as ambiguous and illegible. Like many other tomboys, I was mistaken for a boy throughout my childhood, and like many other tomboy adolescents, I was forced into some semblance of femininity for my teenage years. When gender-ambiguous children are constantly challenged about their gender identity, the chain of misrecognitions can actually produce a new recognition: in other words, to be constantly mistaken for a boy, for many tomboys, can contribute to the production of a masculine identity. It was not until my midtwenties that I finally found a word for my particular gender configuration: butch. In my final chapter, "Raging Bull (Dyke)," I address the ways in which butches manage to affirm their masculinity despite the multiple sites in which that masculinity is challenged, denied, threatened, and violated.

## The Bathroom Problem

If three decades of feminist theorizing about gender has thoroughly dislodged the notion that anatomy is destiny, that gender is natural, and that male and female are the only options, why do we still operate in a world that assumes that people who are not male are female, and people who are not female are male (and even that people who are not male are not people!). If gender has been so thoroughly defamiliarized, in other words, why do we not have multiple gender options, multiple gender categories, and real-life nonmale and nonfemale options for embodiment and identification? In a way, gender's very flexibility and seeming fluidity is precisely what allows dimorphic gender to hold sway. Because so few people actually match any given community standards for male or female, in other words, gender can be imprecise and therefore multiply relayed through a solidly binary system. At the same time, because the definitional boundaries of male and female are so elastic, there are very few people in any given public space who are completely unreadable in terms of their gender.

Ambiguous gender, when and where it does appear, is inevitably transformed into deviance, thirdness, or a blurred version of either male or female. As an example, in public bathrooms for women, various bathroom users tend to fail to measure up to expectations of femininity, and those of us who present in some ambiguous way are routinely questioned and challenged about our presence in the "wrong" bathroom. For example, recently, on my way to give a talk in Minneapolis, I was making a connection at Chicago's O'Hare airport. I strode purposefully into the women's bathroom. No sooner had I entered the stall than someone was knocking at the door: "Open up, security here!" I understood immediately what had happened. I had, once again, been mistaken for a man or a boy, and some woman had called security. As soon as I spoke, the two guards at the bathroom stall realized their error, mumbled apologies, and took off. On the way home from the same trip, in the Denver airport, the same sequence of events was repeated. Needless to say, the policing of gender within the bathroom is intensified in the space of the airport, where people are literally moving through space and time in ways that cause them to want to stabilize some boundaries (gender) even as they traverse others (national). However, having one's gender challenged in the women's rest room is a frequent occurrence in the lives of many androgynous or masculine women;

indeed, it is so frequent that one wonders whether the category "woman," when used to designate public functions, is completely outmoded.[19]

It is no accident, then, that travel hubs become zones of intense scrutiny and observation. But gender policing within airport bathrooms is merely an intensified version of a larger "bathroom problem." For some gender-ambiguous women, it is relatively easy to "prove" their right to use the women's bathroom—they can reveal some decisive gender trait (a high voice, breasts), and the challenger will generally back off. For others (possibly low-voiced or hairy or breastless people), it is quite difficult to justify their presence in the women's bathroom, and these people may tend to use the men's bathroom, where scrutiny is far less intense. Obviously, in these bathroom confrontations, the gender-ambiguous person first appears as not-woman ("You are in the wrong bathroom!"), but then the person appears as something actually even more scary, not-man ("No, I am not," spoken in a voice recognized as not-male). Not-man and not-woman, the gender-ambiguous bathroom user is also not androgynous or in-between; this person is gender deviant.

For many gender deviants, the notion of passing is singularly unhelpful. Passing as a narrative assumes that there is a self that masquerades as another kind of self and does so successfully; at various moments, the successful pass may cohere into something akin to identity. At such a moment, the passer has *become*. What of a biological female who presents as butch, passes as male in some circumstances and reads as butch in others, and considers herself not to be a woman but maintains distance from the category "man"? For such a subject, identity might best be described as process with multiple sites for becoming and being. To understand such a process, we would need to do more than map psychic and physical journeys between male and female and within queer and straight space; we would need, in fact, to think in fractal terms and about gender geometries. Furthermore, I argue in chapter 4, in my discussion of the stone butch, when and where we discuss the sexualities at stake in certain gender definitions, very different identifications between sexuality, gender, and the body emerge. The stone butch, for example, in her self-definition as a nonfeminine, sexually untouchable female, complicates the idea that lesbians share female sexual practices or women share female sexual desires or even that masculine women share a sense of what animates their particular masculinities.

I want to focus on what I am calling "the bathroom problem" because I believe it illustrates in remarkably clear ways the flourishing existence of gender binarism despite rumors of its demise. Furthermore, many normatively gendered women have no idea that a bathroom problem even exists and claim to be completely ignorant about the trials and tribulations that face the butch woman who needs to use a public bathroom. But queer literature is littered with references to the bathroom problem, and it would not be an exaggeration to call it a standard feature of the butch narrative. For example, Leslie Feinberg provides clear illustrations of the dimensions of the bathroom problem in *Stone Butch Blues*. In this narrative of the life of the he-she factory worker, Jess Goldberg, Jess recounts many occasions in which she has to make crucial decisions about whether she can afford to use the women's bathroom. On a shopping outing with some drag queens, Jess tells Peaches: "I gotta use the bathroom. God, I wish I could wait, but I can't." Jess takes a deep breath and enters the ladies room:

> Two women were freshening their makeup in front of the mirror. One glanced at the other and finished applying her lipstick. "Is that a man or a woman?" She said to her friend as I passed them.
>
> The other woman turned to me. "This is the woman's bathroom," she informed me.
>
> I nodded. "I know."
>
> I locked the stall door behind me. Their laughter cut me to the bone. "You don't really know if that is a man or not," one woman said to the other. "We should call security to make sure."
>
> I flushed the toilet and fumbled with my zipper in fear. Maybe it was just an idle threat. Maybe they really would call security. I hurried out of the bathroom as soon as I heard both women leave.[20]

For Jess, the bathroom represents a limit to her ability to move around in the public sphere. Her body, with its needs and physical functions, imposes a limit on her attempts to function normally despite her variant gender presentation. The women in the rest room, furthermore, are depicted as spiteful, rather than fearful. They toy with Jess by calling into question her right to use the rest room and threatening to call the police. As Jess puts it: "They never would have made fun of a guy like that." In other words, if the women were truly anxious for their safety, they would not have toyed with the intruder, and they would not have hesitated to call the police. Their casualness about calling security indicates that they know Jess is a woman but want to punish her for her inappropriate self-presentation.

Another chronicle of butch life, *Throw It to the River,* by Nice Rodriguez, a Filipina-Canadian writer, also tells of the bathroom encounter. In a story called "Every Full Moon," Rodriguez tells a romantic tale about a butch bus conductor called Remedios who falls in love with a former nun called Julianita. Remedios is "muscular around the arms and shoulders," and her "toughness allows her to bully anyone who will not pay the fare."[21] She aggressively flirts with Julianita until Julianita agrees to go to a movie with Remedios. To prepare for her date, Remedios dresses herself up, carefully flattening out her chest with Band-Aids over the nipples: "She bought a white shirt in Divisoria just for this date. Now she worries that the cloth may be too thin and transparent, and that Julianita will be turned off when her nipples protrude out like dice" (33). With her "well-ironed jeans," her smooth chest, and even a man's manicure, Remedios heads out for her date. However, once out with Julianita, Remedios, now dressed in her butch best, has to be careful about public spaces. After the movie, Julianita rushes off to the washroom, but Remedios waits outside for her:

> She has a strange fear of ladies rooms. She wishes there was another washroom somewhere between the mens' and the ladies' for queers like her. Most of the time she holds her pee—sometimes as long as half a day—until she finds a washroom where the users are familiar with her. Strangers take to her unkindly, especially elder women who inspect her from head to toe. (40–41)

Another time, Remedios tells of being chased from a ladies' room and beaten by a bouncer. The bathroom problem for Remedios and for Jess severely limits their ability to circulate in public spaces and actually brings them into contact with physical violence as a result of having violated a cardinal rule of gender: one must be readable at a glance. After Remedios is beaten for having entered a ladies' room, her father tells her to be more careful, and Rodriguez notes: "She realized that being cautious means swaying her hips and parading her boobs when she enters any ladies room" (30).

If we use the paradigm of the bathroom as a limit of gender identification, we can measure the distance between binary gender schema and lived multiple gendered experiences. The accusation "you're in the wrong bathroom" really says two different things. First, it announces that your gender seems at odds with your sex (your apparent masculinity or androgyny is at odds with your supposed femaleness); second, it suggests that single-gender bathrooms are only for those who fit clearly into one category (male) or the other (female). Either we need open-access bathrooms or multigendered bathrooms, or we need wider parameters for gender identification. The bathroom, as we know it, actually represents the crumbling edifice of gender in the twentieth century. The frequency with which gender-deviant "women" are mistaken for men in public bathrooms suggests that a large number of feminine women spend a large amount of time and energy policing masculine women. Something very different happens, of course, in the men's public toilet, where the space is more likely to become a sexual cruising zone than a site for gender repression. Lee Edelman, in an essay about the interpenetration of nationalism and sexuality, argues that "the institutional men's room constitutes a site at which the zones of public and private cross with a distinctive psychic charge."[22] The men's room, in other words, constitutes both an architecture of surveillance and an incitement to desire, a space of homosocial interaction and of homoerotic interaction.

So, whereas men's rest rooms tend to operate as a highly charged sexual space in which sexual interactions are both encouraged and punished, women's rest rooms tend to operate as an arena for the enforcement of gender conformity. Sex-segregated bathrooms continue to be necessary to protect women from male predations but also produce and extend a rather outdated notion of a public-private split between male and female society. The bathroom is a domestic space beyond the home that comes to represent domestic order, or a parody of it, out in the world. The women's bathroom accordingly becomes a sanctuary of enhanced femininity, a "little girl's room" to which one retreats to powder one's nose or fix one's hair. The men's bathroom signifies as the extension of the public nature of masculinity—it is precisely not domestic even though the names given to the sexual function of the bathroom—such as cottage or tearoom—suggest it is a parody of the domestic. The codes that dominate within the women's bathroom are primarily gender codes; in the men's room, they are sexual codes. Public sex versus private gender, openly sexual versus discreetly repressive, bathrooms beyond the home take on the proportions of a gender factory.

Marjorie Garber comments on the liminality of the bathroom in *Vested Interests* in a chapter on the perils and privileges of cross-dressing. She discusses the very different modes of passing and cross-dressing for cross-identified genetic males and females, and she observes that the restroom is a "potential waterloo" for both female-to-male (FTM) and male-to-female (MTF) cross-dressers and transsexuals.[23] For the FTM, the men's room represents the most severe test of his ability to pass, and advice frequently circulates within FTM communities about how to go unnoticed in male-only spaces. Garber notes: "The cultural paranoia of being caught in the ultimately wrong place, which may be inseparable from the pleasure of "passing" in that same place, depends in part on the same cultural binarism, the idea that gender categories are sufficiently uncomplicated to permit self-assortment into one of the two 'rooms' without deconstructive reading" (47). It is worth pointing out here (if only because Garber does not) that the perils for passing FTMs in the men's room are very different from the perils of passing MTFs in the women's room. On the one hand, the FTM in the men's room is likely to be less scrutinized because men are not quite as vigilant about intruders as women for obvious reasons. On the other hand, if caught, the FTM may face some version of gender panic from the man who discovers him, and it is quite reasonable to expect and fear violence in the wake of such a discovery. The MTF, by comparison, will be more scrutinized in the women's room but possibly less open to punishment if caught. Because the FTM ventures into male territory with the potential threat of violence hanging over his head, it is crucial to recognize that the bathroom problem is much more than a glitch in the machinery of gender segregation and is better described in terms of the violent enforcement of our current gender system.

Garber's reading of the perilous use of rest rooms by both FTMs and MTFs develops out of her introductory discussion of what Lacan calls "urinary segregation." Lacan used the term to describe the relations between identities and signifiers, and he ultimately used the simple diagram of the rest room signs "Ladies" and "Gentlemen" to show that within the production of sexual difference, primacy is granted to the signifier over that which it signifies; in more simple terms, naming confers, rather than reflects, meaning.[24] In the same way, the system of urinary segregation creates the very functionality of the categories "men" and "women." Although restroom signs seem to serve and ratify distinctions that already exist, in actual fact these markers produce identifications within these constructed categories. Garber latches on to the notion of "urinary segregation" because it helps her to describe the processes of cultural binarism within the production of gender; for Garber, transvestites and transsexuals challenge this system by resisting the literal translation of the signs "Ladies" and "Gentlemen." Garber uses the figures of the transvestite and the transsexual to show the obvious flaws and gaps in a binary gender system; the transvestite, as interloper, creates a third space of possibility within which all binaries become unstable. Unfortunately, as in all attempts to break a binary by producing a third term, Garber's third space tends to stabilize the other two. In "Tearooms and Sympathy," Lee Edelman also turns to Lacan's term "urinary segregation," but Edelman uses Lacan's diagram to mark heterosexual anxiety "about the potential inscriptions of homosexual desire and about the possibility of knowing or recognizing whatever might constitute 'homosexual difference'" (160). Whereas for Garber it is the transvestite who marks the instability of the markers "Ladies" and "Gentlemen," for Edelman it is not the passing transvestite but the passing homosexual.

Both Garber and Edelman, interestingly enough, seem to fix on the men's room as the site of these various destabilizing performances. As I am arguing here, however, focusing exclusively on the drama of the men's room avoids the much more complicated theater of the women's room. Garber writes of urinary segregation: "For transvestites and transsexuals, the 'men's room' problem is really a challenge to the way in which such cultural binarism is read" (14). She goes on to list some cinematic examples of the perils of urinary segregation and discusses scenes from *Tootsie* (1982), *Cabaret* (1972), and the *Female Impersonator Pageant* (1975). Garber's examples are odd illustrations of what she calls "the men's room problem" if only because at least one of her examples (*Tootsie*) demonstrates gender policing in the women's room. Also, Garber makes it sound as if vigorous gender policing happens in the men's room while the women's room is more of a benign zone for gender enforcement. She notes: "In fact, the urinal has appeared in a number of fairly recent films as a marker of the ultimate 'difference'—or studied indifference" (14). Obviously, Garber is drawing a parallel here between the conventions of gender attribution within which the penis marks the "ultimate difference"; however, by not moving beyond this remarkably predictable description of gender differentiation, Garber overlooks the main distinction between gender policing in the men's room and in the women's room. Namely, in the women's room, it is not only the MTF but *all* gender-ambiguous females who are scrutinized, whereas in the men's room, biological men are rarely deemed out of place. Garber's insistence that there is "a third space of possibility" occupied by the transvestite has closed down the possibility that there may be a fourth, fifth, sixth, or one hundredth space beyond the binary. The "women's room problem" (as opposed to the "men's room problem") indicates a multiplicity of gender displays even within the supposedly stable category of "woman."

So what gender are the hundreds of female-born people who are consistently not read as female in the women's room? And because so many women clearly fail the women's room test, why have we not begun to count and name the genders that are clearly emerging at this time? One could answer this question in two ways: On the one hand, we do not name and notice new genders because as a society we are committed to maintaining a binary gender system. On the other hand, we could also say that the failure of "male" and "female" to exhaust the field of gender variation actually ensures the continued dominance of these terms. Precisely because virtually nobody fits the definitions of male and female, the categories gain power and currency from their impossibility. In other words, the very flexibility and elasticity of the terms "man" and "woman" ensures their longevity. To test this proposition, look around any public space and notice how few people present formulaic versions of gender and yet how few are unreadable or totally ambiguous. The "It's Pat" character on a *Saturday Night Live* skit dramatized the ways in which people insist on attributing gender in terms of male or female on even the most undecidable characters. The "It's Pat" character produced laughs by consistently sidestepping gender fixity—Pat's partner had a neutral name, and everything Pat did or said was designed to be read either way. Of course, the enigma that Pat represented could have been solved very easily; Pat's coworkers could simply have asked Pat what gender s/he was or preferred. This project on female masculinity is designed to produce more than two answers to that question and even to argue for a concept of "gender preference" as opposed to compulsory gender binarism. The human potential for incredibly precise classifications has been demonstrated in multiple arenas; why then do we settle for a paucity of classifications when it comes to gender? A system of gender preferences would allow for gender neutrality until such a time when the child or young adult announces his or her or its gender. Even if we could not let go of a binary gender system, there are still ways to make gender optional—people could come out as a gender in the way they come out as a sexuality. The point here is that there are many ways to depathologize gender variance and to account for the multiple genders that we already produce and sustain. Finally, as I suggested in relation to

Garber's arguments about transvestism, "thirdness" merely balances the binary system and, furthermore, tends to homogenize many different gender variations under the banner of "other."

It is remarkably easy in this society not to look like a woman. It is relatively difficult, by comparison, not to look like a man: the threats faced by men who do not gender conform are somewhat different than for women. Unless men are consciously trying to look like women, men are less likely than women to fail to pass in the rest room. So one question posed by the bathroom problem asks, what makes femininity so approximate and masculinity so precise? Or to pose the question with a different spin, why is femininity easily impersonated or performed while masculinity seems resilient to imitation? Of course, this formulation does not easily hold and indeed quickly collapses into the exact opposite: why is it, in the case of the masculine woman in the bathroom, for example, that one finds the limits of femininity so quickly, whereas the limits of masculinity in the men's room seem fairly expansive?

We might tackle these questions by thinking about the effects, social and cultural, of reversed gender typing. In other words, what are the implications of male femininity and female masculinity? One might imagine that even a hint of femininity sullies or lowers the social value of maleness while all masculine forms of femaleness should result in an elevation of status.[25] My bathroom example alone proves that this is far from true. Furthermore, if we think of popular examples of approved female masculinity like a buffed Linda Hamilton in *Terminator 2* (1991) or a lean and mean Sigourney Weaver in *Aliens,* it is not hard to see that what renders these performances of female masculinity quite tame is their resolute heterosexuality. Indeed, in *Alien Resurrection* (1997), Sigourney Weaver combines her hard body with some light flirtation with co-star Winona Ryder and her masculinity immediately becomes far more threatening and indeed "alien." In other words, when and where female masculinity conjoins with possibly queer identities, it is far less likely to meet with approval. Because female masculinity seems to be at its most threatening when coupled with lesbian desire, in this book I concentrate on queer female masculinity almost to the exclusion of heterosexual female masculinity. I have no doubt that heterosexual female masculinity menaces gender conformity in its own way, but all too often it represents an acceptable degree of female masculinity as compared to the excessive masculinity of the dyke. It is important when thinking about gender variations such as male femininity and female masculinity not simply to create another binary in which masculinity always signifies power; in alternative models of gender variation, female masculinity is not simply the opposite of female femininity, nor is it a female version of male masculinity. Rather, as we shall see in some of the artwork and gender performances to follow, very often the unholy union of femaleness and masculinity can produce wildly unpredictable results.

### Minority Masculinities and the Art of Gender

Minority masculinities and femininities destabilize binary gender systems in many different locations. As many feminist and antiracist critics have commented, femininity and masculinity signify as normative within and through white middle-class heterosexual bodies.[26] Films by artists of color that disrupt this representational code—such as *Looking for Langston* (1988), by Isaac Julien, and *Tongues Untied* (1989), by Marlon Riggs, for example—can undo the hierarchized relations between dominant and minority sexualites, but they also have the power to reorganize masculinity itself. In a recent popular example of the emergence of a minority masculinity within the scopic regime of racialization, we can witness the intersection of stereotyping and counterappropriation at work. In *Set It Off*, a film about four black women who go on a crime spree in response to overwhelming social injustice and personal outrage, rapper Queen Latifah plays what we might call "a butch in the hood." Latifah's character, Cleopatra Simms (Cleo), is a loudmouthed, bullying, tough, criminal butch with a cute girlfriend and a roughneck demeanor. Cleo's depiction of black female masculinity plays into stereotypical conceptions of black women as less feminine than some mythic norm of white femininity, but it also completely rearranges the terms of the stereotype. If blackness in general is associated with excessive and indeed violent masculinity in the social imaginary, then Latifah as Cleo exploits this association with some success. Latifah, a rapper herself, draws from the hyper-masculine moves of black male rappers to round out her character, and she powerfully makes visible what is both attractive and dangerous about a "boyz in the hood" masculine performance.[27]

Other assaults on dominant gender regimes come from queer butch art and performance, which might include drag king shows, butch theatrical roles, or art featuring gender-variant subjects. For example, as we shall see in chapter 7, in terms of drag king performances, stars such as Elvis Her-

Figure 2. Butch in the hood. Queen Latifah as Cleo in *Set It Off* (1997), directed by F. Gary Gray.

selvis or Mo B. Dick turn dominant masculinity around by parodying male superstardom and working conventional modes of performed sexism and misogyny into successful comedy routines. As Mo B. Dick, for example, drag king Maureen Fischer manages to parody masculinity by performing its most unnatural and obviously staged aspect: sexism. Declaiming his heterosexuality and fear of "homos" and desire for "girlies" to audiences in the drag clubs, Mo B. Dick reeks of the tricks of misogyny. Mo B.'s manipulations of a stagy and theatrical masculinity draw attention to not simply the performative aspect of masculinity but also the places where nonperformativity has ideological implications. In other words, by exposing smarmy male attentions to femaleness as staged, the drag king refuses any construction of misogyny as the natural order of things.

In a slightly different kind of butch theater, a queer performance art piece called "You're Just Like My Father," by Peggy Shaw (1995), Shaw represents female masculinity as a pugnacious and gritty staging of the reorganization of family dynamics via the butch daughter. There is no question here that Shaw's masculinity is part and parcel of her lesbianism rather than a drag identity or an imitation of maleness. Shaw becomes

Figure 3. "Stepping Out of the Closet." Drag king Mo B. Dick, photo by Del Grace (New York, 1997). Photo courtesy of the artist.

Figure 4. "You're Just Like My Father." Peggy Shaw's publicity poster (1995).

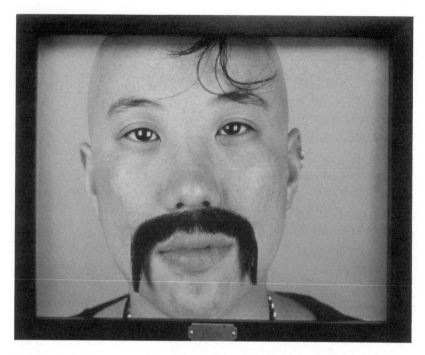

Figure 5. "Ingin," from the series "Being and Having," by Catherine Opie (1991). Photo courtesy of Jay Gorney Modern Art, New York and Regen Projects.

her mother's substitute husband and her lovers' substitute fathers and brothers, and she constructs her own masculinity by reworking and improving the masculinities she observes all around her. Shaw moves easily back and forth between various personae: she is the fighter, the crooner, the soldier, the breadwinner, the romeo, the patriarch. In each of these roles, she makes it clear that she is a female-bodied person inhabiting each role and that each role is part of her gender identity. To play among a variety of masculine identifications, furthermore, Shaw is not forced to become her father or to appropriate his maleness; she is already "just like" her father, and their masculinities exist on parallel plains.

The fleshing out of female masculinities has not been limited to cinematic or theatrical arenas. In the photographic work of artists such as Catherine Opie and Del Grace, we can watch the female body becoming masculine in stunning and powerful ways. Catherine Opie's lush photographic portraits of members of dyke, transgender, and S-M communities put a particular version of female masculinity on display. In one of her

Figure 6. "Whitey," from the series "Being and Having," by Catherine Opie (1991). Photo courtesy of Jay Gorney Modern Art, New York and Regen Projects.

early projects, entitled "Being and Having," Opie created a set of framed portraits of mustachioed or bearded faces against startling yellow back-drops. In each shot, the camera moves up close to the model's face (often even chopping off the top of the head) and brings the spectator right up against a face that, despite the proximity, remains oddly unreadable. The close-up articulates what feels like an intimacy between the model and the artist, an intimacy, moreover, not available to the viewer. The person looking at the photograph is positioned simultaneously as voyeur, as mir-ror image, and as participant, but ultimately it is the spectator who feels caught between looks, between being and having.

Very often the camera comes close enough to the model's face to reveal the theatricality of the facial hair; in other portraits, the facial hair appears to be real, and this sets up a visual trap in which the viewer might attempt to determine whether she or he is looking at a male or a female face. This is a trap because Opie's images are often quite beyond the binary of gender, and each portrait adds a new gender dimension not assimilable within the

Figure 7. "Mike and Sky," by Catherine Opie (1993). Photo courtesy of Jay Gorney Modern Art, New York and Regen Projects.

boundaries of "man" or "woman." In many of the commentaries on Opie's work, however, a critic will suggest that the complexity of Opie's work relies on the "operations that almost unconsciously take place when we determine whether we are looking at a man or a woman."[28] However, when we look at Opie's work within a larger context of productions of female masculinity, the ambiguity of gender seems beside the point. Indeed, these portraits are not ambiguous—they are resolute images of female masculinity in which, as Opie puts it, her cross-dressing models take their performances "both into the bedroom and out to public spaces. They are, I suppose, exhibitionists, and their scene has become a public spectator sport." [29]

Opie's images of bearded, pierced, and tattooed dykes and transgender men create a powerful visual aesthetic for alternative and minority masculinities. Although Opie's work is often compared to that of Diane Arbus because she takes as her subject so-called misfits and freaks, Opie vigorously denies such a comparison. She says: "I try to present people with an extreme amount of dignity. I mean, they're always going to be stared at, but I try to make the portraits stare back. That's what the relationship is all about. I mean, it's not like Diane Arbus or anything like that. Some of the portraits look very sad, I think they have this distant gaze but they are never pathetic." [30] Opie's insistence that her portraits "stare back" creates an interesting power dynamic between both photographer and model, but also between image and spectator. The power of the gaze in an Opie portrait always and literally rests with the image: the perpetual stare challenges the spectator's own sense of gender congruity, and even self, and it does indeed replicate with a difference the hostile stares that the model probably faces every day in the street. One reviewer of Opie's 1994 show, *Portraits,* commented that the isolation of each subject within the stylized frame of the photograph, with its brilliant color backdrops, transformed them into "abstract signs" and leaves the spectator free to be a voyeur. [31] But such an assessment shies away from the disorienting effect of these portraits—the subjects are positively regal in their opulent settings, and their colorful displays of tattoos and body markings seem to single them out for photographic glory. The stare of the spectator is forced to be admiring and appreciative rather than simply objectifying and voyeuristic. The tattoos and piercings and body modifications that mark the Opie model become in her portraits far more than the signifiers of some outlaw status. Whether we are confronted with the hormonally and surgically altered bodies of transgender men or the tattooed and pierced and scarred skin of the butch dyke, we look at bodies that display their own layered and multiple identifications.

Del Grace's images of gender-ambiguous bodies are also stylized portraits in the Mapplethorpe tradition. However, in Grace's photographs, there is often some activity that defines gender ambiguity in relation to a set of sexual practices. Grace's photos often feature two or more bodies in play, and we see gender in these photographs as a complex set of negotia-

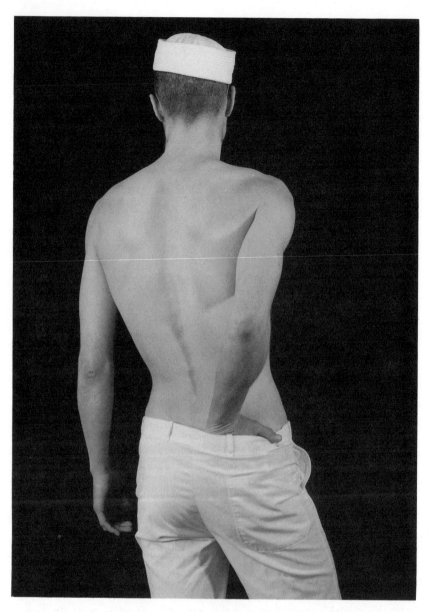

Figure 8. "Jack's Back II," by Del Grace (1994). Photo courtesy of the artist.

Figure 9. "Jackie II," by Del Grace (1994). Photo courtesy of the artist.

tions between bodies, identities, and desire. In "Triad" (1992) three shaven and bald female bodies are intertwined in a three-way embrace. The pallor of the bodies and the smoothness of their shaven skin creates a hard, marble effect and turns skin into stone, refusing the traditional softness of femininity. Grace often gives her subjects an almost mythical treatment and, as in the Opie portraits, always grants her models dignity, power, and beauty even as she exposes them to the gaze. In her photographs of butch bodies, Grace borrows from gay male erotic imagery to construct a context for an unselfconscious female masculinity. In "Jack's Back II" (1994) we see a sailor with his back toward us. The sailor wears white navy-issue pants and a white cap and has a hand tucked into his waistband. The back of the head is closely shaven and the shoulders are broad and manly. This image could be plucked from Paul Cadmus or Fassbinder's *Querelle* or any other classic example of gay homoerotica. However, within Grace's opus, one recognizes the back as belonging to Jackie, a beautifully built and tightly muscled butch whom Grace photographs repeatedly. In "Jackie II" we see Jackie, now from the front, wearing khaki pants and pulling an army T-shirt up over her head. While Jackie's face is still partially obscured in this image, her torso (Jack's front) is exposed, and while the breasts are just pronounced enough to mark Jackie as a "woman," they are small and muscular enough to keep her ambiguity intact.

Catherine Opie also uses back shots to make gender unreadable. In "Dyke" (1994), we see a torso set against an elaborate backdrop. The word *dyke* is tattooed in gothic script just below the neckline of a head of very short hair. On the one hand, the inscription dispels any of the gender ambiguity by rendering the body lesbian, but on the other hand, given the many multigendered images of dykes that Opie has produced, the word *dyke* gives very few clues as to what the front of this body might look like. Opie's and Grace's "back art" are refusals to engage with the all too easy game of gender ambiguity. The artists literally want gender to be a surface for inscriptions, words and drawings, art and desire. In another back shot, "Self-Portrait" (1993), Opie exposes her own back with a cutting etched into her skin. The childlike image of two stick figures in skirts holding hands below a bubble cloud and in front of a stick house is profoundly unsentimental in this location. The drawing is obviously done in blood; it scars the skin and sits in almost uncomfortable proximity to one of Opie's arm tattoos. This back shot makes the back into a canvas and actually defuses any of the curiosity that the viewer might have had about the front of

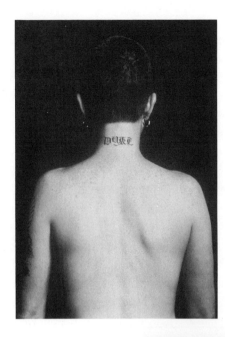

Figure 10. "Dyke," by Catherine Opie (1992). Photo courtesy of Jay Gorney Modern Art, New York and Regen Projects.

Figure 11. "Self-Portrait," by Catherine Opie (1993). Photo courtesy of Jay Gorney Modern Art, New York and Regen Projects.

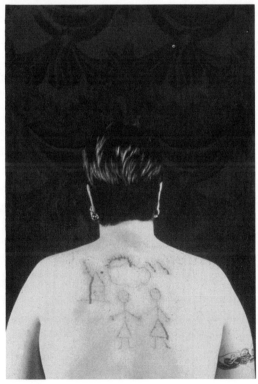

the body. As Opie notes about this self-portrait: "It says a lot of different things. One of them is that I have my back to you."[32] Whereas so many of Opie's photographs literally return the gaze with piercing stares, the back shots circumvent the question of the gaze altogether. Where the gaze is not engaged (from behind), a space seems to open up for gender variation and for different inscriptions of the sexed body.

Opie's cuttings and the tattoos and scars on the bodies of both Opie's and Grace's models stand in direct opposition to another popular image of gender bending. The painted body of Demi Moore on the cover of *Vanity Fair* in August 1992 was considered innovative and challenging when it appeared. Moore wore a painted man's suit on the cover, and inside the magazine were pictures of her in the painted suit leaning over the body of a sleeping man, her husband, Bruce Willis. The juxtaposition of Moore's painted body with the gender art of Opie and Grace reminds us of how fiercely heterosexual and gender-invariant popular culture tends to be. Moore's body suit fails to suggest even a mild representation of female masculinity precisely because it so anxiously emphasizes the femaleness of Moore's body. Whereas Opie's and Grace's portraits often make no effort to make femaleness visible, the Moore images represent femaleness as that which confers femininity on even the most conventional of masculine facades (the suit). The female masculinity in the work of Opie and Grace, by comparison, offers a glimpse into worlds where alternative masculinities make an art of gender.

Del Grace's work on drag kings and trans-butches and Cathy Opie's portraits of male transsexuals highlight another boundary for gender variance: the transsexual body. In chapter 5, I examine the often permeable boundaries between butch women and transsexual men, and I attempt to track the various masculinities produced across these two groups. The boundary between transsexuals and butches becomes important as we try to delineate the differences between being butch and becoming male, becoming transsexual and becoming male; at stake in this discussion is the project of alternative masculinities itself. Not all transsexualities, obviously, present a challenge (or want to) to hegemonic masculinity, and not all butch masculinities produce subversion. However, transsexuality and transgenderism do afford unique opportunities to track explicit performances of nondominant masculinity.[33]

In this introduction, I have tried to chart the implications of the suppression of female masculinities in a variety of spheres: in relation to cultural studies discussions, the suppression of female masculinities allows for male masculinity to stand unchallenged as the bearer of gender stability and gender deviance. The tomboy, the masculine woman, and the racialized masculine subject, I argue, all contribute to a mounting cultural indifference to the masculinity of white males. Gender policing in public bathrooms, furthermore, and gender performances within public spaces produce radically reconfigured notions of proper gender and map new genders onto a utopian vision of radically different bodies and sexualities. By arguing for gender transitivity, for self-conscious forms of female masculinity, for indifference to dominant male masculinities, and for "nonce taxonomies," I do not wish to suggest that we can magically wish into being a new set of properly descriptive genders that would bear down on the outmoded categories "male" and "female." Nor do I mean to suggest that change is simple and that, for example, by simply creating the desegregation of public toilets we will change the function of dominant genders within heteropatriarchal cultures. However, it seems to me that there are some very obvious spaces in which gender difference simply does not work right now, and the breakdown of gender as a signifying system in these arenas can be exploited to hasten the proliferation of alternate gender regimes in other locations. From drag kings to spies with gadgets, from butch bodies to FTM bodies, gender and sexuality and their technologies are already excessively strange. It is simply a matter of keeping them that way.

This book is divided into chapters that proceed not according to a chronology of female masculinity but more within a logic of embodiment. While this introductory chapter has veered between discussions of the most obvious forms of female masculinity (such as tomboyism and butchness) and considerations of methodologies, it has also attempted to convey the urgency of a full consideration of the topic of female masculinity. In the next chapter, I suggest that the project of historicizing female masculinity must evolve by using the inconsistencies that dominate contemporary discussions of gender to temper the kinds of claims we are willing to make about gendered subjectivities from other eras. Using a method that I call "perverse presentism," I try to produce a strategy for deciphering some examples of nineteenth-century female masculinity, and I focus on the "tribade." Turning next to the "invert," in chapter 3, I take my queer methodology into the twentieth century, and I examine the historical context that produced *The Well of Loneliness*. Radclyffe Hall, I suggest, was neither unique in her masculinity nor stranded in a "well of loneliness" because of her gender inversion. I examine Havelock Ellis's case histories and newspaper stories about Hall's contemporaries to show that Hall was surrounded by both communities of masculine women and examples of other individuals who embodied and lived their masculinities in many different ways. Models of inversion, accordingly, must be diversified in order to take the variety of these lives into account.

In chapter 4, I take up a more specific embodiment of female masculinity: the stone butch. Although the stone butch has come to signify the most stereotyped of all butch embodiments, I argue that it is the least understood. By attempting to unravel the contradictions between gender, sex, and desire that characterize the stone butch, I try to resist reading her as an example of the failure of a female masculinity that fantasizes its own maleness, and I reconstitute her as a powerful, self-knowing, and wholly viable sexual subject. The stone butch is often cast as a transitional stage on the way to transsexuality. In chapter 5, I examine the borderlands between lesbian butchness and transsexual maleness. What allows for female embodiment in the case of the butch and refuses such embodiment in the case of the female-to-male transsexual? How do butches and FTMS view their differences? What kinds of community building happen between butches and FTMS?

In chapter 6, I trace a different history of butchness, the history of cinematic female masculinity. In this chapter, I produce six different categories of cinematic butchness, and I outline the requirements and features of each category. I suggest that the butch character need not always be a sign of Hollywood homophobia and may signify a rich history of queer representation. In recent years, however, the most exciting developments in the representation of queer masculinities have taken place not on the screen but in nightclubs within an emergent drag king culture. I have spent a year tracing the form and content of drag king culture in New York, London, and San Francisco, and in chapter 7 I outline the main features of drag king shows, contests, cabarets, and performances. In my final chapter, "Raging Bull (Dyke)," I try to bring together the main theories of female masculinity produced within this book, and I relay them through the image on the book's cover, the beautiful painting of the raging bull dyke. This chapter examines the rich scene of the boxing match both for its production of normative masculinity and for its breakdown and then turns from De Niro's raging bull to the rage of the bull dyke and uses a personal voice narrative to conclude this exploration of female masculinity. The male boxer, from Rocky Balboa to Jake La Motta, represents for me the spectacle of a battered white male masculinity that always finds a way to win. By replacing this pugilist with the butch raging bull, I offer masculinity a new champion, a legitimate contender, ready to fight all comers and determined to go the distance.

*Tuesday 26 Oct. 1824, Paris*

*From 3 to 5, walked [with Mrs. Barlow] in the Tuileries gardens. . . . She said I astonished Mme Galvani at first, who once or twice said to the Mackenzies she thought I was a man & the Macks too had wondered. Mrs Barlow herself had thought at first I wished to imitate the manners of a gentleman but now she knows me better, it was not put on.*

—No Priest but Love: The Journals of Anne Lister *(1992)*

# 2 PERVERSE PRESENTISM

*The Androgyne, the Tribade, the Female Husband, and*
*Other Pre-Twentieth-Century Genders*

## Making Masculinity

In chapter 1, I gave a rather broad overview of the potential impact a theory of female masculinity might have on conventional understandings of masculinity, manliness, and, broadly speaking, the classification of gendered behavior. In a way, I am arguing that the very existence of masculine women urges us to reconsider our most basic assumptions about the functions, forms, and representations of masculinity and forces us to ask why the bond between men and masculinity has remained relatively secure despite the continuous assaults made by feminists, gays, lesbians, and gender-queers on the naturalness of gender. Some popular accounts of female masculinity suggest that the appearance of the virile woman is a relatively recent occurrence and that she is herself a product of feminist ideologies. Other accounts situate her as a sign of the relaxation of gender conformity and a harbinger of greater latitude for gender identification. Few popular renditions of female masculinity understand the masculine woman as a historical fixture, a character who has challenged gender systems for at least two centuries.

As queer historians have repeatedly pointed out, one common limitation of many gay and lesbian as well as feminist models of sexual and gender function is the tendency to be ahistorical. It has proven quite difficult to theorize sexuality and gender deviance in historical ways, and often the field is divided between untheoretical historical surveys and ahistorical theoretical models. Debates about the history of sexuality and the history of gender deviance have also very often reproduced this split, rendering historical sexual forms as either universal or completely bound by and to their historical moment. The challenge for new queer history has been, and remains, to produce methodologies sensitive to historical change but influenced by current theoretical preoccupations. In this chapter, therefore, I offer two examples of female masculinity from the nineteenth century, and I use these examples to show that masculine women have played a large part in the construction of modern masculinity. If the models of masculinity that we use today to bind masculinity to men already depend on the prior production of masculinity by and through women as well as men, then we must account for the ways in which female masculinity has been expelled and deliberately excluded from contemporary theories of masculinity. Furthermore, in relation to latter-day female masculinities, the presumption that they simply represent early forms of lesbianism denies them their historical specificity and covers over the multiple differences between earlier forms of same-sex desire. Such a presumption also funnels female masculinity neatly into models of sexual deviance rather than accounting for the meanings of early female masculinity within the history of gender definition and gender relations. By making female masculinity equivalent to lesbianism, in other words, or by reading it as proto-lesbianism awaiting a coming community, we continue to hold female masculinity apart from the making of modern masculinity itself.

This book rises and falls on two propositions that are utterly simple, and yet, I believe, they have not yet been advanced in any extended way in scholarship on masculinity (or gender, for that matter). The first claim is that women have made their own unique contributions to what we call modern masculinity, and these contributions tend to go completely unnoticed in gender scholarship. The second claim is that what we recognize as female masculinity is actually a multiplicity of masculinities, indeed a proliferation of masculinities, and the more we identify the various forms of female masculinity, the more they multiply. I have no illusions that this book will definitively catalog the entirety of female masculinities, but it does offer models and taxonomies and classifications for future endorsement or rejection. I am well aware of the damaging history of taxonomies within the history of sexuality, but I think that the main problem with taxonomizing was first that it was left to sexologists, and second that we have not continued to produce ever more accurate or colorful or elaborate or imaginative or flamboyant taxonomies, "nonce taxonomies," as Eve K. Sedgwick so eloquently phrases it.[1]

George Chauncey has also suggested that we have perhaps too few, rather than too many, models of sexual behavior. In an essay on a group of sexually active military men at the Newport Naval Training Station in 1919, Chauncey shows that homosexual relations took on many different forms within this social group and that "indeed, the very terms 'homosexual behavior' and 'identity,' because of their tendency to conflate phenomena that other cultures may have regarded as quite distinct, appear to be insufficiently precise to denote the variety of social forms of sexuality we wish to analyze."[2] Chauncey's work in general implies that the medical definitions of sexual behavior that emerged at the turn of the century attempted to give order to what often appeared to the medical researchers as a bewildering array of sexual activity within sexual subcultures.[3] Within the sexual subcultures, there existed much more elaborate taxonomies and models of sexual behavior than the researchers would ever have been able to access. Like Chauncey, Lisa Duggan also downplays the importance of the medical establishment in introducing sexual identities into the culture at large. As Duggan shows in her essay on "sapphic slasher" Alice Mitchell, at the turn of the century, we see the emergence of "modern desiring subjectivities" out of the various overlapping discourses of personal narrative, community awareness, and medical knowledge. Duggan makes us aware of the narrative structures at work within the notion of "identity," and she asks helpfully: "Did hostile sexologists construct the mannish lesbian, or did she, in any meaningful way, construct herself?"[4]

To take this question seriously, it may be time to return to some of the sexological case studies produced by Havelock Ellis and others, as I do in my next chapter, and restore to these case studies some of the complexity that has been lost within the rigidly binary definitions generated by the sexologists. Ellis, for example, interviewed a wide range of women and came up only with a model of inversion divided between feminine and masculine inverts. Is it possible to read the case histories he produced and create a more convincing taxonomy? In my next chapter, I diversify the case histories themselves and set them against the backdrop of the rich and varied communities of inverts in England in the early twentieth century who developed their own identities, sexual categories, self-understandings, and gender aesthetics. In this chapter, however, I confine my analysis to the few examples of same-sex desire between women in the nineteenth century that are readily available to us, and I try to show what is at stake in the contemporary readings of these examples and what we might gain from thinking in terms of tommies, tribades, female husbands, fricatrices, and inverts rather than just "lesbians."

While this book in no way claims to be a straightforward "history" of female masculinity, this chapter presents some ruminations on historically located female masculinities because the meaning and significance of many forms of contemporary female masculinity seem inextricably bound to earlier representations. Furthermore, I do not believe that we can actually understand the meaning of contemporary Anglo-American masculinities (male and female) without considering the history of the production of modern masculinity from the beginning of the nineteenth century to at least the 1920s. In other words, the momentous negotiations about gender that took place at and around the turn of the century, which were created by earlier developments, produced particular forms of femininity and masculinity and clearly showed that femininity was not wed to femaleness and masculinity was certainly not bound to maleness. The transition from affiliation marriages to romantic marriages, the development of the women's rights movement, the trials of Oscar Wilde, the social upheaval caused by World War I, and the development of sexological models of sexual definition all played a part in untangling once and for all the knots that appeared to bind gender to sex and sexuality in some mysterious and organic way. What remains to be demonstrated is how women have contributed powerfully and irreversibly to the constitutive terms of contemporary masculinity and how men have participated in integral ways in the foundations of contemporary femininity.

Many contemporary histories of masculinity seem content to trace the lines of continuity and opposition between concepts of manliness and the production of nation, or between masculinity and class, or even between male sociality and sexuality. But none seems compelled to inquire into what difference the masculine woman might have made to the development of such models of masculinity. To give just one example, in *The Image of Man: The Creation of Modern Masculinity*, George L. Mosse defines masculinity in his first sentence as "the way men assert what they believe to be their manhood."[5] Mosse does mention briefly the effect that the masculinity of the "new woman" had on ideals of manliness, but only to assert that "women who left their ascribed roles . . . joined the countertypes as the enemies against whom manliness sharpened its image" (12). In this way, female masculinity is sharply delineated as separate from the general category of masculinity, as indeed the antithesis of normal masculinity, and the definition of masculinity continues to be articulated in terms of the expression of maleness. Of course, it would make just as much sense to argue, as I do, that the way dominant culture contained the threat that the mannish woman represented to hegemonic masculinity was to absorb female masculinity into the dominant structures. Such an explanation assumes that manliness is built partly on the vigorous disavowal of female masculinity and partly on a simultaneous reconstruction of male masculinity in imitation of the female masculinity it claims to have rejected.[6]

Another study of manliness, Gail Bederman's *Manliness and Civilization*, does express awareness of the possibility that both men and women have participated in the construction of modern masculinity; although such an awareness is valuable in that it lays the foundations for further studies of turn-of-the-century female masculinities, Bederman does not go so far as to provide a sustained examination of the effect of female masculinity on male masculine ideals. In this compelling social history, Bederman defines gender as "a historical, ideological process" through which individuals lay claim to certain kinds of power "based upon their particular type of bodies."[7] Accordingly, "manhood—or 'masculinity,' as it is commonly termed today—is a continual dynamic process" (7), and through this process, men can claim access to public authority. Bederman shows that models of manliness in the late nineteenth century were central to the consolidation of white middle-class power and that the middle-class masculine ideal depended on concepts such as self-restraint and independence. By the turn of the century, however, white middle-class ideals of manliness were severely challenged by working-class men, black men, immigrant men, and even feminist women. This challenge from all sides prompted middle-class men to attempt to "remake manhood": "They began to formulate new ideologies of manhood—ideologies not of 'manliness' but of 'masculinity'" (16).

Although Bederman mentions the impact that emergent models of male homosexuality had on middle-class manhood, she does not focus on the possible effects of a developing discourse of female inversion. While it seems highly likely that new models of masculinity did oppose "excessive femininity" in both men and women (16), the new models must also have opposed masculinity in women and attempted to tie manhood and manliness and masculinity back to the male body in powerful ways. Indeed, that we still have a hard time separating masculinity from men suggests that this attempt to remake manhood as proper to, and limited to, male bodies was one of the most successful aspects of "remaking manhood." As I show in my next chapter, the assault offered by female inverts to the sanctity of male masculinity was prolonged and powerful.

## Perverse Presentism

Lesbian scholarship, as I discuss in more detail later, has generally understood same-sex nineteenth-century and early-twentieth-century desire as either in the model of romantic friendship or along the lines of mannish identification. It now seems highly likely, however, that many other models existed beyond the either-or proposition of an asexual friendship or a butch-femme sexual dynamic. Indeed, before the emergence of what we now understand as "lesbian" identities, same-sex desire worked through any number of different channels. If it seems both obvious and undeniable that probably many models of same-sex desire did exist, then why have we not busied ourselves in imagining their variety? It is my contention that many contemporary lesbian historians cannot extricate themselves from contemporary understandings of lesbian identity long enough to interpret the vagaries of early same-sex desire. Accordingly, we have any number of analyses claiming to find lesbians or protolesbians in any number of different historical periods without proper consideration of the sexual and gender forms in question.[8]

In the late eighteenth century and the early nineteenth century, the mannish woman who actively desired women might have been called a "hermaphrodite," a "tribade," or a "female husband," rather than a lesbian, and none of these labels quite adds up to, or feeds directly into, what we now understand as a lesbian sexual orientation. The name "lesbian" is the term we affix to the pleasurable and cumbersome intersections of embodiments, practices, and roles that historical processes have winnowed down to the precise specifications of an identity. Michel Foucault has named this process the "incorporation of perversions," and he has described the means by which "peripheral sexualities" were channeled into "a new speci-fication of individuals."[9] Whereas Foucault's history of sexuality seems far more pertinent for a history of male sexuality than a history of desiring female bodies, we can certainly borrow liberally from his methodology to produce more specific details about the various forms female masculinity has taken from 1800 to the present. Accordingly, within a Foucauldian history of sexuality, "lesbian" constitutes a term for same-sex desire pro-duced in the mid to late twentieth century within the highly politicized context of the rise of feminism and the development of what Foucault calls a homosexual "reverse discourse"; if this is so, then "lesbian" cannot be the transhistorical label for all same-sex activity between women.

Some historians still try to hold on to the label "lesbian" as a way of clas-sifying a whole range of pre-nineteenth-century sexual practices between women. Emma Donoghue, in *Passions between Women*, writes: "Lesbian does not have the specific connotations of such terms as tribade, hermaph-rodite, romantic friend, Sapphist, and Tommy and so can encompass them all."[10] Of course, it is true that this is often the way that "lesbian" has been used, as almost an umbrella term for all sexual activities carried out be-tween women; however, this use of the term "lesbian" erases the specificity of tribadism, hermaphroditism, and transvestism and tends to make lesbi-anism into the history of so-called women-identified women. We may want to apply the term "tommies," for example, to some histories of the mascu-line (i.e., not female-identified) female.[11] We recognize the word "tommy" from its contemporary use as "tomboy" and in general for its function of conferring masculinity on something, as in "tom cat." In general, "tom" connotes boyishness within women and some disruptive form of uncon-ventional masculinity. Donoghue notes: "By the mid nineteenth century, 'tom' meant 'a masculine woman of the town' or prostitute; by the 1880's it referred to a woman 'who does not care for the society of others than those of her own sex'" (5). In fact, the connection between prostitute and masculine woman seems quite common in the nineteenth century, and we might read this synonymous connection as a function of the nineteenth-century tendency to categorize women in relation to marriageability. The prostitute and the masculine and possibly predatory woman both exhibit extramarital desires and have aggressive sexual tendencies. Tracing the use of the slang term "tommy" in fact gives us access to one particular history of female masculinity and its relation to what emerges by the end of the nineteenth century as "lesbianism" or female inversion. If, at the end of the eighteenth century, "tom" describes loose sexual behavior and a particular form of immorality associated with women not bound by marriage to men (prostitutes), by the end of the nineteenth century, extramarital female masculinity has become synonymous with lesbian or invert. Tracing the history of the tommy as an intertwined narrative of female masculinity and female prostitution allows us to see that a sexual history for the masculine woman will at various moments diverge sharply from what has been called lesbian history.

This chapter proposes a methodology for the study of nineteenth-century and early-twentieth-century same-sex desire. I am not really attempting here to fill out the details of the history of pre-twentieth-century same-sex desire between women, but rather I demonstrate a historical methodology through the close reading of two well-known cases of nineteenth-century female masculinity and through the breakdown of various nineteenth-century female masculinities into their specific categories of embodiment. I acknowledge the existence of many different nineteenth-century masculine female embodiments, but I discuss the details of only two: Under the heading "The Tribade," I discuss a court case from 1811 in which two schoolteachers attempted to sue a woman who accused them of tribadism. Under the heading of "The Female Husband," I examine the personal diaries of a Halifax gentlewoman, Anne Lister. In these diaries, Lister discusses her own masculinity at length. I also briefly discuss the figure of the androgyne. I am certain that other court cases from the same period and other letters and diaries, if discovered, would provide a rich record of cross-identifying women in the nineteenth century; indeed, each category of cross-identification, from passing women to cross-dressing sailors and soldiers, deserves its own particular consideration.[12] What I propose to do in this chapter is not to fill in the details of the historical record or provide new data for future researchers but to confine myself to the much more modest project of constructing a framework within which we can study pre-twentieth-century cross-identifying women without reading them always as lesbians who lack a liberating and identitarian discourse. The other aim of this chapter, therefore, is to insist on historical variation and to note the pitfalls of a rigid insistence that some form or another of female masculinity indicates prelesbianism.

I want to argue for a perversely presentist model of historical analysis, a model, in other words, that avoids the trap of simply projecting contemporary understandings back in time, but one that can apply insights from the present to conundrums of the past. In *Discipline and Punish*, Foucault calls for a "history of the present," and he proposes writing a history of the prison as a history of the present, but not as "a history of the past in terms of the present."[13] The history of the present for Foucault represents, therefore, a refusal of conventional models of history. These models, which he calls presentist, rely on narratives of progression in which all social change contributes to the greater good and arrives at an almost utopian present in which things are always better than they have ever been. Foucault's historiography, on the other hand, is able, as Mitchell Dean puts it, "to undertake an analysis of those objects given as necessary components of our reality."[14] By naming my own model of historiography as perverse presentism, to use a very Sedgwickian formulation, I am questioning in the first instance what we think we already know, and then I move back toward the question of what we think we have found when we alight on historical records of so-called lesbian desire. In *Epistemology of the Closet*, Eve Sedgwick offers as axiom 5 in her axiomatic introduction the idea that "the historical search for a great paradigm shift may obscure the present conditions of sexual identity."[15] She amplifies the axiom by suggesting that the Foucauldian history of sexuality as it has been taken up by scholars such as David Halperin posits earlier models of sexual identity in opposition to the models we "know today." Such a move has the effect of both stabilizing what we think we know today and proposing a history of homosexuality as a "narrative of supersession" (46) in which earlier models are completely replaced by newer models with no overlap and no contradiction. Accordingly, a turn-of-the-century model of inversion is completely replaced by a modern model of gender intransitivity, and those who continue to experience their homosexuality as inversion are marginal even within a homosexual community. Sedgwick's alternative to the narrative of supersession is a denaturalization of the present "to render less destructively presumable 'homosexuality as we know it today'" (48).

Building on Sedgwick's axiom, I propose a perverse presentism as not only a denaturalization of the present but also an application of what we do not know in the present to what we cannot know about the past. I make no general claim for the applicability of this method of perverse presentism, and I use it here only because I think a present-day intuition about the construction of masculinity changes the way we think about the records of latter-day female masculinities. So, what exactly do we not know in the present about masculinity that therefore can (and must) be applied to what we cannot know about the past? If, as I suggest throughout this book, there are multiple forms of female masculinity within our present culture, only some of which are annexed indisputably to lesbianism, might it not also be the case that historically, female masculinity takes on a huge variety of forms? In other words, what we do not know for sure today about the relationship between masculinity and lesbianism, we cannot know for sure about historical relations between same-sex desire and female masculinities.

Some critics actively renounce the Foucauldian model of sexual constructivism, which encourages us to take the invention of sexuality at the end of the nineteenth century as the starting point of modern lesbian identity and to limit the search for "lesbian" desire to the last one hundred years. Terry Castle, for one, finds such a model counterintuitive; she claims that the presence of pre-twentieth-century records of same-sex lives clearly signifies desiring and indeed fully sexualized relations between women. Such records prove, according to her, that lesbians existed long before they were invented as such. Indeed, Castle claims in *The Apparitional Lesbian* that queer theory has made "lesbian" into a much more unstable and incoherent signifier than it really is: "I believe we live in a world in which the word lesbian still makes sense, and that it is possible to use the word frequently, even lyrically and still be understood."[16] I do not think Castle would find too many people who would argue against such a common-sense proposal; indeed, the word "lesbian" does *today* have tremendous definitional power and resonance. However, this was not so in the early nineteenth century, and it is after all early versions of lesbian desire that are in question. As we shall see, many nineteenth-century women whom we may feel we recognize as lesbian would have identified neither as lesbian nor even as sapphic, or whatever the popular term of the day may have been for same-sex desire. The reason "lesbian" resonates for us as a term and as a sexual category is because we have come to see same-sex desire between biological females as a coherent set of terms, but as some theorists, such as Judith Butler, have so forcefully argued, it is "permanently unclear what that sign signifies."[17] Perverse presentism must be carefully distinguished from those presentist models espoused by critics, such as Castle, who actually seek only to find what they think they already know.

Female masculinity in the nineteenth century operated within a different system of sexualities and genders. Randolph Trumbach suggests that we might think in terms of two genders and three bodies in the eighteenth century, and he notes: "The woman who desired women, however, and accompanied this with overt masculine characteristics was in the eighteenth century often supposed to be an actual physical hermaphrodite" ("London's Sapphists," 117). The female hermaphrodite was considered a freak of nature with an enlarged clitoris who desired to penetrate other women who might be drawn to her ambiguity. By the end of the nineteenth century, this biological explanation for female sexual aggression seemed less convincing, especially in light of the increased visibility of cross-dressing among nonhermaphroditic women. Although Trumbach's research on London's sapphists is helpful and important in terms of identifying the emergence of different models of female gender deviance, he tends to downplay the relation between third genders and sexual activity. He suggests, for example, that some cross-dressing women at the end of the eighteenth century may have used dildos and may have taken wives but that "it is also likely that most women who dressed and passed as men for any length of time did not seek to have sexual relations with women; this is probably true even of those who married women" (114). It is important to oppose such a claim with the observation that it is much easier to believe that women who cross-dressed and took wives had fully satisfying sexual relationships with these wives, and there is little or nothing to be gained from insisting that these relations were probably not sexual. Passing as a man and marrying a woman are fairly extensive forms of social subterfuge, and we must give credit to the women who participated in such impersonations—presumably they had compelling reasons for their cross-dressing and took much satisfaction in the results.

Debates among lesbian historians about the roots of modern lesbian identities tend also to focus on the absence or presence of sexual desire and activity among those women who were drawn to same-sex relations, often as so-called romantic friends, in the eighteenth and nineteenth centuries. Or else such histories try to account for the importance and historical place of so-called lesbian role playing. Indeed, Martha Vicinus suggests that "far too much energy has probably been consumed discussing a very American concern—whether romantic friendships or butch-femme relationships are most characteristic of lesbianism."[18] Vicinus critiques the romantic-friendship historians, such as Blanche Wiesen Cook and Lillian Faderman, for ignoring gender variations among women and for assuming the asexual nature of many relations between women, but Vicinus also rejects some of the butch-femme historians for their dependence on empirical evidence of sexual activity, which may never surface: "How are we ever to know, definitely, what someone born a hundred or two hundred years ago did in bed? And as Cook has pointed out, does it really matter so much?" (472).

We might respond to Vicinus's exasperation about questions of sexual activity by saying that some women left records of what they did sexually one or two hundred years ago; other women's sexual practices were recorded in law books when the women were charged with sexual misconduct. Furthermore, in response to Vicinus's provocative question about whether it really matters if we know what women did together sexually, I think that it does indeed matter, if only because lesbianism has conventionally come to be associated with the asexual, the hidden, the "apparitional," and the invisible. There is much evidence to counteract this tendency to think about lesbianism as permanently disappearing, and when, for example, we are considering the history of the masculine woman rather than the "lesbian," we find that she is marked by a kind of hyper-visibility rather than an apparitional quality. Sexual details are important to the history I am trying to chart because lesbianism is after all a "sexual" identity. Once we establish that the kinds of sexual desires and acts that the term "lesbian" claims to represent are multiple and various, the category itself comes under serious pressure. The desires and sexual instincts of a cross-dressing female husband are in no way similar to the desires and sexual instincts of the women she attempts to seduce, and the desires and sexual acts shared by romantic friends may be far different from the sexual relations between masculine women and their married lovers. If this is so, then what do we gain from organizing identity categories around the notion of same-sex desire? As I show in later chapters, sexual identities, when and where they emerge as identities, tend to be exceedingly specific and often refer to a limited range of pleasures rather than an expansive set of pleasures that can be summarized by a term such as "lesbian." Some may argue, in contrast to my point here, that "lesbian" describes a set of social relations between women far more than a set of sexual practices; although this is true, much feminist scholarship has dedicated itself to distinguishing between social and sexual relations between women to mark the specificity of lesbian dynamics and separate them from some universalizing notion of women's community. Furthermore, because so many women whom one may study under the heading "female masculinity" identify only partially or problematically with the category "woman," relations between women and same-sex relations are poor descriptive terms for the physical relations between masculine women and their lovers.

Martha Vicinus's incredibly useful and influential discussion of female gender variance in the nineteenth century provides a preliminary breakdown of the different forms such variance may take. Vicinus, however, stops short of separating out the category of lesbian from female masculinity. She describes various women who were constantly mistaken for men as "androgynous," and she tends to hold to the general category of lesbian in her descriptions of historical same-sex relations.[19] Although my discussions of early forms of female masculinity are clearly indebted to the pioneering work and research by Vicinus and others, I want to extend the implications of Vicinus's radical history: the androgyne, accordingly, represents a different form of gender variance than the masculine woman, and although the androgyne may have faced some kind of social opprobrium, it probably did not come in the form of a response to gender confusion. The androgyne represents some version of gender mixing, but this rarely adds up to total ambiguity; when a woman is mistaken consistently for a man, I think it is safe to say that what marks her gender presentation is not androgyny but masculinity. In other words, I propose that we consider the various categories of sexual variation for women as separate and distinct from the modern category of lesbian and that we try to account for the specific sexual practices associated with each category and the particular social relations that may have held each category in place.

Finally, there are likely to be many examples of masculine women in history who had no interest in same-sex sexuality. While it is not within the scope of this book to do so, there is probably a lively history of the masculine heterosexual woman to be told, a history, moreover, that must be buried by the bundling of all female masculinities into lesbian identity. By holding modern notions of lesbianism apart from the history of female masculinity, I am trying to do two very different things: first, I would like to account for one very specific strand of gender variance without assuming that it neatly corresponds to contemporary formulations of the coincidence of sexual and gender variance; second, I want to allow for the multiple histories of nonnormative subjects. Accordingly, there are many examples of masculinity in women that resonate within a complex of heterosexualities and derive from very different sources. For example, some rural women may be considered masculine by urban standards, and their masculinity may simply have to do with the fact that they engage in more manual labor than other women or live within a community with very different gender standards. The present-day rural masculine woman who lives a heterosexual life and whose masculinity is as much a product of her work as her desire may be related in some way to latter-day cowgirls, tough women who worked with horses and cattle and competed in rodeos. Work on the history of American cowgirls suggests that some of the cowgirls who competed in rodeos in America in the early twentieth century must have been lesbians, but many were not, and these women saw no particular contradiction in being heterosexual and, by some standards, masculine. They would justify their unconventional behavior with appeals to naturalness and health. In a book on cowgirls, one bronc rider is quoted as saying:

> A cowgirl would no more think of wearing spike heels, a tight girdle, a binding brassier, than she would drink poison. It is not that a cowgirl does not want to attract the masculine eyes, but we know cowboys. They like slimness, line, grace—but they want it natural. Women with curved spines and swayed abdomens, with half the muscles in their bodies wasted from lack of exercise and use, who fear childbirth because they have not kept their bodies natural, wonder why their lives are not rich, full, vital—yet they never dream that the violation of natural health laws is the cause of everything.[20]

This testimony to the naturalness of female toughness depends on the equation of modern femininity with artificiality and makes a case for natural and healthy bodies as opposed to wasted and deformed, but properly feminine, bodies. This writer even suggests that a woman can better fulfill her marital role as a tough woman because childbirth is less punishing for a natural body.

Because modern femininity has depended on all kinds of unnatural measures and unhealthy practices, many women over time must have rejected conventional femininity in favor of healthy bodies. For this reason, the female athlete almost inevitably becomes the object of intense gender scrutiny and surveillance. An obviously athletic female body, because it makes visible a willful rejection of feminine inactivity, seems immediately to be associated with lesbianism. Although it is true that unathletic men also fall victim to homophobic suspicion, notice that the demands of proper heterosexual femininity coincide with the renouncing of a healthy body. For this reason, many women, not only inverts and lesbians, over time may have cultivated masculine body aesthetics in order to work, play, compete, or simply survive. The masculine heterosexual woman need not be viewed as a lesbian in denial; she may merely be a woman who rejects the strictures of femininity.

The masculine women whose relationships look like conventional opposite-sex relations—the tommy, the androgyne, and the female transvestite, in other words—all deserve their own specific histories. By engaging a perversely presentist method, one that uses present-day insights to make sense of the complexities of other eras, we can see that multiple modes of gender variance exist in both contemporary society and nineteenth-century society. If contemporary models of gender variance tend to presume some continuity between lesbianism or transsexuality and cross-gender identification, in the absence of sexual identities, gender variance must have meant something different. By tracing the history of the tommy, we might find that gender variance is measured through a woman's marital status; by tracing a history of hermaphroditism, we would have to conclude that gender variance is measured on the body. In what follows, I examine two very different cases of gender variance that produce very different models of perversion and sexual nonconformity.

## The Tribade

The sexual activity of tribadism has commanded far less critical attention than it deserves. "Tribade" is a word of Greek origin meaning a woman who rubs, and it refers to the pleasurable friction of rubbing a clitoris on another person's thigh, pubic bone, hip, buttocks, or any other fleshly surface. In the eighteenth and nineteenth centuries, a known tribade would often also be suspected of having an enlarged and possibly hermaphroditic clitoris, and some early sexologists surmised that a hermaphroditic tribade would attempt clitoral penetration of another female. Tribadism, because it seemed to resemble intercourse in either its motion or its simulation of penetrative sex, was often linked to female masculinity and to particularly pernicious (because successful?) forms of sexual perversion.

Many historians of sexuality use the category of hermaphrodite as a synonym for a third sex because in the seventeenth and eighteenth centuries, the notion of a third sex emerged not only as a biological explanation for so-called same-sex behavior but also as the believed consequence of self-pollution. Seventeenth and eighteenth century anatomists seemed much more interested in the category of the female-to-male hermaphrodite than in the male to female hermaphrodite because it was presumed that nature tends toward perfectibility and the female form is always figured as the imperfect version of the male. Until the eighteenth century, as Thomas Laqueur's work has shown, thinking about the body was dominated by a "one-sex model" in which a woman was understood to be an inverted man; the male and female genitalia, in other words, were considered to be analogous, but in women the genitalia were inside (vagina as penis tucked inside), and in men they were outside.[21] By the late eighteenth century, the one-sex model gave way completely to the two-sex model. Within a one-sex model, then, a hermaphrodite is a woman who becomes male (sometimes a male who becomes female) when her womb drops down. In a two-sex model, she is a woman who has male genitals hidden within her or who has a monstrous clitoris that serves as a penis. Although it is tempting to view the monstrous figure of the hermaphrodite as the focus of, and embodiment of, same-sex desires, I think we have to seriously question even the notion of "same sex" in this case because this formulation assumes that the hermaphrodite was considered as the same sex as a woman. In fact, the hermaphrodite was set apart, as if another sex. The use of the category of hermaphrodite, in general, signals an attempt to locate monstrous nonfemale desire on the body.

Valerie Traub, in a marvelous essay on the history of the clitoris and tribadism, notes that the medical "discovery" of the clitoris occurred in 1559 when two Italian anatomists, Renaldo Columbo and Gabriele Falloppia, gave the organ a name and ascribed to it a function.[22] The clitoris, Traub shows, immediately became the source of great anxiety because it represented another penis on the female body; if the vagina was seen as an inverted penis, the clitoris had to be an external one. Immediately the clitoris was linked to nonreproductive sex, and anxieties arose about women with clitorides capable of penetration; because of these anxieties, the clitoris, its size and function, was immediately linked to same-sex desire. Tribadism, Traub comments in a footnote, is a Greek word, and there was no terminology in the ancient world to refer to same-sex erotic acts between women:

Lesbos was originally associated with fellatio and Sappho with prostitution rather than "lesbian" desire; it was only after the second century A.D. that "Lesbos" was associated with Sappho's expression of desire for women. In fact, there was no established terminology in the ancient world specifically designating same-gender erotic acts between women. Rather, what the ancients found occasion to comment on were penetrative acts (with dildo or clitoris) that women may perform with either women or men.[23]

The ability of a woman to take the role of penetrator and her masculinity are what give rise to the Greek word "tribade," and finally it comes to be associated with same-sex female sexual activity, Traub suggests, in late antiquity.

Traub emphasizes that the tribade is not a lesbian, and she offers the following cautionary note: "I believe that subsuming erotic desire and practices under modern categories thwarts inquiry both into the *construction* of the homosexual/heterosexual divide and the regulatory function of identity" ("Psychomorphology of the Clitoris," 99). The tribade is, however, a part of the history of the masculinization of certain female sexual practices, and she exemplifies the problems of determining their meanings. I would argue that we must also consider tribadism as an important sexual practice among modern masculine women; for such women, it may retain the sense of a masculine sex act even without the belief that it is motivated by the possession of a giant clitoris. Furthermore, it is important to notice the ways in which the tribade partakes in discourses of female pleasure but also violates the category of woman; she must be situated, in other words, in relation to the history of females who cannot conform to the category of woman. Finally, tribadism was and is a sexual practice, not a sexual identity. If we trace the use of the term forward into the present, we find that tribadism is one of those rarely discussed but often practiced sexual activities, and the silence that surrounds it now is as puzzling as the discourse it produced in earlier centuries. Freud had nothing to say on the subject of tribadism, and few contemporary lesbian sex books even discuss it.

Tribadism, with or without a dildo, with or without simultaneous digital penetration of a lover, really constitutes a sexual practice particular to women.[24] It is curious, therefore, that tribadism tends not to be definitively associated with lesbianism. In contemporary lesbian film and within the hetero-pornographic imagination, lesbian sex seems primarily to be summarized as oral sex with mutuality and reciprocation being the main modes of sexual exchange. Within tribadism, there are various modes of sexual gendering at play, and many of them turn on which partner is on top and which is on the bottom; tribadism is also very often accompanied by penetration of a partner with fingers or dildo, and so mutuality and reciprocation tend not to be the main objective, although satisfaction for both partners through different means most definitely is its aim.

Under the entry for "tribadism" in the *OED*, we find a use of the term in 1811 in the court papers of the celebrated case of *Miss Marianne Woods and Miss Jane Pirie v. Dame Cumming Gordon*. This trial has been popularized by Lillian Hellman's play *The Children's Hour* and by Lillian Faderman's extensive re-creation of the court case in her book *Scotch Verdict*.[25] The Woods and Pirie case was tried in Scotland, and it is interesting for our purposes not simply for its depiction of various forms of female masculinity and its relation to tribadism but also for the disagreements it generates, both then and now, over what constitutes sexual activity between women and what makes it "lesbian." The Woods and Pirie case was based on an accusation made by a student at the Woods and Pirie School for Girls, which was countered by a suit for slander filed by Woods and Pirie against the girl's grandmother, Dame Cumming Gordon. In the course of the trial, numerous sexually explicit charges are made against the two women by their former students. The case is remarkable as a document because it provides such detailed information about what people knew or claimed to know (or claimed not to know) about same-sex sexuality.[26] Faderman's book *Scotch Verdict*, on the other hand, is similarly remarkable for the way that it both reproduces some of the original notions about the purity of female erotic expression and relentlessly imposes contemporary understandings of lesbian desire on a text in which lesbian identity cannot be imagined as such.

In *Woods and Pirie v. Cumming Gordon*, a student, Jane Cumming, accuses Marianne Woods and Jane Pirie of sexual indecency, and Cumming and other pupils testify to the extensive sexual activity they have witnessed between the two women. The case goes to trial when Woods and Pirie accuse Jane Cumming's grandmother of slander for circulating rumors about sexual indecency in the schoolhouse. Because of the rumors, the Woods and Pirie School for Girls had to be closed. It is unusual to find a nineteenth-century court case involving such explicit testimony because there were no legal injunctions against sex between women. The indifference showed by the law toward women has meant that there are few official records of same-sex eroticism. Any court cases that do exist tend to involve women who have impersonated men. The peculiarities of this court case are immensely complicated because the accusing girl was Anglo-Indian, and in both the court transcripts and Lillian Faderman's re-creation of them, the girl is repeatedly Orientalized and depicted as suspiciously sexually knowledgeable. Both Faderman and the original judges attribute Jane Cumming's sexual knowledge to her childhood in India. The imbrication of racial difference and sexual perversity in the various representations of this trial become sensational precisely where and when competing definitions of lesbianism are at stake. As Lisa Moore points out in her reading of the case: "The possibility that British female bodies or British female erotic imaginations were capable of sexual congress with each other was thus diverted in the trial through recourse to a racist myth of a deviant, sexualized Eastern woman's body."[27]

The two women are primarily described as tribades who simulate sexual intercourse by lying one on top of the other (mostly Miss Woods on top of Miss Pirie, but very occasionally they switch), and the court presumably imagines that one woman penetrates the other. In their capacity as schoolteachers, the two women each share beds with one or other of the schoolgirls in their charge. Jane Cumming testified that at night, the teachers would visit each other's bed, and the girls would be disturbed by the bed shaking, heavy breathing, and other suspicious sounds and odd conversation. One night, Cumming alleges, when Miss Woods "lay above Miss Jane Pirie and began to move," she heard a sucking sound like "putting one's finger into the neck of a wet bottle" (Faderman, *Scotch Verdict*, 147). On other nights, she claims to have heard whispering and suspicious activity and to have heard Miss Pirie tell Miss Woods, "You are in the wrong place." Miss Woods answers, "I know." Miss Pirie says, "Why are you doing it then?" and Miss Woods answers, "For fun" (147).

Various judges in the lengthy trial question the validity of Jane Cumming's evidence by suggesting that the actual sexual practices that Cumming describes are physically impossible because, the judges believed, women could not give each other orgasmic pleasure and especially not in this tribadic mode. They are all made uneasy by the possibility that the two women engaged in sexual activity with each other that they found "fun" and satisfying. The judges understand Woods and Pirie to have been accused of tribadism, but because no dildo is mentioned, they presume that penetration could take place only if one or both women have abnormally large clitorides or if one of the women is really a man. Such a thing, they all reassure each other, is unheard of in England. Therefore, only one explanation can be given for what Cumming claims: Cumming has made

up her story and based it on illicit knowledge she received while growing up in India. Lord Meadowbank comments that Jane Cumming must
have obtained such information from her "Hindoo female domestics."[28]
Throughout the case, judges and prosecutors accuse Jane Cumming of
importing sexual knowledge from India and tainting pure British women
with her accusations. British women, they insist, practice asexual romantic friendship and know nothing of dildos or enlarged clitorides.

There is something unremarkable, of course, about discovering such
racist sentiments at the heart of British law in the nineteenth century.
What is more remarkable is Lillian Faderman's similar use of Orientalist
rhetoric to downplay the seriousness of Cumming's charges. Faderman
refers to Jane Cumming during her commentary as pernicious and suspect; she refers to "this Indian girl's villainy" in bringing the charge against
the schoolteachers, and she seems to think that Cumming maligned an
innocent and loving friendship. In relation to Jane Cumming's rather convincing description of the sounds and motions that she heard in bed at
night, Faderman says the following:

> But there are other parts of Jane Cumming's description that are
> absurd: if one woman is on top of the other, moving back and forth
> or up and down over her genitals, what would make that noise? There
> would be no room for a hand to be squeezed in between. Somewhere
> the Indian girl must have seen a man and a woman coupling, and she
> must have heard that two females could couple too—and in her utter
> ignorance, she assumed (perhaps not understanding about penetration,
> perhaps having fantastic notions about female tumescence in passion)
> that it was done in the same way. (*Scotch Verdict*, 155)

Leaving aside for the moment Faderman's own assumptions about tribadic
activity—that is, her sureness that tribadic motion leaves no possibility for
simultaneous digital penetration—we can see how completely Faderman
rehearses the same manipulations of race and sexuality as the original
judges of the case did. In her haste to protect romantic friends from lewd
imputations, she too displaces sexual knowledge onto "the Indian girl" (as
she calls Cumming) and suggests that young Indian girls are inevitably
exposed to sexual activity in India.

It is crucial here to note the multiple ironies of this case and of its
interpretations. The case seems to turn on disagreements about what
two women can actually do sexually together: Jane Cumming's testimony

convincingly has the women participating in tribadism and digital penetration. Lillian Faderman is torn between refuting the judges' denial of the
possibility of lesbian sex and refuting the nature of the sex that Jane Cumming describes. At stake for Faderman is a model of lesbian sex that does
not resemble in any way patriarchal sex. The judges, on the other hand,
have to decide which is worse: lesbian corruption of innocents or childish corruptions of pure British women. Faderman protects her belief in a
pure lesbianism by accusing the "evil" Indian girl of sexual fantasy, and the
judges feel secure in the innocence of British womanhood by displacing
all perverse sexual activity onto foreign imaginations. Clearly, translating
sexual activity from one historical moment to another in Faderman's text
is a risky enterprise, and the hazard and jeopardy involved can be relieved
only by recourse to a stabilizing colonial or racist discourse.

The theory of hermaphroditic clitorides and masculine female sexual
aggressions was clearly an idea that threatened English judges and lawyers.
Their assumption that sex between women must involve some penetrating
organ fulfills one set of patriarchal expectations about sex between women,
but the judges' refusal to believe that English women could be involved in
any such activity protects their idea of English womanhood from the possibility of sexually active behavior. Obviously, romantic friendship was a far
more comforting notion, one that has been used time and time again to
cover over the possibility of female sexual aggression in the nineteenth century. One hundred years later, Havelock Ellis also discounted the possibility
of English hermaphroditism by projecting such sexual activity onto non-
European women. Because Freud barely mentions tribadism, we could
argue that the connection between tribadism and same-sex eroticism becomes muted when sexology moves away from physiological explanations
for sexual behavior and comes to depend on psychosexual explanations.
With the rise of psychoanalysis, indeed, tribadism quietly faded from view.

### The Female Husband

I turn now to a particular example of nineteenth-century female masculinity to demonstrate the importance of resisting the label of lesbian for
such early accounts of same-sex desire and to see what emerges from an
analysis of a masculine woman when we examine her life without the comforting and distracting lens of contemporary lesbian identities. This representation of nineteenth-century sexual activity between women occurs

within the remarkable diaries of an English gentlewoman, Anne Lister; the diaries give us another indication of the diversity of sexual activity between women and clearly link certain forms of sexual activity to female masculinity. In places, the diaries produce explicit sexual episodes that are not easily assimilated into modern notions of lesbian sexual practice and seem to have little to do with the kind of autonomous female sexualities that some commentators project onto romantic friends.

Lister's diaries have been used by quite a few commentators to trace a prehistory of lesbian desire. In "They Wonder to Which Sex I Belong," Vicinus calls Lister "a self-consciously mannish lesbian" (481); Lisa Moore usefully refers to Lister's writings as providing the "conditions of production of female homosexual character;"[29] and in an excellent historical essay on the whole of Lister's writings, Anna Clarke suggests that "although she did not use the word lesbian . . . Anne Lister illuminates not only lesbian history but questions of representation and agency in the larger field of the history of sexuality as well."[30] What unites these quite different examinations of Lister's diaries is the unproblematic categorization of Lister and her desire as a lesbian. I will return to this vexed site of historical definition after looking more closely at the diaries themselves.

Recently, historian Helena Whitbread made Anne Lister's diaries from 1819 to 1826 available under the titles *I Know My Own Heart* and *No Priest but Love*.[31] In the diaries, this Halifax gentlewoman gives full accounts of her varied sexual activity, and when we examine carefully the sexual content of Anne Lister's relations with her many different lovers, we can begin to piece together an account of nineteenth-century female same-sex desire that is structured much less by romantic friendships and a shared refusal of patriarchy and more by unequal desires, sexual and gender roles, ritualized class relations, and an almost total rejection of sexual sameness.

Anne Lister (1791–1840) was the daughter of Captain Jeremy Lister and Rebecca Battle, and from about 1815 to 1840, she lived with her bachelor uncle and spinster aunt at Shibden Hall, in Halifax, England. Because all of her brothers had died young, Anne became the sole heir to the Shibden estate, which she did eventually inherit. The diaries were written in an elaborate code in an alphabet of Anne's devising. Helena Whitbread painstakingly went through 6,600 pages of writing and decoded the entire document. The code, of course, is a remarkably suggestive metaphor for the whole enterprise of recording and reading sexual histories, and it is suggestive of the various disguises in which alternative sexual identities may cloak themselves. Anne Lister's diaries reveal a wealth of information about English social life at the beginning of the nineteenth century and about relations between women at this time.

The diaries contain recognizably "sapphic" material, and yet Anne herself did not identify as such and took pains to distinguish between her own "natural" instincts and "sapphic artifices." Her preference for women, she tells one woman she is flirting with, "was all nature. Had it not been genuine the thing would have been different." She goes on, "Got on the subject of Saffic regard. I said there was artifice in it. It was very different from mine & would be no pleasure to me. I liked to have those I loved as near me as possible, etc. Asked if she understood. She said no. I told her I knew by her eyes she did & she did not deny it, therefore I know she understands all about the use of a ———" (*No Priest but Love*, 49). This passage is fairly elliptical in terms of its sexual description, and we can only speculate about how Anne is distinguishing between her own desire and "Saffic regard." "I liked to have those I loved as near me as possible" could refer to her use of a dildo but definitely refers to her preference for tribadism over other forms of sexual activity, oral or otherwise. As we will see, in other passages, she is more explicit about what she does and how she understands sex between women.

Anne never married, but she had constant female companionship of one kind or another. Although the term "female husband" is often used to describe outright female transvestism and male impersonation, here I use it to describe women who played husband to married women who were either abandoned or neglected by their male husbands. In Henry Fielding's famous play *The Female Husband* (1746), he dramatizes the story of Mary Hamilton, alias George, a passing woman who married another woman while in disguise and was arrested for doing so in 1746. Fielding, of course, uses this plot to ridicule the masculine woman and to try to deny her power. But, as Terry Castle argues, Fielding does not completely demonize the female husband; he is also drawn to the particular kind of social disorder that she represents: "Fielding is both repulsed and attracted to his heroine, concerned to distance himself from her morally, but also unconsciously drawn to her."[32] Such an attitude on the part of Fielding perhaps expresses the social position of the female husband; she was both a kind of folk hero who lived a daring life of subterfuge and dissimulation, and a rebellious figure who usurped male power. Whereas Anne Lister was not a female transvestite per se, her masculinity worked precisely by constantly inserting itself into the cracks that inevitably result from the gendered separation of spheres for men and women, and her sexual seductions took place precisely in the spaces left by men unwilling or unable to fulfill their wives. A local gentleman says of Anne Lister that he would as soon "turn a man loose in his house" as have Anne around his wife and daughters (*No Priest but Love*, 127). Anne is constantly mistaken for a man or treated like one during her daily life, but she sees her gender ambiguity as neither imitative nor deficient. Indeed, she notes in response to a letter from a female admirer, "Tis well I have not a penis. I could never have been continent." Anne's lack of a penis—what we might call the privileged gadget of male masculinity—allows her "pleasure without danger," almost unlimited access to women she desires and the joys of sex without marriage. She is not troubled by the social danger of impregnating her partners, in other words. Significantly, when she and her lover Marianne become infected with a venereal disease, it is traced back to Marianne's husband, Charles.

From 1812 to about 1828, Anne was emotionally and physically involved with Marianne Percy Lawton, a young woman whom Anne met in York and continued to court even after Marianne married Charles Lawton in 1815. During the course of the marriage, the women sent love letters to each other and slept together whenever possible. In one significant scene, the two women are reunited after a long absence in which Anne has been gallivanting around Paris with various women and Marianne has been stuck in the loveless and apparently sexless marriage. Anne makes love to Marianne and finds after penetrating Marianne that her finger is covered in blood; this leads her to suspect that Charles has "never broken the membrane" (*No Priest but Love*, 125). Marianne confirms that she is probably still a virgin because "Charles . . . has never been able to do the business" (125). This presents Anne with a challenge she cannot refuse, and the next week, she describes pushing in her middle finger, "not pushing hard, merely pushing up and down." When no more blood appears, she declares: "I believed I had done the business better than I had thought & she was no longer a virgin, at which we were both well satisfied. My having done this for her seems to have delighted us both. It proves that Charles has had not much power & she has never belonged to anyone but me" (126).

The deflowering of Marianne by Anne, or Fred, as Marianne calls her, confirms the sexual insignificance of marriage for Marianne and for Anne gives her access to a virility separate from penile sexuality. This remarkable scene is just one of many instances in the diaries in which Anne and Marianne revel in the superiority of their sexual liaison over any liaison involving a man. Far from imitating heterosexuality, in fact, this scene registers the lack of a functional model of heterosexuality or of male masculinity to imitate. It is also one of a few incidents in which Anne and Marianne celebrate Anne's potent masculinity. More often, Anne remarks on the stares she draws from people in the street who think she might be a man (this despite the fact that she always wears women's clothing), and on one occasion, Marianne is actually embarrassed by her lover's masculinity. The two go away to Scarborough, a seaside resort, for a holiday; while there, they are socially snubbed on account of Anne's masculinity, and Anne records that Marianne wishes Anne had "a feminine figure." At another moment, however, Marianne confesses that if Anne were more feminine, Marianne would not desire her sexually.

Anne herself feels no desire to change her own masculinity. She does wish, at this point in the diaries, that she could access the wealth and social status necessary to ignore social slanders. Once she inherits her uncle's estate, indeed, her social position actually protects her from the kind of disapprobation that she routinely undergoes as a masculine woman without her own income. Social status obviously confers mobility and a moderate freedom from the disgrace of female masculinity. Anne's discomfort in this scene suggests why so many working-class masculine women would have had to go undercover and pass as men. Anne, in a sense, can live out the contradiction of female masculinity because she is upper-class. As Anna Clarke comments, "Anne's androgynous appearance—she was obviously a woman in skirts, yet she walked like a man—threatened contemporaries because she did not completely cross-dress but still took male freedoms" (46). Those "male freedoms," Clarke goes on to note, were not simply the freedom of a particular gait; they were economic freedoms associated with aristocratic landowning power. Based on Lister's own descriptions of her public humiliations, however, it is clear that she finds the limits of her class power all too quickly when it comes to her far from "androgynous" appearance. The snubs she experiences are not on account of some blend between femininity and masculinity in her appearance; they are the direct consequence of public recognitions of her masculinity.

Although Lister was primarily preoccupied during this period with Marianne Lawton, she also became involved with a woman she met in

Paris called Mrs. Barlow, and interspersed with these two women, Anne recounts another relationship with an older woman, Isabelle Norcliffe. Anne's relationship with Isabelle and her relationship later to another masculine woman called Miss Pickford suggest the existence of a gendered code *between* women. Anne shows little sustained interest sexually in other masculine women, and she also does not bond with these women as kindred souls. In an interaction with Miss Pickford, Anne denies her desire for women. "My manners may mislead you," she tells Pickford, "but I don't in reality go beyond the utmost verge of friendship" (*I Know My Own Heart,* 273). Isabelle, also a masculine woman, pursues Anne quite vigorously over the course of about a decade. Anne rejects Isabelle repeatedly and finally sums up her disinterest in Isabelle by saying, "two Jacks would not suit together" (127).

Anne, in fact, invariably flirts with feminine women who are or who have been married, and she engages in long, drawn out seductions of them. When she is in Paris during 1824 to 1826, she embarks on a long affair with Mrs. Barlow, a widow who catches Anne's fancy. This affair is quite typical of Anne's exploits. The seduction begins with Anne taking Mrs. Barlow onto her lap and attempting to feel under her petticoats. While they are out in public, Anne fondles Mrs. Barlow and tries to excite her. Anne tells her diary one day: "Kissed her in a little dark passage as we came out of the dining room. She lets me kiss her now very quietly & sits with her feet close to mine. . . . If I had a penis though of small length, I should surely break the ice some of these times before I go" (*No Priest but Love,* 42). Anne alludes to various fantasies of having a penis, but she mainly seems to see a penis as useful for sex in public places rather than necessary to her whole sexual enterprise. Eventually, she gets Mrs. Barlow into bed to their mutual satisfaction. Most of their sexual activity seems to involve Anne touching Mrs. Barlow's "queer" (as she calls the female genitals) and tribadically rubbing on her.

Anne gives several hints to Mrs. Barlow about how she works sexually. One day, Mrs. Barlow comments that Anne seems sexually ready for anything, and Anne replies: "No, I do what I like but never permit them to do so" (*No Priest but Love,* 85). Based on what follows, this exchange relays Anne's understanding of sexual roles. She does what she likes to women, but they are never permitted to do the same in return. This, she adds, seems to please Mrs. Barlow. Another hint that there are clear sexual roles for Anne occurs one day as Anne and Mrs. Barlow are getting out of bed:

In getting out of bed, she suddenly touching my queer, I started back. "Ah," said she "that is because you are a pucelle (virgin). I must undo that. I can give you relief. I must do to you as you do to me." I liked not this & said she astonished me. She asked if I was angry. No, merely astonished. However, I found I could not easily make her understand my feeling on the subject and I dropped the matter altogether. Marianne would not make such a speech. This is womanizing me too much. Marianne will suit me better. I cannot do much for Mrs Barlow except with my finger. I am more sure of going on well with Marianne who is contented with having myself next to her. (*No Priest but Love*, 85)

This is a fairly remarkable passage both in its directness and in terms of the sexual roles Anne describes. Clearly, for Anne, that she and Mrs. Barlow are both women does not mean that sexual activity between them is completely reciprocal. Anne touches Mrs. Barlow's queer but does not expect Mrs. Barlow to touch hers. Anne manipulates Mrs. Barlow digitally but would prefer full-body tribadism, queer to queer, as she says elsewhere. This emphasis on roles and tribadism and in other places on penetration perhaps suggests how Anne understands her own sexuality to be different from "Saffic regard." Clarke comments of this exchange that "it is interesting that Mrs Barlow expected to be able to touch Anne, perhaps having experienced or desiring more reciprocal lovemaking" (44). There is little evidence in the diaries of such desire or experience on Mrs. Barlow's part, and the implication of the scene, for Anne at least, seems to be that Mrs. Barlow is naive and untutored in these extremely gendered exchanges.

There are many more instances in the diaries where Anne refers to her gendered desires, her fantasies of having a penis, her desire to be Marianne's "husband," and her "sensitiveness of anything which reminded me of my petticoats" (*No Priest but Love*, 173). She details the great orgasmic satisfaction (she calls orgasms "kisses") that she and Marianne give each other every night that they spend together, and in general Anne claims and affirms her own masculinity as a powerful attractor of women and a potent marker of her own desires: "Slept very little last night," she tells us, "talked almost the whole time till about 4 in the morning. Went to Marianne four times, the last time just before getting up. She had eight kisses, I counted ten" (163).

Critics such as Terry Castle have used Anne Lister's diaries to argue with constructivists who, as she sees it, perpetuate the "no-lesbians-before-

1900-myth."[33] Castle conflates here an argument about the invention of homosexuality by sexologists at the end of the nineteenth century and the arguments by some lesbian historians about the conventionality of asexual romantic friendships between women in the eighteenth and nineteenth centuries. Although few critics would make the nonsensical claim that women did not have sex with other women before 1900, Castle uses Lister simply as proof of lesbian sexual activity. When Castle does mention Lister's pronounced masculinity, it is only to aver that "in a society that typically ghosts or occludes images of women desiring women, the homosexually inclined woman will inevitably be attracted to the next best thing: to images of men desiring women" (104). By seeing masculine identification as merely a stand-in for a properly female desire for women, Castle eliminates the possibility that masculinity may function independently of men and through biologically female bodies. She also ignores Anne's constant references to the potency of her own masculinity next to the impotency of male masculinity as it functions within middle-class or aristocratic marriages. Anna Clarke also suggests that Anne grafts her own desires onto the machinery of masculine desire in the absence of a functional model of lesbianism: "For Lister, therefore, imagining having a phallus was a way of representing her desire for a woman (and for male privilege) in a culture that gave her almost no other ways of representing a *sexual* lesbian desire" (44). Although Clarke is much more carefully attentive to the specificities of historical location, she, like Castle, assumes that there is such a thing as lesbian desire, independent of desiring subjects who identify as such, which is merely waiting to enter discourse and find adequate representation. As long as such a mode of representation is absent, lesbian desire must masquerade as other things. However, in contemporary lesbian culture, there are still many women whose desire works through masculinity and through phallic fantasy and through sexual practices that phantasmically transform their female bodies into penetrating male bodies.[34] Lister's tribadic practices, the restrictions she places on her lovers' sexual access to her body, and her self-identification with masculinity should be read for what they are—signs of an active and functional but preidentitarian female masculinity embedded within a highly ritualized marriage culture and struggling with the active cultural biases against female masculine expression.

There is obviously much more work to be done on the incredible revelations of Anne Lister's diaries. Similarly, court cases of women on trial for male impersonation or sexual impropriety beg to be examined in terms of affirmative histories of sexual deviance. Although turn-of-the-century sexologists would later try to classify all lesbian activity as inversion, in the early nineteenth century, it is obvious, sexual activity between women flourished in spaces where the masculine woman trespassed on male sexual privilege and created not "a female world of love and ritual"[35] but an exciting sexual landscape dominated by the female husband and the tribade.

*And it may be that being myself a "misfit," for as you know beloved, I am a born invert, it may be that I am a writer of "misfits" in one form or another—I think I understand them —their joys & sorrows, indeed I know I do, and all the misfits of this world are lonely, being conscious that they differ from the rank and file.—John Radclyffe Hall, letter to Evguenia Souline, 24 October 1934,* Your John: The Love Letters of Radclyffe Hall *(1997)*

# 3  ''A WRITER OF MISFITS''

*John Radclyffe Hall and the Discourse of Inversion*

## The Invert

At the turn of the twentieth century, as Michel Foucault has argued, the discourse of sexuality became a medical discourse, and sexual acts were transformed through complex discursive practices into stable notions of identity.[1] As we saw with Anne Lister, her understanding of herself as masculine certainly seemed to hint at an identity formation and allows us to think about the emergence of a notion of sexual identity as a long process rather than the result of one intense period of medical research and social reform. As early as 1910 and into the 1920s, communities of inverts and their "wives" had developed into visible and elaborate subcultures, and with the publication in 1928 of Radclyffe Hall's novel of inversion, *The Well of Loneliness,* the topic of inversion became highly publicized. Hall's complex understanding of her own sexual subjectivity has been handed down to modern readers in her novels, her letters, and recollections of her life made by her partner Una Troubridge and many other literary luminaries. The recent publication of Hall's letters allows for new insights about the psychic mechanisms of inversion and the romantic relations between inverts and their lovers. It is also important to consider, as I do in this chapter, the many different forms and practices associated with female masculinity during the era of inversion. By contextualizing the life of Radclyffe Hall—or John, as she insisted on being called—I call attention to the multiple and contradictory models of female masculinity produced by not only John but also her many inverted friends and contemporaries.

When the idea of sexual identities did come to dominate people's thinking about sex and gender, it was not some idea of an autonomous lesbian desire between women or a notion of outward hermaphroditism that provided the basis of those notions of identity; it was gender inversion. "Inversion," then, was the medical term used in the late nineteenth and early twentieth centuries to explain the phenomenon of homosexuality as Anne Lister may have experienced it. Female inversion and the accompanying masculinity was considered at length first by Richard von Krafft-Ebing and then in much greater detail by Havelock Ellis.

In *Psychopathia Sexualis* (1886), Krafft-Ebing identified four types of lesbians: women who were available to the attention of masculine inverts but not masculine themselves, cross-dressers, fully developed inverts who looked masculine and took a masculine role, and degenerative homosexuals who were practically male. Krafft-Ebing did not seem to think that slippages occurred between these states but thought that each one was fixed in place and in relation to a stable sense of female masculinity.[2] In "Sexual Inversion in Women" (1895), Havelock Ellis built on Krafft-Ebing's taxonomy of masculine and feminine inverts, and while retaining the multitiered taxonomic structure, Ellis emphasized the split between masculine and feminine inverts. The feminine invert was a social, rather than a sexual, deviant who had been rejected by men and pushed therefore into the arms of the masculine invert. They were the "odd women," or as he puts it, "they are the pick of the women whom the average man would pass by."[3] The masculine invert was the congenital invert who was born to an essential female masculinity.

In the move to simplify the sprawling taxonomy in *Psychopathia Sexualis* into masculine and feminine types, Ellis betrays the underlying motivation of sexological study. Certainly, at least part of the motivation to study so-called sexual anomalies was to argue for the naturalness of these desires and thereby achieve some kind of sexual tolerance. However, there was a larger cultural imperative at work, namely, the desire to reduce sexuality to binary systems of gender difference. Of course, what Ellis and other sexologists began, Freud and the machinery of psychoanalysis finished with the establishment of a system of psychic development that hinged completely on binary gender and binary sexual identity. Some critics have attempted to read sexual complexity back into the psychoanalytic account by developing Freud's case histories of minority perversions such as fetishism. However, the psychoanalytic system is ultimately hostile to truly enriched understandings of female masculinity in particular because female sexual and gender behavior in general is already understood to be derivative of male identity.[4] Given my premise in this book, namely, that female masculinity is a specific gender with its own cultural history rather than simply a derivative of male masculinity, psychoanalytic approaches that assume that female masculinity mimics male masculinity are not especially helpful. Furthermore, as I show, critics who use psychoanalytic methods to decipher texts preoccupied with female masculinity begin and end with the essential femininity of the female body.

More productive than psychoanalysis for my purposes is the return to the sexological texts. I think the sexological studies of Ellis in particular, rather than simply being guilty of stereotyping lesbian behaviors on a heterosexual model, fail to render the full range of perverse sexual behaviors in women in all their complexity. These studies glossed over differences that may have made all the difference to women within the sexual subcultures in question, and the studies missed subtle differences between types of female masculinity; in general, sexological studies could not remark on the many different levels of sexualization and gendering in intimate relations between women. To use my perverse presentist model of analysis here, we might note that when observed from the outside, even a contemporary lesbian community cannot be depicted accurately if the observer has no sense of the vernaculars of that culture or its hierarchies, gender codes, or sexual practices. The outsider, simply put, does not have access to the structures of social, sexual, and casual interaction that organize any sexual subculture. Although work is being done to restore the historical fullness of various lesbian communities of this century, the damage has been done and tends to be irreversible in terms of the full effect of denying and ignoring differences between and within communities of women who are attracted to women. The notion of inversion, I am arguing here, must be greatly expanded to recognize the multiple models of female masculinity in circulation at the turn of the century.

"Sexual Inversion in Women" is Ellis's main work on female homosexuality. This study definitely had a liberal agenda, and the work avoids demonizing inverts while it retains the notion of elements of dysfunction. "Sexual Inversion" provides an odd mix of social and biological reasons for homosexuality. On the one hand, Ellis finds lesbianism to be rampant in female homosocial environments such as convents and schools; on the other hand, he finds a degree of masculinity to be responsible for inversion. His understanding of female homosexuality is facilitated at least in part by the belief that social aspirations fuel the inverts' desire to be masculine; in other words, Ellis presumes that in a male-dominated world, everyone at least symbolically would want to be a man. Accordingly, Ellis points to the many lesbians in history (such as Catherine the Great) who have been monarchs and leaders.

Esther Newton discusses the misogyny, or at least "anti-feminism," of Ellis's text in terms of his "reluctance to see active lust in women."[5] But we might also point to the misogyny embedded in the implicit assumption that masculinity always and everywhere constitutes superiority, even when found in women; Ellis writes: "It has been noted of distinguished women in all ages and in all fields of activity that they have frequently displayed some masculine traits" (196). However, we notice that there are distinct limits to this notion of masculine superiority, and those limits are class bound. In the upper-class or royal inverts, Ellis infers, their masculinity corresponds to high levels of intellect and distinction. In lower-class or middle-class women, however, the masculine instinct, he claims, could as easily lead to criminality.[6]

Although these examples suggest that Ellis seems to be considering female masculinity as a social construct, he also searches for bodily signs of congenital dispositions toward inversion. Ultimately, however, he is forced to conclude that the "impression of mannishness or boyishness" conveyed by some inverts seems to have no "anatomical characteristics associated with" it (251). Accordingly, a beard on a woman gives no indication of inversion, but at the same time, Ellis asserts that some kinds of excessive hairiness (hypertrichosis) and masculine distribution of hair can be associated with inversion. Similarly, inverts, he finds, are not necessarily bigger than "normal" women, but "the muscles tend to be everywhere firm" (255). Finally, Ellis looks for genital abnormality in female inverts: "As regards the sexual organs it seems possible, so far as my observations go, to speak more definitely of inverted women than of inverted men. In all three of the cases concerning whom I have precise information . . .

there is more or less arrested development and infantilism" (256). In other words, contradicting the eighteenth- and nineteenth-century opinions about tribades with enlarged clitorides, inverts tend to have small clitorides and underdeveloped sexual characteristics. Such a notion links female homosexuality to immaturity and premature womanhood and concurs, therefore, with Freud's sense of female homosexuality as arrested female development. As Newton argues, Ellis's discussion of the feminine invert drops completely out of sight in his discussions of anatomical signs of inversion: "Like most examples that do not fit pet paradigms," Newton notes, "she is dropped" (568).

Because the anatomical differences between inverts and "normal" women are not to be relied on when attempting to make inversion visible, Ellis counts on the narratives of masculine identification or of the failures of femininity to mark the invert. The case histories he collects all tell of masculine identifications and early tomboyism. The case histories that Ellis provides, in fact, are remarkably similar to the childhood narrative of Radclyffe Hall's *The Well of Loneliness*, and they suggest a shared narrative among masculine women of early childhood boy identification, adolescent dysphoria, and adult adaptation with some successful relationships. But while many of the narratives share traits, they also differ in significant ways, ways not accounted for in a model of feminine and masculine inversion.

In "History XXXIV," Miss S, aged thirty-eight, is an American urban businesswoman who seems to be sexually active with women "whom she loves as a man loves a woman" (Ellis, "Sexual Inversion," 223). Miss S is described as "rather retiring in disposition, with gentle, dignified bearing," and she sees her sexuality as "a gift of loving" that she generously "tries not to give all . . . to one person" (223). Miss S "cannot care for men." The next case features Miss B, an artist who would like to try marriage even though she has made one unsuccessful attempt at it already; Miss B seems to be a little more feminine, and she "is attracted to women of various kinds even though she realizes that there are some women to whom only men are attracted" (223). This cryptic statement can only mean that Miss B is attracted to women whom men do not find attractive, that is, masculine women. However, the one relationship she describes involves a feminine and passive woman. Miss B is described as a woman toward whom "men are not usually attracted" (224). In another case, a Miss H had experienced male identification since childhood "and in her games always took the part of the man" (224). She has distinct sadomasochistic tendencies that often involve her as the "bottom," and she has a definite "love of domination" (225). She seems to like voluptuous women who will dominate her and has a social interest in men but feels "repugnance" about marriage. She specifically articulates a desire for younger "womanly women" and likes to play a "protecting role" with them. Miss M was also a tomboy, and she realized her desire for women when she was eight or nine years old. Miss M has highly specific desires and describes an interest in some combination of beauty and sadness in a lover: "Her sense of beauty developed early, but there was always a sense of melancholy associated with it" (227). Ellis describes this woman as marked by "boyish tricks of manner and speech which seem to be instinctive" (229). Miss M, he thinks, tries to cover over her masculinity but gives herself away to Ellis when he uses a rather idiosyncratic test of her gender identification: "with arms, palms up, extended in front of her with inner sides of hands touching, she cannot bring the inner sides of the forearms together as nearly every woman can, showing that the feminine angle of the arm is lost" (229).

In just these four cases, we find a remarkable range of sexual expressions and female masculinities. Some women, such as Miss S, are gentlemanly inverts whose masculinity is a combination of manners and male identification. When Miss S says she loves women as "a man loves women," we might understand her to be saying not that she copies men but that her desires are not feminine or emanating from a sense of a female body. Other women, such as Miss B, are less distinct in their masculinity than the gentlemanly Miss S and the masochistic and manly Miss H. And women such as Miss H articulate desires that emerge through contradictory impulses: namely, to protect the beloved but also to be dominated by her. Miss M is the melancholy invert whose masculinity is not manly but boyish, but whose body gives her away. Miss M also makes a claim for sexual tolerance, saying that inverts "have perfect right to live in freedom and happiness. . . . One must bear in mind that it is the soul that needs to be satisfied and not merely the senses" (Ellis, "Sexual Inversion," 229).

One case gives a replica history to Stephen Gordon's in *The Well of Loneliness*. Miss V spent her early life as "a mystery to herself," but ever conscious that she was different. Finally, in early adulthood, she found a book on sexual inversion that showed her that she was not "an anomaly to be regarded with repulsion" (229). Miss V taught in a women's college; she looks young for her age and has a mannish walk and a low voice. She has been told repeatedly that she does things "just like a man" (229), and she whistles and smokes. As a child, Miss V insisted that people call her John, and she climbed trees and tried to imitate her father in all things. Among her adult forays into sexuality, Miss V recalled sleeping with a female prostitute, trying to seduce a female friend, and falling in love with two different women. She describes sexual pleasure in terms of tribadism and touching her partner's genitals. Miss V concludes: "I regret that I am not a man, because I could then have a home and children" (235).

In a final, very long case history of Miss D, Ellis lets her speak in her own words rather than retelling her narrative. Ellis suggests that she is boyish rather than mannish and that she has "feminine development," but she says: "I could never think of myself as a girl and I was in perpetual trouble, with this as the real reason" (235). Miss D expresses a complicated version of gender dysphoria, and she claims: "When I was 5 or 6 years old I began to say to myself that whatever anyone said, if I was not a boy at any rate I was not a girl" (235). At a later point, she refers to "my non-girl's attitude" (239). Miss D also understands the intensification of masculinity when it appears in a female form: "I fancy I was more strongly 'boyish' than the ordinary little boy" (235). Miss D describes a childhood filled with boyish activities until she is sent by her parents to boarding school. Here she has feelings for a teacher, although the relationship fails to develop along romantic lines. As an adult, Miss D narrates, she lives in a fantasy world: "Dreaming was forced upon me. . . . I was always the prince or the pirate rescuing the beauty in distress or killing the unworthy" (239). This heroic masculine identification is deepened by Miss D's sense of the political injustice of a world that manufactures women as "fools": "I felt more and more that men are to be envied and women pitied" (239). She takes up women's causes but also begins to think about sex; between the ages of eighteen and twentyfour, Miss D goes through what she considers to be late puberty, and her sexual awakening leaves her thinking that she must represent a "third sex" and that to live her life without trouble, she should just avoid sexual encounters. She decided that she was far less interested in the question of why she felt the way she did about sex and gender and more concerned with finding "a way of life" (241). With money and opportunity, she thinks, "I would dress in men's clothing and go to another country" (241).

Miss D finally does court women, and when she becomes sexually involved, she stresses that "I never wanted them to kiss me half so much as I wanted to kiss them," and she occasionally reports feeling "slight erections" when excited (Ellis, "Sexual Inversion," 243). Miss D always "imagined my-self as a man loving a woman" in these encounters but at the same time does not express the desire to be a man (243). She speaks of herself more as troubled by having to play the part of the normal woman and as "an actor never off the boards" (243). She emphasizes that she would not want to be a "normal woman" and (like Anne Lister) boasts about her power to attract women. When she is with women, Miss D states, they become shy and flirtatious, and she in no way identifies with them and notes, "I always feel that I am not one of them" (244). Miss D's story is a remarkable com-bination of self-knowledge, self-sufficiency, and self-invention. Her sense of herself as a "third sex" and even "homosexual" obviously comes to her later in life from books and other medical references, but even without these terms, Miss D manages to find a way of living the life she wants. She obviously feels that wealth and social status would have immeasur-ably helped her to indulge her masculinity and find lovers, but she bravely makes do with what is available and apparently finds no shortage of part-ners. She does not refer to herself as wanting to be a man, although she does seem to think that she may have a man's spirit in a female body. More interesting is that she is not anxious to discover why she desires women and feels masculine; she only wants to find ways of living out her desires. Obviously, then, the question of what causes homosexuality was a ques-tion asked by doctors, not inverts; the invert asked, rather, how can I be a homosexual and satisfy my desires and not be forced into womanhood, marriage, and childbearing?

Inversion as a theory of homosexuality folded gender variance and sexual preference into one economical package and attempted to explain all deviant behavior in terms of a firm and almost intuitive belief in a binary system of sexual stratification in which the stability of the terms "male" and "female" depended on the stability of the homosexual-heterosexual binary. When, some fifty years later, lesbian feminists came to reject inversion as an explanation for same-sex sexuality, they also rejected female masculinity as the overriding category of lesbian identification, putting in her place the woman-identified woman, who is most often gender androgynous. To reconstitute the history of female masculinity, we actually have to accept that the invert may not be a synonym for "lesbian" but that the concept of inversion both produced and described a category of biological women who felt at odds with their anatomy. In this section, I have revisited the lit-erature on inversion to show that the medical category of invert collapsed many different distinctions between masculine women, distinctions that we can read back into our understanding of sexual variance and gender deviance by examining just a few different kinds of female masculinity from the 1920s. The most elaborate of all the depictions of early-twentieth-century female masculinity, of course, came from John Radclyffe Hall.

## Officers and Gentlemen

In an odd and even fantastical short story titled "Miss Ogilvy Finds Herself," written in 1926 and published in 1934, John Radclyffe Hall tells the story of a "sexually inverted woman" who had served in the army during the Great War and had then been cast aside after the war ended. Both this short story and *The Well of Loneliness* explore the supposedly melancholic existence of women who feel themselves to be men. In and around Hall herself were dozens of masculine women, many living under male names, some cross-dressing and passing, some switching back and forth between male and female drag, some serving in the army, some in the Women's Auxiliary Police Force, some living with other masculine women, some settling down with more feminine "wives," some even settling into odd threesomes. Most of these women were aristocratic or middle-class or had inherited wealth; many were artists. In the past, their stories have been read into, and out of, the story of sexual inversion, and their specificities have been lost in what we might call the parsimony of science. Medical experts, in other words, tried to force multiple expressions of sexual and gender deviance into a very narrow range of categories and tried to explain a huge array of physicalities in relation to the binary system of sexual difference that they were absolutely committed to bolstering and preserving. Closer examination of the lives of even a few inverts restores some of the complexity of early-twentieth-century sexual identifications to the historical record. Although it is by no means satisfactory to study only the lives of rich and even aristocratic inverts, it is much harder to trace the patterns of identification of lower-class women. Given the many stories of passing women infiltrating the military and other male-dominated spaces at this time, we can assume that working-class women took other routes to masculinity.[7]

"Miss Ogilvy Finds Herself" is about the suicide of a woman who avows, "My God! If only I were a man," and who feels herself to be "deeply defrauded" in having missed the experience of manhood.[8] Miss Ogilvy is, as Hall herself admits in her introduction, different from, but related to,

Stephen Gordon in *The Well of Loneliness*. Like Stephen, Miss Ogilvy has a "tall, awkward body," and like Stephen, she had been a "queer little girl" (5–6). Stephen and Miss Ogilvy both occupy themselves with weight lifting and sports in their childhood only to discover that their muscular bodies are not an asset but a mark of shame; Miss Ogilvy finds that developing muscles "seemed to lead nowhere, she being a woman" (7). But then came the war, and in her fiction, Hall allows both Stephen and Miss Ogilvy to play heroic parts in the military; for Miss Ogilvy, the war allowed her to forget "the bad joke that Nature seemed to have played her" (12). After the war is over, Miss Ogilvy tries to settle down again but finds that her masculinity, a cause of celebration when she was leading a British military ambulance unit, has become once again absurd. Miss Ogilvy is unable to adapt to civilian life and eventually goes off on a holiday and retreats into a fantasy of primordial maleness, during the course of which she dies in a cave.

"Miss Ogilvy Finds Herself" was both a trial run for *The Well of Loneliness* and a sort of tribute to Hall's good friend Toupie Lowther. Hall and her partner, Una Troubridge, had met Toupie in 1920, and Hall was quite taken with Toupie's military career and her generally gallant demeanor. Toupie Lowther was an overtly masculine aristocratic woman who had flourished during the war, when she ran a women's ambulance unit. Hall's biographer Michael Baker cites a "probably apocryphal" story about Toupie Lowther that told of her arrest at the "Franco-Italian frontier for cross-dressing as a man." On the way home, the story has it, Lowther was arrested again "for masquerading as a woman" (125). In a letter relating the history of the formation of the Hackett-Lowther Ambulance Unit, Lowther wrote: "My object was to form an ambulance section on exactly the same lines, subject to the same conditions as the allied men's sections." As Lowther puts it, opposition to the unit came in the form of "sentimental feeling on the part of the French; vis: the idea that women ought not to be subjected to the risks of bombardment and shell-fire, or the hardships which ambulance drivers doing front-line work had to undergo."[9] Lowther overcame the initial opposition to her plan and was awarded twenty cars and twenty-five to thirty women drivers. She was assisted by Miss Desmond Hackett and Miss Frances Denisthorpe in finding drivers. The unit arrived in France only to be denied access to the front lines. At this point, Lowther went to visit Commandant Domenc, the French officer in charge; in her later narrative of the incident, she provides a humorous account of the momentous meeting between herself and fifty French male officers: "They were all seated at various tables staring at me and I am sure regarding me as some extraordinary bold freak who had dared under some mad impulse to beard 'le grand chef' in his own den."[10] Domenc then asks her, "Am I to send you to possible death?" Lowther gives a quick response: "I am of the opinion that a few women less in the world is of no importance." Lowther's argument finally found an audience, and "11 days later we were on our way to Compiegne attached to the 2nd Army Corps of the 3rd (General Humbert's) Army."

After the war, Lowther, unlike Miss Ogilvy, did not disappear into oblivion and ignominious death; in fact, she received a Croix de Guerre for her service and enjoyed considerable notoriety as a war hero.[11] A newspaper article from 1919 describes Lowther as "one of the first women in England to have ridden a motorcycle" and celebrates her as a "sportswoman who could hold her own at anything that required skill and brains."[12] Lowther was also a first-class tennis player and a champion fencer. According to Una Troubridge's diaries, John and Toupie went car shopping together and would spend time together working on their vehicles. Una and John came to call Toupie "Brother" and referred to her using male pronouns. World War I obviously gave some masculine women the opportunity to live out the kinds of active lives that in peacetime they could only fantasize about. Although Lowther's ambulance unit was constantly hampered by conventional notions of female activity, they also did see active combat, and many of these women were applauded for the first time in their lives for behaving more like men than women. The newspaper stories celebrating Lowther's heroics praise her for precisely those activities that may earlier in the century have been opposed to notions of true womanhood. Furthermore, the public celebration of Lowther suggests that the masculine woman, at least briefly in the postwar years, was not always reduced to being a misfit or a figure of abject loneliness.

Toupie and Miss Ogilvy, the women in Havelock Ellis's surveys, and even Stephen Gordon seem much more closely related to what we now call a transsexual identity than they do to lesbianism. Indeed, the history of homosexuality and transsexuality was a shared history at the beginning of the century and only diverged in the 1940s, when surgery and hormonal treatments became available to, and demanded by, some cross-identifying subjects. In her history of transsexuality, Bernice Hausman reads Havelock Ellis's case histories of inversion carefully to argue that we can separate the intricately entwined histories of homosexuality and transsexuality by paying attention to the difference between "expressing a desire to be the other sex" and "demanding to be made into the other sex."[13] In his history of sexology in the twentieth century, George Chauncey specifically comments on the transition that leads to the construction of transsexualism, the move, in other words, from a model of sexual inversion to a model of homosexuality, from gender role to object choice. He finds that the medical interest in female inversion in the early twentieth century comes at a time when male masculine supremacy was being challenged politically by the rise of a women's movement, domestically by a huge population of unmarried women, and in the workplace by changing notions of gendered labor: "The sudden growth in the medical literature on sexual inversion, I would argue, was part of the general ideological reaction by the medical profession to women's challenge to the sex/gender system during this period."[14]

While Chauncey's essay usefully accounts for the social contexts that produce and ratify particular models of sexual behavior, it does not directly relate the invention of transsexuality to the separating out of gender inversion and same-sex desire. Hausman dates the emergence of a transsexual identity to the 1940s because she claims that there is no transsexuality without the medical technologies that became available at this time for sex reassignment, but this model is perhaps too rigid, because there were clear transsexual fantasies and cross-identifications in some of Hall's contemporaries. Even if we just compare Hall's fictional characters Miss Ogilvy and Stephen Gordon, it is clear that Miss Ogilvy quite distinctly desires to be a man, whereas Stephen Gordon desires masculinity and female companionship. Similarly, there are clear differences and even rivalries between masculine women, who note differences between themselves that others may not pick up on. Hall, for example, seemed to envy Lowther her heroism and her mechanical aptitudes. Hall also had rivalrous relations with other masculine friends: she and her friend Mickie Jacobs, for example, had a long-standing competitive relationship. In 1937 Hall wrote to her lover Souline and related a story about a visit from one of Mickie's lovers. Apparently the woman was quite stricken with Mickie, and Hall comments: "It would really seem that Mikkie must have a most deadly Sex Appel [sic]—sex appeal Mikkie. What price false teeth, an enormous back and front view, a cockney accent and all the rest! Thank God she hated you at sight or I might have had a most fearsome rival!"[15] Clearly, the differences between and among inverts, as well as the similarities between them, contributed to the strengthening of the sense of sexuality as an identity. These differences also provide different trajectories for the experience of female masculinity. Some women may have seriously wanted to change their sex; others, we must conclude, were less intent on the notion of a sex change and more interested in sexual tolerance for masculine women.

As we saw in the case of Anne Lister, identities do not suddenly emerge from some protean slime at the appropriate time; the possibility of a sexual identity or category is in fact years in the making and depends on all kinds of other factors in the culture at large. In the second decade of the twentieth century, of course, Europe was engulfed by the Great War, and as at other times of national crisis, World War I allowed some women (such as Toupie Lowther) to experience their fantasies of being men within the rigid strictures of military life. Changing sex for Hausman is a medical and surgical ordeal, but in the 1920s, many women were living their lives as, if not men, wholly masculine beings. Many women in the 1920s did effectively change sex inasmuch as they passed as men, took wives as men, and lived lives as men. It is inadequate to call such women lesbians, and in fact to do so is to ignore the specificity of their lives. It is, of course, also inadequate simply to label them pretranssexual; what they were, in fact, were women who wanted to be men before the possibility of sex change existed. Most satisfied their desires for masculine identification through various degrees of cross-dressing and various degrees of overt masculine presentation. It is hard to know which of these women would have desired a change of sex if such an option had existed, just as it is difficult to know today which masculine young women will identify as lesbian or butch and which will become transsexuals.

Masculine identification with social impunity required money and social status. As independently wealthy people with high social standing and money to travel, Una Troubridge and John Radclyffe Hall lived the good life. What is more, they lived among a large community of other couples and other "inverts," all of whom were managing to find their place and leave their marks. In *Our Three Selves*, Michael Baker remarks on Una and John's community, and he gives details from a reading of Una's diaries of some of the other masculine women, such as Toupie Lowther, and their lovers who populated John and Una's life. John and Una knew the masculine artist Romaine Brooks and the salon diva Natalie Barney; they were friends with the cross-dressing Vita Sackville-West and many other less public "sexual deviants." Among their personal friends were a strange ménage à trois made up of Edy Craig (the actress Ellen Terry's daughter), the writer

Christopher St. John (Christabel Marshall), and painter Clare Atwood, who was known as Tony. Chris and Tony both wore men's clothing and, obviously, took men's names. They also knew the policewomen Mary Allen and Margaret Damer Dawson, both of whom were masculine women and rarely appeared in public without their mannish police uniforms.[16]

Some aristocratic inverts, or what we may call "gentlemen inverts," were content to live their lives in masculine clothing and take male names without completely letting go of their claim to femaleness. Radclyffe Hall, as I have said, herself was called John and spent much time in men's clothing, but she also did not try to pass herself off as a man and often appeared in skirts. Michael Baker comments cryptically: "Ironically, John never attempted to masquerade as a man—not by her own standards at any rate. Though she never carried a handbag and had special pockets sewn into her skirt, she drew the line at wearing trousers in public. To have done so would, in her book, have been to act out a deception. Therefore, from the waist down at least, she made no attempt to disguise her true sex. But it did not stop her from wanting to be a man."[17] Baker's commentary is a bit unreliable because although his biography is detailed and well researched from letters and diaries of Una Troubridge in particular, he often also makes grand assumptions about Hall's desire without giving sources for his inside knowledge. In this passage, we do not know what it means that Hall wants to be a man, and we would like to know more about her thoughts about gender "disguise."

Critics have disagreed profoundly on the meaning of Hall's masculinity. Newton, obviously, reads Hall's masculinity as part of her sexual persona and as an expression of a true self. Terry Castle, in a book on the otherwise obscured relationship between Noel Coward and Radclyffe Hall, reads Hall's masculinity as, at least in part, an imitation of Coward's look. "Was Hall—whose studious cultivation of the same 'slick and satiny' masculine look throughout the '20's made her famous—one of Coward's many imitators?"[18] Of course, Castle is not suggesting that Hall simply copied Coward's style, but she is arguing for the importance of "vibrant cross-gender relationships" within the history of homosexuals (12). Calling them "kindred spirits," Castle reads Coward and Hall through and alongside each other's work and biography. Whereas this is an admirable project in some respects, with regard to the question of Hall's masculinity and indeed Coward's femininity, Castle links female masculinity to the imitation of queer maleness and male femininity to the imitation of queer female-ness and thereby renders cross-gender expressions as wholly derivative.

Another commentator also remains an unbeliever on the topic of Hall's masculinity. Joanne Glasgow has produced an edited volume of some of Hall's obsessive love letters to Evguenia Souline from the last decade of Hall's life. The volume, *Your John,* is an amazing addition to the record of Hall's life and to the history of inversion in general. Glasgow provides an introduction to the letters and, apart from establishing the history of Hall's relationship with Souline, also attempts to situate Hall's thoughts on inversion. Stephen Gordon, Glasgow proposes, is clearly not an autobio-graphical protagonist or "John's last word on the nature of inversion."[19] As Glasgow understands John's views on inversion from her letters, it lies in "the profound difference in her erotic desires" rather than in an inverted expression of masculinity.

> As the letters reveal, it is precisely this difference in erotic desires that defines the invert in John's view—not "mannishness," certainly not dress or personal style or mannerisms or activities. She believed that sexual orientation was not determined by how one acts, but rather by whom one's desires, an object-relations theory of inversion. Thus, she believed that most people were probably bisexual, Souline among them. The congenital invert, like herself, was one who never had any erotic attraction to a member of the "opposite" sex. (10)

This summary of John's notions of inversion is helpful, but a bit confusing. While John may well have thought that congenital inversion expressed itself in the desire for same-sex relations, she also fairly clearly stated that this expression was channeled through an essential masculinity. It was both masculinity and the desire for more feminine women that defined inversion for John. Furthermore, John's masculine aspirations are clearly stated in the letters.

At numerous points in these letters to Souline, John compares herself to a man or a husband and states various desires to father Souline's chil-dren and to marry Souline. In 1934 John writes to Souline: "Had I been a man I would have given you a child—as it is I am angry that I cannot do so" (97). Later she describes herself as "jealous as a school boy" (107). In a humorous note to Souline in 1935, John tells her lover: "I think it's a good thing for a woman to be able to cook, even if she has no need to do so"; to make it clear that "a woman" in this context refers not to herself but only to Souline, John adds: "Don't laugh. I am laughing a little myself—as I write this I feel that I am thinking like an early Victorian man: 'A woman's place is in the nursery and kitchen.' No—but there's something homey about the thought of you frying ham & eggs!" (135).

Glasgow also refutes the notion that John wanted to be a man at all. She notes that in the context of the triangular relations between John, Una, and Souline, many commentators "have read John as the 'husband' in this triangle" (12). Hall's biographer, Baker, in particular argues that John played the role of the unfaithful husband with a wife and mistress. Glasgow responds: "I believe that Baker is simply wrong, primarily because he believes John wanted to be and tried to 'be' a man, which the letters show to be patent nonsense. John was a lesbian—not the same thing at all" (12). Glasgow may be quite right that John did not in any simple way want to be a man, and she is also right to resist simply reading this complex love triangle on the model of patriarchal marriage; however, there is certainly something of the husband in John and something very mannish and not so mythic about her masculinity. Glasgow, I believe, wants to protect John's letters from a very literal reading, which would find them to be a melancholic rendition of failed heterosexuality. Rather than deny all masculinity to John, however, I think the letters must be read as expressions of a complex female masculinity, one that neither copies male homosexuality nor male heterosexuality but that carves out its own gender expression.

In relation to her desire for manhood, Michael Baker suggests that John steadily became more and more masculine in her dress and appearance throughout the twenties and that when her periods stopped in August 1922, she and Una saw menopause symbolically as John's "advance towards manhood" and now felt that they were truly "man and wife." [20] Obviously, for John, manhood was a private identity rather than a public self, and it was one she celebrated and cultivated in concert with Una. As we shall see in *The Well of Loneliness*, John linked her masculinity or manhood not simply to men's clothing but to a sartorial aesthetic that actively opposed the notion of a "true sex" by equating gender and costume. As Baker notes, she and Una loved clothes and often shopped for their clothing at Nathan's, a theatrical costume shop. But clothing and costume and "masquerade" were not the same thing for John, and she seems not to have equated her costumes with masquerade. Masquerade, for her, seems to have been about passing.

John, in fact, seems to have had a curious disdain for passing women. In 1929 she wrote to her literary agent, Audrey Heath, denouncing a person who had stood trial for male impersonation and for marrying a woman under false pretenses. This male impersonator was known as Colonel Barker, and s/he was sentenced to nine months in a women's prison.[21] The story of Colonel Barker is curious and fascinating. Born Lilian Irma Valerie Barker in 1895, Barker was raised a girl but developed into a real tomboy. Her father was disappointed in his son and so taught his tomboy daughter fencing, boxing, and cricket.[22] During the war, Barker joined a "big Canadian army cavalry unit," and although she did not try to pass as a man, everyone "treated me as a man and as one of themselves."[23] During the war, Barker was married briefly and unsuccessfully to Harold Arkell Smith, but she soon left him: "[G]radually life with my husband became intolerable and I broke away. I joined the Women's Auxiliary Air Force and became a driver."[24] Later Barker became involved with another man and even had two children by him. She left this man, too, and ran off to take refuge with a female friend, Freda. At this point, Barker decided to begin her life as a man. The reason she gives in her autobiographical narrative in the *Empire News and Sunday Chronicle* is wholly pragmatic: Barker argues that as a man, she will be able to "screen myself from all the tortures, miseries and difficulties of the past and work out my own salvation."[25] But given that Barker goes on to live her life as a man and marries and expresses little regret about her "cross-over," we must assume that there are also less practical and more psychological motivations behind her transition. Indeed, in the last installment of the autobiography in the *Empire News*, Barker comments: "[S]o long have I lived as a man, that I have come to think as one, behave as one, and be accepted as one. For the life of me, I would not know how to put on women's clothes now!"[26]

In 1923 Barker married her friend Freda Haward by explaining that s/he was really a man who had been injured in the war. S/he explained the children as the result of an earlier marriage and told Freda that although s/he had tried to live as a woman, s/he was now determined to resume life as a man. Barker comments in her memoir: "Reading over this now, I marvel that such an incredibly fantastic story could ever have been accepted. Yet Freda believed every word of it, and from the moment I told it to her she accepted me without question as a 'man.'"[27] Barker lived now as Sir Victor Barker and married Freda under this name. Some years later, Barker became Colonel Barker and deserted Freda. Colonel Barker served in the British Expeditionary Force in France and received military medals. The colonel was discovered to be a woman when s/he was arrested for bankruptcy and medically examined in jail. The charges then became per- jury, and the case garnered widespread publicity in 1929, only one year after John Radclyffe Hall had stood trial on charges of obscenity following the release of *The Well of Loneliness*. John commented on Barker's trial to her agent:

> I would like to see [Colonel Barker] drawn and quartered. . . . A mad per- vert of the most undesirable type, with her mock war medals, wounds, etc.; and then after having married the woman if she doesn't go and desert her! Her exposure at the moment is unfortunate indeed and will give a handle to endless people—the more so as what I ultimately long for is some sort of marriage for the invert.[28]

In this remarkable commentary, John seems as offended by Barker's im- personation of a military officer as she does by his/her impersonation of a man. And what are we to make of John Radclyffe Hall's obvious distinc- tion between herself as invert and "the mad pervert" Colonel Barker? In a chapter on masculine fashions for women in the 1920s, Laura Doan points to this letter and surmises that Hall is making a distinction between ac- quired and inborn sexual instinct. Doan writes: "[W]hile Hall cannot help herself and has no choice about her sexual inversion, Barker—if taken at her word in the court and to the press—assumes male clothing to better herself financially and to support her child. Because of Barker's total con- trol over her predicament, she is by Hall's definition, a pervert rather than an invert."[29] If Doan is correct about Hall's distinction between invert and pervert, this is one place where Hall was not in agreement with either Ellis or Krafft-Ebing, both of whom saw inversion as a subcategory of perver- sion or as the result of a perversion of the sexual instinct. Michael Baker theorizes that Hall's distinction between herself and Barker hinges on a notion of masquerade: "The key difference for John was one of deception" (*Our Three Selves*, 254). In her book on passing women, *Amazons and Mili- tary Maids*, Julie Wheelwright also comments on the surprising nature of John's outrage:

> Both the novelist and the bogus "Colonel" were interested in claiming male social privileges, including the right to sexual relationships with women, but they remained diametrically opposed in their methods:

Valerie Arkell-Smith continued her masculine disguise and lesbian relationships even after her release from prison, while Radclyffe Hall never
pretended to be anything but "a woman with a masculine psyche." [30]

Wheelwright seems to concur here with Baker and Doan, and they all
conclude that the difference between John and Barker has to do with deception and inauthenticity and with the way that Arkell makes use of
masculine disguise to access "male social privileges" and, as Wheelwright
put it, to carry on "lesbian relationships." Wheelwright is puzzled, therefore, as to why "the word lesbian was never used during the Colonel's case"
(3). Colonel Barker, I would argue, cannot be slotted neatly into the history
of lesbians in the twentieth century, and indeed the coincidence of John's
trial and Colonel Barker's trial argues ever more strongly for the consideration of a far more finely calibrated system of sexual identity.

John clearly saw herself and Barker as miles apart and even viewed the
publicity surrounding Barker's trial as a serious setback to her campaigns
for sexual tolerance. We can certainly chalk up some of John's discomfort
with Barker to a kind of snobbery; John clearly thought it was bad form
and just "not done" to pose as an officer, pose as a man, and then un-
ceremoniously desert the woman one has deceived. But there was also a
sense in which John recognized what is perhaps not so clear today, namely,
that a world of difference separated the inverted woman from the passing
woman and that the two would not have shared common cause. Also, I
think it does not make sense to interpret Barker as someone who simply
masquerades to bypass the social restriction of womanhood. Barker sustained her chosen gender role for almost thirty years and did not give it up
later in life when the role no longer served its purpose.

One can read a kind of assimilationist position into John's rejection of
Barker because John seems to feel that the publicity garnered by Barker's
case would reflect badly on other sexual minorities. In general, John was
a social conservative who did not link the outrage of sexual intolerance to
other forms of political intolerance. She was, for example, not much of a
feminist, and quite anti-Semitic, and at the outbreak of World War II, she
was all too sympathetic to the fascist cause. Ironically, Colonel Barker also
found his/her way to a fascist politics. In 1927 s/he joined the National
Fascisti and participated in their sports clubs (mostly boxing) and their
political demonstrations on Sundays designed to interrupt Communist
meetings in Hyde park. [31] It is quite chilling to note the appeal of fascism

and anti-Semitism for many cross-dressing aristocratic women at this time.[32] Wheelwright notes that gender rebellion does not necessarily translate "into a broader social analysis of oppression" and that often the cross-identifying woman may well embrace "an extreme of masculinity" (11). This seems quite true in the case of Colonel Barker, although Barker's flirtation with fascism seems to have been, like her flirtation with the military in general, an expression of her desire for active service in the company of other men. When s/he recalls being asked to join the Fascists, Smith writes: "'Why not?' I wondered. The role would help me in my pose as a man. Besides I was told that as a secretary I would get free board and lodgings at H.Q., though I would not be paid."[33] In the case of Radclyffe Hall, her anti-Semitism and fascist sentiments were almost certainly a product of her class sympathies and her horror of the prospect of socialism and communism. In a way, Hall's freedom to express her gender deviance was afforded by her class standing, and any change in social hierarchy could easily remove the leverage and mobility on which she utterly depended. Barker, obviously, could not and had never depended on inherited wealth, and so s/he had to find mobility in other ways. At one moment, this mobility was provided by the English Fascist party; at another, toward the end of his/her life, s/he was reduced to a sideshow in a Blackpool carnival.

When s/he was exposed to all as a woman in the 1929 trial, Colonel Barker announced: "Today when the world knows my secret I feel more a man than a woman."[34] At other times, s/he reiterated this claim to be more man than woman and indeed to have become a man by playing one for so long. As I said earlier, there were different degrees of male aspiration articulated by those women whom society labeled masculine inverts at this time. Barker's sense of being a man is articulated in far more emphatic terms than Hall's is, and Hall herself notes the difference and calls it "perversion." But Barker, in the 1956 confessional piece in the *Empire News and Sunday Chronicle*, refutes the charge of perversion: "Was it some kind of perversion?" s/he asks rhetorically and responds, "nothing of the kind!"[35] S/he also denies that she has some kind of "complex" or "phobia" and reassures her/his readers that s/he has "undergone no surgical operation to turn me from woman into man." In 1956, of course, a discourse of transsexuality was obviously available to the average reader, and Barker has to carefully distinguish between her masculine life and the decision to change one's sex. Although his/her life may read now like the life of a nonoperative transsexual, we have to understand the complications of living on the cusp of sexual definition. When Arkell-Smith became Colonel Barker in 1923 there was no such definition as transsexual available; when s/he recounts his/her life some thirty years later, the discourse of transsexuality has almost engulfed the category of the passing woman. Almost, but not quite—in fact, as I was reading over Barker's story in the 1956 editions of the *Empire News and Sunday Chronicle,* another headline caught my eye: "The 'Miss' Who Is Now a 'Mr.' "[36] This little story tells of a science teacher, Donald Oliver Bury, who had changed his birth certificate from female to male and then lived as a man. When discovered, Bury commented that the change on the birth certificate "is simply a legal correction and no change of sex." The article does not elucidate the meaning of this statement.

The claims to male identity or cross-gendered understandings of self made by Colonel Barker and others cannot be easily dismissed and should be understood not as simply transsexual but at least as the beginning of the emergence of a transsexual identity.[37] We may not want to claim Stephen Gordon or John Radclyffe Hall ultimately as a model for a prototypical transgender hero, but certainly figures such as Colonel Barker seem to live lives far removed from the lives of the other inverted women of the time. While women such as Toupie Lowther also served as soldiers, also cross-dressed, and also wore trousers and dressed exclusively in male clothing, they did not all try to marry women as men, and they tended to live with other inverts or at least with women who knew that they were biologically female. Just as the passing women of the eighteenth and nineteenth centuries must be seen as categorically different from women such as Anne Lister, so the passing women of the twentieth century must be distinguished from the communities of same-sex couples who were beginning to demand political and social recognition as lesbians.

## A Writer of Misfits: *The Well of Loneliness* (1928)

*The Well of Loneliness,* by Radclyffe Hall, is the best record we have of masculine inversion in women, and it is worth examining this novel to find the terms on which John mounted her campaign for sexual tolerance. As we shall see, the constituent features of inversion in this novel have to do with inversion or a masculine identity expressed through a female self and perceived by society as a whole as unnatural and wrong. The distinction that I have been examining between male masquerade and masculine costume becomes crucial in this novel to the definition of the functional invert. That *The Well of Loneliness* closely resembles Havelock Ellis's model of female inversion should come as no surprise, for John had read Ellis and was quite influenced and convinced by his thinking. But before we attribute enormous power of definition to the medical discourse, we must remember and note well the actual discrepancy between John's life and her fiction. Her life, as critics have noted, was far from lonely and isolated, and she and Una knew many other masculine women as well as many other same-sex couples. They frequented lesbian bars, which were not the vile places she describes in the novel but provided a lively base for a rather flourishing community. We can use the novel not to define inversion and outline its subjective forms but rather to emphasize the ongoing construction of a modern lesbian identity from the already visible and socially functional role of the masculine woman. As the notion of lesbianism gathered strength, so the masculine woman became a paradoxical figure within lesbian communities; she was representative of those communities as the "butch," but she was also ultimately rejected as an anachronistic reminder of the rejected discourse of inversion. Indeed, to this day, many contemporary lesbian communities signal their modernity by denying the stereotype of the mannish lesbian.

*The Well of Loneliness* occupies a complicated place in the history of lesbian fiction. Simultaneously, it seems to represent *the* classic novel of lesbian identity in the twentieth century and *the* classic representation of homophobia. It is both the best-known novelistic depiction of a lesbian and the most problematic. The female masculinity of the novel's protagonist, Stephen Gordon, finally leads the reader to question whether the novel is really about lesbian subjectivity at all, or whether it is actually an account of what we would now call transsexual aspiration or transgender subjectivity. Stephen Gordon identifies clearly as an invert according to the sexological models of the day, and she loves women very specifically *as* a man would. The novel both activates sexological definitions of homosexuality and provides a stark illustration of how limited the medical model actually was in both its descriptive efforts and its applicability.

In the essay that has influenced all subsequent readings of *The Well of Loneliness*, Esther Newton dubbed Stephen Gordon the "mythic mannish lesbian." In "Radclyffe Hall and the New Woman," Newton uses this label to suggest that Stephen's "inversion" has come to contradict certain lesbian feminist ideals about the "woman-identified-woman." Newton writes: "Embarrassed by Radclyffe Hall but unable to wish her away, sometimes even hoping to reclaim her, our feminist scholars have lectured, excused or patronized her."[38] Indeed, in an essay written in 1982 about teaching *The Well of Loneliness,* Toni McNaron describes the discomfort with which her class responds to the novel: "No one had liked anything about the book. The nonlesbians objected to it as non- or even anti-feminist, while the lesbians hotly rejected it as heterosexual in its notions of relationships and negative in its presentation of lesbians."[39] The class is able to reconcile themselves to the novel eventually only by reading Stephen Gordon as quintessential outsider rather than as EveryLesbian, but still the reactions of hostility are somewhat typical for that readership.

Newton attempts to define what is embarrassing about Hall's novel by arguing that Stephen represents "the stigma of lesbianism" and the explicitly sexual nature of relations between women ("Mythic Mannish Lesbian," 560). Whereas Newton acknowledges that women had cross-dressed and passed as men before the late nineteenth century, it was the medical model of inversion that provided an alternative, fully sexualized model of lesbianism that some women embraced "to break out of the asexual model of romantic friendship" (560). The mannish woman activates and embodies a phallic sexuality that makes visible the erotic component of female bonds. Newton suggests finally that "Hall's association of lesbianism and masculinity needs to be challenged not because it doesn't exist, but because it is not the only possibility" (575).

Twelve years after its publication, Newton's reading of the mythic mannish lesbian remains by far the most significant text on early-twentieth-century female masculinity. However, in the light of recent scholarship on transgendered subjectivities and on eighteenth- and nineteenth-century female masculinities, it is definitely worth returning to *The Well of Loneliness* to ask again the questions Newton raised: "Did the doctors invent or describe the mannish lesbian?" (558) and "Why does this novel make so many lesbian feminists and their allies squirm?" (559). I want to argue that Stephen represents something more than the "mannish lesbian": she embodies a sexual and gender identity that is not fully contained by the term "lesbian," and hence we must examine the characteristics of inversion and take seriously Hall's representation of female masculinity as part of an ongoing transformation of gender binarism. I am challenging the widely accepted notion that a John Radclyffe Hall needs the mannish lesbian to disassociate her heroine from the asexual tradition of romantic friendship—Hall may not have placed herself only in relation to this tradition. Because we now have evidence of rich female sexual cultures in the eighteenth and nineteenth centuries that revolved around gender deviance and nonheterosexual sex (such as tribadism), Stephen Gordon is fully readable within such a history. Hall need not have known about Anne Lister to find historical continuity for her character, but Hall may well have known about the mannish Ladies of Llangollen.[40] Needless to say, traditions of female masculinity must have intersected with and crisscrossed the nineteenth century categories of romantic friendship and female transvestism.

When *The Well of Loneliness* made its appearance in 1928, the novel was immediately charged with obscenity, and the home secretary, Sir William Joynson-Hicks, began legal proceedings to stifle the publication of the book. After a brief hearing, the book was declared obscene, and all English copies were destroyed.[41] The trials of Hall's *The Well of Loneliness* are to lesbian definition what the trials of Oscar Wilde were to gay male definition in the early part of the twentieth century.[42] Both Hall's novel and Wilde's *The Picture of Dorian Gray* were charged with obscenity, and both were characterized in the popular press as poisonous and contagious.[43] Both novels depict homosexuality as congruent with some kind of gender inversion, and both depict the subterranean worlds of homosexuals as lonely drug dens filled with moral perversion. Antihomophobic critics have rehabilitated *The Picture of Dorian Gray* by discussing its treatment of secrecy and sexuality, of representation and the real in the context of a queer aesthetic.[44] Some lesbian critics have begun the work of recuperating *The Well of Loneliness* by referencing it as a brave depiction of butch sexuality that replaces a model of lesbianism as a sin with medical and sociological models of the lesbian as invert and victim respectively.[45] Both texts announce the emergence of homosexuality at the turn of the nineteenth century as scandal, as pornography, and as obscenity; they both implicate homosexual desire in some rescripting of gender roles, and they both situate the homosexual within a process that Foucault has called "the implantation of perversions."[46] Because of their particular historical contexts, both novels can be situated within both homophobic and homophilic discourses, and both straddle the divide between the canonical and the popular.

If *The Picture of Dorian Gray* allows us to access what Sedgwick has named "the epistemology of the closet,"[47] *The Well of Loneliness* charts a rather different sexual topography. Not the closet, but the wardrobe, we might say, constitutes the epistemological terrain of *The Well of Loneliness*; Stephen Gordon in no way lives her life as an open secret, and she in fact represents the unmistakable visibility of female sexual perversion when it appears in male clothing.[48] Stephen positively wears her sexuality, and accordingly the novel dwells in luxurious detail on her fetish for men's clothing and the ways in which she covets and wears it. A sartorial semiotic provides this novel with its system of knowing and unknowing, conceal-ment and disclosure, and the trace of secrecy in this text involves not secret desires but the secret female body—Stephen's body—which of ne-cessity remains covered. In my reading of the novel, I want to focus on the relations between the invert and her male costume and argue for the im-portance of recognizing an elaborate construction of gender, sexuality, and self that takes place through a dressing that is not exactly cross-dressing and that positions itself against an aesthetic of nakedness. The object of this reading is first to question the coherence of the category of "masculine invert"; second, to examine the very specific contours of Stephen Gordon's desire and embodiment and measure it against contemporary notions of lesbianism and transsexualism; third, to posit a gender identity that consti-tutes itself through clothing, not simply fetishistically, but in such a way as to equate nakedness with binary sexual and gender codes and the clothed self with the construction of gender itself.[49]

*The Well of Loneliness* operates through a number of different semiotic systems that relate sexuality to nature in various ways. One such trope is inversion, and the novel deploys inversion as a narrative strategy as well as a description of Stephen Gordon's condition. For example, Stephen finds domesticity repulsive, and she prefers the outdoors, the hunt, and nature to the domestic hearth. Similarly, in relation to her beloved home, Mor-ton, she identifies with the house itself, not the domesticity it encloses; however, she experiences Morton as a spirit "that would always remain somewhere deep down within her."[50] After she is forced to leave Morton, she carries its memory within her, so that inversion now becomes a kind of mourning technique by which Stephen incorporates the places and the people she loses.

Stephen's relation to, and rebellion from, her mother is also repre-sented as a kind of inversion. When her mother is pregnant with Stephen, she assumes (along with her husband) that the child will be a boy; thus she carries within her own body an image of inversion, of the boy in the woman. Pregnancy, of course, is the kind of productive inversion that con-trasts with the sterility of homosexual inversion. It is also interesting that Stephen's inversion is a secret to her, but not to the reader, for a large part of the early narrative, and we witness her first love for the housemaid Collins with an understanding that she is denied. While this seems to conform to the structure of the closet whereby knowledge and ignorance both produce queer identity, in actuality, the novel suggests that Stephen is never closeted, but only ignorant. There is no double structure of revelation and secrecy that the subject plies, but only a system of deception in which everyone else keeps the crucial information from Stephen herself. When Stephen finally sees the housemaid kissing the footman, she responds violently to the revelation of what has been kept hidden from her alone, that is, her difference. Stephen describes the scene of heterosexual love as "catastrophic" because sexuality has been revealed to her as an act that excludes her" (28). Sir Philip, Stephen's father, reads books about inversion, and he knows what Stephen does not know about herself. In other words, the secret is a secret only to Stephen because her physical form, which she does not examine closely early on, gives her away to everyone else who sees her. The problem of self-knowledge in this novel is presented as much more difficult than the recognition of difference by others.

Because self-knowledge is the secret kept by society from the invert, it is not surprising that the climactic scene in *The Well of Loneliness* takes place in front of a mirror. Building up to this scene, Stephen visits her mirror image several times along the way to self-knowledge. At the age of seventeen, Stephen attempts to manage her queerness by dressing in ways that feel appropriate: "Sometimes Stephen would appear in a thick woolen jersey, or a suit of rough tweeds" (73). Meanwhile her mother would insist that she try to wear "soft and very expensive dresses." Stephen observes her image in a mirror as this war of clothes rages on, and she notes: "*Am* I queer looking or not?" (73). The omniscient narrator answers the question for her by confirming that Stephen's efforts to dress in the way her mother approved produced results that were "always far from becoming." The narrator observes: "It was open warfare, the inevitable clash of two opposing natures who sought to express themselves in apparel, since clothes after all are a form of self-expression" (73). Clothing, indeed, becomes the means by which Stephen covers her queerness and finds a comfortable gender expression. Clothing is her way of making her masculinity both real and potent, convincing and natural; without her male clothes, she is either awkward (in women's clothes) or inadequate next to the "real" embodied masculinity of a man. While Stephen's inherent masculinity does work sometimes to undermine the social conventions that allow Roger Antrim, her childhood nemesis, "his right to be perfectly natural" (47), more often it places her in competition with men in a battle that she is doomed to lose.

In a scene that has been much discussed by lesbian critics, Stephen Gordon examines her female body in the mirror and "longed to maim it for it made her feel cruel" (187). The scene, the apex of what looks like Stephen's self-hatred, has been understood by critics to represent the tragic meaning of the invert: lost in "the no-man's-land of sex" (79), the invert must constantly negotiate between her male spirit and her female body, her status as female and her masculine bearing. Esther Newton sees the scene as an expression of Stephen's "alienation from her body" ("Mythic Mannish Lesbian," 570), an alienation that she covers with men's clothing. As Newton astutely notes: "Cross-dressing for Hall is not a masquerade" (570). The mirror scene, indeed, is preceded by a short chapter detailing Stephen's shopping spree, in which she buys among other things "pajamas made of white crepe de Chine," a man's dressing gown that she describes as "an amazingly ornate garment," and gloves and an umbrella.[51] In the next section, Hall describes Stephen's confrontation with a self she claims not to understand:

> That night she stared at herself in the glass; and even as she did so she hated her body with its muscular shoulders, its small compact breasts, and its slender flanks of an athlete. All her life she must drag this body of hers like a monstrous fetter imposed on her spirit. This strangely ardent yet sterile body that must worship yet never be worshiped in return by the creature of its adoration. She longed to maim it; for it made her feel cruel; it was so white so strong and so self-sufficient; yet withal so poor and unhappy a thing that her eyes filled with tears and hate turned to pity. She began to grieve over it, touching her breasts with pitiful fingers, stroking her shoulders, letting her hands slip along her straight thighs—Oh poor and most desolate body! (187)

This is an immensely complicated passage, expressing as it does strange combinations of self-hate, self-pity, and awe. Stephen expresses her feelings about her body as essentially contradictory. On the one hand, the body is a female "fetter" to her masculine "spirit." On the other hand, it is quite masculine in its muscularity, "compact breasts," and "slender flanks." Her body makes her feel like maiming it and yet is already maimed by her sense of its incompleteness. It is "so strong" and "so self-sufficient" and yet makes her feel pity for its strength and its sterility. Stephen, furthermore, feels that her body is doomed to a lifetime of worshiping without being worshiped. What are we to make of these complex contradictions, this wild swerving between self-admiration and self-hatred?

We recall that Anne Lister spoke in quite similar terms about her desire to touch her beloved without ever permitting her beloved to do the same to her for fear that it would "womanize" her too much. As we shall see in the next chapter, this particular version of female masculinity comes to be named "stone butch" within a lesbian vernacular in the 1950s, and as such it represented a privileged and ideal version of butch gender and sexuality among butch-femme communities.[52] In fact, we could say that stone butchness—Lister's untouchability in the 1820s, Hall's role as worshiper in the 1920s, the impenetrable butch in the 1950s—marks one particular historical tradition of female masculinity. What is noticeable about Hall's representation of stone butchness in 1928 is that it tends to be read as a sign of self-hatred and shame by contemporary critics; if we read it alongside Anne Lister's diary, however, we can see it as a signifier of virility; furthermore, if we consider the passage in tandem with John's letters to Souline, we can understand the dynamic between the lover and the beloved within a complex matrix of emotional economics.

Teresa de Lauretis has argued that the dynamics of this scene in *The Well of Loneliness* must be located in a "fantasy of dispossession" in which Stephen mourns her lack of femininity and must seek this femininity constantly in other women's bodies.[53] Thus, her desire for women is always a melancholic attempt to make up for her masculinity that is not male and her femaleness that is not feminine. I want to resist such a reading vigorously because I believe it confirms the most conservative attempts to shore up the essential and historical relations between masculinity and men and condemns masculine women once more to the pathos of male mimicry. It is not surprising that de Lauretis is committed to this reading because her book in general is an attempt to fashion a theory of lesbian desire out of Freud's "negative theory of sexuality—sexuality as perversion" (1). De Lauretis asserts that lesbian theory in general has avoided psychoanalytic readings of desire and that this avoidance has allowed Freud's assertion of the lesbian "masculinity complex" to remain undisputed and therefore potent.[54] The masculinity complex, she suggests, "has consistently precluded the conceptualization of female sexuality autonomous from the male" (xiii) and has simultaneously failed to offer any explanations for the "non-masculine lesbian" or "feminine invert." Obviously, then, de

Lauretis's mission becomes the retooling of a psychoanalytic theory of lesbian desire that resists the centrality of the masculine woman and begins with the feminine lesbian—the lesbian, in other words, whose sexuality is more likely to function autonomously from men.

The premise of de Lauretis's model is flawed at its inception: in what model of culture could one conceive of a sexuality that functions autonomously of anything, let alone a female sexuality that functions separately from male sexuality, or masculinity that functions apart from femininity? One might expect that her critique of Freud's theory of the "masculinity complex" would force de Lauretis to give up on psychoanalytic accounts of lesbianism or any version of female sexuality, but on the contrary, her book is an effort to recuperate psychoanalysis for lesbian and queer theory. Furthermore, de Lauretis's sense that the masculine woman has been wrongly installed at the center of theories of perverse female desire also leads to a version of homophobia or butchphobia that forces her constantly to read the masculine woman into a narrative of cultural conservatism (masculine women are like men and therefore not radical in any way). Moreover, she discounts over and over the masculine woman's account of her desire and her gender in favor of a model of false consciousness in which the masculine woman really wants to be feminine, but because she cannot be, she must hate herself and women in general.

We know that de Lauretis's reading of *The Well of Loneliness* may be counterintuitive when she deems the novel "culturally conservative" and warns that "my reading of *The Well of Loneliness* in light of Freud's account of fetishism diverges sharply from Hall's own views of sexuality (informed by Havelock Ellis) as it does from most feminist readings of the novel" (xviii).[55] Apart from the fact that it makes no sense to read the novel "against Hall's own views of sexuality," one wonders why one would want to read it also against other feminist readings. Furthermore, de Lauretis's diagnosis of *The Well of Loneliness* as culturally conservative is both a hard claim to back up and a strange kind of historical judgment to hand down to a complicated novel that was banned for obscenity and constituted the first internationally distributed discussion of the plight of the masculine woman. As I have already acknowledged, John herself was a politically conservative person, and her political affiliations were constantly suspect; however, it is not at all clear that the novel she produced on the topic of sexual tolerance was conservative, and to read the novel as such is again to presume essential and inevitable continuities between male and female masculinities.

De Lauretis uses the mirror scene in which Stephen confronts her "sad" body to emblematize her theory of the fantasy of dispossession that dooms the invert to loneliness and unbelonging. De Lauretis comments that because Stephen's body is not feminine, it cannot receive desire from an other; however, "because it is masculine but not male, it is also inadequate to bear the subject's desire in the masculine mode" (212). One question arises here: Why is the masculine female body inadequate to bearing the subject's desire "in the masculine mode"? Whereas male masculinity all too often depends on the functionality of the penis and its ability literally to be phallic; the masculine woman, on the other hand, is not limited to the unpredictable movements of phallic desire; she can "bear the subject's desire in a masculine mode" through an artificial phallus, in her fingers, through tribadism, and so on. Although the male also has access to these prosthetic forms of lovemaking, his use of them is often seen as a sign of impotence, rather than an index of his virility. As we saw in Havelock Ellis's case histories as well as in Anne Lister's diaries, both the masculine woman and her partner regularly find the masculine female body to be more than adequate to bearing desire in a masculine mode. In relation to the scene in which Lister deflowered her lover, her act of penetration actually emphasized the inadequacy of the male body in its attempt at masculine lovemaking. Indeed, John also speaks of taking her lover's virginity as a sign of the functionality of female masculinity: John claims, in her letters, to have deflowered her lover Souline, and this act becomes very important in their relationship because it allows John to think of herself as the person who introduced Souline to her own passion. On 7 June 1935, John wrote to Souline: "And I thought of how virginal & innocent you were, how ignorant of physical passion—you the most passionate of all women. Oh, Soulina it is a wonderful thing that has come to me through you, for I was your first lover. Through me you are no longer a child."[56] Obviously, in her own life, John did not experience her masculinity as lack.

Finally, de Lauretis argues that this mirror scene registers that for Stephen "the body she desires not only in Angela but also autoerotically for herself, the body she can make love to and mourns for, is a feminine, female body" (213). Nowhere, of course, does the narrative even hint at such a notion of the inadequacy of Stephen's masculinity. In fact, in terms very similar to Lister's description of deflowering Marianne, and John's later description of making love to Souline, John describes Stephen taking Mary's virginity: "Like a barrier of fire her [Mary's] passion for [Stephen] flared up to forbid her the love of the man; for as great as the mystery of virginity itself, is sometimes the power of the one who destroyed it, and that power still remained these days with Stephen" (431). In *The Well of Loneliness*, it is social disapproval that causes Stephen finally to "give away" her lover to a man and resign herself to loneliness. The novel never allows us to think that Stephen really wants to be feminine; she certainly expresses the desire to be a man but not the desire to be a womanly woman. Furthermore, for Stephen the martyr (as her name suggests), the acts of worshiping her beloved and sacrificing for her beloved are pleasurable activities; certainly, sacrifice and worship and desire are contradictory activities for Stephen, but she accepts them as such and calls her romantic style "this bitter loving" (187).

Worshiping and loving the beloved fall into an economic system of exchange for John Radclyffe Hall. Giving is not simply sacrificing, although the notion of sacrifice lends a little nobility to the form of lovemaking that John describes in relation to Stephen Gordon. In her letters to Souline, again, John gives great insights into the dynamics of giving and receiving that motivated the relations between the invert lover and her bisexual beloved. John is writing to Souline to try to explain the difference between "inverts" and "bisexuals"; she begins the letter as she begins many others: "My beloved."[57] John wants Souline to see inversion as "natural" and explains that "nothing in nature's scheme is ever wasted." In other words, everything in nature has its place and its purpose, and inverts and bisexuals both occur as part of some natural principle. That, by John's reckoning, bisexuals far outnumber inverts does not render the invert "morbid" or "lonely"; as long as love is unselfish, she opines, love is natural. Unselfish desire, within John's theory of inversion, involves complex systems of giving and receiving between the invert and her lover. John writes: "If I am the 'giver' then take what I give—love and deep, deep friendship, and take it without misgiving. If I am the 'Master' then obey me in this: don't worry yourself ill by doubts and fears" (52). But the role of master can also slip into the role of slave, and John tells Souline a short time after this last letter: "I'm not going to have you anyone's slave. If your [sic] anyone's slave your [sic] going to be mine, only I'd hate to have you my slave—I prefer to have that the other way round" (53). Later still, John tells Souline: "I give because I love, please accept because you love" (158). John financially supported Souline throughout their involvement and then left money for her after her death. The emotional economics of the drama between the beloved and the lover were therefore also backed by a financial arrangement, and throughout John positioned herself as the one who gives, as a generous lover and as a giving partner within a give-and-take arrangement. This in no way makes Souline selfish and John selfless, or John noble and Souline base; nor does it guarantee even that Souline could feel secure in her role as the other woman. What it does signify, however, is an elaborate system of desire in which mutuality is not a principle and in which giving on the part of the lover does not signify her own depletion or her beloved's inadequacy, or her own morbidity and her beloved's desperation.

Rather than consent in any way to the idea of a "fantasy of dispossession," it makes more sense to read Stephen Gordon's mirror scene in *The Well of Loneliness* in relation to a fantasy of transformation and an economic model of desire based on exchange value. As I mentioned earlier, the category of invert predicts the category of transsexual as it emerges in the 1940s and 1950s. However, whereas the modern invention of the transsexual turns on the medical capability to produce sex reassignment, the invention of the invert rests on the impossibility of the sex change. Because one cannot change sex in the 1920s, the fantasy of a male body becomes the basis for a transformation of the female body into a masculine one. For Stephen, this transformation occurs through the act of dressing. Stephen's coming to consciousness, in the novel, about her female masculinity is accompanied by a greater and greater need for masculine clothing. Whereas early on in her life, as we saw, Stephen attempts to make feminine clothing fit her body, as she achieves adulthood, she realizes that she is not in thrall to her female body. Stephen literally redresses the wrongs of her embodiment by taking on male clothing, meticulously tailored and fashioned to fit her masculine spirit. What she confronts, then, in this crucial mirror scene is not the frustrated desire for femininity or her hatred of her body but her disidentification with the naked body. Stephen's repudiation of nakedness or the biological body as the ground for sexual identity suggests a modern notion of sexual identity as not organically emanating from the flesh but as a complex act of self-creation in which the dressed body, not the undressed body, represents one's desire.

While some critics have obscured crucial differences between atypical women from different times periods, others, as we see in de Lauretis's text, suffer from an inadequate sense of the historical specificity of certain modes of self-understanding. The scene that I have analyzed from *The Well of Loneliness* makes much more sense when we recall the complex ideas about clothing and masquerade that circulated between masculine women in the early twentieth century. In fact, perhaps only the contemporary reader understands this mirror scene as a dreadful representation of self-hatred. Anne Lister, a century before Hall's time, wrote deliberately and in detailed ways about her clothing and its importance. She insisted on wearing black and gave her tailor explicit instructions about making her skirts. Furthermore, Lister did not discuss her own body but focused obsessively and in detail on the bodies of her lovers. And, very often when Lister and her lover were making love, they were both partially clothed. Indeed, the idea of naked union is, to begin with, a modern notion shaped by 1960s-era notions of openness and literally fueled by the invention of such things as central heating. In early eras, simply put, nakedness would not have meant what it means today, and consequently we must not simply equate the naked with the sexual.

Finally, in Hall's circle were many women who felt that their masculine clothing represented their identities. The newly formed Women's Police Service was filled with women who seemed to want to join up to wear the handsome uniforms.[58] One of the first women in the force, the extremely masculine Mary Allen (who later took the name Robert) "seems never to have taken her uniform off, even wearing it for traveling."[59] Michael Baker, reading from Una Troubridge's diaries, comments that Robert "was never happier than when wearing her uniform and highly polished boots."[60] Una and John became quite friendly with Robert and her lover Miss Taggert, and they sympathized with Robert, who felt that an earlier incarnation of the Women's Police Service, the Women's Volunteer Police Force, had been disbanded because "all they wanted were fluffy policewomen."[61] In an excellent chapter on British lesbians in the 1920s, Emily Hamer discusses the wps and wvpf at length. On the subject of clothing, she writes: "Before the mid-1920's the only way a middle-class woman stood any chance of wearing clothes which were not feminine, let alone trousers, was by wearing a uniform. Belonging to an organization such as the wps which required members to wear a military-style uniform gave to the watching heterosexual world a justification of why a woman was wearing men's clothes."[62] But Hamer also tries to resist the notion that male aspiration motivates these policewomen. She suggests that the only way to dress like a lesbian was to look mannish but that "this is not to say that lesbians felt like men" (46). Clearly many of these women did feel like men, did look like men, and presented a threatening image to a world that feared female masculinity in any form.

In her own book, *The Pioneer Policewoman,* Mary Allen includes a photograph of herself with her first lover, policewoman Damer Dawson. Mary Allen is seated on the motorbike, and Damer Dawson is in the sidecar. Both are wearing peaked hats, shirts and ties, and military overcoats, and both are looking toward a child seated on the street curb. The caption reads: "How Women Police Deal with a Lost Child." In the chapter in which this photo appears, Allen is arguing that sometimes female police officers are more appropriate than male officers; in the case of lost children, for example, she suggests that policemen scare the children, and that "it is questionable whether the intervention of a policeman would not add to the child's confusion and terror."[63] The photograph of Robert and Damer Dawson ("the Chief") on the motorbike is a remarkable image of the power of female masculinity (and it is an image, I might add, that must surely "add to the child's confusion and terror" despite Allen's claims). On the one hand, it situates women in the heart of power, but on the other hand, it suggests the disruption that can be done by allowing for the inclusion of women in male bastions of domination. In this photograph and others in *The Pioneer Policewoman,* Allen and Damer Dawson look completely at home in their uniforms. They give the impression of clean-shaven military men with a hint of difference. It is hard, looking at these images, not to think also of John Radclyffe Hall and Colonel Barker and their fascist inclinations nearly a decade later, and one wonders, at least in relation to Barker, how much the lure of fascism had to do with the lure of the uniform and showy display of costume for the mannish woman. One does not want to gloss over the fact that the police force and the army are conservative institutions dedicated to the often violent preservation of law and order, and yet the presence of mannish women in the ranks of these governing bodies does not always signify politically conservative aims. Masculine women in the 1920s sought widely for political and social equality and for contexts in which their masculinity could flourish. They chose uniforms and homosocial environments, they chose occupations where they could drive cars and trucks and motorbikes, and they formed a formidable force of cross-identifying women who wore their gender and sexualities literally on their sleeves.

Among these women was John Radclyffe Hall, and so we should not be surprised to find a climactic scene in her classic novel on inversion in which a woman rejects the naked image of herself. The invert rejected the female body but did not always give up on femaleness; instead, she fashioned it into a masculinity she could live with. John understood herself as "a writer of misfits," but her writing very often worked toward finding complex ways of finding a fit. When modern lesbian critics, historians, and theorists try to read an idealized history of lesbian identification into and out of the bodies and lives of masculine women, a great violence is done to the meaning of those lives in the name of a politically pure lesbianism. As long as masculinity is annexed in our society to power and violence and oppression, we will find some masculine women whose gender expression becomes partially wedded to the worst aspects of a culturally mandated masculinity. However, as the complicated lives of some masculine women show, there are also ways for women to pioneer forms of masculinity that change the meaning of modern gender and sexual identity.

## Conclusions

Much work remains to be done on masculine women who lived before the late twentieth century; much is in progress. In this chapter and the last chapter, I have argued for the need to keep the label "lesbian" at bay throughout the first half of the twentieth century. Neither Fred (Anne) Lister, Woods and Pirie, John (Radclyffe) Hall, Colonel Barker, Robert (Mary) Allen, the women in Havelock Ellis's case histories nor their lovers would have identified as lesbians. When we describe them unproblematically as such, we tend to both stabilize contemporary definitions of lesbianism and produce highly unrealistic histories of pure and asexual relations between women. The emphatic defense of modern notions of lesbianism, furthermore, as we saw in relation to Faderman's discussion of Woods and Pirie, may also result in the disavowal of certain historical events and the projection of the terms of that disavowal onto racialized others. A vocabulary does exist to describe the social and sexual and gendered formations that we want to examine, but these words are historically specific and cannot stretch between historical periods or among very different communities of women. Although categories inevitably overlap and are continually under construction, it is possible to provide rough taxonomical definitions of the many different kinds of masculine women that we may encounter throughout history. Accordingly, Lister was a female husband, a masculine woman

who wore skirts but was continually mistaken for a man; she desired feminine women, did not identify with other sapphic women, and practiced
scripted modes of tribadic lovemaking, often with married women. Lister
commented on her desire for a penis but did not want to be a man. Hall
was an invert, a masculine woman who used her money and independence
to dress in elaborate masculine clothing and moved comfortably within an
extensive community of cross-identified women; she seems to have had an
aggressive sexual response and took a protective attitude toward her lovers.
Hall thought of herself as a man but did not try to pass as one. Colonel
Barker was a passing woman who came to think of himself as a man; he
married other women and used a dildo to maintain his male identity. He
seems not to have been connected to a community of masculine women,
and he maintained a seamless male identity when possible. Robert Allen
was an invert who was involved with first another masculine woman and
later a feminine woman; she seems to have satisfied her desire for masculinity by pursuing a police force career and wearing police uniform. She
was part of several communities of inverts, including Hall's circle and the
company of other policewomen.

These women are not all the same kinds of masculine women. Obviously, there is no way to identify exhaustively every kind of masculine
woman any more than it is possible to identify every kind of masculine
man. However, just as we recognize distinctive types of masculinity in
men, we must recognize them in women, and we must do so in place of
organizing all these women in relation to a catch-all category such as lesbianism. As I have tried to show throughout this survey of historical female
masculinities, a perversely presentist method reveals the multiplicity of
female masculinities now as then.

*Lust, light, love, life all tumbled into grief.*

—*Marilyn Hacker,* Love, Death, and the Changing of the Seasons *(1986)*

# 4 LESBIAN MASCULINITY

*Even Stone Butches Get the Blues*

Stephen Gordon, in Radclyffe Hall's *The Well of Loneliness,* looks at her body in the mirror and sees it as a body that "must worship yet never be worshiped in return by the creature of its adoration" (187). And Anne Lister, writing in her diaries in the early nineteenth century, comments on how she asks her lovers to refrain from touching her during lovemaking: "I do what I like but never permit them to do so" (*No Priest but Love,* 85). These two formulations of desire bear a remarkable resemblance to what came to be called the "stone butch" role in the 1950s. One stone butch, Sandy, describes this role as follows: "I love to make love. I still say that's the greatest thing in the world. And I don't want them to touch me. It spoils the whole thing. . . . I am the way I am. I'm not doing this because I am pretending. This is my way."[1] It is tempting, having lined up these three descriptions of female masculine desire, to argue for a coherent, transhistorical consistency within the role of stone butch. Indeed, one could argue that the role of stone butch has far more transhistorical consistency than the sexual identity we call "lesbian." However, according to the model of perverse presentism I have developed so far, we should be wary of linking very different historical expressions of desire. While I do not wish to argue that Anne Lister's untouchability is the same as Sandy's untouchability in terms of its relation to a sexual identity, or that Radclyffe Hall's conception of the butch as worshiper echoes Lister's articulation of her sexual practices, I will at least mark certain consistencies in various historical understandings of embodiment and sexual practice.

In this chapter, I examine the ways in which masculine untouchability in women has become immutably linked to dysfunction, melancholy, and misfortune. Stephen Gordon's mirror scene, as I argued in my last chapter, is all too often read as a quintessential scene of lesbian self-hatred, and Anne Lister's desire to remain untouched has presented certain problems for contemporary historians of same-sex love. In some way, across very different historical locations, stone butchness has been understood as a dysfunctional rejection of womanhood by a self-hating subject who cannot bear her embodiment. Stoneness becomes the literalization of castration (rather than castration anxiety), and the stone butch has been characterized as more blocked, more lacking, and more rigid than all other sexual identities. Indeed, the psychoanalytic notion that all desire is founded in lack seems to solidify in relation to the stone butch as true lack, as real castration, and as the exact place where, to paraphrase Marilyn Hacker, lust tumbles into grief.

In my last two chapters, I have tried to develop a method—perverse presentism—for the analysis of historical accounts of gender-variant women. I examined case histories from a period of more than one hundred years and concluded that female masculinities have held very different meanings in different eras and that they promote different kinds of anxieties in both the women who embody them and the cultures that reject them. Accordingly, histories that homogenize these multiple experiences of gender variance under the heading of "lesbian history" risk erasing preidentitarian forms of female masculinity and make it harder to make sense of modern masculinity. In this chapter, I turn to one particular form of female masculinity, the stone butch, to examine the ways in which gender identity and sexual nonconformity can be rendered illegible and discounted as improbable. My purpose in this chapter is not only to dispute this melancholic formulation of stone butch desire (although I also do just that) but also to challenge the way in which we demand accountability from some sexual roles but not from others. Furthermore, a thorough examination of the construction of the stone butch reveals the ways in which some sexual roles are irrevocably linked to inauthenticity while others are

entwined so thoroughly with the real that we cannot conceive of them as
"roles." The stone butch role consistently draws criticism for being unten-
able. But as the 1950s stone butch Sandy says emphatically: "I'm not doing
this because I am pretending. This is my way. And I figure if a girl is attracted to me, she's attracted to me because of what I am" (Kennedy and
Davis, *Boots of Leather,* 204). Sandy's formulation of desire here holds a
certain commonsense appeal, one indeed that has been much overlooked
in most discussions of the stone butch. In what follows, I try to examine
why it has been so difficult to talk about sexuality in queer studies in general and in relation to female masculinity in particular.

## Talking Sex

Although contemporary gay/lesbian/transgender studies have produced
great insights about modern queer identities and the communities in
which they flourish, it has been noticeably more difficult to talk in very
specific ways about the kinds of sexual practices and sexual meanings associated with specific queer identities. Paying close attention to the peculiarities and variable pleasures of an identity long associated with sexual
dysfunction, I use the stone butch to expose the production of new sexual
hierarchies associated with even queer pronouncements on sex. Politics
and sex have much more complicated and contradictory relations than we
would like to think. For example, whereas people may well invest in values
such as equality and reciprocity in their political lives, they may not want
those same values to dominate their sexual lives. The rise of lesbian feminism in the 1970s, for example, presented women with some very thorny
questions about the noncontinuities between sex and politics and resulted
ultimately in internal sex wars within feminist and lesbian and lesbian
feminist communities. These debates produced both sexual morality and
sex radicalism and ultimately led to the overturning of a strongly sex-
negative strain within lesbian politics.

The institutionalization of queer theory has raised questions about its
political affiliations and its increasing distance from queer cultures; as we
begin to break down the pros and cons of institutional recognition, we
should also attempt to account for what happens within the academy to
discussions of the actual practices of queer sex. Surprisingly, we talk about
sex—sexual practices and erotic variation—much less than we might imagine, and this is at least partly because we talk a great deal about categories

such as "lesbian" and "gay." We almost seem to assume that particular practices attend particular sexual identities even as we object to the naturalization of the homosexual-heterosexual binary. In fact, knowing that someone is gay or lesbian tells you nothing or, at least, very little about his or her sexual practices, and yet we still seem to think that anal sex between men and oral sex between women provide paradigms for gay and lesbian sexual behavior in much the same way that vaginal intercourse might for heterosexuals. Perhaps in our frenzy to de-essentialize gender and sexual identity, we failed to de-essentialize sex. The analysis of sexual practices does more than simply fill in the dirty details; it also destabilizes other hierarchical structures of difference sustained by the homosexual-heterosexual binary system. For example, in "Dinge," an essay on the inattention of white queer critics to the question of cross-racial desire, Robert Reid-Pharr notes: "It is surprising, then, that queer theory has so infrequently addressed the question of how we inhabit our various bodies, especially how we fuck, or rather, what we think when we fuck."[2] Reid-Pharr finds the absence of explicit discussions of specific queer desires to be continuous with the ideological processes that maintain whiteness as a cultural dominant and render white sexuality transparent and invisible. "Dinge" makes apparent the urgency of descriptive queer projects regarding sex by showing how difference becomes readable only in the details and the specifics of sexual practices. Reid-Pharr's essay also provides a caution against universalizing gay and lesbian experience along the lines of white gay and lesbian definition.

Within present-day cultural stereotyping, gay men tend to be associated with excessive sexuality, and white lesbians are still linked to frigidity and spectrality, and white lesbian desire becomes entwined with suffusive eroticism rather than overwhelming sex drives. But lesbians of color tend to be stereotyped along racial, as well as sexual, lines: the black lesbian, for example, is often stereotyped as the butch bulldagger or as sexually voracious, and so it makes no sense to talk about such a construction in terms of invisibility and spectrality. As Anna Marie Smith has pointed out: "It is simply not true that all lesbians are equally 'invisible.' Black lesbians, working class butches, and lesbian prison inmates pay a very high price for their extraordinary visibility."[3] But even visibility is not the defining principle of the pathologization of black lesbian sexuality. As Evelynn Hammonds remarks, black lesbian sexuality "has been constructed in a binary opposition to that of white women: it is rendered simultaneously invisible, visible (exposed), hypervisible, and pathologized in dominant discourses."[4] For this reason, when white lesbians continue to invest exclusively in this construction of lesbian sex as elusive, apparitional, silent, and intangible, other hyper-visible lesbian sexualities with highly complex relations to silence and exposure are totally discounted.

Lesbian feminist Marilyn Frye makes explicit the conventional formulation of lesbian invisibility in an essay titled "Lesbian Sex," in which she claims that in comparison to gay men and heterosexuals, lesbians seem not to articulate their desires. Her lesbian feminist reading of this inarticulate desire blames the patriarchy for silencing lesbians and suggests that patriarchal language cannot account for specialized and unique lesbian love. Frye writes: "Lesbian 'sex' as I have known it most of the time I have known it is utterly inarticulate. Most of my lifetime, most of my experience in the realms commonly designated as 'sexual' has been prelinguistic, noncognitive."[5] While Frye's tone suggests that lesbian sex has been experienced in general as "inarticulate" or "noncognitive," her comments on lesbian sex reveal only that some white women of a certain generation and class have lacked a sexual vocabulary. Furthermore, the inarticulateness of white lesbian sexuality is quite different from what Hammonds describes as the imposed "problematic of silence" that characterizes the colonization of black lesbian bodies. In other words, there are different silences and different forms of invisibility in relation to different lesbian bodies, and whereas some lesbians feel shrouded in silence, others feel overexposed and hyper-visible.

Historically speaking, white lesbian communities seem not to have always lacked sexual vocabularies. Indeed, when we compare the desolation of Frye's vision of an "inarticulate" sex to the positively garrulous languages of sex in the nineteenth and early twentieth centuries, not to mention the elaborately coded subcultures of butch-femme in the 1950s, we must ask how lesbians such as Frye have come to feel so disconnected from the vibrant sexual subcultures that preceded them. As I showed in earlier chapters, mannish lesbians such as Radclyffe Hall were the visible members of elaborate and articulate emergent lesbian communities; in the second half of the twentieth century, it has been the butch-femme couple that has signified and made visible and articulate an active and complex desire between women. Joan Nestle's work on femme desire and Elizabeth Kennedy and Madeline Davis's oral histories of butch-femme communities in Buffalo, New York, in the 1940s and 1950s both provide detailed portraits of how lesbian life was organized and how it thrived before gay and lesbian liberation and the so-called sexual revolution.[6]

The project of "thinking sex" was initiated more than a decade ago by cultural anthropologist Gayle Rubin, and her intellectual legacy still animates contemporary work on the specificities of desire and on the intricate webs of racial, class, and gendered identities within which desire may be embedded. In "Thinking Sex," Rubin laid out in great detail the discursive foundations that hamper "radical thought about sex," and she called for new levels of "erotic creativity."[7] "Sex," Rubin reminded her readers, "is always political." She went on to show, however, that there is no linear or cause-and-effect relationship between sex and politics, and to posit such a relation is to mimic the religious fundamentalists who believe in a congruence between perverse sexual identity and moral corruption.[8] Of course, to argue that sexual perversity has no essential relation to criminality means also conceding that sexual transgression does not feed directly into radical politics. The relationship between sex and politics remains contestatory and contradictory and continues to defy attempts to force organic links between sexual and other forms of behavior.[9] Discussions of sex in queer contexts have come to focus less on discrete identities and more on fantasy, pleasure, and acts. Furthermore, the more we talk explicitly and in intellectually responsible ways about sex, the more we learn about the damage that can be done in the name of sexual morality. As Rubin's pioneering work has repeatedly shown, "there is a hierarchy based on sexual behavior," and this hierarchy does not simply place heterosexuality at the top of the scale and homosexuality at the bottom but accounts for all kinds of sexual difference from sex work to sadomasochism. In 1984 Rubin wrote: "It is time that radicals and progressives, feminists and leftists, recognize this hierarchy for the oppressive structure that it is instead of reproducing it within their own ideologies" (226). I think the challenge to recognize sexual hierarchies has still not been met, but there are some strands within contemporary queer theory that have been influenced by the history of a sex radical discourse and are dedicated to finally producing appropriate languages and discourses for the dissemination of sexual information and toward the depathologization of perverse sex practices.

Producing sexual discourses, of course, does not mean producing some truth about sex or seeking some ideal level of sexual accuracy; it means becoming serious about a discourse of acts rather than identities.[10] As my last two chapters demonstrated, although certain acts between men seem to have generated an enormous amount of documentation, others, such as tribadism between women, have generated very little. There are all kinds of reasons why gay male sex acts garner so much critical attention and lesbian sex acts attract comparatively little interest—the existence of gay male public sex, gay prostitution and an extensive gay male pornography industry, for example, when combined with the lack of lesbian public sex networks certainly contributes to degrees of visibility and invisibility. But whatever the reason for the fetishization of gay male sex, we must be careful not to replace a hierarchy of identities with a hierarchy of acts.

A discourse of acts in and of itself, of course, does not really solve the problem of heterosexism or rampant homophobia; nor does it remove us from the world of sexual identities. However, it can and does uncover sexual scenes and sexual practices and pleasurable identifications that are often rendered invisible by the homosexual-heterosexual continuum. Finding out what people do sexually and, furthermore, what kinds of erotic narratives they apply to what they do sexually can rewrite both psychoanalytic theories of desire and scientific theories of sexuality. It can also clear up homogenizing notions of gay and lesbian desire that hold that all lesbians are attracted to all other lesbians and all gay men to other gay men. In an essay in *Pleasure and Danger* called simply "The Misunderstanding," for example, Esther Newton and Shirley Walton collaborated on a call for more precise sexual vocabularies. Simple as such a call may be, I am willing to argue that their call for new vernaculars has not been met. Newton and Walton describe a simple misunderstanding in which they both assumed that they should be sexually compatible because Newton was a butch and Walton was femme (albeit heterosexual). Their sexual incompatibility was a direct result of a coarsely calibrated shared sexual code that could account for gender polarity but not positions such as "top" and "bottom." As Newton and Walton comment: "We can't assume we are all the same, or that we all mean the same thing by 'good sex,' 'perversion,' 'attraction' or any other sexual concept. We need a more precise vocabulary to take us out of a Victorian romanticism in sexual matters and toward a new understanding of women's sexual diversity and possibility."[11] More precise vocabularies, then, are not simply helpful; they may actually facilitate understandings between women of sexual diversity.

It is also important, I believe, to remain aware of the ways in which sexualities and sexual self-understandings tend not to lend themselves to linear models of human identity. I am not calling here for a remedy to the problem of nonlinear desires in the form of something like a sex chart that can identify potential lovers according to some mixing and matching of traits, aims, and identifications of both partners. Obviously desire works in much more complicated (but not necessarily mysterious) ways, but if it cannot be charted, it also cannot just be expected to work automatically. One reason that psychoanalytic theories of desire have remained valid is that desire, basically, does not make sense. Desire, as psychoanalysis would have it, is a narrative embedded in the unconscious and coded through elaborate functions of repression, sublimation, and fantasy. But although psychoanalysis clearly recognizes the crazy loops of sexual desire, as an explanatory system, psychoanalysis has increasingly proven inadequate to the particular narratives of desire common to the late twentieth century. Freud's model of sexual psychopathology was created specifically within and for his historical moment, and it is difficult to invest in terms such as "castration anxiety" and "penis envy" at a time when sex seems to be most obviously prosthetic and seems to operate according to a very different sexual economy: this may be the age of artificial genitalia in the wake of surgical reproduction, or a posttranssexual era, and our sexual present is marked by bodies with multiple organs, virtual bodies, even posthuman bodies.[12] In this chapter, I want to argue for a sexual discourse that pays particular attention to the constellations of acts that make up increasingly queer gender identities.

## The Stone Butch

Despite feminist and queer rearticulations of the meanings and effects of sexuality and gender, we continue to live in an age of gender conformity and therefore heteronormativity. More women, perhaps, feel able to push at the limits of acceptable femininity, and more men, maybe, find ways of challenging dominant forms of masculinity, but the effects of even gentle gender bending have not been cataclysmic. We still script gender for boys and girls in remarkably consistent and restrictive ways, and we continue to posit the existence of only two genders. Gender outlaw Kate Bornstein refers to this practice as a kind of compulsory gendering that leaves out all kinds of gender perverts who do not clearly identify as male or female or even as a combination of the two.[13] And Leslie Feinberg, a self-proclaimed gender warrior, suggests in a new project that gender is a history of change and has always been determined by anomalies.[14] If gender has become a battleground at this time, it is worth asking who fights the battles, who receives the wounds and bears the scars, who dies? The gender struggle, furthermore, has a way of collapsing gender and sexuality because for gender outlaws, their gender bending is often read as the outward sign of an aberrant sexuality.

Feminists have, in the last decade, complicated immensely the multiple relations—biological and cultural, fleshly and abstract—between sex and gender and generally agree that there is nothing "natural" about sex or gender or, for that matter, the body.[15] Far from holding on to the notion that sex refers to one's biology, and gender to one's acculturation, feminist theorists have tended to use "sex" only to refer to sexuality, and gender to refer to the mutual construction of both biology and social role.[16] However, the revelation that gender is a social construct does not in any way relieve the effects of that construction to the point where we can manipulate at will the terms of our gendering. Judith Butler says as much when she argues with critics of *Gender Trouble* who had confused construction with voluntarism. A construction, she emphasizes, is not "a kind of manipulable artifice" because the subject of gender "neither precedes nor follows the process of this gendering, but emerges only within and as the matrix of gender relations themselves."[17] In other words, we are embedded in gender relations, and gender relations are embedded within us, to the point where gender feels inescapable. Because gender and its effects are inescapable, a degree of what has been called "gender dysphoria" characterizes most embodiments although this "syndrome" has been used to describe only pretranssexual forms of gender discomfort.[18] I want to argue against a pathological theory of gender dysphoria; within certain brands of lesbian masculinity, the effects of gender dysphoria produce new and fully functional masculinities, masculinities, moreover, that thrive on the disjuncture between femaleness and masculinity. By detaching the lesbian role of stone butch from dysfunctional sexuality, we establish a zone of gendering in which sexual practices and sexual identities may emerge from and within unstable gendering.

Although it may ultimately prove unfruitful to theorize lesbianism and female masculinity synonymously, it is important to acknowledge that historically within what we have called lesbianism, masculinity has played an important role. Masculinity often defines the stereotypical version of lesbianism ("the mythic mannish lesbian," to use Esther Newton's term);[19] the bull dyke, indeed, has made lesbianism visible and legible as some kind of confluence of gender disturbance and sexual orientation. Because masculinity has seemed to play an important and even a crucial role in some lesbian self-definition, we have a word for lesbian masculinity: butch. As Gayle Rubin states: "Butch is the lesbian vernacular term for women who are more comfortable with masculine gender codes, styles, or identities than with feminine ones."[20] Rubin goes on to show that butches vary wildly in their investments in masculinity: some butches are invested in masculine accoutrements such as clothing and hairstyle, and others actually experience themselves as male; some are gender dysphoric, some are transvestites, some pass as men. But many lesbians have seen and still do see the butch dyke as an embarrassment and furthermore as a dupe of sexological theories of inversion.[21] Ultimately, because the butch tends to see herself as something other than a woman-identified woman, we may want to reserve the label "lesbian" for women who identify with women and desire other women and mark out different semiotic and sexual terrain for butches. For the moment, however, I use the term "lesbian masculinity" to refer to women who perform their masculinity within what are recognizably lesbian relations.

Lesbian masculinity has always encompassed a multiplicity of forms. In Joan Nestle's oral history compilation *The Persistent Desire*, various women recall their particular constructions of butch identity. One black butch, Mabel Hampton, describes herself as a butch who liked to wear men's clothes, but she distinguishes between her performance of butch identity and the "studs" of the 1950s who were absolutely meticulous about their masculinity from the short haircut to the men's shoes.[22] A white working-class butch, Merrill Mushroom, in another recollection of butch-femme bar culture, provides a glossary for the contemporary reader. She defines the butch as "the aggressive partner in a lesbian relationship," but a strict butch is a "woman who insistently maintains the butch role at all times and who only goes with femmes." A "drag butch" is a kind of passing woman who takes on the form of a heterosexual male in clothes and style, but a "stone butch" is "a butch who does not let her partner touch her sexually." There are also "femmie-looking butches" and "butch-looking femmes."[23] There are indeed a plethora of categories available, and just as the term "lesbian" tends to subsume multiple sexual styles under the heading of same-sex desire, so "butch" has become a receptacle for all lesbian masculinity. Even if we hold on to butch as a master signifier of lesbian masculinity, we can still modify it when necessary and speak quite specifically. In addition to the modifications mentioned in Merril Mushroom's catalogue of terms, we may also think in terms of soft, baby, and old-style butches, not to mention studs, daggers, and diesels.[24]

As many social histories of lesbianism have now shown, after the rise of lesbian feminism in the 1970s, some women rejected butch-femme and its forms of sexual role playing as a gross mimicry of heterosexuality. The rejection of the butch as a repulsive stereotype by some lesbian feminists also had the unfortunate effect of pathologizing the only visible signifier of queer dyke desire; the rejection of the femme produced limits for lesbian feminine expression and grounded middle-class white feminism within an androgynous aesthetic. The suppression of role playing, therefore, by lesbian feminists in the 1970s and 1980s further erased an elaborate and carefully scripted language of desire that butch and femme dykes had produced in response to dominant culture's attempts to wipe them out.

In *Loving in the War Years*, Chicana writer Cherríe Moraga points out that the attack on butch-femme role playing made by white feminists also erased cultural and ethnic differences between women.[25] Moraga details her own sexuality and sexual consciousness in relation to her hybrid ethnic identity: she discusses growing up as the daughter of a Mexican mother and a white father, and she attempts to account for both her whiteness and her sense of herself as Chicana. Alongside her open and courageous critique of sexism within communities of color, Moraga carefully describes the various forms of feminist racism that she is forced to experience. One particular form has to do with feminist sex. Moraga comments on the presumption within lesbian feminism that "lesbian sexuality was *naturally* different from heterosexual sexuality."[26] She struggles with the notion that power should automatically vanish from sexual relations between women and wonders about the charge of "male-identification" against those women who retain desires for sexual power. Moraga concludes that her sense of her sexuality may well be structured as much by Mexican cultural norms as by lesbian standards and therefore may bear closer relation to what men and women of color do sexually than what white lesbians prescribed.

What I need to explore will not be found in the feminist lesbian bedroom, but more likely in the mostly heterosexual bedrooms of South Texas, L.A., or even Sonora, Mexico. Further, I have come to realize that the boundaries white feminists confine themselves to in describing sexuality are based in white-rooted interpretations of dominance, submission, power-exchange etc. (126)

If "chingon" and "chingada" describe the commonly understood gender roles within Mexican culture, Moraga says, then Chicana lesbians cannot suddenly be expected to cast off these sex roles in favor of a lesbian feminist egalitarianism. Prescribed sexual behavior along lesbian feminist lines enacts a form of cultural imperialism and ignores the specificities of different sexual cultures.

As I discuss later, lesbian feminists took aim at butch-femme as a particularly insidious form of cultural imitation. Much of the lesbian feminist reaction to butch-femme took the form of disbelief, and women expressed bewilderment about what looked to them like slavish copying of heterosexual roles. To restore the complexity to butch-femme systems of sex and gender, it is important to note the wide range of activities and identifications that each label—butch and femme—contained. In a prescient article from 1971, Rita Laporte confirms a sense of butch variability: "The qualities, femininity and masculinity, are distributed in varying proportions in all Lesbians. . . . A butch is simply a Lesbian who finds herself attracted to and complemented by a Lesbian more feminine than she, whether this butch be very or only slightly more masculine than feminine. Fortunately for all of us, there are all kinds of us."[27] Laporte's commonsense approach to what she calls the "butch-femme question" makes for fascinating reading twenty-five years later because it advances over and over the variation among butches and femmes and argues for a nonjudgmental understanding of the butch-femme marriage. Decades before Judith Butler's refusal of the notion that lesbian genders imitate heterosexual originals, Laporte wittily rejects the imitation hypothesis as simply too easy: "It would indeed simplify matters if butch/femme were no more than the imitation of male/female. Then we could dispense with those two traits as nothing more than cultural convention. The scientific principle of parsimony, that the simplest theory is the best, will seldom work where human nature is concerned" (6).[28]

In *Stone Butch Blues,* a novel by Leslie Feinberg, one of Feinberg's characters, a femme called Edna, tells the stone butch Jess about how many different kinds of butches there are:

I don't think femmes ever see butches as one big group. After a while you see how many different ways there are for butches to be. You see them young and defiant, you see them change, you watch them harden up or be destroyed. Soft ones and bitter ones and troubled ones. You and Rocco were granite butches who couldn't soften your edges. It wasn't in your nature.[29]

Butch, in this description, is a category that alters across time and bodies, and, we might add, it definitely shifts across social class and ethnicity. Predictably, the degrees of butchness are measured in terms of hardness and softness or in terms of permeability; the hard butch or stone butch, furthermore, has a masculine "nature" as opposed, one presumes, to a masculine style or exterior. The soft butch is a dyke with butch tendencies who has not completely masculinized her sexuality; then there are the "granite" butches, the stones who will not melt and are impenetrable.

Stone butch is a particularly appropriate place to begin a genealogy of butch variation because it is a profoundly enigmatic category: as we shall see, the "stone" in stone butch refers to a kind of impenetrability and therefore oddly references the nonperformative aspects of this butch's sexual identity. The stone butch has the dubious distinction of being possibly the only sexual identity defined almost solely in terms of what practices she does *not* engage in. Is there any other sexual identity, we might ask, defined by what a person will not do? What does it mean to define a sexual identity and a set of sexual practices that coalesce around that identity within a negative register? What are the implications of a negative performativity for theorizing sexual subjectivities? Furthermore, could we even imagine designating male sexual identities in terms of nonperformance? Many men do not invite sexual penetration as part of their sexual routines, and yet such an omission occasions little to no comment and certainly has not been diagnosed as part of a sexually dysfunctional complex. Perhaps we need recourse to the term "stone male" when the fear of penetration combines with a delusional sense of innate superiority and leads to sexual and other kinds of violence. Stone male could become a diagnostic tool for identifying male sexual pathology in early adulthood. Obviously, such categories have not been used to assess male sexual response, nor should we expect them to be in the near future, nor should we advocate such a practice; but it is certainly worth contemplating how rarely this culture identifies male heterosexuality as aberrant even where it is built on unreasonable sexual prohibitions and unsocial sexual demands. There are also heterosexual women and femme lesbians who may also eschew penetration, and we can label such women "stone femmes." Stone femininity gives rise to a whole set of interesting questions about the noncontinuities between feminine identification and passivity or femininity and receptivity.[30]

The stone butch, as I will argue, is a dyke body placed somewhere on the boundary between female masculinity and transgender subjectivity and seems to provoke unwarranted outrage not only from a gender-conformist society that cannot comprehend stone butch gender or stone butch desire but also from within the dyke subculture, where the stone butch tends to be read as frigid, dysphoric, misogynist, repressed, or simply pretranssexual. The stone butch defines an enigmatic core of lesbian sexual and social practice in that even other lesbians often ask about the stone butch, "what does she do in bed?" In fact, there is nothing particularly odd or unreadable about the desires of the stone butch *as long as she is understood in the more general context of female masculinity,* and as long as we have viable and comprehensive theories and accounts of lesbian masculinity. The stone butch occupied, and continues to occupy, a crucial position in lesbian culture, and despite numerous attempts by lesbian feminists and others to disavow her existence, indeed her persistence, the stone butch remains central to any and all attempts to theorize sexual identity and its relations to gender variation.

The stone butch complicates immensely the imitation hypothesis—or the idea that butches are bad copies of men—and codifies at least one register of difference between some general notion of male sexual roles and butch sexual roles. To both maintain the complexity of the stone and elucidate her relation to pleasure, I turn to her sexual practices and explain her untouchability in terms of a functional desire. Clearly, being untouchable did not and does not signify an absence of desire or pleasure for the stone butch. Historically, the term "stone butch" has been used for a butch lesbian who would make love to her femme partner but would not allow herself to be "touched." I put "touched" in quotation marks because there are of course many ways of being touched beyond direct genital manipulation, and in general the untouchability of the stone butch refers to a lack of *unmediated* genital contact. Although some stones chose (and choose) not to orgasm with a partner, others have and do receive pleasure from their partners through a variety of sex practices such as tribadism (also known as "friction" or "dyking") or dildo wearing. Historically speaking, however, "stone" referred to those butches who were unmistakably masculine in appearance and felt compromised by being made love to as women.

The women that Elizabeth Kennedy and Madeline Davis talked to in Buffalo for their oral history of butch-femme lesbian communities in the 1940s and 1950s had a wide range of responses to questions about the varieties of butchness and the breadth of its social meanings. Throughout the discussions of butch subjectivity, the narrators and authors themselves take great care to distinguish between heterosexual gender polarity and the carefully constructed and maintained gender polarities in lesbian dynamics. Kennedy and Davis stress in particular one difference between butches and men: butches, even though they took the active or aggressive role sexually, aimed solely—unlike men—to please their partner sexually rather than simply to please themselves. This emphasis on the pleasure of the femme was embodied within the stone butch, the partner who "does all the doin' and does not ever allow her partner to reciprocate in kind."[31] This kind of butch within 1950s working-class bar culture was both honored and ridiculed: although many claimed to be stones because of the status associated with the position, not all actually sustained a stone butch practice of untouchability. As one butch interviewed by Kennedy and Davis puts it: "There's no such thing as a stone," and as another says, "You can't be a giver and can't be a taker. You've got to be a giver and a taker" (206). Nonetheless, untouchability remained an ideal butch standard for the butch-femme communities of the 1940s and 1950s.

Why should untouchability have become an ideal standard for butch behavior? Untouchability, we might respond, guards against disruptions in the butch woman's performance of gender—the question is not really why would a butch not want to be touched but rather how do butches switch between being masculine on the streets and female in the sheets? The answer, of course, is that many do it quite easily and with great pleasure; others, however, experience the disjuncture as problematic and even dangerous, and for various reasons they are unable to lose the masculinity that they wear everywhere else when they enter the bedroom. To take the question further: why should we necessarily expect butches suddenly to access some perfect and pleasurable femaleness when everywhere else in their social existence they are denied access to an unproblematic feminine subjectivity? The stone butch represents a functional inconsistency or a productive contradiction between biological sex and social gender. In other words, the stone butch manages the discordance between being a woman and experiencing herself as masculine by creating a sexual identity and a set of sexual practices that correspond to and accommodate the disjuncture. The stone butch makes female masculinity possible.

We have become accustomed to thinking of gender in terms of performativity: Judith Butler's incredibly influential formulation of gender as "a compulsory performance"[32] describes the ways in which gender and sexuality are scripted within heterosexist culture and produced through non-volitional performances. Butler's theory of gender performance contradicts what we might call "the expressive fallacy," or the notion that "sexuality and gender," as Butler puts it, express "in some indirect or direct way a psychic reality that precedes it" ("Imitation and Gender Insubordination," 24). The stone butch again challenges even this complicated theory of performativity because her performance is embedded within a nonperformance: stone butchness, in other words, performs both female masculinity and a rejection of enforced anatomical femininity. Nonperformance, in this formulation, signifies as heavily as performance and reveals the ways in which performativity itself is as much a record of what a body will not do as what it might do.

If we apply this argument to the stone butch, gender becomes visible within the stone butch as a performance that is not only a repetition but one that is necessarily imperfect, flawed, and rough. This imperfect performance reveals, furthermore, that gender is always a rough match between bodies and subjectivities; when and where that mismatch shows itself, we tend to talk about pathology. In actual fact, the stone butch has made the roughness of gender into a part of her identity. Where sex and gender, biology and gender presentation, fail to match (female body and masculine self), where appearance and reality collide (appears masculine and constructs a real masculinity where there should be a "real" femininity), this is where the stone butch emerges as viable, powerful, and affirmative.

Butler actually makes an odd reference to the stone butch and her particular gender performance toward the end of "Imitation and Gender Insubordination." Butler is discussing "the logic of inversion" to try to describe seemingly contradictory relations between "gender and gender presentation and gender presentation and sexuality."

This logic of inversion gets played out interestingly in versions of lesbian butch and femme gender stylization. For a butch can present herself as capable, forceful, and all-providing, and a stone butch may well seek to constitute her lover as the exclusive site of erotic attention and pleasure. And yet, this "providing" butch who seems *at first* to replicate a certain husband-like role, can find herself caught in the logic of inversion whereby that "providingness" turns into a self-sacrifice, which implicates her in the most ancient trap of feminine self-abnegation. She may well find herself in a situation of radical need, which is precisely what she sought to locate and find and fulfill in her femme lover. (25)

I have quoted this passage at length because it seems at odds with Butler's radical constructivism. By the logic of inversion, Butler tells us, a stone butch comes to occupy the role of female because she neglects her own desires in the process of fulfilling her lover.

There are several inconsistencies within the formulation of stone butch in this passage. First, Butler allows for no distinction between "feminine self-abnegation" and "butch self-abnegation." In that so-called "ancient trap" of female self-sacrifice, we might assume, there are few if any rewards for the woman who disregards her own needs to provide for another's. But for the stone butch, pleasure lies in, and indeed springs from, her ability to satisfy her partner *without reciprocation in kind*. Second, the traditional form of female self-abnegation involves a woman self-sacrificing on behalf of a man; a stone butch, however, seems self-abnegating on behalf of another woman, and the radical nature of this performance can be further impacted depending on many other coordinates such as race and class. For example, what is the meaning of a stone butch performance of self-abnegation within an interracial butch-femme couple? Obviously, that "ancient trap of feminine self-abnegation" is neither simply "ancient" (transhistorical) nor simply "feminine" (embedded within the power relations of heterosexuality). Just as butch-femme gender dynamics do not merely rehearse a prior model of heterosexual gendering (as Butler herself has convinced us), butch self-abnegation and femme satisfaction have little if anything to do with "ancient" heterosexual arrangements.

Returning to *Stone Butch Blues,* we find that in her first sexual encounter with a woman in the novel, the stone butch, Jess, is making love with a prostitute called Angie. Jess makes love to Angie passionately, and then Angie turns to her lover and says: "I just wish I could make you feel that good. You're stone already aren't you?" In this context, stone is a response to continual sexual abuse or challenges: the butch closes down because she has to, because the world has charged her already with perversion and insupportable sexual ambiguity. Angie hastens to reassure Jess: "Don't be ashamed of being stone with a pro, honey. We're in a stone profession. It's just that you don't have to get stuck in being stone either. It's OK if you find a femme you can trust in bed and you want to say that you need something, or you want to be touched" (73). Being stone is not exactly depicted here as an affirmative erotic category, although the rest of the novel does attempt to assert the power of the stone butch. Given that Feinberg's novel has become enormously popular, it is important to recognize the ways in which it represents stoneness as a limit, a response to abuse, a wall that has been built up and could come down with the right femme, but also as a viable sexual subjectivity. At various times in the story, for example, Jess has sex with women and is able to come as a stone through dildo use or tribadism. Her stone butchness, therefore, is problematic in some places where it represents the residue of abuse, and powerful in others where it constitutes a successful construction of a sexual self. Stone butch, in this novel and in historical accounts in general, is often linked irrevocably to the blues because it was associated only with abuse and not with the individual's rewriting of her own sexual identity. *Stone Butch Blues* clearly recognizes and calls into being another narrative for the stone butch that does always code this position as a sexuality that has become "closed."

"Closed" and "open" are not really very helpful categories when it comes to sex; they tell us nothing about the function or dysfunction of categories. Insofar as sexualities are specific to bodies, psyches, and experiences, all sexualities are both closed and open, repressive and productive. The stone butch is a body closed to penetration but open to rubbing or friction, closed to conventional femininity but evocative of queer masculinity; the stone's prohibition against genital touching might allow for other forms of touching or might create a sexual loop through the desire of the femme— the stone butch in many ways is femme dependent, and there are multiple modes of complementarity between stone butches and various forms of femme pleasure that stake out a central place for the stone butch within both historical butch-femme bar life and present-day queer sexual subcultures.

## Abjecting the Stone

The stone butch, as we know, has often been represented as the abject within lesbian history. For lesbian feminists who argue against butch-femme role playing, and for others who argue for the commonsense rejection of only being a giver or a taker, the stone butch becomes an example of the pitfalls of rigidity of categories. The stone butch, such critics might aver, embodies the dysfunction of gender rigidity by taking her masculinity so seriously that she denies her female body. One twist in the narrative of *Stone Butch Blues* involves the breakup of Jess and her lover Theresa, which comes about at least in part owing to Theresa's involvement in the burgeoning women's movement. The year is 1973, and work is hard to come by for he-shes. Jess decides she must start passing as a man or else risk death by violence or suicide. Theresa cannot accompany her butch on this particular journey and explains painfully: "I'm a woman, Jess. I love you because you're a woman too. . . . I love your butchness. I just don't want to be some man's wife, even if that man's a woman" (148). As Jess begins her hormone treatments, Theresa identifies more and more as a lesbian, and the rift becomes unbridgeable. The erotics of lesbianism, as Theresa describes them, have everything to do with mutuality, reciprocity, and equality. She hangs a poster of two naked women on the wall of their kitchen, and it is clear to the reader that this image precisely excludes Jess and her kind. He-shes, women who are not received anywhere in society simply as women, cannot suddenly experience themselves as women within their private and personal emotional and sexual encounters. The burden of butchness manifests as sexual confusion that *is resolved* by the assumption of a stone sexual identity. To be stone, then, is not simply to have shut down and closed off to "normal" sexual contact between women; it is a courageous and imaginative way of dealing with the contradictory demands and impulses of being a butch in a woman's body.

The lesbian feminists in *Stone Butch Blues* are depicted as rabid detractors of butch-femme, and indeed it is no surprise to learn that the stone butch has received particularly harsh criticism from some separatist branches of lesbian feminism. Sheila Jeffreys, in an essay on the return of butch-femme in the 1990s, argues that stone butchness is about "internalized lesbophobia" and self-hatred.[33] Jeffreys understands role playing as part of a "sexologist prescription" (163) for lesbian sexual relations and claims that sexologists such as Havelock Ellis are responsible for creating the stereotypes of the mannish lesbian and the feminine invert. Jeffreys's logic in this article is astoundingly rigid in that she sets up an either-or model of lesbian sexual response: either lesbians eroticize difference and therefore engage in role playing, sadomasochism, or other forms of dominance and submission, or lesbians might eroticize sameness and engage in "the real pleasures of a sexual relationship . . . full of the double-takes and wounds of all their female and lesbian experience" (184). Obviously, within Jeffreys's model, true lesbian desire is beyond role playing. Jeffreys also attributes enormous power to the sexologists and no power to butch self-definition. As I tried to show in my last chapter, sexological theories of inversion were wholly dependent on, and interactive with, a plethora of complex self-definitions circulating within emergent communities of inverts and their lovers.

Another cultural lesbian feminist, Julia Penelope, looked on a 1980s revival of butch-femme roles with horror. Penelope sees this revival as a lesbian form "of the contemporary rightwing backlash, further encouraged by '50's nostalgia . . . and the illusion of security we get by going back to what we imagine to have been better days."[34] Remembering her own role-playing days and her fifteen years spent as a stone butch, Penelope obviously feels that community butch-femme standards and prescriptions for sexual activity had forced her into a sexual identity that then held her in thrall.

> For 15 years no matter how badly I might have wanted to let another woman touch me, no matter how badly I craved sexual release, I remained untouched and untouchable. By refusing to allow another Lesbian to give me any measure of pleasure, I felt in my guts that I thereby retained my power and my autonomy. (27)

Penelope sees her stoneness as a protection against "losing control" and as a way of having sexual power over a femme, but she felt that her stone image was a facade that protected her from "the strength of my sexual desire" and allowed her only "an occasional indulgence in tribadism" (27–28). For Penelope, feminism was the way out of the prison of stone butchness, and she felt that a new feminist consciousness about power and pleasure led her to a more positive and pleasurable sense of lesbian identity. One feels a certain empathy for Penelope's particular struggle, and it is clear that she felt role playing and stone butchness to be burdensome because they were mandated by her sexual community. However, as did Jeffreys, Penelope sees stone butchness as the epitome of lesbian self-hatred and as an example of the harmful associations made within butch identities between toughness and lack of emotion, touch and vulnerability, sex and power. Obviously, in my defense of the stone butch, I am not trying to deny the harm some women such as Penelope may have suffered from mandatory role playing; however, I am asking that we look again at the supposedly intuitive connections that some butch-femme detractors make between stoneness and lack of intimacy or vulnerability, stoneness and sexual dysfunction, and stoneness and the excesses of male masculinity.

In a 1975 issue of a "lesbian/feminist newspaper" called *WICCE*, Victoria Brownworth wrote an article called "Butch/Femme, Myth/Reality or More of the Same?" This article articulated all too clearly the notion that lesbian role playing was a harmful form of false consciousness that has nothing to do with pleasure or freedom of expression. Brownworth presented interviews with some butch-femme couples and then solicited commentary from women who had rejected role playing. The article unequivocally located female oppression in the assumption of roles and regarded with complete incomprehension testimonies by butches signaling that they do not want to be sexually touched.[35] Brownworth's intent in this article was to nurture the myth that in the 1970s, after "gay liberation" and "women's liberation," lesbians are no longer "into role playing." She confessed: "As a lesbian and a feminist I am also aware that for some the butch-femme attitude is as much a part of the scene as it was ten and twenty years ago. It is less blatant, more insidious, but nevertheless it does exist" (7). In an attempt to discover "what prompts women to act out roles," Brownworth interviewed some women were role players and others "who are trying to or who have transcended it" (7). Predictably, the role players are cast as butch misogynists and femme victims, and those women who have cast off roles are viewed as liberated and even revolutionary. The final interviewee, Patricia, has never been into roles; she sees herself unproblematically as a woman and sees butch-femme roles as limited and boring. Her words conclude the article. Brownworth prompts her, asking: "Do you think role playing will continue or do you think women are getting out of it?" Patricia responds: "I believe in the power, breadth and scope of the women's movement. The only hope for revolution and the true humanization of life is for the movement to continue and to reach all women" (10).

The sentiments expressed in this article are quite typical. Much of the literature of the 1970s expresses disbelief at the continuance of lesbian role playing, and role players were seen as insecure, immature, and unevolved.

Lesbian feminists of this ilk believed that by casting off roles, women became free of patriarchal and capitalist constraints and could find their way
to new and liberated and fully human forms of social and sexual interaction. Articles such as this one also use the stone butch as an example
of the absurdity of role playing. Brownworth, for example, asks Mickey, a
twenty-four-year-old butch, what she does sexually with her girlfriend. "I'm
in control," Mickey tells her. "I do what I want with my girlfriend." Brownworth pushes her: "Does she do what she wants with you?" "No. She's not
expected to. I don't think she should touch me." Brownworth then asks:
"How do you achieve any kind of sexual satisfaction if she never touches
you?" Later Brownworth asks a femme whether she touches her butch
lover by asking: "Do you reciprocate in bed?" The femme says that she does
not. Brownworth challenges her: "Don't you have any desire to touch the
woman you're with; don't you feel it is selfish not to?" (8). There is no good
way of answering such a question. If the femme says, "No, I don't want to
touch my lover in a way that discomforts her," she must be "selfish," so this
femme responds defensively, saying that she and many other femmes are
willing and eager to reciprocate but are not allowed to do so. This femme
says she feels bad about the lack of reciprocation but also acknowledges
that her partner does feel sexual pleasure and "she enjoys being with me"
(8). What is most notable about the Brownworth article is the author's attempt to ridicule and pathologize stone butchness although both partners
confess to a degree of satisfaction with their sexual arrangement.

Audre Lorde's classic biomythography *Zami: A New Spelling of My Name*
also names stone butch desire as some combination of emotional abuse
and selfishness, but within a very different context. In her first sexual encounters, Lorde's autobiographical protagonist, Audre, finds herself playing the role of baby butch to both black and white lovers and often in the
position of love maker rather than the object of another woman's sexual
attentions. When she gets involved with an older white woman who identifies very specifically as a lesbian rather than a "gay girl," this woman shows
Audre how to allow herself to be touched: "When I told Eudora I didn't
like to be made love to, she raised her eyebrows. 'How do you know?' she
smiled as she reached out and put down our coffee cup. 'That's probably
because no one has ever really made love to you before.'"[36] Audre learns
to abandon a role that she felt was simply handed to her rather than one
that she actively chose. Furthermore, her discomfort with the role of stone
butch had to do with some of the racialized dynamics that accompanied

being stone. In an early relationship with a white lover, Audre expresses great dissatisfaction with the nonreciprocating dynamic and with her role as servicer to a white woman who seems incapable of either satisfaction or reciprocation. In her relationship with Bea, Audre describes their mutual frustration: "So weekend after weekend . . . I ran my hot searching mouth over her as against a carved mound of smooth stone, until lip bruised and panting with frustration I fell back for a brief rest" (151). The stone partner here, of course, is the unresponsive body of the beloved rather than the closed body of the lover, but it is also the smooth whiteness of the stone body. The inactivity of her lover causes Audre to also experience herself as stone.

In *Zami* Lorde criticizes the bars for their rigid butch-femme codes, which stranded the non-role-playing dykes in a kind of sexual limbo. Going into the bar, she writes, "was like entering an anomalous no-woman's land. I wasn't cute or passive enough to be a 'femme,' and I wasn't mean or tough enough to be a 'butch'" (224). She sees the role playing among black women as a "masquerade" of power. The role playing for Lorde only feeds into and stabilizes the other race and class dynamics at work in the complicated social terrain of the queer bar. Although Audre Lorde's experience of the tyranny of role playing need not be either definitive of, nor exceptional to, the actuality of butch-femme role playing, it does suggest what the dangers of role playing could be for women of color. Stoneness, in particular, when forced on a black woman in relation to a white lover, could signify more than simply choosing to embody a particular form of masculinity; it could also signify the sacrificing of the black butch's desire to the white woman's pleasure. Stoneness in *Zami*, as in *Stone Butch Blues*, often means a tough exterior developed in the face of oppression and repeated humiliations. In her essay "Eye to Eye: Black Women, Hatred, and Anger," Lorde clearly expresses this meaning of stone: "In order to withstand the weather, we had to become stone."[37]

Clearly, lesbian feminists of many ilks have had good and varied reasons for their rejections of the scripted roles of early lesbian bar culture, but one complaint in particular that butches and femmes have lodged against middle-class lesbian feminist versions of sex culture is that the dominant strands, at least of cultural lesbian feminism, never replaced the erotic codes and practices of the butch-femme bar culture from the 1950s and 1960s with anything but negative sex recommendations. In their history of butch-femme community, Kennedy and Davis report on and celebrate the diverse sexual culture that blazed a trail for later lesbian communities. They document and record the social organizations, court-ship rituals, class and race divisions, and sexual practices of a group of self-identified butches and femmes. Despite severe oppression in the form of homophobia at work and at home, economic hardship, and social ostracism, this group of lesbians were creative and daring in their sexual and social experiments. Because lesbian feminists of the 1970s "defined these butch-femme communities as an anathema to feminism," we must assume that lesbian feminists had conceived of some social and sexual codes and systems to replace what they saw as anachronistic and derivative self-presentations (*Boots of Leather*, 11). It is interesting, therefore, to find that the lesbian feminist journals of the late 1970s and early 1980s, as I show later, seem to lack a sexual language for lesbianism.

It is quite common nowadays to claim that we have overdone the critique of this brand of lesbian feminism and that in fact just as many women in the 1970s and the 1980s were sexually adventurous as they may be today. Biddy Martin, for example, opines: "For a long time I have been concerned about the tendency among some lesbian, bisexual, and gay theorists and activists to construct 'queerness' as a vanguard position that announces its newness and advance over and against an apparently superseded and now anachronistic feminism with its emphasis on gender."[38] Martin, in this essay, is justifiably concerned about what she sees as a queer celebration of fluidity that projects fixity onto "feminism or the female body" (104). Emphasizing the transgressive nature of antinormative cross-identifications, Martin feels, obscures again the punitive measures cast against the femme and totally ignores the constraints of gender conformity itself. It is difficult to respond to such criticisms, if only because Martin uses Eve Sedgwick and Gayle Rubin as representatives of this antifeminist strand of queer theory without adequately recognizing the motivations that cause Sedgwick and Rubin to detach sexuality from gender in the first place. Moreover, there is no historical account of the ways in which a certain strand of feminist thought has rigidly prescribed "correct" forms of sexual desire. Finally, whereas it may be true that gender cross-identification has been identified as transgressive within queer projects, this need not come at the expense of comparable accounts of the discomfort of non-cross-identifying lesbian genders.[39] The transgression of the stone butch, for example, signifies only against the backdrop of a certain amount of pain and discomfort. If stone butch is claimed as a transgressive sexual subjectivity, then, it is not because of some notion of trendy rebellion but because there is a degree of hardship and contradiction embedded in this sexuality.

Even a quick glance at some of the literature from the 1970s and 1980s makes clear the kinds of feminist imperatives that led to the production of a clear feminist sexual morality and also shows that some feminists tended not to represent their sexual practices, in lesbian feminist venues at least, as anything other than thoroughly proper, romantic, mutual, and loving. At the risk of reifying a history that is of course complex and multifaceted, I want to argue that the cultural feminist strand of lesbianism is not a myth or a convenient bogey created by queers to make their own sexual politics appear all the more transgressive. Cultural feminism, as Alice Echols and other feminist historians have shown, has had a long-lasting effect on lesbian self-definition, and at the time that the sex wars raged, cultural feminists seemed to be in the majority.[40] It is worth examining some of the history and some of the dominant ideals of cultural feminism, if only to show how thoroughly contemporary queer dyke communities have rejected such models of sexual culture.

Some of the positions within white lesbian feminist circles around sexuality in the 1970s tended toward a conservative essentialism. Even radical and fringe feminists such as Valerie Solanas tended to cede raw sexuality to men, equate femininity with intimacy rather than sexuality, and argue for the purity of lesbian sex as a full expression of feminism, egalitarianism, and the joys of mutual desire untainted by the power dynamics inherent in patriarchal heterosexuality.[41] In a section on sex in the *S.C.U.M. Manifesto,* Solanas writes:

> Sex is not part of a relationship; on the contrary, it is a solitary experience, non-creative, a gross waste of time. The female can easily—far more easily than she may think—condition away her sex drive, leaving her completely cool and cerebral and free to pursue truly worthwhile relationships and activities; but the male, who seems to dig women sexually and seeks constantly to arouse them, stimulates the highly-sexed female to frenzies of lust, throwing her into a sex-bag from which few women ever escape . . . when the female transcends her body, rises above animalism, the male, whose ego consists of his cock, will disappear. (18–19)

Sex, in other words, is what men do to women, and women who enjoy sex have somehow succumbed to patriarchal brainwashing and are trapped forever. Postrevolution, Solanas suggests, sex can engage in "grooving," a more creative conception of intimate relations between women and one not reduced to the power relation of sex.

The antipornography movement solidified the notion that sexuality within patriarchy tended to further the oppression of women.[42] Feminists felt that pornography was an expression of patriarchal attitudes toward women and toward the female body and that pornography both represented and produced sexism, or worse, violence against women and rape.[43] Instead of the antipornography position developing into a call for sex education or for the fostering of sexual diversity, as Carole Vance's work has shown, it actually fed into moralistic fears about perversity and a religious right effort to legislate against certain forms of sexual expression.[44] As had happened at the beginning of the century in relation to first-wave feminism, sexual purity and moralism became a feature of lesbian feminism.[45]

In case readers think that this idea of a pure feminist desire is all speculation, I would like to turn briefly to one account of lesbian desire that appeared in the pages of a well-known lesbian feminist publication. It is not clear how representative this piece is, but it is certainly worth remarking on how cloying, sterile, and generally unappealing it is by way of making a case against what we might call "feminist sex." In their attempts to avoid sexist or pornographic language, some lesbian feminist writers who wanted to depict loving sex scenes were reduced to talking about "vaginas" and "digital manipulations" in tones that sounded highly clinical. This particularly asexual piece of lesbian erotica is from *Common Lives, Lesbian Lives* (1983). In the story, "Making Adjustments," by Teresa Lilliandaughter, the narrator and her lover are having trouble agreeing on when to have sex and how to coordinate their desires around their schedules. The lover has less desire than the narrator, so the narrator attempts to find creative solutions to the dilemma. One involves talking it out and trying to find out why her lover does not desire her. She tells her lover: "I guess I feel like we should always feel the same, so if I'm horny, you should be horny."[46] Another solution that the lovers hit on is that the narrator should masturbate more, but she says she doesn't want to because she really wants her lover. The lover responds: "Maybe we can work out a joint effort. . . . Why don't you masturbate while I stroke you or something?" (37). Finally, they decide to do it; the lover does not mind, she says, "because you come fast." To the sex scene:

She begins to massage my breasts and tickle the side of my neck. Then she starts to nibble and chew on my ear lobe. I start using the vibrator. Ummmm. Her hands feel so good.

"Can I just have a little finger in my vagina?"

"You want a little finger? How about a regular size finger?"

"Yeah gimme a regular size finger in the vagina. To go." Like ordering in a fast food place. (39)

After she comes, the narrator notes with satisfaction, "It only took a few minutes, six to be precise." The scene continues in this way, and now the lover takes a turn with the vibrator, and the narrator tickles her neck, nibbles her ear, and inserts fingers into vagina, being careful never to give the impression of fucking and never to lose control in such a way that the scene would degenerate into something pornographic.

This sex scene has more in common with a Kinsey report than a porno story. And this is an example of the kind of feminist sex that was supposed to avoid the patriarchal pitfalls of fucking, sucking, rubbing, biting, dildo wearing, and role playing. The absence of all gender and sex play from this scene and its assumption of sameness and equality as the basis for desire can only really produce this particular narrative over and over again: in other words, the narrative of waning desire and the attempts of the participants to revive or inspire sexual reawakenings. The scene is asexual, in fact—if a sex scene can be asexual—because it de-eroticizes sex and assumes a sameness in desires. Furthermore, the adjustments to which the title refers involve adjusting expectations to accommodate the nondesire of one's partner. There is an overwhelming sense of sexual defeat in the story, and one feels that many lesbians paid a high price for this kind of adjustment and for the more general adjustment from a working-class butch-femme role-playing community to a politicized middle-class woman-loving-woman community.

Nowadays butch-femme has made something of a comeback, and many younger women do identify affirmatively with roles. Curiously, then, despite the renewed interest in butch-femme, we still find a generalized critique or misunderstanding of the stone butch as representative of a kind of failure of lesbian desire or self-hatred. In a recent anthology called *Dagger*, a collection of contemporary essays on the theme of butchness and lesbian identity, several of the contributors take exception to the notion of stone butches. Surprisingly, Susie Bright of "sexpert" fame and Pat Califia, the macho slut, both express some discomfort with the notion of butches who won't flip: Susie Bright is careful to emphasize that it is her own personal preference that causes her discomfort, but she asserts: "If I don't get my quarter time of being the one who fucks, who *parts* her legs, who makes *her* bend to me in that really aggressive way, then I get really bent out of shape."[47] Pat Califia goes even further, accusing the "Stone Butch Police" of stigmatizing butches who like to get fucked: "If you aren't running the fuck and being in charge," she claims, "your butch identity is likely to be revoked the second the Stone Butch Police catch up with you."[48] Califia actually asserts that self-hate might be the reason butches are stone, and on this point, she concurs with Sheila Jeffreys, setting up a problematic alliance between sex radical and sex conservative. Both Bright and Califia seem to subscribe to a Freudian notion of polymorphous perversity that understands desire to be completely fluid in its ideal state but blocked in its actual physical manifestations. According to Bright, the butch who won't flip just needs to get in touch with her inner libertine, and according to Califia, the stone butch must actually despise women on some level. Of course, what both these sexual theorists ignore is that if sexuality were so fluid, then it would not even make sense to talk about lesbians and heterosexuals.

To a certain degree, the category of the stone butch lies on the boundary between lesbian and transgendered, a boundary I explore in more detail in the next chapter. The stone butch attempts to create direct access to masculinity from within a female embodiment, and as long as there is a community to facilitate and validate her choice of sexual practices and gender rigidity, the stone butch can thrive within a queer lesbian community. However, as Feinberg's novel dramatizes, the dominance of lesbian feminist models of sexual mutuality, reciprocity, and exchange turns stone butches into pariahs. Foreclosing on functional forms of lesbian masculinity prevents some butches from identifying as lesbians and creates a displacement that can be partly resolved by the category of transgendered. While it would be inaccurate to claim that all transgender butches are erstwhile lesbians, it would be equally absurd to claim that there is no relation between some transgender butches and a broader definition of lesbian.

## Conclusion

The stone butch, finally, represents a mode of female masculinity that has been categorized as unreadable. For many feminist historians, the stone butch embodies the excesses and indeed the liabilities of a role-playing lesbian culture, and she resides within a form of false consciousness about her "true" lesbian desires. However, the stone butch is as legible as any other fixed set of sexual practices if we have a functional model of female masculinity. The stone butch refuses in a way to sublimate her masculinity and to channel it through any of the conventionalities of femininity.

In conclusion, the sexual discourse we have settled for is woefully inadequate when it comes to accounting for the myriad practices that fall beyond the purview of homo- and hetero-normativity. The development of a new sexual vocabulary and a radical sexual discourse is happening already in transgender communities, in sexual subcultures, in clubs, in zines, in queer spaces everywhere. Female masculinity within queer sexual discourse allows for the disruption of even flows between gender and anatomy, sexuality and identity, sexual practice and performativity. It reveals a variety of queer genders, such as stone butchness, that challenge once and for all the stability and accuracy of binary sex-gender systems. Because we tend to type nonconformist genders as pathology, it is easy to understand how the stone butch can be read simply as a sign of sexual dysfunction and gender dysphoria; indeed, stone butch does signify both dysfunction and dysphoria, but as I have claimed here, dysfunction and dysphoria actually become part and parcel of this complicated and fully actualized sexual identity. This is not to say that stone butch is forever annexed to loss and dissymmetry and disturbance, but these markers of trauma and melancholy do haunt the stone butch and mark her, and after all, even stone butches get the blues.

*In addition to the definitional and legal wars, there are less obvious forms of sexual*

*political conflict which I call the territorial or border wars. The processes by which erotic*

*minorities form communities and the forces that seek to inhibit them lead to struggles over*

*the nature and boundaries of sexual zones.* —*Gayle Rubin, "Thinking Sex,"* Pleasure

and Danger: Exploring Female Sexuality *(1984)*

# 5  TRANSGENDER BUTCH

*Butch/FTM Border Wars and the Masculine Continuum*

## The Wrong Body

In 1995 the BBC broadcast a series called *The Wrong Body*. One episode in the series dealt with a young person called Fredd, a biological female, who claimed to have been born into the wrong body. Nine-year-old Fredd claimed that "she" was really a male and demanded that his family, friends, teachers, and other social contacts deal with him as a boy. The program followed Fredd's quest for gender reassignment over a period of three years until at age twelve, Fredd trembled on the verge of female puberty. Fredd expressed incredible anxiety about the possibility that his efforts to be resocialized as a male were to be thwarted by the persistence of the flesh, and he sought hormone-blocking drugs to stave off the onset of puberty and testosterone shots to produce desired male secondary characteristics in and on his body. The BBC program dealt with Fredd's condition as a medical problem that presented certain ethical conundrums when it came to prescribing treatment. Should Fredd be forced to be a woman before he could decide to become a man? Could a twelve year old know enough about embodiment, gender, and sexuality to demand a sex change? What were the implications of Fredd's case for other seemingly commonplace cases of tomboyism?

Over the three-year period covered by the documentary, Fredd spent a considerable amount of time attending a child psychiatrist. We watched as Fredd carefully reeducated his doctor about the trials and tribulations of gender dysphoria and led his doctor through the protocols of gender reassignment, making sure that the doctor used the correct gender pronouns and refusing to allow the doctor to regender him as female. The doctor suggested at various moments that Fredd may be experiencing a severe stage of tomboy identification and that he may change his mind about his gender identity once his sexuality developed within a female adolescent growing spurt. Fredd firmly distinguished for the doctor between sexuality and gender and insisted that his sexual preference would make no difference to his sense of a core male gender identity. The doctor sometimes referred to Fredd by his female name and was calmly corrected as Fredd maintained a consistent and focused sense of himself as male and as a boy. Fredd's case made for a rivetting documentary, and although the BBC interviewers did not push in these directions, questions about childhood cross-identification, about the effects of visible transsexualities, and about early childhood gender selection all crowded in on the body of this young person. What gender is Fredd as he waits for his medical authorization to begin hormones? What kind of refusal of gender and what kind of confirmation of conventional gender does Fredd's battle with the medical authorities represent? Finally, what do articulations of the notion of a wrong body and the persistent belief in the possibility of a "right" body register in relation to the emergence of other genders, transgenders?

In this chapter, I take up some of the questions raised by contemporary discussions of transsexuality about the relations between identity, embodiment, and gender. In an extended consideration of the differences and continuities between transsexual, transgender, and lesbian masculinities, I approach the thorny questions of identity raised by the public emergence of the female-to-male transsexual (FTM) in the last decade or so. If some female-born people now articulate clear desires to become men, what is the effect of their transitions on both male masculinity and on the category of butch? What will be the effect of a visible transsexual population on young people who cross-identify? Will more tomboys announce their transsexual aspirations if the stigma is removed from the category?

In the last part of this century, the invention of transsexuality as a medical category has partly drained gender variance out of the category of homosexuality and located gender variance very specifically within the category of transsexuality. Whereas in earlier chapters I have attempted to trace and historically locate some of the intersections between medical definitions of transsexuality and homosexual inversion, I want to analyze here the surprising continuities and unpredictable discontinuities between gender variance that retains the birth body (for example, butchness) and gender variance that necessitates sex reassignment. Medical descriptions of transsexuality throughout the last forty years have been preoccupied with a discourse of "the wrong body" that describes transsexual embodiment in terms of an error of nature whereby gender identity and biological sex are not only discontinuous but catastrophically at odds. The technological availabilities of surgeries to reassign gender have made the option of gender transition available to those who understand themselves to be tragically and severely at odds with their bodies, and particularly for male-to-female transsexuals (MTFS), these surgical transitions have been embraced by increasing numbers of gender-variant people. The recent visibility of female-to-male transsexuals has immensely complicated the discussions around transsexuality because gender transition from female to male allows biological women to access male privilege within their reassigned genders. Although few commentators would be so foolish as to ascribe FTM transition solely to the aspiration for mobility within a gender hierarchy, the fact is that gender reassignment for FTMs does have social and political consequences.

If we study the fault lines between masculine women and transsexual men, we discover, I point out, that as transsexual men become associated with real and desperate desires for reembodiment, so butch women become associated with a playful desire for masculinity and a casual form of gender deviance. Although homosexuality was removed from the DSM III manual in 1973, transsexuality remains firmly in the control of medical and psychological technologies.[1] However, all too often, such a fact is used to argue that more cultural anxiety focuses on the transsexual than on the homosexual. I believe that the confusing overlaps between some forms of transsexuality and some gender-deviant forms of lesbianism have created not only definitional confusion for so-called medical experts but also a strange struggle between FTMs and lesbian butches who accuse each other of gender normativity. I am attempting here to unravel some of the most complicated of these arguments.

I use the term "transgender butch" in this chapter to describe a form of gender transitivity that could be crucial to many butches' sense of embodiment, sexual subjectivity, and even gender legitimacy. As the visibility of a transsexual community grows at the end of the twentieth century and as FTMS become increasingly visible within that community, questions about the viability of queer butch identities become unavoidable. Some lesbians seem to see FTMS as traitors to a "woman's" movement who cross over and become the enemy. Some FTMS see lesbian feminism as a discourse that has demonized FTMS and their masculinity. Some butches consider FTMS to be butches who believe in anatomy, and some FTMS consider butches to be FTMS who are too afraid to make the "transition" from female to male. The border wars between transgender butches and FTMS presume that masculinity is a limited resource, available to only a few in ever decreasing quantities. Or else we see masculinity as a set of protocols that should be agreed on in advance. Masculinity, of course, is what we make it; it has important relations to maleness, increasingly interesting relations to transsexual maleness, and a historical debt to lesbian butchness. At least one of the issues I want to take up here is what model of masculinity is at stake in debates between butches and FTMS and what, if anything, separates butch masculinity from transsexual masculinities. I will examine some of the identifications that we have argued about (the stone butch in particular) and attempt to open dialogue between FTM and butch subject positions that allows for cohabitation in the territories of queer gender. I will also look at the language of these arguments and try to call attention to the importance of the metaphors of border, territory, crossing, and transitivity.

Recently, transsexual communities have become visible in many urban areas, and a transsexual activist response to transphobia (as separate from homophobia and not assimilable under the banner "queer") has animated demands for special health care considerations and legal rights. Although one might expect the emergence of transsexual activism to fulfill the promise of a "queer" alliance between sexual minorities by extending the definition of sexual minority beyond gay and lesbian, in fact there is considerable antipathy between gays and lesbians and transsexuals, and the term "queer" has not managed to bridge the divide. Whereas transsexuals seem suspicious of a gay and lesbian hegemony under the queer banner, gays and lesbians fear that some forms of transsexualism represent a homophobic restoration of gender normativity. But there is possibly another group in this standoff who maintain the utility of queer definition without privileging either side of the gay/lesbian versus transsexual divide. This group may be identified as transgender or gender-queer. The gender-queer position, often also called queer theory or postmodernism, has been cast in many different theoretical locations as the blithe opponent of the real, the player who fails to understand the life-and-death struggle around gender definition. While I contest such a characterization of the transgender position, I do want to consider what kind of symbolic burden we force on the transsexual body within postmodernism and how such bodies resist or defy the weight of signifying the technological constructions of otherness.

## Transgender Butch

Transsexuality has become something of a favored topic for gender studies nowadays because it seems to offer case studies for demonstrations of various gender theories. Because transsexual self-accountings are all too often left out of the theorizations of gender variance, some critical animosity has developed between transsexual and nontranssexual theorists. Jacob Hale has informally published a set of rules for nontranssexuals writing about transsexuality (http://www.actlab.utexas.edu/~sandy/hale.rules.html), and these rules suggest that parameters are necessary and important for non-identity-based writings. As a nontranssexual who has written about transsexuality, I would like to comment in this section about the important skirmishes between FTM and butch theorists, my role in those skirmishes, and the kinds of knowledge they produce.

In 1994 I published an essay called "F2M: The Making of Female Masculinity" in a volume called *The Lesbian Postmodern*.[2] The avowed intention of the article was to examine the various representations of transsexual bodies and transgender butch bodies that surfaced around 1990 to 1991, largely within lesbian contexts. The essay was speculative and concentrated on films, videos, and narratives about gender-ambiguous characters. Much to my surprise, the essay was regarded with much suspicion and hostility by some members of FTM International, a San Francisco–based transsexual men's group; these reactions caused me to look carefully at the kinds of assumptions I was making about transsexuality and about the kinds of continuities or overlaps that I presumed between the categories of FTM and butch. My intention here is not to apologize for that essay or simply to explain again my position; rather, I want to use the constructive criticism I received about that article to reconsider the various relations and nonrelations between FTM and butch subjectivities and bodies. Ultimately, I believe that "F2M" was actually trying to carve out a subject position that we might usefully call transgender butch to signify the transition that the identity requires from female identity to masculine embodiment. At present, the moniker "FTM" names a radical shift in both identity and body base within the context of transsexuality that by comparison makes "butch" look like a stable signifier. But the shifts and accommodations made in most cross-gender identifications, whether aided by surgery or hormones or not, involve a great deal of instability and transitivity. Transgender butch conveys some of this movement.

In "F2M," I attempted to describe the multiple versions of masculinity that seemed to be emerging simultaneously out of both lesbian and transsexual contexts. My project was not a fact-finding ethnography about FTM; nor did it examine the mechanics, trials, tribulations, benefits, and necessities of body alteration. Rather, I asked discursive and possibly naive questions such as: Why, in this age of gender transitivity, when many queers and feminists have agreed that gender is a social construct, is transsexuality a widespread phenomenon? Why has there been so little discussion of the shared experiences of masculine lesbians and FTMs? And, finally, why are we not in what Sandy Stone has called a "posttranssexual era"?[3] My questions presumed that some forms of transsexuality represented gender essentialism, but from this assertion, some people understood me to be saying that butchness was postmodern and subversive whereas transsexualism was dated and deluded. I think, rather, that I was trying to create a theoretical and cultural space for the transgender butch that did not presume transsexuality as its epistemological frame. I was also implicitly examining the possibility of the non-operated-upon transgender person.

My article was received, as I suggested, as a clumsy and ignorant attack on the viability of FTM transsexuality, and there was a small debate about it in the pages of the *FTM Newsletter*. The editor, James Green, took me to task for speaking for FTMs, and in a review essay, a writer called Isabella cast me in the role of the lesbian feminist who wanted transsexuals to disappear within some postmodern proliferation of queer identities.[4] Isabella noted that I focused on film and video in my essay (on representations, in other words, as opposed to "real" accounts), and she accused me of failing to integrate the real lives and words of "the successfully integrated post-op FTM" into my theory.[5] She went on to suggest that I was not interested in the reality of transsexuality because "it is the fluidity, the creation and dissolution of gender 'fictions' that is so fascinating" (14). I took this criticism very seriously, if only because I had been trying to do the very opposite of what she accused me of doing and because my position on transsexuality is not really akin to the kinds of lesbian feminist paranoias articulated by the likes of Janice Raymond.[6] By arguing that "desire has a terrifying precision" ("F2M," 212), I was trying to get away from the tendency within queer popular culture and some queer writing to privilege gender fluidity (being butch *and* femme for example) as the goal of some ongoing gender rebellion, and I was trying to talk about the ways in which desire and gender and sexuality tend to be remarkably rigid.[7] Rather than consent to the terms of this debate, I wanted to question the belief in fluid selves and the belief, moreover, that fluidity and flexibility are always and everywhere desirable. At the same time, I was trying to show that many, if not most, sexual and gender identities involve some degree of movement (not free-flowing but very scripted) between bodies, desires, transgressions, and conformities; we do not necessarily shuttle back and forth between sexual roles and practices at will, but we do tend to adjust, accommodate, change, reverse, slide, and move in general between moods and modes of desire. Finally, Isabella's charge that I had not accounted for the experiences of "the successfully integrated post-op FTM" assumes that this particular mode of transsexuality—integrated and post-op—represents the apex of cross-gender transition and indeed represents its success. The in-between bodies that I had focused on in my essay can only be read in such a context as preoperative versions of the real thing, as bodies that fail to integrate.

Another more recent article critiquing "F2M" also accused the essay of advocating some simple celebratory mode of border crossing. In "No Place like Home: The Transgendered Narrative of Leslie Feinberg's *Stone Butch Blues*," Jay Prosser sets up "F2M" as a prime example of queer theory's fixation on the transgender body.[8] This article pits queer theory against transgender identity in a polemic: queer theory represents gender within some notion of postmodern fluidity and fragmentation, but transgender theory eschews such theoretical free fall and focuses instead on "subjective experience" (490). Queer theories of gender, in Prosser's account, emphasize the performative, and transgender theories emphasize narrative. Queer theories of gender are constructivist, and transgender theories are essentialist. Ultimately, Prosser proposes that transgender be separated from "genetic queerness" to build a transgender community (508).

The shaky foundation of Prosser's polemic is revealed in his reading of Feinberg's novel, in which it becomes clear that *Stone Butch Blues* represents both essential and constructed genders, both performative gender and genetic embodiment. Accordingly, when the main character, Jess Goldberg, chooses to halt his transition from female to male, we see the necessary insufficiency of binary gender rather than the solidity of transsexual identification. But Prosser uses Goldberg's transition to claim a continuity between this novel and transsexual autobiography. Even though Jess says, "I didn't feel like a man trapped in a woman's body, I just felt trapped," Prosser reads this as a transsexual paradigm "driven by the subject's sense of not being home in his/her body" ("No Place like Home," 490). The point here is that many subjects, not only transsexual subjects, do not feel at home in their bodies, and Prosser even cites from Feinberg a list of such gender outlaws at the end of his essay: "Transvestites, transsexuals, drag queens and drag kings, cross-dressers, bull-daggers, stone butches, androgynes etc."[9] But this was exactly my point in "F2M," and it is also what I recognize by using the term "transgender butch"—there are a variety of gender-deviant bodies under the sign of nonnormative masculinities and femininities, and the task at hand is not to decide which represents the place of most resistance but to begin the work of documenting their distinctive features. The place from which I chose to begin the work of examining the specificity of embodied desires was the butch, indeed the stone butch; I examined FTM subjectivity in that essay only as it compared to butch identifications. The place from which one theorizes "home," as Prosser calls it, completely alters the models of gender and sexuality one produces. As I discuss later, when theorized from the perspective of the FTM, the stone butch becomes pre-FTM, a penultimate stage along the way to the comfort of transsexual transformation; however, when theorized from the perspective of the butch, the stone butch becomes a nonsurgical and nonhormonal version of transgender identification and does away with the necessity of sex reassignment surgery for some people.

My essay also found a supporter in the *FTM Newsletter*. Jordy Jones, an FTM performance artist from San Francisco, responded to some of the criticisms of my article by suggesting that the notion that I had advanced of gender as a fiction did not necessarily erase the real-life experiences of transsexuals; rather, he suggested, it describes the approximate relation between concepts and bodies.[10] Furthermore, Jones objected to the very idea that transsexual experience could be represented in any totalizing or universal way:

Not everyone who experiences gender dysphoria experiences it in the same way, and not everyone deals with it in the same way. Not all transgendered individuals take hormones, and not everyone who takes hormones is transgendered. I have a (genetically female) friend who identifies as male and passes perfectly. He's never had a shot. I certainly know dykes who are butcher than I could ever be, but who wouldn't consider identifying as anything other than women. (15)

Jones, eloquently and forcefully, articulates here the limits of a monolithic model of transsexuality. His description of the wild variability of masculinities and identifications across butch and transsexual bodies refuses any notion of a butch-FTM continuum on the one hand, but on the other hand, it acknowledges the ways in which butch and FTM bodies are read against and through each other for better or for worse. Jones's understanding of transgender variability produces an almost fractal model of cross-gender identifications that can never return to the binary models of before and after, or transsexual and nontranssexual, or butch and FTM.

Needless to say, I have learned a great deal from these various interactions and textual conversations, and I want to use them here to resituate "F2M: The Making of Female Masculinity" in terms of a continuing "border war," to use Gayle Rubin's term, between butches and FTMs. In this chapter, I try again to create an interpretive model of transgender butchness that refuses to invest in the notion of some fundamental antagonism between lesbian and FTM subjectivities. This is not to ignore, however, the history of lesbian feminist opposition to transsexuals, which has been well documented by Sandy Stone. In "A Posttranssexual Manifesto," Stone shows how Janice Raymond and other feminists in the 1970s and 1980s (Mary Daly, for example) saw male-to-female transsexuals as phallocratic agents who were trying to infiltrate women-only space.[11] More recently, some lesbians have voiced their opposition to FTM transsexuals and characterized them as traitors and as women who literally become the enemy.[12] More insidiously, lesbians have tended to erase FTMs by claiming transsexual males as lesbians who lack access to a liberating lesbian discourse. So, for example, Billie Tipton, the jazz musician who lived his life as a man and who married a woman, is often represented within lesbian history as a lesbian woman forced to hide her gender to advance within his profession rather than as a transsexual man living within his chosen gender identity. In "The Politics of Passing," for example, Elaine K. Ginsberg rationalizes

Tipton's life: "He lived his professional life as a man, presumably because his chosen profession was not open to women."[13] Many revisionist accounts of transgender lives rationalize them out of existence in this way or through the misuse of female pronouns and do real damage to the project of mapping transgender histories.

So while it is true that transgender and transsexual men have been wrongly folded into lesbian history, it is also true that the distinctions between some transsexual identities and some lesbian identities may at times become quite blurry. Many FTMS do come out as lesbians before they come out as transsexuals (many, it must also be said, do not). And for this reason alone, one cannot always maintain hard and fast and definitive distinctions between lesbians and transsexuals. In the collection *Dagger: On Butch Women*, for example, the editors include a chapter of interviews with FTMS as part of their survey of an urban butch scene.[14] The five FTMS in the interview testify to a period of lesbian identification. Shadow admits that "the dyke community's been really great, keeping me around for the last 12 years" (154); Mike says that he never really identified as female but that he did "identif[y] as a lesbian for a while" because "being a dyke gave me options" (155). Similarly, Billy claims that he feels neither male nor female but that he did "go through the whole lesbian separatist bullshit" (155). Like Shadow, Eric feels that for a while, "the lesbian place was really good for me" (156), and finally Sky suggests that although certain individuals in the dyke community are hostile to him, "I'm forty years old and I've been involved with dykes for nearly half my life. I'm not going to give that up" (158). Obviously, these FTM voices are quite particular and in no way represent a consensus or even a dominant version of the relations between FTM and dyke communities. Also, these versions of FTM history have been carefully chosen to fit into a collection of essays about lesbian masculinities. However, these transgender men do articulate one very important line of affiliation between transsexualities and lesbian identities. Many transgender men, quite possibly, successfully identify as butch in a queer female community before they decide to transition. Once they have transitioned, many transsexual men want to maintain their ties to their queer lesbian communities. Much transsexual discourse now circulating tries to cast the lesbian pasts of FTM as instances of mistaken identities or as an effort to find temporary refuge within some queer gender-variant notion of "butchness."[15]

In this FTM chapter of *Dagger*, just to complicate matters further, the transgender men also tell of finding the limits of lesbian identification. Billy, for one, hints at the kinds of problems some pretransition transgender men experience when they identify as lesbians. Billy recalls: "I've had this problem for ten years now with women being attracted to my boyishness and my masculinity, but once they get involved with me they tell me I'm too male" (156). Billy crosses the line for many of his lovers because he wants a real moustache and a real beard and does not experience his masculinity as temporary or theatrical. Billy's experience testifies to the ways in which masculinity within some lesbian contexts presents a problem when it becomes too "real," or when some imaginary line has been crossed between play and seriousness. This also makes lesbian masculinity sound like a matter of degree. Again, this kind of limited understanding of lesbian masculinity has a history within lesbian feminism. As many historians have pointed out, male identification was an accusation leveled at many butches in the early days of lesbian feminism, and so it is hardly surprising to find a residue of this charge in the kinds of judgments made against FTMs by lesbians in contemporary settings.[16] The real problem with this notion of lesbian and transgender masculinities lies in the way it suggests a masculine continuum that looks something like this:

Androgyny—Soft Butch—Butch—Stone Butch—Transgender Butch—FTM

Not Masculine ————————————————— Very Masculine

Such a model clearly has no interpretive power when we return to Jordy Jones's catalog of transgender variety. For Jones, the intensity of masculinity was not accounted for by transsexual identification. Furthermore, as Jones points out, "not everyone who experiences gender dysphoria deals with it in the same way"; gender dysphoria can be read all the way along the continuum, and it would not be accurate to make gender dysphoria the exclusive property of transsexual bodies or to surmise that the greater the gender dysphoria, the likelier a transsexual identification. At the transgender end of the spectrum, the continuum model miscalculates the relation between bodily alteration and degree of masculinity; at the butch end, the continuum model makes it seem as if butchness is sometimes just an early stage of transsexual aspiration. Stone butchness, for example, is very often seen as a compromise category between lesbian and FTM and is therefore defined by sexual dysfunction rather than sexual practice. As a compromise category, stone butch may be seen as a last-ditch effort to maintain masculinity within female embodiment: the expectation, of course, is that such an effort will fail and the stone butch will become fully functional once she takes steps toward transitioning to be a transsexual man.

In the essay "Stone Butch Now" (as opposed to stone butch in the 1950s), Heather Findlay interviews stone butches about their various modes of gender and sexual identification. For the purposes of the article, stone butch occupies "a gray area" between lesbian and FTM.[17] One of Findlay's informants simply calls him/herself Jay and relates that s/he is considering transitioning.[18] Jay tries to define the difference between being stone and being transsexual: "As a stone butch you have a sense of humor about your discomfort in the world. As an FTM, however, you lose that sense of humor. Situations that were funny suddenly get very tragic" (44). Obviously, in this comment, Jay already seems to be speaking from the perspective of an FTM. To do so, s/he must cast the stone butch as playful in comparison to the seriousness of the FTM transsexual. The stone butch laughs at her gender discomfort whereas the FTM finds his discomfort to be a source of great pain. The stone butch manages her gender dysphoria, according to such a model, but the FTM cannot. Again, these oppositions between FTM and butch come at the expense of a complex butch subjectivity and also work to totalize both categories in relation to a set of experiences. As other stone butches interviewed in the article attest, being stone may mean moving in and out of gender comfort and may mean a very unstable sense of identification with lesbianism or femaleness. To separate the category of FTM from the category of butch, Jay must assign butch to femaleness and FTM to maleness.

My aim here and in my earlier essay has been to focus on certain categories of butchness without presuming that they represent early stages of transsexual identity within some progressive model of sexual transidentity and without losing their specificity as masculine identifications within a female body. Just as there is obviously much tension between the categories "lesbian" and "FTM," there are even tensions between "lesbian" and "butch." As I have been using butch here, it obviously refers to some form of dyke masculinity and refers to a historical equation of female homosexuality with female masculinity. But this history of overlap between sexual and gender variance does not mean that female masculinity has not often been cast as a thorn in the side of contemporary lesbian definition. All too often, as Billy suggests, the lesbian butch has been pressured to forgo her masculinity and attest to positive female embodiment. In Stone Butch Blues, for example, as we saw in my last chapter, the he-she,

Jess Goldberg, fights with her femme-turned-feminist girlfriend about acceptable forms of female masculinity. "You're a woman," Theresa tells Jess, but Jess responds, "I'm a he-she, that's different."[19] Jess goes on to tell her girlfriend that s/he is not a lesbian in the terms that Theresa has used for lesbian definition. The distinction that butches have made throughout the last twenty years between lesbianism and female masculinity hinges on a mounting perception of distinct differences between gender and sexual identities. "Lesbian," since the rise of lesbian feminism, refers to sexual preference and refers to some version of the "woman-loving woman." Butch, on the other hand, bears a complex relation to femaleness and, in terms of sexual orientation, could refer to a "woman-loving butch" or a "butch-loving butch."

The places where the divisions between butch and FTM become blurry, on the other hand, have less to do with the identity politics of lesbian feminism and more to do with embodiment. As Jordy Jones suggests, many individuals who take hormones may not be transgendered, and many transgendered men may not take hormones. In fact, although in "F2M" I tried to make visible some of the gender fictions that prop up contemporary gender binarism, in the disputes between different groups of queers, we see that the labels "butch" and "transsexual" mark another gender fiction, the fiction of clear distinctions. In "F2M" I used the refrain "There are no transsexuals. We are all transsexuals" to point to the inadequacy of such a category in an age of profound gender trouble. I recognize, of course, the real and particular history of the transsexual and of transsexual surgery, hormone treatment, and transsexual rights discourse. I also recognize that there are huge and important differences between genetic females who specifically identify as transsexual and genetic females who feel comfortable with female masculinity. There are real and physical differences between female-born men who take hormones, have surgery, and live as men and female-born butches who live some version of gender ambiguity. But there are also many situations in which those differences are less clear than one might expect, and there are many butches who pass as men and many transsexuals who present as gender ambiguous and many bodies that cannot be classified by the options transsexual and butch. We are not all transsexual, I admit, but many bodies are gender strange to some degree or another, and it is time to complicate on the one hand the transsexual models that assign gender deviance only to transsexual bodies and gender normativity to all other bodies, and on the other hand the hetero-normative models that see transsexuality as the solution to gender deviance and homosexuality as a pathological perversion.

### Female-to-Male

While many female-to-male transsexuals (FTMS) live out their masculinity in deliberately ambiguous bodies, many others desire complete transitions from female to male (and these people I will call transsexual males or trans-sexual men). Some of those transgender people who retain the label "FTM" (rather than becoming "men") have mastectomies and hysterectomies and take testosterone on a regular basis and are quite satisfied with the male secondary characteristics that such treatments produce. These transgender subjects are not attempting to slide seamlessly into manhood, and their retention of the FTM label suggests the emergence of a new gender position marked by this term. However, another strand of male transsexualism has produced a new discourse on masculinity that depends in part on startlingly conservative pronouncements about the differences between themselves and transgender butches. These conservative notions are betrayed in the tendency of some transsexual males to make distinct gender assignations to extremely and deliberately gender-ambiguous bodies, and this tendency has a history within transsexual male autobiography; indeed, the denigration of the category "butch" is a standard feature of the genre.

In Mario Martino's autobiography *Emergence* (1977), Martino goes to great lengths to distinguish himself from lesbians and from butches in particular as he negotiates the complications of pretransition identifications. Before his transition, Mario falls in love with a young woman; s/he tells the girlfriend, Becky: "You and I are not lesbians. We relate to each other as man to woman, woman to man."[20] One day, Becky comes home from work and asks: "Mario, what's a butch?" (141). Mario writes, "I could actually feel my skin bristle" (141). Becky tells Mario that the head nurse on the ward where Becky works asked her about her "butch," and in effect she wants to know the difference between Mario and a butch. Mario gives her a simple answer: "A butch is the masculine member of a lesbian team. That would make you the feminine member. But, Becky, honest-to-God, I don't feel that we're lesbians. I still maintain I should have been a male" (141). Becky seems satisfied with the answer, but the question itself plagues Mario long into the night: "The word *butch* magnified itself before my eyes. *Butch* implied female—and I had never thought of myself as such" (142). In *Emergence*, lesbianism haunts the protagonist and threatens to swallow his gender specificity and disallow his transsexuality. Unfortunately, as we see in the passages I have quoted, Martino's efforts to disentangle his maleness from lesbian masculinity tend to turn butchness into a stable female category and tend to overemphasize the differences between butch womanhood and transsexual manhood.

Another transsexual autobiography also magnifies the gulf between butch and transsexual male to mark out the boundaries of transsexual masculinity. In *Dear Sir or Madam*, Mark Rees obsessively marks out his difference from lesbians. On attending a lesbian club before transition, sometime in the early 1960s, he feels assured in his sense of difference because, he notes, "the women there didn't want to be men; they were happy in their gender role."[21] He goes on to identify lesbianism in terms of two feminine women whose attraction is based on sameness, not difference. It is hard to imagine what Rees thinks he saw when he entered the lesbian bar. In the 1960s, butch-femme would still have been a cultural dominant in British lesbian bar culture, and it is unlikely that the scene that presented itself to Rees was a kind of "Bargirls" scene of lipstick lesbians. What probably characterized the scene before him was an array of gender-deviant bodies in recognizable butch-femme couplings. Because he needs to assert a crucial difference between himself and lesbians, Rees tries to deny the possibility of cross-identifying butch women.

In his desperation to hold the terms "lesbian" and "transsexual" apart, however, Rees goes one step further than just making lesbianism into a category for women who were "happy in their gender role." He also marks out the difference in terms of sexual aim as well as sexual and gender identity; he focuses, in other words, on the partner of the transsexual male for evidence of the distinctiveness of transsexual maleness. Rees claims to find a medical report confirming that lesbians and transsexuals are totally different. The report suggests that transsexuals "do not see themselves as lesbians before treatment, hate their partners seeing their bodies. It added that the partners of female-to-males are normal heterosexual women, not lesbians, and see their lovers as men, in spite of their lack of a penis. The partners were feminine, many had earlier relations with genetic males and often experienced orgasms with their female-to-male partners for the first time" (*Dear Sir or Madam*, 59). This passage should signal some of the problems attendant on this venture of making transsexual man and transgender butch into totally separate entities. Although one is extremely sympathetic to the sense of being misidentified, the need to stress the lack of identification inevitably leads to a conservative attempt to reorder the sex and gender categories that are in danger of becoming scrambled. Here Rees attempts to locate difference in the desires of the transsexual male's partner and unwittingly makes a distinction between these women as "normal heterosexual women" and lesbians. Lesbianism suddenly becomes a category of pathology next to the properly heterosexual and gender-normative aims of the transsexual man and his feminine partner. Furthermore, this "normal heterosexual woman" finds her perfect mate in the transsexual man and indeed, we are told, often experiences orgasm with him "for the first time."

The jarring need to identify the feminine partner of the transsexual man with normal sexual aims and desires unravels a little later in the book when Rees reports his difficulty in finding a relationship. After several disastrous relationships, he resigns himself to living alone and asexually, and he tries to admit his own responsibility in the string of bad relationships: "My conclusion is that my lack of success must be due to my lack of acceptability as a person" (134). However, he quickly turns this judgment onto his partners: "One flaw has been my appalling lack of judgement." In other words, Rees has not found a good relationship because he has made bad choices, and ultimately the women are to blame. The distinction between lesbian and transsexual is undoubtedly an important one to sketch out, but there is always the danger that the effort to mark the territory of transsexual male subjectivity may fall into homophobic assertions about lesbians and sexist formulations of women in general.

Rees's categorical distinctions between lesbians and partners of transsexual men and both his and Martino's horror of the slippage between homosexual and transsexual also echo in various informal bulletins that circulate on transsexual discussion lists on the Internet. In some bulletins, transsexual men send each other tips on how to pass as a man, and many of these tips focus almost obsessively on the care that must be taken by the transsexual man not to look like a butch lesbian. Some tips tell guys[22] to dress preppy as opposed to the standard jeans and leather jacket look of the butch; in other instances, transsexual men are warned against certain haircuts (punk styles or crew cuts) that are supposedly popular among butches. These tips, obviously, steer the transsexual man away from transgression or alternative masculine styles and toward a conservative masculinity. One wonders whether another list of tips should circulate advising transsexual men of how not to be mistaken for straight, or worse a Republican or a banker. Most of these lists seem to place no particular political or even cultural value on the kinds of masculinity they mandate.[23]

Finally, in relation to the conservative project of making concrete distinctions between butch women and transsexual males, such distinctions all too often serve the cause of hetero-normativity by consigning homosexuality to pathology and by linking transsexuality to a new form of heterosexuality. In a popular article on transsexual men that appeared in the *New Yorker*, for example, reporter Amy Bloom interviews several transsexual men and some sex reassignment surgeons to try to uncover the motivations and mechanics of so-called "high intensity transsexualism."[24] Bloom comments on the history of transsexualism, the process of transition, and the multiple, highly invasive surgeries required for sex reassignment from female to male. She interviews a young white transsexual male who sees his transsexualism as a birth defect that needs correction and several older white transsexual males, one Latino transsexual man, and one black transsexual man, who have varying accounts of their gender identities. Bloom spends much time detailing the looks of the men she interviews: a young transsexual man, Lyle, is "a handsome, shaggy graduating senior," and James Green is a chivalrous man with a "Jack Nicholson smile" (40); Loren Cameron is "a not uncommon type of handsome, cocky, possibly gay man" with "a tight, perfect build" (40); Luis is a "slightly built, gentle South American man" (40). So what, you might think, these are some important descriptions of what transsexual men look like. They look, in fact, like other men, and Bloom quickly admits that she finds herself in flirtatious heterosexual dynamics with her charming companions, dynamics that quickly shore up the essential differences between men and women. Bloom, for example, reports that she was sitting in her rental car with James Green and could not find the dimmer switch for the headlights; when James finds it for her, she comments: "He looks at me exactly as my husband has on hundreds of occasions: affectionate, pleased, a little charmed by this blind spot of mine" (40). Later, over dinner with Green, she notices: "He does not say, 'Gee, this is a lot of food,' or anything like that. Like a man he just starts eating" (40).

Bloom's descriptions of her interviewees and her accounts of her interactions with them raise questions about mainstream attitudes toward male transsexuals versus mainstream attitudes toward masculine lesbians. Would Bloom, in a similar article on butch lesbians, comment so approvingly on their masculinity? Would she notice a woman's muscular build, another butch's wink, another's "Jack Nicholson smile"? Would she be aware of their eating habits, their mechanical aptitudes? The answer, of course, is a resounding "no," and indeed I find confirmation for my suspicions further down the page. Bloom reflects on her meetings with these handsome transsexual men as follows:

> I expected to find psychologically disturbed, male-identified women so filled with self-loathing that it had even spilled into their physical selves, leading them to self-mutilating, self-punishing surgery. Maybe I would meet some very butch lesbians, in ties and jackets and chest binders, who could not, would not accept their female bodies. I didn't meet these people. I met men. (41)

What a relief for Bloom that she was spared interaction with those self-hating masculine women and graced instead by the dignified presence of men! Posttransition, we must remember at all times, many transsexual men become heterosexual men, living so-called normal lives, and for folks like Amy Bloom, this is a cause for some celebration.

In her interaction with a black transsexual man, Bloom asks questions that actually raise some interesting issues, however. Michael, unlike James and Loren, is not part of an urban FTM community; he lives a quiet and somewhat secretive life and shies away from anything that may reveal his transsexuality. Michael finds a degree of acceptance from his family and coworkers and strives for nothing more than this tolerance. He articulates his difference from some other transsexuals:

> I was born black. I don't expect people to like me, to accept me. Some transsexuals, especially the white MTF's—they're in shock after the transition. Loss of privilege, loss of status; they think people should be thrilled to work side by side with them. Well, people do not go to work in mainstream America hoping for an educational experience. I didn't expect anyone to be happy to see me—I just expected, I demanded a little tolerance. (49)

Michael is the only person in the whole article to mention privilege and the change in social status experienced by transsexuals who pass. He clearly identifies the differences between transsexuals in terms of race and class, and he speaks of lowered expectations on account of a lifetime of experiencing various forms of intolerance. Bloom makes little comment on

Michael's testimony, and she does not make a connection between what he says and what the other white men say. But Michael's experience is crucial to the politics of transsexualism. In America there is a huge difference between becoming a black man or a man of color and becoming a white man, and these differences are bound to create gulfs within transsexual communities and will undoubtedly resonate in the border wars between butches and transsexual men. The politics of transsexuality, quite obviously, reproduce other political struggles in other locations, and while some transsexuals find strength in the notion of identity politics, others find their identities and loyalties divided by their various affiliations. As in so many other identity-based activist projects, one axis of identification is a luxury most people cannot afford.

We are presently in the midst of a "reverse discourse" of transsexuality. In *The History of Sexuality*, Michel Foucault analyzes the strategic production of sexualities and sexual identities, and he proposes a model of a "reverse discourse" to explain the web of relations between power, discourse, sexuality, and resistance. He argues that resistance is always already embedded in power "as an irreducible opposite" and that therefore resistance cannot come from an outside; the multiplicity of power means that there is no opposite, no site of resistance where power has not already been.[25] There is, Foucault suggests, a "reverse discourse" in which one empowers a category that might have been used to oppress one—one transforms a debased position into a challenging presence. As a reverse discourse takes shape around the definitions of transsexual and transgender, it is extremely important to recognize the queerness of these categories, their instability and their interpretability. While identity obviously continues to be the best basis for political organizing, we have seen within various social movements of the last decade that identity politics must give way to some form of coalition if a political movement is to be successful. The current discourse in some transsexual circles, therefore, of setting up gay and lesbian politics and communities as the enemy to transgender definition is as pernicious as the gay and lesbian tendencies to ignore the specificities of transsexual political needs and demands.[26] Furthermore, the simple opposition of transsexual versus gay and lesbian masks many other lines of affiliation and coalition that already exist within multiple queer communities: it masks, for example, that the gay/lesbian versus transsexual/transgender opposition is very much a concern in white queer contexts but not necessarily in queer communities of color. Many immigrant queer groups have successfully integrated transgender definition into their conceptions of community.[27]

## The Right Body?

My intent in this chapter is not to vilify male transsexualism as simply a reconsolidation of dominant masculinity. But I do want to point carefully to the places where such a reconsolidation threatens to take place. In academic conversations, transsexualism has been used as both the place of gender transgression and the marker of gender conservatism. Obviously, transsexualism is neither essentially transgressive nor essentially conservative, and perhaps it becomes a site of such contestation because it is not yet clear what the politics of transsexualism will look like. Indeed, the history of FTM transsexuality is still being written, and as FTM communities emerge in urban settings, it becomes clear that their relations to the history of medicine, the history of sexuality, and the history of gender are only now taking shape. One attempt to chart this history in relation to a more general history of transsexualism and medical technology reveals what we might call the essentially contradictory politics of transsexualism. In *Changing Sex*, Bernice Hausman meticulously details the dependence of the category "transsexual" on medical technologies and in turn the dependence of the very concept of gender on the emergence of the transsexual. Several times in the book, Hausman rejects the notion that we can read gender as an ideology without also considering it as a product of technological relations. This argument marks a crucial contribution to the study of gender and technology, but unfortunately Hausman quite simply tends to attribute too much power to the medical configuration of transsexual definition. She claims that the transsexual and the doctor codependently produce transsexual definitions and that therefore transsexual agency can be read "through their doctor's discourses." She develops this notion of an interdependent relationship between transsexuals and medical technology to build to a rather astounding conclusion:

> By demanding technological intervention to "change sex," transsexuals demonstrate that their relationship to technology is a dependent one . . . demanding sex change is therefore part of what constructs the subject as a transsexual: it is the mechanism through which transsexuals come

to identify themselves under the sign of transsexualism and construct themselves as subjects. Because of this we can read transsexuals' agency through their doctor's discourses, as the demand for sex change was instantiated as the primary symptom (and sign) of the transsexual.[28]

Sex change itself has become a static signifier in this paragraph, and no distinction is upheld between FTM sex change and MTF sex change. No power is granted to the kinds of ideological commitments that doctors may have that influence their thinking about making vaginas versus making penises, and because sex change rhetoric has been mostly used in relation to MTF bodies, the FTM and his relation to the very uncertain process of sex change, demanding sex change, and completing sex change is completely lost.

Hausman's book, I should stress, is careful and historically rich and will undoubtedly change the way that gender is conceived in relation to transsexual and nontranssexual bodies. But the particular border wars between butches and transsexual men that concern me both here and in my earlier essay have been lost in a study of this kind. Future studies of transsexuality and of lesbianism must attempt to account for historical moments when the difference between gender deviance and sexual deviance is hard to discern.[29] The history of inversion and of people who identified as inverts (Radclyffe Hall, for example) still represents a tangle of cross-identification and sexual preference that is neither easily separated nor comfortably accounted for under the heading of "lesbian." There is not, furthermore, one history to be told here (the history of medical technology) about one subject (the transsexual). There are many histories of bodies that escape and elude medical taxonomies, of bodies that never present themselves to the physician's gaze, of subjects who identify within categories that emerge as a consequence of sexual communities and not in relation to medical or psychosexual research.

Because these categories are so difficult to disentangle, perhaps, a new category has emerged in recent years, "transgender." Transgender describes a gender identity that is at least partially defined by transitivity but that may well stop short of transsexual surgery. Inevitably, the term becomes a catchall, and this somewhat lessens its effect. Toward the end of her book, Hausman attempts to stave off criticisms of her work that may be based on an emergent notion of transgenderism. She acknowledges that transgender discourse seems to counter her claims that transsexuals are produced solely within medical discourse and that this discourse actually suggests "a fundamental antipathy to the regulatory mode of medical surveillance" (*Changing Sex*, 195). Hausman manages to discount such an effect of transgender discourse by arguing that "the desire to celebrate and proliferate individual performances as a way to destabilize 'gender' at large is based on liberal humanist assumptions of self-determination" (197). This is an easy dismissal of a much more complicated and ongoing project. Transgender discourse in no way argues that people should just pick up new genders and eliminate old ones or proliferate at will because gendering is available as a self-determining practice; rather, transgender discourse asks only that we recognize the nonmale and nonfemale genders already in circulation and presently under construction.

Hausman's real stakes in this seemingly historical project slip out at the end of her chapter "Transsexual Autobiographies." Having argued strenuously that transsexual autobiographies collude in the construction of notions of an authentic sex, Hausman attempts to ease off her critical tone and express some empathy for the transsexual condition. She comments earnestly: "Those of us who are not transsexuals may wonder what it is like to feel oneself in the 'wrong body'" (174). The idea that only transsexuals experience the pain of a "wrong body" shows an incredible myopia about the trials and tribulations of many varieties of perverse embodiment.[30] It neatly ascribes gender confusion and dysphoria once again to transsexuals and efficiently constructs a model of "right body" experience that applies, presumably, to people such as Hausman. Part of the motivation of a transgender discourse is to produce what Sedgwick calls in *Epistemology of the Closet* "universalist" models of gender identity in which all gender identities fall under scrutiny rather than simply the unorthodox ones. Hausman resists a universalist model of gender identification and ensures that transsexual and pathology remain annexed while her book maintains the fiction of proper and normal genders.

## Border Wars

Because the production of gender and sexual deviance takes place in multiple locations (the doctor's office, the operating room, the sex club, the bedroom, the bathroom) and because the discourses to which gender and sexual deviance are bound also emerge in many different contexts (medical tracts, queer magazines, advice columns, films and videos, autobiographies), the categories of transsexual, transgender, and butch are constantly under construction. However, in the border wars between butches and transsexual men, transsexuals are often cast as those who cross borders (of sex, gender, bodily coherence), and butches are left as those who stay in one place, possibly a border space of nonidentity. The terminology of "border war" is both apt and problematic for this reason. On the one hand, the idea of a border war sets up some notion of territories to be defended, ground to be held or lost, permeability to be defended against. On the other hand, a border war suggests that the border is at best slippery and permeable. As I mentioned earlier, in "No Place like Home," Prosser critiques queer theory for fixing on "the transgendered crossing in order to denaturalize gender" (484), and he claims that queer border crossing positions itself against "the homeliness of identity politics" (486). For Prosser, such a move leaves the transsexual man with no place to go and leaves him languishing in the "uninhabitable space—the borderlands in between, where passing as either gender might prove quite a challenge" (488–89). Whereas queers might celebrate the space in between, Prosser suggests, the transsexual rushes onward to find the space beyond, "the promise of home on the other side" (489). "Home," as one might imagine in relation to Prosser's model, is represented as the place in which one finally settles into the comfort of one's true and authentic gender.

Prosser thinks that queer theory (specifically, actually, my earlier essay "F2M") celebrates the in-between space as full of promise and "freedom and mobility for the subject" ("No Place like Home," 499), whereas transsexual theory embraces place, location, and specificity. The queer butch, in other words, represents fluidity to the transsexual man's stability, and stability (staying in a female body) to the transsexual man's fluidity (gender crossing). Prosser makes little or no recognition of the trials and tribulations that confront the butch who for whatever reasons (concerns about surgery or hormones, feminist scruples, desire to remain in a lesbian community, lack of funds, lack of successful phalloplasty models) decides to make a home in the body with which she was born. Even more alarming, he makes little or no recognition of the fact that many FTMS also live and die in those inhospitable territories in between. It is true that many transsexuals do transition to go somewhere, to be somewhere, and to leave geographies of ambiguity behind. However, many post-op MTFS are in-between because they cannot pass as women; many FTMS who pass fully clothed have bodies that are totally ambiguous; some transsexuals cannot afford all the surgeries necessary to full sex reassignment (if there is such a thing), and these people make their home where they are; some transsexual folks do not define their transsexuality in relation to a strong desire for penises or vaginas, and they may experience the desire to be trans or queer more strongly than the desire to be male or female.

If the borderlands are uninhabitable for some transsexuals who imagine that home is just across the border, imagine what a challenge they present to those subjects who do not believe that such a home exists, either metaphorically or literally. Prosser's cartography of gender relies on a belief in the two territories of male and female, divided by a flesh border and crossed by surgery and endocrinology. The queer cartography that he rejects prefers the charting of hybridity: queer hybridity is far from the ludic and giddy mixing that Prosser imagines and more of a recognition of the dangers of investing in comforting but tendentious notions of home. Some bodies are never at home, some bodies cannot simply cross from A to B, some bodies recognize and live with the inherent instability of identity.

So far, I have noted the ways in which transsexual males and butch lesbians regard each other with some suspicion and the ways in which the two categories blur and separate. I have argued against stable and coherent definitions of sexual identity and tried to suggest the ways in which the lines between the transsexual and the gender-deviant lesbian inevitably crisscross each other and intersect, even producing a new category: transgender. I want to turn now to the rhetoric itself in the debate between transsexuals and butches to try to identify some of the dangers in demanding discrete and coherent sexual and gender identities. Much of the rhetoric surrounding transsexualism plays with the sense of transitivity and sees transsexuality as a passage or journey. Along the way, predictably enough, borders are crossed, and one leaves a foreign country to return, as we saw in Prosser's essay, to the home of one's true body.

If we return for the moment to the BBC series *The Wrong Body*, it offers an interesting example of the power of this kind of rhetoric. In one remarkable confrontation between Fredd and his psychiatrist, the psychiatrist used an extended simile to try to express his understanding of the relation of Fredd's female and male gender identities. He said: "You, Fredd, are like someone who has learned to speak French perfectly and who immigrates to France and lives there as a Frenchman. But just because you speak French and learn to imitate Frenchness and live among French people, you are still English." Fredd countered with: "No, I don't just speak

French having moved there, I AM French." In this exchange, the doctor deploys what has become a common metaphor for transsexualism as a crossing of national borders from one place to another, from one state to another, from one gender to another. Fredd rejects such a rhetorical move and insists that his expression of his boy self is not a transition but rather the expression of a self that he has always inhabited. That Fredd is young and indeed preadolescent allows him to articulate his transsexualism very differently from many adult transsexuals. He is passing into manhood not from one adult body to another but from an almost pregendered body into a fully gendered male body. The rhetoric of passing and crossing and transitioning has only a limited use for him.

Metaphors of travel and border crossings are inevitable within a discourse of transsexuality. But they are also laden with the histories of other identity negotiations, and they carry the burden of national and colonial discursive histories. What does it mean, then, to discuss gender variance and gender transitivity as a journey from one country to another or from a foreign country toward home or from illegal status to naturalized citizenship? How useful or how limiting are metaphors of the border and crossing and belonging to questions of gender identity? How does gender transitivity rely on the stability of other identity markers?

Within discussions of postmodernism, the transsexual body has often come to represent contradictory identity per se in the twentieth century and has been discussed using precisely the rhetoric of colonialism. Whereas Janice Raymond identified the transsexual body in 1979 as part of a patriarchal empire intent on colonizing female bodies and feminist souls,[31] Sandy Stone responded in her "Posttranssexual Manifesto" by allowing the "empire" to "strike back" and calling for a "counterdiscourse" within which the transsexual might speak as transsexual. Whereas Bernice Hausman reads transsexual autobiographies as evidence that to a certain extent "transsexuals are the dupes of gender,"[32] Jay Prosser sees these narratives as "driven by the attempt to realize the fantasy of belonging in the sexed body and the world."[33] Many contemporary discussions of plastic surgery and body manipulation take transsexuality as a privileged signifier of the productive effects of body manipulation, and many theories of postmodern subjectivity understand the fragmentation of the body in terms of a paradigmatic transsexuality. Transsexuality, in other words, seems burdened not only by an excess of meaning but also by the weight of contradictory and competing discourses. If we sort through the contradictions, we find transsexuals represented as "empire" and the subaltern, as gender dupes and gender deviants, and as consolidated identities and fragmented bodies.

Jay Prosser, as we saw, critiques postmodern queer theory in particular for fixing on "the transgendered crossing in order to denaturalize gender" ("No Place like Home," 484), and he claims that queer affirmations of the "trans journey" celebrate "opposition to a narrative centered upon home" (486). Female-to-male transsexual theorist Henry Rubin provides an even more polarized opposition than the queer versus transgender split produced by Prosser. For Rubin, the division that is most meaningful is between transsexuals and transgenders: "Although it is often assumed that 'transgender' is an umbrella term that refers to cross-dressers, drag queens, butch dykes, gender blenders, and transsexuals, among others, there is a tension between transsexual and transgenders."[34] For Rubin, the tension lies between the transsexual's quest for " 'home,' a place of belonging to one sex or the other," and the transgender quest for "a world without gender" (7). According to such logic, the transgender person is just playing with gender and trying to deconstruct the naturalness of gender, but the transsexual bravely reaffirms the notion of stable gender and fortifies the reality of biology. The people who fall under the "umbrella" of transgender definition represent for Rubin a nonserious quest for gender instability that comes at the expense of a transsexual quest for "a place of belonging." To hold up what might seem an unlikely division between transgender and transsexual, Rubin models his argument on the various debates about lesbian identity. In the 1970s, it became quite common for women to call themselves "lesbian" as a mark of solidarity rather than a statement of sexual practice, and Rubin suggests that transgenders are like political lesbians. Again, such an argument collapses the historical differences between the lesbian sex debates and contemporary identity skirmishes, and it also renders transgenders as well-meaning, but transsexuals as the real thing.

One other essay that typifies this concern about gender realness and the symbolic uses of transsexualism within postmodernism is "Fin de Siecle, Fin de Sexe: Transsexuality, Postmodernism, and the Death of History," by Rita Felski. Felski notes the ways in which transsexuality is invoked at this fin de siècle to "describe the dissolution of once stable polarities of male and female."[35] But she warns against the elevation of transsexualism to the status of universal signifier because it runs the risk of "homogenizing differences that matter politically: the differences between men and women, the difference between those who occasionally play with the trope of trans-sexuality and those others for whom it is a matter of life and death" (347). In other words, if queer theorists take up transsexualism as a trope for the breakdown of identity, they unwittingly shore up a postmodern evacuation of political activism by detaching transsexualism from the hard facts of gender and embodiment. Felski's warning is well taken, but to whom is it directed? Who, in other words, occasionally plays with transsexuality rather than taking it seriously? Felski finds such play to be dangerous and necessarily a sign of privilege: "Not all social subjects, after all, have equal freedom to play with and subvert the signs of gender, even as many do not perceive such play as a necessary condition of their freedom" (347). Felski identifies Arthur and Marilouise Kroker and Jean Baudrillard as being those postmodernists playing with transsexuality and therefore, we presume, failing to take seriously the differences between men and women and the differences between gender players and gender realists.[36] I have no wish to defend Baudrillard's vacuous postmodern visions or the Krokers' notions of pomo sex, but I do want to challenge the depiction of a postmodern queer constituency who play happily in some gender borderlands while others diligently and seriously refuse to take part in the celebration. What or who is missing from Felski's earnest picture of the "fin de sexe" at the "fin de siècle"?

The people, presumably, who play with transsexuality and gleefully subvert the signs of gender are nontranssexuals who "see such play as a necessary condition of their freedom." They are indeed the transgenders of Henry Rubin's article and the queers in Jay Prosser's. I wonder if it strikes anyone else as ironic that the very people, gays and lesbians and gender deviants, who have been identified as historically the victims of hetero-normativity are here invoked as dilettantes and recreationalists in the game of gender. Suddenly the transsexual has been resituated as the central figure in gender deviance, the one body that suffers, the only body that believes in gender and as an antidote to queer mobility. But the transgender butch in particular has long been a literary tragic hero who is martyred by her sense of being out of place. Whether it is Stephen Gordon in Radclyffe Hall's *The Well of Loneliness* (1928) discovering that "the loneliest place in this world is the no-man's-land of sex,"[37] or the 1950s butch Jess Goldberg in Leslie Feinberg's *Stone Butch Blues* (1993) finding herself out of time and place in contemporary lesbian New York, the narrative of the transgender or inverted butch has been one of loss, loneliness, and disconnection.[38] The butches in these narratives are hardly playful gender hedonists, and indeed they share with many FTMS a serious quest for place and belonging. In the novel *Sacred Country* (1992), Rose Tremain's female-to-male transsexual character, Marty, counters her grandfather's claim that "everything important in life was dual, like being and not being, male and female, and that there was no country in between." Marty thinks to him/herself: "Cord is wrong, there is a country in between, a country that no one sees, and I am in it."[39] The literary narrative of gender transitivity and gender dysphoria, then, has understood the experience of the "wrong body" in terms of a complex rhetoric of unbelonging and nonidentity. In response to this fundamental sense of being out of place, Tremain's transsexual man and Hall's invert and Feinberg's transgender butch conjure up images of imaginary lands, both countries in between and border worlds of the dispossessed.

Transition and mobility have themselves long been the alibi of many a female-to-male cross-dresser: female adventurers and fortune hunters have, over the last three hundred years, donned men's clothing, very often military uniforms, and made their way in the world passing back and forth between places and genders. Some passing women in the eighteenth and nineteenth centuries went to sea and lived as pirates; others joined the army and lived as men among men; still others used their disguises to enter male professions, take female lovers, or travel the world.[40] In other words, cross-dressing, passing, and gender transitivity work in and through other forms of mobility: a woman who accesses mobility through cross-dressing may well destabilize economies of masculinity, but she may simultaneously restabilize certain forms of racism or particular class antagonisms. To give just one example of such a nest of contradictory crossings, we could consider the abundance of turn-of-the-century cross-dressing and cross-identifying aristocratic women in Europe who took up the fascist cause in very active ways that I discussed in chapter 3.

The contradictions of cross-identification and its mobilities are further exemplified in a highly renowned autobiographical transsexual text, Jan Morris's *Conundrum*. Jan Morris was at one time known as James Morris, a travel writer and, in the 1950s, foreign correspondent for the *London Times*. Morris uses her skills as a travel writer to take the metaphor of travel and migration to its logical end in relation to questions of gender transition. She describes every aspect of her transition from male to female as a journey and characterizes not only gender identity in terms of countries but also national identities in terms of gender. "I was a child of imperial times," writes Morris at one point to explain her impression of "Black Africa" as "everything I wanted not to be."[41] While cities like Venice represent the feminine (and therefore a desired female self) to the pre-transsexual James Morris, Black Africa represents a masculinity that scares him because it is "alien" and "vicious." In this transsexual autobiography, the space in between male and female is represented as monstrous. Jan Morris describes herself between genders as "a kind of nonhuman, a sprite or monster" (114), and the space of gender is described as "identity itself."

Morris, world traveler and travel writer, understands national identity in much the same way that she understands gender identity; national identities are stable, legible, and all established through the ruling consciousness of empire. Accordingly, Morris collates different reactions to her gender ambiguity according to country: "Americans," she tells us, "generally assumed me to be female" (111); however, in a manner reminiscent of a whole history of colonial travel narratives, Morris tells us casually: "Among the guileless people, the problem was minimal. They simply asked. After a flight from Darjeeling to Calcutta, for instance, during which I had enjoyed the company of an Indian family, the daughter walked over to me at the baggage counter and asked . . . 'whether you are a boy or a girl' " (111). In her essay on transsexuality, Sandy Stone does mention the "Oriental" quality of Morris' travel narrative, and Marjorie Garber upgrades this assessment to "Orientalist" in her discussion of Morris' description of her sex change in Casablanca. In general, however, there has been little consideration of this transsexual autobiography as a colonial artifact, as, indeed, a record of a journey that does not upend either gender conventionality or the conventions of the travelogue.[42] Ultimately, *Conundrum* is a rather unremarkable modernist narrative about the struggle to maintain identity in the face of a crumbling empire. It is, paradoxically, a narrative of change that struggles to preserve the status quo. I want to stress that Morris's narrative in no way represents "*the* transsexual autobiography." Plenty of other transsexual fictions and autobiographies contradict Morris's travelogue, and many such narratives combine a profound sense of dislocation with a brave attempt to make do with the status of unbelonging. The narrative of the female-to-male transsexual, furthermore, differs in significant ways from, and in no way mirrors, the narrative of the male-to-female. Morris's book serves less as a representative narrative and more as a caution against detaching the metaphors of travel and home and migration from the actual experience of immigration in a world full of borders.

Indeed, we might do well to be wary of such a unidirectional politics of home and of such divisions between sexual minorities. As Fredd's story shows, transsexuality requires often long periods of transition, periods within which one must live between genders. The place where transgender ends and transsexual begins is not as clear as either Morris's text or Rubin's essay assumes, and the spaces between genders, which some queer theory claims, do not represent giddy zones of mobility and freedom but represent lives reconciled to gender queerness and bodies committed to making do with the essential discomforts of embodiment. Although the language of home and location in Prosser's and Henry Rubin's essays sounds unimpeachable, as in the Morris text, there is little or no recognition here of the danger of transposing an already loaded conceptual frame—place, travel, location, home, borders—onto another contested site. In *Conundrum*, the equation of transsexuality with travel, and gender with place, produced a colonialist narrative in which both gender identity and national identity are rendered immutable and essential. Of the male, Morris writes: "It is this feeling of unfluctuating control, I think, that women cannot share, and it springs of course not from the intellect or the personality . . . but specifically from the body" (82). On becoming female, she comments: "My body then was made to push and initiate, it is made now to yield and accept, and the outside change has had its inner consequences" (153). The politics of home for Morris are simply the politics of colonialism, and the risk of essentialism that she takes by changing sex turns out to be no risk at all. The language that Prosser and Rubin use to defend their particular transsexual project from queer appropriations runs the risk not only of essence and even colonialism but, in their case, of using the loaded language of migration and homecoming to ratify new, distinctly unqueer models of manliness.

Analyses of transsexual subjectivity by critics such as Prosser and Rubin, I am arguing, are implicated in the colonial framework that organizes Morris's account of transsexuality, if only because both texts seem unaware of the discussions of borders and migration that have raged in other theoretical locations. In Chicano/a studies and postcolonial studies in particular, the politics of migration have been fiercely debated, and what has emerged is a careful refusal of the dialectic of home and border. If home has represented the comfort of place and the politics of location and the stability of belonging within such a dialectic, the border has stood for the politics of displacement, the hybridity of identity and the economics of undocumented labor. There is little to be gained theoretically or materially from identifying either home or border as the true place of resistance. In the context of a discussion of Asian American theater, Dorinne Kondo notes "home for many people on the margins is what we cannot not want."[43] In this context, home represents the belated construction of a safe haven in the absence of such a place in the present or the past. Home becomes a mythic site, a place to anchor some racial and ethnic identities even as those identities are wrenched out of context or pressured into assimilation. But for the queer subject, or what Gloria Anzaldúa calls the border dweller, home is what the person living in the margins cannot want: "She leaves the familiar and safe home ground to venture into the unknown and possibly dangerous terrain. This is her home / this thin edge / of barbwire."[44] Clearly, home can be a fantasy space, a remembered place of stable origin and a nostalgic dream of community; it can as easily be a space of exclusion whose very comforts depend on the invisible labor of migrant border dwellers. To move back to the debate around transsexualism and queers, the journey home for the transsexual may come at the expense of a recognition that others are permanently dislocated.

When nine-year-old Fredd rejects his doctor's simile of naturalized citizenship for his transsexual condition, Fredd rejects both the history of the rhetorical containment of transsexuality within conventional medical taxonomies and a recent attempt to translate the rhetoric of transsexuality into the language of home and belonging. Fredd does not, however, reject the popular formulation of being a "boy trapped in a girl's body," and he holds on to his fantasy of male adulthood even as his body begins to betray him. We might do well to work on other formulations of gender and body, right body, and right gender to provide children such as Fredd, queer cross-identifying children, with futures and bodies that seem habitable. Obviously, the metaphor of crossing over and indeed migrating to the right body from the wrong body merely leaves the politics of stable gender identities, and therefore stable gender hierarchies, completely intact. The BBC program avoided the more general questions raised by the topic of transsexuality by emphasizing Fredd's individual needs and his urgent desire for maleness. When Fredd was shown in dialogue with other transsexual men, the group as a whole expressed their desire simply to be "normal" boys and men and to live like other male subjects. None of the group expressed homosexual desires, and all expected to live "normal lives" in the future once their sex reassignment surgery was complete.

Transsexuality currently represents an immensely complicated web of identifications and embodiments and gendered phenomena and cannot reduce down to Fredd's narrative of prepubescent angst or Jan Morris's narrative of colonial melancholy. However, as "transgender" becomes a popularly recognized term for cross-identification, the sexual politics of transgenderism and transsexualism must be carefully considered. Because much of the discussion currently circulates around the male-to-female experience of transsexuality, we have yet to consider the gender politics of transitioning from female to male. In this section, I have tried to argue that wholesale adoptions of the rhetoric of home and migration within some transsexual aesthetic practices alongside the rejection of a queer border politics can have the uncanny effect of using postcolonial rhetorics to redeem colonial texts (such as Morris's) or of using formulations of home and essence advanced by feminists of color to ratify the location of white transsexual men. Such rhetoric also assumes that the proper solution to "painful wrong embodiment" (Prosser) is moving to the right body, where "rightness" may as easily depend on whiteness or class privilege as it does on being regendered. Who, we might ask, can afford to dream of a right body? Who believes that such a body exists? Finally, as long as migration and borders and home remain metaphorical figures within such discourse, transsexuals and transgendered people who actually are border dwellers or who really do work as undocumented laborers or who really have migrated from their homelands never to return must always remain just outside discourse, invisible and unrecognized, always inhabiting the wrong body.

### Conclusion

As Gayle Rubin remarks in her essay on the varieties of butchness: "Butches vary in how they relate to their female bodies" ("Thinking Sex," 470). She goes on to show that "forms of masculinity are molded by experiences and expectations of class, race, ethnicity, religion, occupation, age, subculture, and individual personality" (470). Rubin also casts the tensions between butches and FTMs as border wars (she calls them "frontier fears") and notes that the border between these two modes of identification is permeable at least in part because "no system of classification can successfully catalogue or explain the infinite vagaries of human diversity" (473). Rubin's conclusion in this essay advocates gender and sexual (and other kinds of) diversity not only as a political strategy but as simply the only proper response to the enormous range of masculinities and genders that we produce.

I also want to argue against monolithic models of gender variance that seem to emerge from the loaded and intense discussions between and among transgender butches and transsexual males at present, and I also want to support some call for diversity. However, at the same time, it is important to stress that not all models of masculinity are equal, and as butches and transsexuals begin to lay claims to the kinds of masculinities they have produced in the past and are generating in the present, it is crucial that we also pay careful attention to the function of homophobia and sexism in particular within the new masculinities. There are transsexuals, and we are not all transsexuals; gender is not fluid, and gender variance is not the same wherever we may find it. Specificity is all. As gender-queer practices and forms continue to emerge, presumably the definitions of "gay," "lesbian," and "transsexual" will not remain static, and we will produce new terms to delineate what they cannot. In the meantime, gender variance, like sexual variance, cannot be relied on to produce a radical and oppositional politics simply by virtue of representing difference. Radical interventions come from careful consideration of racial and class constructions of sexual identities and gender identities and from a consideration of the politics of mobility outlined by that potent prefix "trans." Who, in other words, can afford transition, whether that transition be a move from female to male, a journey across the border and back, a holiday in the sun, a trip to the moon, a passage to a new body, a one-way ticket to white manhood? Who, on the other hand, can afford to stay home, who can afford to make a home, build a new home, move homes, have no home, leave home? Who can afford metaphors? I suggest we think carefully, butches and FTMs alike, about the kinds of men or masculine beings that we become and lay claim to: alternative masculinities, ultimately, will fail to change existing gender hierarchies to the extent to which they fail to be feminist, antiracist, and queer.

*When I was little, I could recognize myself in the faces and screen characters of Tatum O'Neal, Jodie Foster, and Kristy McNichol. These little tomboys empowered me to think of myself as a hero. They were strong and smart like the movie cowboys and gangsters I emulated. . . . On screen, tomboys were socially acceptable. As a young butch dyke coming out in 1986, I looked for their grown-up counterparts. I couldn't find anything. My trio of tomboy heroes hadn't turned out like I had. Instead, I turned to Marlon Brando and James Dean as my models of butchness.* — Jenni Olson, "Butch Icons of the Silver Screen," Dagger: On Butch Women (1994)*

# 6 LOOKING BUTCH

*A Rough Guide to Butches on Film*

**The Queer Gaze**

In this chapter, I explore the history of butch women on film to reclaim a tradition of cinematic female masculinity that lesbians have tended to disavow within a discourse of "positive" and "negative" images. I begin with a consideration of definitions of the lesbian image, and I also try to present a map of recent debates within queer cinema over positive and negative images, spectatorship, and the role of feminist psychoanalytic film theory. The rest of the chapter I devote to a survey of butch images from both mainstream and independent film, and I argue for a reconsideration of what it means to "look" butch, to look at butches, and even to engage a "butch" gaze.

The August 1993 issue of *Vanity Fair* featured a rather remarkable cover photo of lesbian singer k. d. lang sitting in a barber's chair in a suit with shaving cream on her face. Supermodel Cindy Crawford is standing behind lang, poised to give her a "face job." This image is wonderfully provocative for a number of reasons. First, by positing a conventional heterosexual pinup as the object of butch lesbian desire, the photo-fantasy makes an unholy alliance between the male gaze and a more queer butch gaze. Second, the picture flaunts stereotypes and by doing so explodes the tension between homophobic and queer representation. Finally, it calls for many different identificatory strategies from viewers: a heterosexual male must access his desire for Crawford only through the masculinity of a lesbian; a straight woman might identify with Crawford and desire lang; a queer viewer finds that dyke desire is mobile here and may take up butch, femme, masculine, or feminine spectator positions.

The point I want to make by drawing attention to this queer cover is that the ample possibilities offered by spectatorship make concepts such as lesbian images, and hence lesbian art or lesbian cinema, harder and harder to define. The butch on the *Vanity Fair* cover can immediately be read as a lesbian image, if only because of k. d. lang's particular visibility as a dyke; the femme, represented here by Cindy Crawford, reads as lesbian only alongside the butch and therefore occupies only a temporary and contingent relation to lesbian imagery. If femme reads as lesbian only in the presence of a butch partner, then femme becomes a wholly dependent category, borrowing an aura of authenticity from the masculine woman. In turn, the masculinity of the butch can become a trap for lesbian imaging because it depends on stereotypical homophobic constructions of what Esther Newton has called "the mythic mannish lesbian."[1] But flawed as each image might be, ultimately the *Vanity Fair* cover is about unconventional or perverse channels of pleasure. Sometimes, in other words, it is precisely the stereotype that can access pleasure: the juxtaposition of two stereotypical images—the butch in drag and the femme in hyper-feminine costume—resonates with a particularly queer history of representation and simultaneously upends the conventional scene of hetero-normativity that the picture mimics. The picture of k. d. lang and Cindy Crawford can certainly be claimed as a lesbian image but also as an image that exceeds the imperatives of lesbian representation (i.e., to make lesbianism visible, to make it desirable, to make it powerful).

Many writers have recently commented on the damage done by labeling diverse forms of cultural production and representation as "lesbian" or "gay." Gloria Anzaldúa, for example, asks, "What is a lesbian writer?"[2] Implicit in the question, she suggests, is the assumption that a "lesbian" writer is a white writer. A lesbian writer of color will automatically require further identifying labels. Better to ask, she says, "What is the power and what is the danger of writing and reading like a 'lesbian' or a 'queer?'" (252).

In a theoretical inquiry into the same problem of naming, Judith Butler writes, "I'm permanently troubled by identity categories, consider them to be invariable stumbling-blocks, and understand them, even promote them, as sites of necessary trouble."[3] Identity, it seems, as a representational strategy produces both power and danger; it provides both an obstacle to identification and a site "of necessary trouble." As such, the stereotype, the image that announces identity in excess, is necessarily troublesome to an articulation of lesbian identity, but also foundational; the butch stereotype, furthermore, both makes lesbianism visible and yet seems to make it visible in nonlesbian terms: that is to say, the butch makes lesbianism readable in the register of masculinity, and it actually collaborates with the mainstream notion that lesbians cannot be feminine.

I begin my discussion of butch imagery with an emphasis on reception and on the function of the stereotype because gay and lesbian film history has been bound to the institutionalized suppression of unsuitable images. From 1932 to 1962, the Hays Hollywood Production Code banned the representation of "sex perversion" and insisted that "no picture shall be produced which will lower the moral standards of those who see it. Hence the sympathy of the audience shall never be thrown to the side of crime, wrongdoing, evil or sin."[4] This censorship measure ensured that between 1934 and 1962, representations of gays and lesbians would always appear under the cover of strict and often almost impenetrable codes. But just because explicit representation was impossible, this did not mean that queer images and themes and narratives were forced into silence. As Chon Noriega notes in his article on film reviews during this period, the same kind of censorship did not apply to the printed word, and therefore when a film was adapted from a book or play with an explicitly homosexual theme, the reviewers could restore the homosexual context in their critical summations of the films.[5] For Noriega, the presence of reviews that made explicit references to homosexual themes reduces our dependence on careful readings of highly elaborate queer subtexts: "The question, then, becomes not whether certain films have—in retrospect—gay and lesbian characters, subtexts, stars, or directors as an anodyne to censorship, but how homosexuality was 'put into discourse' and the role censorship played during the Production Code Era" (21). I find Noriega's research on the Production Code compelling, but I think it is unnecessary to reject, as he does here, the usefulness of reading "gay and lesbian characters, subtexts, stars, or directors." Although we would do well to follow the Foucauldian imperative analyze how homosexuality was put into discourse rather than concentrating on its repression, we must simultaneously realize that repression, indeed legal repression, was precisely what the code mandated. Finally, no single strategy can exhaust the possibilities of queer reception, and as we construct atypical histories of queer imagery, we must deploy many strategies, methods, and technologies of spectatorship.

Feminist and queer theories of spectatorship may proceed through historical accounts of actresses, studios, directors, and production, or they might concentrate on the star system or biographical material about particular stars. Some studies will try to account for audience response to certain films, and still others will examine the mechanics of the gaze through mostly psychoanalytic theories of visual pleasure. In an example of a particularly successful attempt to pressure the notion of "lesbian spectatorship," Valerie Traub argues forcefully for a queer strategy of appropriation in "The Ambiguities of 'Lesbian' Viewing Pleasure."[6] In this essay, she reads a mainstream heterosexual film, *Black Widow* (1987), as a potential site of lesbian pleasure by paying equal attention to both "the signifying powers of the text" and "the interpretive interventions and appropriations of the film spectator" (309). While she remains conscious of the heterosexist framework of the film, Traub suggests that *Black Widow* represents lesbian desire between its two protagonists and "solicits a 'lesbian' gaze at the same time that it invites male heterosexual enjoyment" (308). By making visible the ambiguity that structures both viewing pleasure and narrative pleasure in this film, Traub is able to imagine access to a plenitude of spectator positions rather than binary codes of gazing. She proposes finally that we identify "lesbian" as "less a person than an activity, less an activity than a modality of pleasure, a position taken in relation to desire" (324).

I read Traub's proposition, that we use words such as "lesbian" or "heterosexual" as adjectives rather than as nouns, as a convincing challenge to the binary codes of visual pleasure offered by psychoanalytic film theory. It does not make sense to rehearse here the many debates about the gaze that have preoccupied feminist film criticism since the 1970s; however, much feminist film criticism responds to Laura Mulvey's essay "Visual Pleasure and Narrative Cinema."[7] In this essay, Mulvey argued that Hollywood cinema had coded erotic pleasure into immutably patriarchal and sexist forms, and therefore she called for a "new language of desire" that would disrupt the pleasure of a male gaze directed at a female object (59). There have been many responses to Mulvey's excessively neat formula for the increasingly messy business of erotic identification, including Mulvey's own recasting of the terms of her argument.[8] Most rewritings of this formulation of visual pleasure, however, comment on the ways in which a spectatorship is necessarily more heterogeneous than psychoanalysis allows and also less neatly organized around identity categories. As Judith Mayne writes in *Cinema and Spectatorship:* "It is one thing to assume that cinema is a discourse (or a variety of discourses), to assume, that is, that the various institutions of the cinema *do* project an ideal viewer, and another thing to assume that these projections *work.*"[9]

The significance, then, of reformulations of spectatorship by queer film critics such as Traub and Mayne lies in their ability to multiply the gendered positions afforded by the gaze and to provide a more historically specific analysis of spectatorship. A less psychoanalytically inflected theory of spectatorship is far less sure of the gender of the gaze. Indeed, recent discussions of gay and lesbian cinema assume that the gaze is "queer" or at least multidimensional.[10] It is important, I think, to find queer relations to cinematic pleasure that are not circumvented by the constrictive language of fetishism, scopophilia, castration, and Oedipalization. At this historical moment, we may simply have to avoid psychoanalytic formulations (rather than, say, negate them through a methodical critique) to get beyond them and forge the new cinematic vocabulary that Mulvey seemed to be calling for but seemed not to be able to imagine. Queer cinema, with its invitations to play through numerous identifications within a single sitting, creates one site for creative reinvention of ways of seeing.

## The Positive Images Debate

One strategy that gay and lesbian film criticism took from early feminist film criticism was the emphasis placed on "positive images."[11] As a consequence, there are many useful but limited studies of the demonization of gays and lesbians in Hollywood.[12] The desire for "positive images" places the onus of queering cinema squarely on the production rather than the reception of images. It also makes representation into a kind of unmediated event that shows either truth and reality or else skewed versions of them. But representation and its effects are never so simple. In an essay on the stereotyping of gays in film, Richard Dyer takes issue with the positive images position. He claims that "thinking about images of gayness needs to go beyond simply dismissing stereotypes as wrong or distorted."[13] While stereotyping is obviously a hurtful practice, it is not remedied by asking for nonstereotyped images.

> What we should be attacking in stereotypes is the attempt of heterosexual society to define us for ourselves, in terms that inevitably fall short of the "ideal" of heterosexuality (that is taken to be the norm of being human), and to pass this definition off as necessary and natural. Both these simply bolster heterosexual hegemony, and the task is to develop our own alternative and challenging images of ourselves. (31)

Stereotypes, then, are not in and of themselves right or wrong. Rather, they represent a particularly economic way of identifying members of a particular social group in relation to a set of quickly recognizable characteristics. Dyer goes on to discuss the stereotype as both a term of abuse and a useful ideological tool. The stereotype basically constitutes a set of traits within an individual as representative of the behavior and appearance of a particular (often minority) group. The stereotype is usually thought of as a pejorative mode of representation because it can be used to reduce the heterogeneity of any given group to a select few types. However, stereotyping does not always and only work on behalf of a conservative representational agenda: the stereotype does often represent a "true" type, a type, in other words, that does exist within the subculture. In relation to gay and lesbian subcultures, "the butch" and "the queen" are the two most common stereotypes used to represent these groups, but that does not mean that wherever we find butches and queens, we are in the presence of a homophobic code of representation. It is important to judge the work that the stereotype performs within any given visual context—accordingly, if the queen or the butch is used only as a sign of that character's failure to assimilate, then obviously the stereotype props up a dominant system of gender and sexuality.[14] But often the butch or the queen exceeds the limits of representation imposed by the law of the stereotype and disrupts the dominant systems of representation that depend on negative queer images.

Black or Latina butch images, for example, represent a particularly complicated location when we try to resolve the tension within stereotyping between offensive imaging and productive visibility. The image of the black or Latina butch may all too easily resonate with racial stereotyping in which white forms of femininity occupy a cultural norm and nonwhite femininities are measured as excessive or inadequate in relation to that norm; however, the butch of color may also be an image with the power to defamiliarize white masculinity and make visible a potent fusion of alternative masculinity and alternative sexuality. Because black female sexuality, in particular, has historically been measured through and against a fantasy of white womanhood, this history should warn us to be careful in discussions of black female masculinities; conversely, because white manhood has been identified as an unmarked location of power and privilege, black or Latina female masculinity may be a site within which dominant modes of power can be resignified with subversive and even potentially revolutionary results.[15] In my last section of this chapter, "Postmodern Butches," I look at the portrayal of a gangsta butch by Queen Latifah in *Set It Off* and examine the explosive and violent restructuring of the social order that occurs temporarily in the presence of black butchness. However, there is a difference between racist representations of supposedly failed femininity and a potentially queer or at least subcultural representation of a potent black butchness.

As we will see in the section on "Fantasy Butches," in *Aliens* (1986), the Latina butch Vasquez provides an interesting example of the double stereotype, the butch who is stereotyped, in other words, along racial as well as gender lines. Vasquez displays her butch iconicity in this film through an elaborate ritual of physical prowess, smart talk, and her ability to handle firearms. In her first scene in the film, the camera catches Vasquez working out in the main cabin; a male soldier says slyly to her: "Hey Vasquez, have you ever been mistaken for a man?" She answers, in mid-pull-up: "No, have you?" The tough comeback nicely denaturalizes gender and literally returns the gaze, refusing to allow the white soldier to claim the place of universality and indeed humanity. Vasquez's butch performance hints at an "alien" logic of gender within which masculinity is as much a production of ethnicity as it is of gender and sexuality, but although the film permits the momentary exhilaration of Vasquez's butch prowess, it also quickly snuffs it out by making her the alien's first victim and by finally attaching her unorthodox gender performance with a perversely alien identity. Furthermore, the particular valence of Latina masculinity is underscored by the fact that a Jewish actress, Jeanette Goldstein, is used to play this role. Although Goldstein makes a convincing Latina, it is worth asking why the butch could not have been Jewish or white in this film or why a Latina could not have been cast in the role.

To give one other example of a butch stereotype that both represents lesbianism in a negative register and fails to remain confined within the

Figure 12. "Hey Vasquez! Have you ever been mistaken for a man?" Jeanette Goldstein as Vasquez in *Aliens* (1986), directed by James Cameron.

bounds of the negative image, we can turn to Robert Aldrich's *The Killing of Sister George* (1968). Aldrich's film of the aging butch actress (played by Beryl Reid) whose character is being killed off on a soap opera represents George as an aggressive bully, a loudmouth dyke, and an abusive lover who is nonetheless vulnerable and dignified. Although I look at the film more closely in the section "Predatory Butches," I will say here that *The Killing of Sister George* makes stereotyping into just one part of the film's general preoccupation with roles, performances, and theatricality. In a film about the eroding boundaries between representation and reality, Beryl Reid's character moves back and forth between roles: the alcoholic, middle-aged June Breckridge; the cheery nun of the soap opera world of "Applehurst" known as Sister George; and George, the butch persona caught between her TV life and her real life, her lesbian life and her closeted relationship with her longtime lover Childie. If we only notice the iconography of butchness in this complex film, we may read *The Killing of Sister George* as a film that traffics in stereotypes in order to highlight the grotesqueries of lesbian interaction. In a scene early in the film, for example, George punishes Childie by making her eat the butt of her cigar. The music in the background is oddly sinister and sad, and the camera crowds in on the face of Childie as she bites into the cigar butt. We watch her contorted face chew the tobacco and then suddenly change from disgust to pleasure. Childie suddenly begins to enjoy the cigar, and as George screams, "Stop it! Stop it!" Childie writhes in pleasure and answers, "What, stop eating this lovely cigar?" Of course, Childie has turned a punishment into her own pleasure here and consequently ruined the ritual for George. George marches out, leaving Childie standing on the stairs.

This scene tends to exemplify the dangers of negative images for queer audiences. It depicts lesbianism as a strange, ritualistic exchange involving S-M power dynamics and gross humiliation for the femme-identified partner. Childie is reduced to childish helplessness, and George's larger-than-life bullying persona seems hideous and monstrous. However, in the context of the larger film, this scene actually reveals one of the main mechanisms of the Childie-George dynamic. Childie is far more aware and conscious of her seemingly abased role than we first think, and her transformation here of punishment into pleasure bespeaks an agency that we assume she lacks. Whereas in this scene it is George who leaves the house and Childie who is left, in later scenes, Childie repeatedly leaves George. We first imagine that Childie is housebound and that George is tied to a world beyond, a public sphere, but we soon discover that Childie's world is, if anything, less circumscribed than George's, and she goes to places that the film cannot even show. George travels between the TV studio, the apartment, and the pub, and Childie goes to work and to the theater and has secret meetings with the slimy Mercy Croft. Ultimately, of course, Childie leaves George, and George is the one confined to a place and a time. In the film's final, tragic scene, George returns to the TV studio after Childie has left her and after she has been fired from the set and offered a part as the voice of a cow in a children's program. George enters the TV studio and wrecks the TV equipment, knocking over lights and cameras and pushing down props. She sits in the ruins of her TV world, and as the camera ascends and drifts out of George's world, she lets out a plaintive "mooo!" The reduction of the bully to the drunk and ultimately to the pathetic over-the-hill actor may indeed signal her stereotypical function. And, furthermore, the final reduction of butch to "cow" or nonhuman also suggests a gross oversimplification of complex individuality. However, there is a symbolic dimension to George's roles that takes us far beyond the purview of the negative image. George's final howls are the sounds of

Figure 13. Sister George tears down the set. Beryl Reid as George in *The Killing of Sister George* (1968), directed by Robert Aldrich.

her anguished failure to assimilate, and as nonhuman and nonverbal, they signify excess, rage, and the refusal of orderly representation.

Queer stereotypes are supposed to render visible what has been represented as invisible. The damage they do lies less in the way they depict homosexuality in relation to pathology and more in the way they render "gay" or "lesbian" as coherent terms. The opposite of the stereotype has long been thought of as "the positive image," and yet it may well be that positive images also deal in stereotypes and with far more disastrous effects. Furthermore, a cinema of positive images is simply not a very interesting cinema.[16] We tend to consider films such as *Fried Green Tomatoes* (1991) as positive, or as gay or lesbian sensitive. But as I argue later in this chapter, *Fried Green Tomatoes* earns its appellation of positive at the expense of the butchness of its main character. In the course of converting the Fannie Flagg novel into a mainstream film, the director completely makes over the butch mannish Idgie into a straight-looking feminine heroine. *Fried Green Tomatoes* has been given awards by GLAAD and other gay and lesbian groups for its "outstanding depiction of lesbians in a film" even though it was quite possible to watch the film without recognizing the sexual nature of the relationship between Idgie and Ruth. In the novel, Idgie is often mistaken for a boy; the film erases all of Idgie's fundamental masculinity and does so precisely because her butchness would have suggested the lesbian nature of the relationship.

Invisibility, in fact, can often do much more damage than visibility. But we do not hear about protesters outraged by the invisible butch and the muted lesbianism in *Fried Green Tomatoes* because this movie is a feel-good film (even though it, too, implicates lesbians in the killing of men) and we think of it as "positive." Positivity and negativity, finally, are obviously not the best standards to use when measuring the political impact of any given representation. We need to be more creative in our interpretations, more willing to use Hollywood, and quicker to "queer" supposedly hegemonic and traditional depictions of masculinity and femininity. Gay and lesbian filmmakers do not always, when given the chance, produce so-called positive images. In the same year that GLAAD was protesting gay stereotyping in *The Silence of the Lambs* (1991) and *Basic Instinct* (1992), gay filmmaker Tom Kalin produced *Swoon* (1992), a film about the gay child killers Leopold and Loeb. *Poison* (1991), by Todd Haynes, and *The Living End* (1992), by Gregg Araki, also offered up less than idealized images of gay men. The cult success of lesbian vampire movies also attests to the appeal of horrific and outlaw queer character typing. Of course, it can be argued that stereotyped or compromised images by gays of gays are far more acceptable than stereotyping that originates in a heterosexist industry. Although this is true, it still overlooks the fact that positive images are no more realistic than negative ones and that positive and negative are simply not standards that are productively applied to representation.

Moving from the positive-images debate to an attempt to reclaim queer cinema from the trash pile of negative images, I am arguing for a queer cinema that recycles as much as it produces. Positive images, we may note, too often depend on thoroughly ideological conceptions of positive (white, middle-class, clean, law-abiding, monogamous, coupled, etc.), and the emphasis on positivity actually keeps at bay the "bad cinema" that might productively be reclaimed as queer. We can look back at the history of "negative images" and find a plethora of queer images: I suggest that we look again at *The Killing of Sister George* (1968), *Cruising* (1980), *The*

*Children's Hour* (1961), and other reviled films and try to patch together a queer history of film. In what follows, I attempt to provide a genealogy of the butch in film history precisely to show that a cinema of negative images may also provide a history of the representation of sexual minorities. The films that I examine here do not in any way add up to a history of lesbian representation or lesbian filmmaking or even lesbian images; they do provide, however, another chapter in the history of female masculinity.

## Butches on Film

Before there were lesbians, there were butches. The masculine woman prowls the film set as an emblem of social upheaval and as a marker of sexual disorder. She wears the wrong clothes, expresses aberrant desires, and is very often associated with clear markers of a distinctly phallic power. She may carry a gun, smoke a cigar, wear leather, ride a motorbike; she may swagger, strut, boast, flirt with younger and more obviously feminine women; she often goes by a male moniker: Frankie, George, Willy, Micky, Eli, Nicky. She is tough and tragic, she was a tomboy, and she expresses a variety of masculinities. The history of the butch dyke in film, as I have suggested, has long been regarded by gay and lesbian film historians as the history of cinematic homophobia; however, the butch does not simply function within a negative register. Before the emergence of an independent lesbian cinema, the butch was the only way of registering sexual variance in the repressive environment of Hollywood cinema. Indeed, much of what we call "independent" film in this country has been queer, and the history of film production outside of the studio system has everything to do with the development of a queer cinema. In what follows, I want to trace the peregrinations of the butch in film to track not homophobia but a queer dyke identity associated as much with aggression as with pathology, with strength as well as shame, with boyishness rather than girlishness, and with a form of powerful female masculinity rather than simply as the disgrace of the gender bender. I have divided butch cinema into six categories: Tomboys, Predators, Fantasy Butches, Transvestites, Barely Butches, and Postmodern Butches. These categories are somewhat arbitrary and a bit rough, but each attempts to locate the butch generically and historically as well as sexually.[17]

I use these categories to suggest distinct butch genres and again to suggest the incredible variation of gender display that we tend to cram under single headings. "Butch" is, to say the least, an overdetermined category at this particular historical moment, and as I have already suggested in this chapter, it cannot be explained away simply as the most common form of lesbian stereotyping. As I have been arguing throughout this book, female masculinities have not been accounted for until now because they have been represented as a singular otherness to the propriety of male masculinity on the one hand and the conformity of female femininity on the other. The presence of masculine women in our culture in ever increasing numbers makes it necessary to reassess even what we think we know about the visual representation of a supposedly hackneyed stereotype. My few genres of cinematic butch only scratch the surface of visual butch variation. Each category sketches the contours for a type, and each attempts to reckon with the tension between stereotype and subcultural identity. Ultimately, however, the categories are offered as ways of exploring the pleasures as well as the dangers of looking butch. Within each section, I may combine Hollywood films with foreign films with independent cinema and even with experimental video productions. My aim here is not to gloss over the historical differences between each cinematic genre and its specific history but to show that butch images are used for a complex range of purposes within the history of cinema. In Hollywood film made during the Production Code era, for example, a butch character was a window onto the sexual variance that the camera could not reveal. In independent features of the 1980s, conversely, the butch character has been almost completely excised to rid lesbian cinema of what was thought to be a hated stereotype. By mixing different kinds of cinema within each category, I am able to show that independent films were not necessarily the site of creative imagery and that ironically, during the years of most strict surveillance, the Production Code era, butch imagery signified an often creative tactic for introducing censored material to queer audiences.

### Pre-Butch: The Tomboy Era

The first category of importance to a history of cinematic butches contains a set of films from the late 1950s to the early 1980s that we could call the tomboy films.[18] To a certain extent, the tomboy film is an offshoot or variation of another more mainstream genre, the boy film. Hollywood, as we know, *loves* stories about little boys. It doesn't really matter what the little boys are doing; they might be growing up or refusing to, bonding with a pet or torturing it; they could be playing with aliens, struggling to get by without a father or a mother or both; they might be good or evil, smart or impaired, left alone or reunited with a family. The timeless popularity of the boy movie suggests that the transformation of boy into man is endlessly interesting to this culture. Predictably enough, there seems to be little to no interest in girls in Hollywood unless they are becoming the sexual objects of male desire. But this has not always been the case.

The girl movie has not always been such a debased category. In *Hollywood Androgyny*, Rebecca Bell-Metereau suggests that "the popularity of the tomboy reached its peak in the years after the second World War" (96), and she points to films such as Clarence Brown's *National Velvet* (1945) and George Cukor's *Pat and Mike* (1952) as examples. I think it is fair to say, however, that the heyday for the tomboy film was the 1970s and 1980s, when a plethora of tomboy films were made featuring butch, wise-cracking, aggressive little tykes such as Jodie Foster (*Foxes* [1980] and *Alice Doesn't Live Here Anymore* [1974]), Tatum O'Neal (*Paper Moon*, 1973), and Kristy McNichol (*Little Darlings*, 1980). These movies made girlhood interesting and exciting and even sexy. They also, of course, tended to imagine girlhood as tomboyhood.

In the 1970s and 1980s, the effects of the rise of feminism in the 1960s were finally beginning to affect child rearing. Tomboyism flourished in a climate of liberal parenting where parents were questioning sex role orientation and challenging the conventional wisdom about girls and boys. Within such a climate, people (feminists and others) may well have thought that change begins at home and that the way to intervene most effectively in the seemingly concrete and rigid societal standards for female behavior (and misbehavior) was to bring up children differently. In the 1970s, moreover, there was finally a visible gay and lesbian community in the United States, and in the wake of the Stonewall rebellion, many "gay power" groups sprang up across the country.[19] As gays and lesbians became more visible throughout the decade, of course, the effects of that visibility changed. Although at first queer visibility offered the promise of some kind of proliferation of sympathetic representations of gays and lesbians, as time wore on, the tomboy and the sissy boy, within a public psychologized discourse on homosexuality, became the visible markers for the potentially queer child. I believe that the tomboy film faded from view by the end of the 1980s partly owing to the implicit link between tomboys and lesbians.

In the early 1970s, child stars such as Tatum O'Neal, Kristy McNichol,

Figure 14. "They're gonna see who I am." Robin Johnson as Nicky in *Times Square* (1980), directed by Alan Moylan.

and Jodie Foster regularly played spunky tomboys with attitude and smarts; there were also, by the end of the decade, teen actresses such as Robin Johnson and Pamela Segall who portrayed the anguish of adolescence within an oddly gendered body. "They're gonna see who I am," shouts Robin Johnson as Nicky in the classic punk girl movie *Times Square* (1980). Her desire to be seen as something or someone other than a presexual woman propels her on a rocky search for fame that takes on heroic proportions. And, like the tragic hero, she suffers for her ambition. *Times Square* featured two girls on the run from parents, the law, and boys. To the accompaniment of a fine punk-influenced sound track, Nickie and Pammie very specifically aim their attack at the media. Their signature rebel act is to throw TVs off the top of buildings. This image of two wild girls—Thelma and Louise for juniors—destroying televisions is a perfect representation of girls bashing back loudly, angrily, and violently against their invisibility.

But the original tragic hero of adolescent growing pains has to be Frankie Addams as played by Julie Harris in *The Member of the Wedding* (1953). This film and the novel it was adapted from are all the more remarkable for the fact that they emerge out of the repressive cultural climate of the American South in the 1950s. Carson McCullers was born Lula Carson in 1917 in Columbus, Georgia, and she grew up with a sense of her own freakishness and inability to fit the mold of conventional femininity. She was often called "weird," "freakish," and "queer," and she felt herself to be outlandish and different.[20] McCuller's girl hero Frankie Addams is similarly preoccupied with her own freakishness, which is often depicted as a lack of commonality with other girls. Fred Zinneman's adaptation of Carson McCuller's novel perfectly captures the balance between comedy and tragedy in this story. The set is sweaty and claustrophobic, and the camera stays almost exclusively in the hot confines of the family kitchen. In one of the few outside scenes, Frankie runs onto the porch to greet the girls in the neighborhood girl club. "Am I the new member?" Frankie demands urgently as the girls march through her yard. The camera moves back and forth between the real girls, the emblems of true femininity, and the ragtaggle tomboy Frankie, who awaits their answer. "No," answers one particularly groomed girl, "you're not the new member." But, of course, Frankie has never been and will never be a member, has never belonged and will never succumb to the pressure to be a heterosexual and feminine girl.

In her novel (written in 1946), Carson McCullers describes Frankie as "an unjoined person," and it is the lack of connection, the awkward failure to fit, that makes up Frankie's identity. *The Member of the Wedding* draws attention to the clubby nature of gender. Berenice (played by Esther Waters) reminds Frankie of the definition of a club: "There must be members and non-members." Berenice also articulates membership in relation to racial relations in the South in the 1950s, and the film and the book strenuously link racial oppression to gender oppression within the matrix of prejudices that characterize the South in the 1950s. The nonmembers of the club of girls are the tomboys and pre-butches, the not-girls who struggle to make gender fit and who attempt to squash their angular and flat bodies into the curves of naturalized femininity. Failure to assimilate to the demands of femininity, of course, spells out trouble for the tomboy by imagining a queer future for her butch body. *The Member of the Wedding* emphasizes the tragic nature of the tomboy quest and quietly confines the tomboy to a past better forgotten and left behind as the girl blossoms into a quiescent young-adult femininity.

But the drama of the tomboy is not all tragic. As "tomboy lite" films such as *Paper Moon* and *Something Special* show, gendering can also be family fun. In *Paper Moon* (1973), Tatum O'Neal as Addie Pray follows her con-man daddy all over the Midwest selling Bibles and charming women.

Figure 15. "There must be members and non-members." Julie Harris as Frankie Addams in *The Member of the Wedding* (1953), directed by Fred Zinneman.

Gender in this film is just another con game, just another costume to make a buck. Tatum plays a rather endearing tomboy who leaves old ladies wondering whether she is a girl or a boy, and her father (Ryan O'Neal) struggles to make her gender readable with big hair bows and feminine clothing. *Paper Moon* depicts tomboyism as the result of the lack of a dominant maternal presence that can easily be corrected within a firm family structure. Indeed, the absent mother is often given as a trite explanation of tomboyism, an explanation, moreover, that sidesteps the whole issue of cross-gender identification and the pain of girlhood. Tatum O'Neal shows up again in the classic tomboy film *Little Darlings* (1980), starring Kristy McNichol. McNichol and O'Neal play opposite ends of tomboyism in this film about a group of girls spending the summer together at Camp Little Wolf. McNichol plays Angel Bright, a fatherless girl from the wrong side of the tracks. Her mother smokes and wears sexy dresses and drives a big American car. Angel plays the tomboy in an Oedipally inflected relation to her mother, and she swaggers around the neighborhood in denims beating up boys. O'Neal plays a motherless rich girl, Ferris Whitney, whose father is somewhat negligent and drives her to camp in a big Rolls Royce. When the two girls meet, sparks fly.

Angel and Ferris are immediately linked by the other girls at camp as different kinds of outsiders. In a classic bathroom confrontation scene, the pretty girl of the group asks Angel and Ferris whether they are still virgins. "I think guys are a pain in the ass," intones Angel. Another girl snickers, "They are probably lezzies," and Ferris responds quickly: "She may be but I am straight!" Significantly, Angel does not deny the charge of lesbianism but instead defiantly makes a grab for the older girl's breasts and wrestles with her. The rest of the film degenerates into a competition between Angel and Ferris over who can lose their virginity first, but the bond between Ferris and Angel is nicely established in this central bathroom scene. Whereas in women's prison films the bathroom tends to be the scene of torture and sexual assault, in the tomboy film, the bathroom, with its woman's sign on the door and its mirrors all over the interior, becomes a gender zone. Females are literally divided here into women and girls, girls and not-girls, straights and dykes. Kristy McNichol's tough stand in this bathroom scene echoes Julie Harris's outrage against the girls in her neighborhood club. And Tatum O'Neal's role as the nonmasculine tomboy reprises her role from *Paper Moon*.

In a comedic tomboy film, *Something Special* (1986, directed by Paul Schneider),[21] a tomboy is granted her deepest and darkest wish one night, and she wakes up with something very special—a penis. Millie Niceman changes her name, appropriately, to Willy and attempts to acclimate herself to boyhood. Gender trouble in this made-for-TV movie, however, comes in the form of family pressures to be one of two available genders. Mr. and Mrs. Niceman confirm the doctor's opinion that Willy must choose a gender and stick with it. Willy asks pragmatically, "Can't I be both?" Mr. Niceman explodes with outrage and says, "There will be no girlish boys and no boyish girls in this house!" This scene is humorous in the way it depicts a struggle between the parents as they try to convince their child that s/he must pick either his or her "side," but it is troubling in the way that it resolves the problem of intersexuality or transsexuality by abjecting gender ambiguity. It is in-betweenness here and elsewhere in the history of butches in film that inspires rage and terror in parents, co-workers, lovers, and bosses. As soon as the tomboy or the butch locates herself in an other gender, trouble begins, and science, psychology, family, and other social forces are all applied to reinforce binary gender laws. As Willy, Milly Niceman is at first lulled into the pleasures of boyhood: clothing, new freedoms, new privilege. However, the film reverses its originally transgressive premise by creating a rather predictable obstacle to the transition Willy seems to be making with no trouble from female to male. Suddenly Willy is forced to confront the fact that his best male friend is also the object of his desire, and although Willy may have changed sex, he has not escaped compulsory heterosexuality. With the specter of homosexuality looming in the not too distant future, Willy wishes to return to his girl self, and gender normativity is restored.

The tomboy film has long since disappeared as a distinct genre, and it is worth asking why. Where are the next generation of girl actors, sassy girls playing tough tomboys and pushing the limits of compulsory femininity? And what exactly is the threat of the little-girl film and the tomboy aesthetic? One can only speculate, but it seems reasonable to suppose that the tomboy movie threatened an unresolved gender crisis and projected or predicted butch adulthoods. There is always the dread possibility, in other words, that the tomboy will not grow out of her butch stage and will never become a member of the wedding. Today we have only boy movies (think of *Free Willy*), and the girls are relegated to dumb sisters, silly cry babies, and weak playmates. Quite obviously, Hollywood sees tomboy films as a queer cinema for preteens. Boys can be shown bonding, hiking together, fighting, discovering dead bodies, killing people, and killing each other, but even the suggestion that girls might be shown doing similar things raises the specter of the dyke. Girls in films tend to fight each other for boys (*Heathers*) or fight each other for older men (*Poison Ivy*) or just catfight each other. They do not bond, they do not rebel, they do not learn, they do not like themselves, and perhaps most importantly, they do not like each other.

### Predatory Butches

What if the tomboy grew up with her masculinity intact? Hollywood film offers us a vision of the adult tomboy as the predatory butch dyke: in this particular category, we find some of the best and the worst of Hollywood stereotyping. Most predatory butches roamed the screen during the era of the Hollywood Production Code. Because explicit representations of gay or lesbian material were expressly forbidden, very often a queer subtext would be created through an evil cross-identified character. In some

Figure 16. Unarmed and Dangerous. Mercedes McCambridge as Emma in *Johnny Guitar* (1954), directed by Nicholas Ray.

of these films, the predatory butch is a woman who has lived alone too long; in others she is the full-blown lesbian who seeks out naive young women for sexual companionship; she might have a nontraditional occupation or be forced because of her job into a homosocial environment. She is, in other words, the gunslinger, the prison warden, the gang member, the female pimp; in short, the bulldagger.[22] Very often the predatory butch's identity is explained through rudimentary psychoanalytic models as an immature femininity, a femininity that failed to blossom. In Nicholas Ray's classic tough-girl film, *Johnny Guitar* (1954), for example, Joan Crawford plays Vienna, the rough cowgirl who needs to be tamed and seduced into a mature femininity. In one scene, she stands tall above her angry neighbors, dressed all in black, holding a gun and telling them to back off. "That's big talk for a little gun," says Mercedes McCambridge, her archrival and double, Emma. It is hard not to hear a Freudian admonition in here: the little gun, of course, is the woman's version of a man's big gun. When Vienna learns to be less trigger-happy, her man Johnny drops his guitar, gets his gun, and gender order returns. The one remaining symbol of immature and butch female embodiment now is Emma, and Vienna shoots her as if she is killing off her butch self and emerging triumphant, unarmed but a woman. In this scene, the camera hovers below Vienna, making her into a powerful and almost phallic figure who towers over the scene. When Vienna finally comes down the stairs to meet Emma, the camera frames Emma and Vienna in a two-shot and binds them together as doubles; Emma and Vienna echo each other's words, suggesting that they are not individual subjects but that one represents the extension of the other's masculine self. "I'm going to kill you," says Emma. "I know," Vienna responds, "but not if I can kill you first."

As Bell-Metereau points out, "the sexual ideology of (this) film is strangely paradoxical" (*Hollywood Androgyny,* 93). On the one hand, Vienna finds herself in danger whenever she takes up a feminine role and feminine attire, and it is only in masculine attire and with a tough and aggressive attitude that she can survive. On the other hand, even as she returns to her masculine self, she is forced to kill Emma and thus symbolically refuse her outlaw self. She maintains her masculinity, but at a high cost. Although Bell-Metereau finds it ironic that "Vienna's freedom from femininity results in the same kind of enslavement to violence that she begs Johnny to avoid" (93), I am less concerned with the violence and more concerned that Vienna's little gun must be turned onto her alter ego. The death of Emma signifies the death of a female masculinity unmoored from male companionship and uncompromised by the marks of the feminine.

Mercedes McCambridge, incidentally, has made this category of the predatory butch her very own. In Orson Welles's creepy classic *A Touch of Evil* (1958), Mercedes plays an uncredited role as a Mexican butch. Orson Welles was most certainly quoting from Ray's use of McCambridge, whom Ray had cast in *Johnny Guitar*. In the later film, McCambridge quietly but insistently takes up the role of butch gang member. In her first scene, the camera catches sight of Mercedes in a mirror, and then she walks into the frame, where her masculinity is made more visible by her position next to a more obviously feminine woman, probably her girlfriend. The move of situating the butch in the mirror marks many different presentations of female masculinity. In *Johnny Guitar*, Emma and Vienna literally mirrored each other, and as we shall see, in *Calamity Jane,* Calamity is thrown into crisis when she glimpses herself in a dressing room mirror. While the mirroring in *Johnny Guitar* signified the division of masculinity between the two women, in *A Touch of Evil*, the mirroring probably signifies a kind of

Figure 17. Looking Butch. Mercedes McCambridge as a street butch in *A Touch of Evil* (1958), directed by Orson Welles.

"through the looking glass" moment in which the spectator understands that multiple reversals and transversals and inversions are about to take place. This is emphasized by the next scene, in which Mercedes whispers to Janet Leigh through the thin motel walls and tells her what is about to happen. When Mercedes comes around from the other side of the wall to the room, the film enters its fantasy mode, in which the Mexican gang members, including Mercedes, simulate a rape.

Mercedes is present when the gang members gather in Janet Leigh's hotel room to drug her and make her think she has been gang raped; here, it is Mercedes who oversees the administration of the drugs and growls at the lusty boys, "Lemme stay, I wanna watch." In her leather jacket and next to her femme girlfriend, Mercedes is more than convincing as a tough street butch. In a film about borders, crossing, double-crossing, and national identities, we should probably locate Mercedes's character at the carefully policed borders of citizenship, femininity, and criminality. Perhaps the snarling butch dyke that she depicts is supposed to represent non-American femininity (a good joke by Welles, since he uses non-

Mexican actors, McCambridge, Marlene Dietrich, and Charlton Heston, to depict Mexicans). Perhaps, as I have suggested, she is just part of the looking glass world of Welles's Tijuana, a world where values and people and ethics are all inverted. Mercedes is *A Touch of Evil*'s special invert.

The most famous invert in lesbian film, however, is probably Sister George, played by Beryl Reid in the 1968 film *The Killing of Sister George*. This magnificent film was made in England, and therefore director Robert Aldrich was not so confined by the Production Code; however, when the film was released in America, the sex scene between Coral Browne and Susannah York had to be cut, and the film received an X rating.[23] *The Killing of Sister George* tells the tragic story of the TV actress whose character, Sister George, is about to be killed off on the air. The association made in this film between acting and being queer is common enough, as is the connection between homosexuality and the unreal, but the power of *The Killing of Sister George* lies in the way it insists on the absolute confusion between theater and life. Sister George is both an acting role and a real role, just as George's butch persona is both a role and an identity. In the course of the film, George accosts a clutch of nuns in a taxicab, visits a prostitute, and goes to a dyke bar costume party with her lover as Laurel and Hardy: everything and nothing is an act. George's brushes with various sisterhoods (the nuns, the whores, the dykes) truly identify her with female homosociality and lend the weight of the real to her stage name Sister George. Indeed, the actress Beryl Reid was herself completely identified forever afterward with the role of Sister George, and when Reid died in 1996, her obituary in the *New York Times* described her as someone who specialized in "eccentric characters" and who had her greatest success "as June Buckridge in Frank Marcus's play *The Killing of Sister George*."[24] The obituary also suggests that Reid was warned not to touch the play "with a barge pole" but went on to turn her success as Sister George into an international reputation.

*The Killing of Sister George* occupies a peculiar place in most lesbian film history. It is often regarded as a kind of showcase for lesbiphobia. The film's depiction of the lonely butch who holds her younger femme lover hostage, drinks too much to drown her sorrows, and goes out dressed in drag seems overdetermined as a pathetic stereotype of dyke despair. However, as I discussed earlier, in the infamous cigar scene, George's predations are part of an elaborate ritual played out between George and Childie (Susannah York), and it is a ritual, moreover, that is markedly sexual. Furthermore, when Childie does finally leave George, she does not flee to the arms of

Figure 18. George in London. Notice the graffiti on the wall behind Reid. Beryl Reid as George in *The Killing of Sister George* (1968), directed by Robert Aldrich.

Figure 19. "Another fine mess." Beryl Reid as George in drag in *The Killing of Sister George* (1968), directed by Robert Aldrich.

some man but succumbs to the attentions of another predatory butch, suggesting that she feels some desire precisely for this form of domination. Also, the bar scene at the London dyke club Gateways is far from a representation of abject loneliness. The club scenes are almost carnivalesque with women in butch-femme couples as well as women in costume for the costume party. A girl band is playing in the background, and the whole scene is a lively display of lesbian community. Few other lesbian bar scenes in film history depict the lesbian club as a place of pleasure, and such scenes are usually used to show the pathos of lesbian life.

One sisterhood that George does not frequent is the caged sisterhood of prison life. The prison, within the homophobic imaginary, is a privileged site of butch predation and lesbian lowlife. It is no surprise, then, that any number of lesbian-themed films use a prison setting. Women's prison films are fairly formulaic, and they present butch predation as a fact of prison life. Often the predation is embodied by a sadistic and butch warden (*Caged Heat, Bad Girls Dormitory*) who seeks out innocent young inmates, but sometimes it may be constituted through a dynamic between the warden and her sidekick (*Caged Heat*). The story will sometimes revolve around the struggles of one particular inmate, an innocent victim of miscarriage of justice who becomes inured to prison life, and at others, the story is a campy narrative about the inability of a warden to keep control of the women under her command. On account of the homosocial setting, however, the women's prison film offers a rare opportunity for multiple codings of intragender categories. While obviously the films are in no way documenting prison life for women, there is some correspondence between the elaborate genderings of women's prison films and gender systems within real women's prisons. As Juanita Diaz-Cotto points out in a study of real prison life involving Chicana inmates, the women set up elaborate family systems within the prison for their own protection. Some of the prisoners adopt the roles of father, brother, or husband; others take on the role of wife, mother, or sister. Diaz-Cotto goes on to explain that the prevalence of masculine roles can be attributed to the brutality of prison life and the need for women to take care of themselves: "One of the motivations that led prisoners to adopt an 'aggressive' or 'masculine' role was to protect themselves from other prisoners or at least give the impression that they could take care of themselves physically. As a result it was not uncommon for prisoners who identified as heterosexual on the outside to adopt 'male' roles in prison." [25]

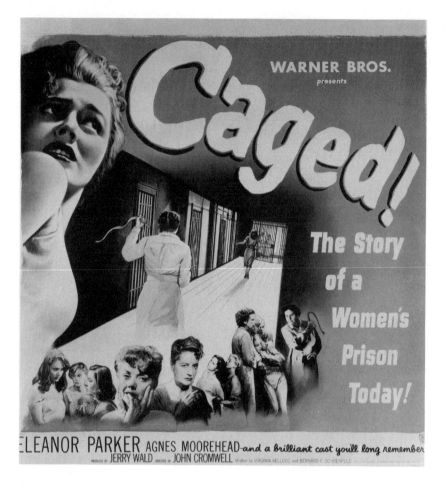

Figure 20. Movie poster for *Caged* (1950), directed by John Cromwell.

In prison films, the prisoners tend to be sorted into two main types: the innocent femme who needs to toughen up and the predatory butch who will either protect the femme or take advantage of her. In *Bad Girls' Dormitory* (1985), a young woman is sentenced to a term in the New York Juvenile Reformatory. In the course of her quest for survival, the victim must avoid both the brutality of the other inmates and the brutality of the staff; she is torn between committing suicide, maintaining her innocence, and becoming a hardened survivor who has learned the ropes of prison life. *Bad Girls' Dormitory* is really just a remake of *Caged* (1950), the original and most stylish women's prison film, and is also derivative of other B movie prison films such as *Caged Heat* (1974). *Caged Heat* was Jonathan Demme's directing debut, and the film was produced by trash king Roger Corman. It features the mainstays of the genre: a crippled and sadistic female warden who has an equally corrupt assistant (and this pairing of female officers suggests that lesbianism is part of their evil repertoire), a sympathetic innocent inmate, and action brought to a head (as it usually is) by a particularly brutal act on the part of the prison staff toward a vulnerable inmate. In this case, an inmate is scheduled to be lobotomized for stealing food. The inmates prove to be both resourceful and courageous, and they rescue their comrade from her fate. The scenes of rebellious women in prison films always allow for the possibility of an overt feminist message that involves both a critique of male-dominated society and some notion of female community.

One of the earliest and most successful films in the genre was *Caged*. In *Caged* (1950), directed by John Cromwell, Eleanor Parker plays a young pregnant woman incarcerated for robbery. After a series of rough encounters with other inmates and guards, she becomes desensitized and fully a part of prison life. Her main tormentor is played by Hope Emerson in a sadistic performance that became the standard model for women's prison films. Queer actress Agnes Moorehead also has a role in this drama as a warden.[26] In his anthology *Prison Pictures from Hollywood*, James Robert Parish called *Caged* "one of the most remarkable studies of women behind bars ever to be presented onscreen. . . . Not since the late 1930's, with such films as *Condemned Women* (1938), had Hollywood dealt so starkly with the traumatic existence that female prisoners endure so frequently."[27] *Caged* is a beautifully moody black-and-white film with excellent acting and none of the over-the-top exploitation features that have come to characterize the genre. While later prison films such as *Prison Girls* (1973) turn the all-women set into an opportunity for soft-core pornography, *Caged* is serious treatment of both the plight of poor women and the problems with the prison system. Femininity, in prison, is simply a luxury the women cannot afford, and the butch warden Evelyn Harper (Hope Emerson) indulges herself in "feminine comforts" such as romance novels and dressing up not, one feels, for the pleasure that she gains from femininity but because femininity is what is denied to the inmates. A central scene illustrates this premise when the butch and well-connected vice queen Elvira dis-

Figure 21. The sadistic prison matron. Hope Emerson in *Caged* (1950), directed by John Cromwell.

tributes lipsticks to the women as a Christmas present. Harper tries to intervene, but the sympathetic warden, Benton (Agnes Moorehead) allows the women to keep the cosmetics.

The innocent prison women—the femmes, in other words—in most prison films, enter prison as young ingenues but leave as street-tough dykes. The older inmates prey on the newer ones, and the predatory dyke is not only lurking around every corner; she is also the destiny of the young inmate, who must lose her femininity to survive. Although a conservative message is embedded in this plot structure, namely, that female criminality must be contained because it erodes femininity, these films also make a hard-hitting critique of both class and gender politics. By making femininity into a luxury and a privilege, the prison film makes clear links between poverty, female masculinity, female criminality, and the predatory butch.

## The Fantasy Butch

"Fantasy" in this section will refer to nonrealistic films, horror films, space films, B movies. The B movie almost by definition focuses on the unsavory, the alien, the horrific, and the extreme. The butch can be found lurking with other misfits in the dark shadows of B movie land: like the freak and the zombie, the butch is nonhuman but nonanimal. The fantasy butch, unlike the prison butch, actively destroys femininity within her own body and remakes it as a stunning and defiant female masculinity. "I'm the dyke, blow me," intones the dyke chopper chick in *Chopper Chicks in Zombie Town*. Although it is a drag that the rest of her girl gang indulge in dull straight sex, this film's equation of heterosexual townspeople with zombies makes for exciting queer comedy. *Chopper Chicks in Zombietown* (1990) represents the Chopper Chicks as six wild women with 1,000 cc's between their legs. Campy, trashy, tough, and violent, *Chopper Chicks* is everything you could ever want in a "women's movie" and more. This morality tale of wrong against right, evil against good, chopper chicks against zombies, finally gives the bad guys/gals a chance to win out in the age-old struggle against peace and justice. The Chopper Chicks, led by their courageous lesbian leader, roar into a sleepy town only to discover that the townspeople are zombies out for blood and guts. Our fearless sheroes become chopper chicks with a vengeance, and heads roll as they chop, slash, shoot, and generally fight blood with more blood. A subplot involving a busload of blind kids only heightens the tension.

*Chopper Chicks* plays less with the overt butchness of one character and more with the predatory and menacing effect of the girl motorbike gang. Only one of our sheroes is actually a lesbian, and she presents a kind of Suzi Quatro leather image rather than any straightforward butch aesthetic. However, I put *Chopper Chicks* in this category because the film so obviously plays with and against the classic boy bike movies from the 1950s and 1960s—*The Wild One* (1954) or *Easy Rider* (1969) as well as the classic gay motorbike films such as Kenneth Anger's *Scorpio Rising* (1964) and Fred Halston's *Sex Garage*—and one could even argue that *Chopper Chicks* cites earlier predatory butch films like *Johnny Guitar*. *Chopper Chicks* resists simply transforming male homoeroticism into female homoeroticism and instead capitalizes on multiple forms of female rebellion. One form is definitely the butch on her bike, but another is the housewife who has taken to the open road to escape a certain future of laundry and housework.

This film builds on the almost otherworldly fear produced by the notion of the predatory butch dyke but reverses the terms of that fear: here it is the townspeople who become zombies and the dykes on bikes who must rescue them.

The horror film has often been cast as a close relative of pornography: both genres are obsessed with seeing the perverse body in all its erotic and violent glory. It is not surprising, therefore, that we should find butches and pseudobutches in many horror films. Carol Clover calls attention to the ambiguity of the girl who always manages to survive the monster's rampage, and she calls this character "the final girl."[28] The final girl is slightly butch and is often considered to be undesirable by the men and boys in the film. Her lack of appeal saves her from both sex and violence and, in Clover's theory, allows her to be a stand-in for the male spectator, who experiences a masochistic thrill from the identification. But Clover's neat theory of this male masochistic gaze fails to account for a much more subversive and threatening butch gaze, a gaze allowed for by the presence of the final girl and maintained by her survival and persistence.

Although the butch is standard fare in the horror film, we should not expect to find her in pornographic films, if only because the pornographic imagination tends to imagine lesbian sex as the spectacle of two feminine women engaged in sex play for a male gaze. However, some pornography from the 1960s did use nonconventional female bodies and images for heterosexual viewing pleasure. In one remarkable 1968 porn flick called *The King*, the entire narrative turns around a butch and her two femme lovers. The film obviously uses the butch as a male stand-in, but in her role as masculine sex partner, the butch exceeds such a utilitarian function. This sexually explicit feature introduces us to a sexy trio made up of two feminine women and a hippy butch called Mickey. Mickey, played by an actress called King Drummond, is called "the King" by the two women, who take turns in receiving his/her attention. The press packet describes this king butch as follows: "The King is a woman who has the body of a female and the desires of a man." Throughout the opening section of the tape, Mickey remains clothed while both of the femmes are in various states of undress. An ecstatic voice-over narrates the thoughts of one of the girls and articulates both her jealousy about sharing the King and her dependence on the other girl, who, she admits, goes down on her when Mickey is not around.

*The King* clearly plays with the standard threesome of heterosexual pornography by making the butch the focus of the femmes' attentions and by making the dynamic between the two femmes completely subsidiary to anything that happens between Mickey and either of the women. In heterosexual porn, of course, very often a triangle involving lesbian sex establishes lesbianism as an opening act for heterosexual intercourse. In *The King*, femme-to-femme action is foreplay for the main event of butch-femme sex. The film also involves a strange interracial dynamic that displaces the butch-femme arrangement at various moments. The woman through whom the scenes are narrated by the voice-over is black, and she is constantly the third wheel to Mickey and the white femme. The exclusion of the black woman is only intensified when she describes herself in the voice-over as sexually voracious and never satisfied. Obviously, the racist trope of excessive black female sexuality forces us to question the racial dynamics of the sexual scene: one could argue that the white butch and white femme become a "natural" match when compared to the perverse racialized triangle. Whereas in heterosexual porn the presence of a male body authorizes and legitimizes the sex play between the two women, in the butch-femme scene, the interracial femme sex play is interrupted by the white butch, who provides both a masculine sexual presence and a white partner for the blond feminine woman.

As I mentioned earlier, a surprising source of butch imagery is provided by *Aliens* (1986). *Aliens* counts as a fantasy film here in terms of its interest in otherworldly contexts, alien sex, alien erotics, and alien bodies. In deep space, Ripley (Sigourney Weaver) wakes from hibernation, and she and the company of marines ready themselves for the task at hand. As the characters wander around in various states of undress, the gaze of the camera brushes up against a hard-muscled body doing pull-ups on a rail in the cabin. When the camera returns moments later to this character, we realize it is a tough Latina. Vasquez proceeds to cruise Ripley and whispers "qué bonita" as she walks by. Of course, Vasquez's studly appreciation for the rather asexual Sigourney Weaver does not save the Latina from being one of the first victims of the voracious aliens; neither pull-ups nor a moment of butch bonding with a male marine can pull her from the jaws of death, and this butch meets a gory and untimely end.

Finally, what fantasy survey would be complete without an entry from the master of camp smut, John Waters? In *Desperate Living* (1977), Waters depicts a loving relationship between the foulmouthed, zit-covered butch Moe and her porn queen girlfriend Muffy. Moe and Muffy are a match made in Mortville, and their love life, according to the size queen Muffy, lacks only a good hard dick. Only too eager to please, Moe uses her lottery prize money to go out and purchase the real thing. Moe, tragically, discovers her inner man and her outer dick, or wang, only to generate disgust and loathing from the lovely Muffy. As usual in John Waters's films, these characters represent not simply camp versions of some recognizably queer types but the absolute extreme of that type, and they tip all too often into shock value. In *Desperate Living*, Moe represents not only unapologetic butchness but also the site of transsexual aspiration. Waters plays with penis envy by giving Moe a penis and then forcing her to castrate herself. The final shot in this scene, of a dog eating the discarded penis, explodes notions such as castration anxiety and turns castration itself into comedic horror.

### Transvestite Butches

We have become more than accustomed to seeing images of cross-dressed men in Hollywood—the standard plot of the transvested-man genre features a moral lesson in which we learn that men make better women than women do. Predictably, however, when women appear cross-dressed as men in mainstream cinema, they are coded as flawed women rather than perfect men. The genre of the transvested woman demands careful attention because the various themes of gender theatricality, gender dysphoria, androgyny, and butch masquerade all produce very different narratives. In some films, the cross-dressing woman has been forced into male costume by social restrictions on her gender or by the need for mobility. In others, cross-dressing produces an image of essential androgyny and constructs the transvested woman as a meeting of the sexes. In others still, the male drag has become more than a costume, and the butch inside it has an erotic relation to her clothes and uses masculine clothing to complete her gender presentation.

Female masculinity in film has often been rendered synonymous with male impersonation or female transvestism. In *Hollywood Androgyny*, for example, Rebecca Bell-Metereau makes nice distinctions between the imitation of maleness, tomboyism, and masculine women, but she still includes all these manifestations under the heading of "male impersonation."[29] Chris Straayer, on the other hand, in her chapter titled "The Temporary Transvestite Film," looks at cross-dressing and assumed female masculinity in relation to the notion of disguise.[30] Both Straayer and Bell-Metereau do an incredible job of laying out the conventions of the cross-dressing genre and of the place of the female transvestite within it; what I add to their analyses, however, is the relation of the butch character to the cross-dressing narrative, and I observe when and where transvestism tips into transsexualism or where and when the theater of gender disguise gives way to the hard realities of masculine identification.

Bell-Metereau traces a historical narrative of the pre-1960s male imper-sonator and argues that "regardless of the decade, the majority of films involving women dressed as men are attempts to reconcile the mascu-line woman to her role in society" (*Hollywood Androgyny,* 73). Accordingly, these films have to represent the allure of the cross-dressed woman but also the limited nature of her transgression. She may revel momentarily in the uncertainty of gender and gender roles, but ultimately order must be restored in terms of full heterosexual womanhood. The pre-1960s and post-1960s periodization obviously refers to the difference between films produced during the ban on homosexual imagery and films produced after the ban was lifted. During the Hollywood Production Code era, indeed, the cross-dressing woman was a common feature of Hollywood film. After the ban was lifted, she became much more of an oddity and indicated some form of extreme eccentricism. Because much cross-dressing on film tends to be a short-lived form of gender transgression, Straayer refers to trans-vestite films as "temporary" and notes: "These films offer spectators a mo-mentary, vicarious trespassing of society's accepted boundaries for gender and sexual behavior. Yet one can relax confidently in the orderly demarca-tions reconstituted by the films' endings" ("Temporary Transvestite Film," 42–43). Along the way, however, gay and lesbian audiences in particular are offered the possibility of numerous viewing pleasures and multiple de-constructions of the "natural" order of things. Bell-Metereau divides her "male impersonation" films into categories such as "The Career Woman" and "The Western Heroine" and concludes with her favored category, "The True Androgyne." Straayer divides her survey into analyses of the generic conventions and pays particular attention to "The Hetero/Homo Collapse" as well as "Trans-body" and "Trans-sex" films. The logic driving my analy-sis of the transvestite film relies not so much on generic conventions or historical function; rather, I note the opportunity afforded by transvestism for the particular expression of female masculinity.

In 1961 William Castle's curious film *Homicidal* was released on the very cusp of the post–Production Code era. Viewers were thrilled by an elaborate gothic tale of murder, mayhem, gender disguise, and family misfortunes. Set in California, the film features an icy blond who first picks up a hotel bellhop and pays him to marry her and then stabs the county clerk as he performs the ceremony. The blond, Emily, drives off into the night, leaving the corpse and the disappointed groom far behind her, and does not stop until she reaches her family home. Here we are introduced to her husband, Warren, a slight, stern man; her sister-in-law, Mariam Webster, who is to be married to the town's pharmacist; and Warren's mother, Helga, a wheelchair-bound, mute paraplegic. As the plot unfolds, we discern tensions between Mariam and Emily: Mariam apparently did not approve of Warren's marriage to Emily. Warren met Emily during a trip to Sweden and brought back his bride to California. Odd flashback scenes of Warren punctuate the film's main story line and hint at the subterranean narrative of family secrets, buried violences, and childhood disturbance. Finally it becomes clear that Emily is trying to kill Helga and possibly Mariam, and Mariam rushes to the family home to warn Warren of his wife's homicidal tendencies. Emily has already killed Helga when Mariam arrives, but as she calls to Warren for help, Emily removes her wig and reveals the ghastly secret: Emily and Warren are the same person. Warren, we find out, was born female but raised male by his mother, Helga, because his father would leave his fortune only to a son. Warren kills himself in the film's closing moments by falling down the stairs and landing on his own knife.

*Homicidal* is, as Bell-Metereau points out, a clear imitation of *Psycho*, and like Hitchcock's masterpiece, Castle's film implicates cross-gender identification with twisted family dynamics and a murderous attitude toward women.[31] Both films also suggest that some kind of thwarted homosexual tendency erupts through cross-dressing into homo-cidal tendencies, and in both films, murder, desire, and gender are all bound to each other in a classic psychoanalytic narrative of Oedipal rage. The twist in *Homicidal*, however, concerns the cross-dressing performance of Jean Arliss in the roles of Warren and Emily. It is impossible to know from watching the film whether Jean Arliss is male or female, a male impersonator or a female impersonator, transsexual or transgender; the uncertainty of Arliss's gender only emphasizes the gender confusion in the film and heightens the tension. Straayer does not mention *Homicidal*, but we could place it in her "Films with Trans-sex Casting" category, although we do not know whether Jean Arliss is a woman playing a man or a man playing a woman. For Straayer, the trans-sex role requires that "the performed transvestism be effective both within and outside the diegesis. Transgender gestures, behaviors and secondary sex markers are maintained throughout the film" ("Temporary Transvestite Film," 75). *Homicidal,* of course, goes way beyond a simple trans-sex casting decision because the film itself is about transsexual aspiration. We might assume, for example, that the trip Warren takes to Sweden in his early adulthood refers to the trip Christine Jorgensen took in the 1950s to Denmark for sex reassignment surgery. If Christine left as a woman and returned as a man, Warren left as a girl who had been forced to become a boy and returned a murderous woman. Transsexualism in *Homicidal* has been thoroughly confused with homosexuality and childhood gender disorders in general. If it is difficult to locate the sexual deviance in the film, it is even harder to locate the precise nature of the gender deviance, and under the weight of so much gender-crossing, gender identity becomes totally unreadable. In other words, even if clues exist to tip off the viewer as to the gender of Jean Arliss, the actor, they are scrambled in the film by the cross-sex theme.

Another unique film in which gender becomes transparent and unreadable features cross-dressed women but refuses to draw attention to the transvestism or make it visible in any way. The Japanese film *Summer Vacation 1999* (1988), by Shusuke Kaneko, traces a series of homoerotic encounters between a group of schoolboys at boarding school during the summer. The effect of adolescent sexual and gender ambiguity is rendered by using girls to play the male parts. Such a practice borrows from the Japanese theatrical tradition of using girls for boys (the Takarazuka Review, for example), but it also plays against Kabuki and Shakespearean drama and the practice of using boys for women's parts.[32] Gender substitution in this odd film creates an uncanny effect as a barely submerged femininity becomes part and parcel of male adolescence and a surface masculinity comes to define the girl actors: gender is literally rendered invisible.

Obviously, the usual effect of watching a cross-dresser in film is to make gender visible and legible, often with comic results. For example, in the classic musical Western *Calamity Jane* (1953), Doris Day plays a butch cowgirl who has become one of the guys in Deadwood and shoots, rides, spits, and drinks as well as they do. Historically there is a fair amount of evidence that the real Calamity Jane was a passing woman, but Hollywood transforms this transgender hero into a rather fluffy character who eventually settles into a properly feminine form of domesticity with Wild Bill

Figure 22. Calamity Jane. Doris Day in *Calamity Jane* (1953), directed by David Butler.

Hickcok. On her way to finding a true heterosexual femininity, however, Calamity has some seriously queer encounters: she is mistaken for a man and cruised by women in Chicago, and in a beautifully ironic scene, she sets up house with an actress called Kate while they sing a gorgeous butch-femme duet called "A Woman's Touch."

In one important scene that emphasizes the importance of the gender-deviant role, Calamity has burst into Kate's theater dressing room, and while Kate mistakes Calamity for *Mr.* Calamity, Calamity mistakes Kate for an actress instead of the actress's maid. The camera focuses for a moment on the two characters looking in a mirror as if to suggest that neither one is "real." But the mirror reflects to Calamity Jane an image that scares her—an image that seems incongruent with her sense of self. The mirror scene suggests that neither woman is really being true to herself; they are both impostors of one kind or another. This scene promises that when we leave the world of the looking glass (and this resonates with mirror scenes in other butch films such as *A Touch of Evil*), the calamity of multiple role reversals will be contained by the real necessities of life—home and hearth.

The potentially disruptive and transgressive nature of the cross-dressed woman is the way she reveals the fragility of gender coding but also the

Figure 23. "I shall die a bachelor." Greta Garbo in *Queen Christina* (1933), directed by Rouben Mamoulian.

oppressive weight of gender conformity. In *Queen Christina* (1933), Greta Garbo depicts a lonely monarch torn between being a woman and being a king. "I shall die a bachelor," she tells her valet sorrowfully. *Queen Christina* is often held up as an example of lesbian representation under the constraints of the Production Code. Garbo's androgynous and ambiguous heroine pushes at the limits of acceptable femininity and carries it off through the agency of her royal position. Director Rouben Mamoulian allegedly tried to tone down the masculinity of Garbo's performance and reworked a script written by Garbo's lover Mercedes De Acosta. But Mamoulian's efforts were all to no avail. *Queen Christina* remains a queer classic, not simply for the full-mouth kiss that Garbo plants on her lady-in-waiting Countess Ebba Sparre (Elizabeth Young), but rather on account of the swagger that Garbo injects into this trouser role.

One scene of cross-dressing confusion makes clear that the gender ambiguity of the queen does not simply imply a lesbian current. Queen Christina is passing as a man while traveling in Sweden, and her male costume disguises not only that she is a woman but also that she is the queen. She finds herself forced to share a room with the Spanish ambassador, Antonio, (John Gilbert). As Antonio and Queen Christina size up the room, a barmaid enters and makes a slyly indecent proposal to the queen while helping her off with her boots. Rather than hinting simply at some lesbian undercurrent, however, this complicated scene demonstrates a complex array of homoerotic dynamics. The film certainly does indulge in homoerotic fantasy, but this fantasy is not limited to a lesbian imaginary: while the queen is still disguised as a man, there is a male homoerotic dynamic between her and Antonio owing to the obvious sexual tension between the disguised queen and the envoy. When Queen Christina reveals herself to be a woman, Antonio exonerates himself for his earlier transgressive desire by saying, "I knew it!" This suggests, of course, that heterosexual instinct cannot be wrong, and so if he was attracted to her, she must have been a woman—his desire literally genders her, and when the love scene unfolds between them, Queen Christina comments that she "has just become a woman."

Because this is a heterosexual romance about a woman rescued from frigidity by a "hot" Spaniard and from the duty of monarchy by the anarchy of love, where is the queer gaze in this film and how does it underwrite the heterosexual romance? Obviously, there are clear moments of sexual tension, as I have noted, within the cross-dressed scenes, and the general atmosphere of gender transgression in the film is created by Queen Christina's resistance in the first half of the film to a political marriage or indeed to any kind of marriage. Furthermore, we are told early on that monarchy establishes its power through masculinity; hence Queen Christina is "raised a boy" and born to be "king." When she is crowned early on, she is proclaimed "king." The epithet of "queen" is almost an afterthought, and in the title, it serves to emphasize that her womanhood is in conflict with her title. The role ultimately emphasizes that certain forms of power demand masculine subjects.

The first half of the film, with its emphasis on female masculinity and monarchy, is in direct conflict with the second half of the film, with its emphasis on femininity and womanhood. Indeed, the difference between, and incompatibility of, these two narratives can be seen through a comparative reading of two scenes, both of which position the queen in bed. The bed scenes demonstrate the different claims of privacy, desire, ambition, and power that work through the clash between being queen and being a private person. In the first bed scene, we see her in her four-poster, reading in the early morning, sharing her bed with a book; this signals her love of art and privacy and makes a link between the two. The scene of the queen reading in the half-light of dawn is also a scene of her bachelorhood. The bed literally represents her private self (as opposed to the public self of monarch). The second scene in bed occurs at the hotel, and now she is in bed with Antonio; in the cross-dressing scene, the two had argued long and hard about sharing a bed, but after she has revealed herself to him as female, the bed sharing ceases to be problematic. The curtains are drawn about the bed, and Antonio's manservant enters the room and asks if his master will be getting up soon or would like some hot chocolate. The voice that answers from behind the curtain, Antonio's voice, speaks for both himself and his companion; as far as the manservant knows, Antonio's roommate was a man, and the manservant appears shocked by the appar- ent homoeroticism of the scene. Of course, the homoeroticism that was latent the night before may now be invoked because Antonio and Queen Christina and the audience know better. The queerness of the homoeroti- cism is undercut by the erasure of the queen; she has relinquished her bachelorhood and no longer speaks for herself. Now she is spoken for, and her voice has been subsumed by his.

Following their love scene, Queen Christina says, "I will always remem- ber this room, I will return to it many times in the future." This evocation of future nostalgia, an impossible space—"I will look back"—marks the impossibility of Queen Christina's desire to be a bachelor and a king and a lover. This weird collision of past and future is captured perfectly in the film's final shot of Christina, no longer queen, looking back and moving forward or away. Ultimately this film suggests that monarchy rests on mas- culinity or an asexual femininity. If she wants to be a woman, Christina cannot be queen or monarch, and if she wants to be a monarch, she cannot be a woman.

This point about the essential masculinity of monarchy is emphasized in another cross-dressing film, *Orlando* (1993). The director of this film, Sally Potter, is quite clearly referencing *Queen Christina*, particularly in her cast- ing decisions. In *Orlando*, Quentin Crisp plays Queen Elizabeth to Tilda Swinton's androgyne Orlando. Almost in homage to Garbo, Swinton plays her princely role as a drooping and melancholic antihero. Orlando em- bodies the unbearable loneliness of being neither and both, eternally. For him, happiness collapses into sorrow as one century collapses into the next. Orlando is hardly butch in his masculine form; the perfect androgyne, Tilda Swinton captures to perfection an in-betweenness of gender, which again looks more like the eradication of gender than its staging. Adapted

Figure 24. Neither and both. Tilda Swinton in *Orlando* (1993), directed by Sally Potter.

from Virginia Woolf's novel, Potter's *Orlando* is the story of a person who lives through centuries, through wars, through monarchies, and through at least two genders. The film is lush and spectacular, and Potter paints gorgeous cinematic backdrops for her hero/ine for all seasons. From the frozen Russian winter to a golden English summer, Orlando flits through history and across geographies like a gender-bending time traveler.

But how queer is Potter's Orlando? When we are not being seduced by the visual opulence of Potter's scenery, we suddenly notice that Tilda Swinton's cross-dressing androgyny has distinctly unqueer limits. As a male Orlando, Swinton performs an oddly androgynous character who can be read comfortably as a "boy" but less comfortably as a "man." Still, this presents interesting possibilities for a love scene between Orlando and Sasha, a Russian princess. The androgyny of Orlando means that we cannot forget that we are looking at a woman in drag, and therefore the love affair between Orlando and Natasha has serious lesbian overtones. This also makes sense if you recall that Woolf wrote the novel *Orlando* for her lover Vita Sackville-West, who often wore male drag. But Potter completely refuses to capitalize on the queer sexuality invoked by this love affair, and she refuses to screen the lesbian sex scene that the romance demands. Potter, in fact, saves the film's sex scene for a rather conventional encounter between a female Orlando and an all too male young American called Shelmerdine (Billy Zane). Because each section of the film is introduced by titles such as "Death," "Poetry," "Politics," and "Love," Potter only adds insult to injury when she places the encounter with Shelmerdine under the heading of "Sex." Chris Straayer also finds *Orlando* to be less than a queer film because Swinton's androgyne ultimately emphasizes the feminine over the masculine. As a woman, Orlando appears naked, but as a man, he is always dressed and not a little impotent. Straayer ultimately decides that "Orlando is not primarily a queer film; it is a feminist film" ("Temporary Transvestite Film," 77). Although Rebecca Bell-Metereau does not discuss *Orlando,* we might expect this film to fall in well with what she dubs "Hollywood androgyny." Ultimately, for Bell-Metereau and to a certain extent for Sally Potter in her film, androgyny is seen as the apex of gender flexibility. Androgyny is, in fact, figured as the perfect blend of the masculine and the feminine and the creation of gender harmony. Bell-Metereau summarizes her vision of androgyny as follows: "The androgynous figure gives audiences a sense of hidden possibilities, of the potential for change and renewal. Films allow us to enter into the forbidden worlds of the imagination, and when we find ourselves identifying with the other sex, we learn more of what it is simply to be human" (*Hollywood Androgyny,* 237). Ultimately, androgyny always returns us to this humanist vision of the balanced binary in which maleness and femaleness are in complete accord. Of course, the image of the blatant butch upsets such a balance and offers no hope of temperate gendering; to really explore the power of visual images of female masculinity, we have to leave the androgyne behind and grapple with the implications of butch and transgender realness.

For the transgender butch or the dysphoric woman, gender ceases to be theater, performance, harmonious blending, or aesthetic presentation; for the dysphoric butch, clothing becomes a temporary resolution for a severe identity crisis. In the Brazilian film *Vera* (1987), a butch is rescued from a reform school and put to work in a library by her guardian; once established as a functional employee, she remakes herself as Bauer, a slick young man in a neat suit and tie. This film finds nothing about gender to be artificial and suggests that the weight of gender realness burdens the transsexual or transgender body with disastrous effects. Bauer cannot find recognition for his new gender, and he is met everywhere with disbelief or refusal.[33] Bauer begins a relationship with Clara, a woman at the library, and she at first re-

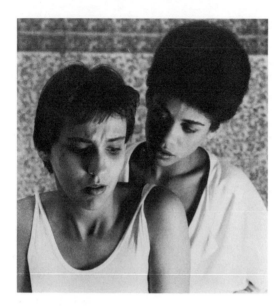

Figure 25. Ana Beatrice Nogueria as Bauer in *Vera* (1987), directed by Sergio Toledo.

buffs his overtures, reading them as "lesbian"; however, after a remarkable scene in which Bauer arrives at Clara's house and passes as a man in front of her parents, Clara seems endeared to her admirer. As the relationship picks up steam, Clara and Bauer begin to be sexual, and chaos ensues. Clara sees Bauer as a masculine woman who needs to be carefully drawn into naked lovemaking; when Bauer, who sees himself as male, refuses to undress, Clara rejects him. In another painful mirror scene, Bauer undresses slowly, looking at his own reflection while Clara coaxes him on. As he carefully unbinds his breasts, he watches himself become alien in the mirror, and when finally confronted with a naked and female image, he panics and grabs his clothes and runs from the room. This scene, ultimately, suggests that unlike Calamity Jane, who felt at odds with her cross-dressed image, Bauer cannot stand the reflection of the naked female body that he reduces down to when his lover refuses his transgender self. It is significant that this film is Brazilian and that it references a different and highly gendered code of sexual variance. In 1986, when this film was released, most of the lesbian films in the United States had removed the butch from the frame of reference, and transgender films were nowhere to be found.

That the story of the transgender butch is a tragedy should not suggest that she or he fails to find other gender options; rather, it signifies the refusal of heterosexist gender clones to read and recognize new and exciting genders when and where they emerge. In the tragic tale of *Vera,* Orlando's androgynous pathos, Moe's "desperate living," Frankie Addams's "unjoined" status, and Sister George's butch bully identity are echoed through Bauer's plea for recognition: "You don't understand," Bauer yells in one crucial encounter with his guardian, "I am different. I am something else, something else." Difference and the desire to have one's difference heard, registered, seen, and felt are the real themes of the transvested butch and the transgender man.

## Barely Butch

In the 1980s, films about dykes, bulldaggers, cross-dressers, and butch perverts were replaced with a self-conscious "lesbian cinema." Two lesbian films in particular, *Lianna* (1982) and *Desert Hearts* (1986), managed to drum up a modest mainstream appeal despite being moderate-budget independently produced features. The group of lesbian films that I examine in this section were all intended as contributions to a nonpathologizing lesbian cinema made up of positive images and role model material. However, there is a startling development in this group: the butch character is played as a shadow of her former self. The shades of butch are still readable (Patrice Donnelly as a jock, Mary Stuart Masterson as a rough-and-tumble southern dyke), but their embodiments are definitely feminized. Wherever a novel has been turned into a film (*Fried Green Tomatoes, Desert of the Heart*), the characters in the novels who were coded as butch have been noticeably softened into femmey butches or soft butches. This "positive" cinema works only at the expense of masculine women.

How do we account historically for such an erasure? One could argue that since the butch dyke had long symbolized a homophobic stereotyping of lesbians, her disappearance within lesbian cinema was supposed to signal the arrival of positive and responsible images of everyday lesbians. But by relegating the butch to the trash heap of homophobic cinema, lesbian cinema made butch women into the scapegoat for homophobic representation. In other words, the butch is a *type* of lesbian as well as a lesbian stereotype; the butch, moreover, makes dyke desire and dyke sexuality visible and exemplifies a dyke variation on hetero-normative gender roles. This trend in the 1980s should not surprise us. As I showed in chapter 4, the 1980s was a time of considerable backlash within white lesbian feminist communities against butch-femme imagery. The rejection of so-called role-playing lesbians was duplicated in lesbian cinema by the depiction of lesbian desire through the modality of sameness. The women in these self-consciously lesbian films, in other words, are shown to desire sameness, not difference.[34]

Within the "barely butch" films—*Lianna, Desert Hearts, Personal Best,* and *Fried Green Tomatoes*—we find traces of the butch dyke and her various modes of alternate gendering. The narrative of the predatory dyke lives on as the tale of the lesbian who seduces and tutors or "brings out" a straight woman. The phallic signifiers that marked dyke masculinity in earlier films reappear in lesbian cinema as simply an unconventional femininity. The barely butch might do something considered to be traditionally male—she may have muscles, she may be a heartbreaker or a philanderer. There are only occasional hints of cross-dressing or erotic attachment to male clothing in these films, and all of the barely butches are recognizable as women. This is a particularly significant development in *Desert Hearts* and *Fried Green Tomatoes* because in the novels on which these films are based, both butch characters are constantly mistaken for men.

One of the earliest "barely butch" films, *Lianna* (1982), tells the story of one woman's coming out almost as a universal tale of human discovery. In the course of the narrative, Lianna comes out, leaves her husband, and begins a life for herself as a lesbian. The barely butch in this scenario is an older teacher, Ruth, who in another era would have been the predatory butch preying on female innocence. Here she is a husband substitute who facilitates Lianna's escape from the clutches of heterosexuality. Ruth has short hair and a face that would be boyish were it not for the makeup and femme earrings. Like Lianna's husband, Ruth is a teacher; Lianna met her husband in graduate school and became his research assistant before dropping out to marry him. Now she becomes Ruth's research assistant, and the film suggests a parallel development between the role of husband and the role of barely butch lover. In a scene that shows the growing attraction between the two women, Lianna gazes with adoration at the barely butch teacher who replaces her husband—the already obvious substitution is emphasized in a rather heavy-handed fashion by filmmaker John Sayles, who shows writing on the blackboard behind Ruth that reads "parallel development."

*Personal Best* (1982) and *Desert Hearts* (1986) also make parallels between the barely butch character and another male figure in the barely femme heroine's life. In *Personal Best*, Tori is a female version of the coach/mentor figure with whom Mariel Hemingway eventually falls in love.[35] In this film about female athletes, Robert Towne's camera lovingly details female musculature but ultimately seems to categorize it as a weak version of male athleticism. Tori's little muscles, like Joan Crawford's little gun in *Johnny Guitar,* can never compete with a real male muscle. The film, as critics pointed out on its release, spends more time catching crotch shots of the women athletes than really concentrating on their athleticism, and ultimately, rather than taking a peek at the obvious lesbianism within women's sports, *Personal Best* serves up a voyeuristic account of female physicality.[36]

*Personal Best* tries to emphasize the inevitability of heterosexuality even within the most homosocial female spaces; *Desert Hearts,* by lesbian director Donna Deitch, refuses this narrative of inevitable heterosexuality and offers instead the lesbian potential of even the most avowedly heterosexual of women. In the novel on which this film is based, *Desert of the Heart,* by Jane Rule, multiple themes lend themselves to a butch aesthetic. The novel tells of a relationship between a younger woman, Ann, and an older woman, Evelyn. The two meet while Evelyn is in Reno waiting for her divorce to be finalized. Ann is a cartoonist, and Evelyn an English professor. Evelyn scours Ann's books for clues to her lover's character and finds a few lines from Sappho underlined by Ann: "But I say, / Whatever one loves one is."[37] The novel, at first glance, seems to embrace an aesthetic of sameness, but it ultimately undermines sameness and identification as models of lesbian desire by accentuating the differences between Ann and Evelyn. One axis of difference is an overt mother-child dynamic that animates the bonds between the two women. Ann's last name is Childs, and she lacks a mother; Evelyn lacks a daughter. Ann, Evelyn feels, is like her child, and she commences on a strange and erotic parenthood in which she and Ann are like and unlike at the same time: "What she saw was no longer an imperfect reflection of herself but an alien otherness she was drawn to and could not understand" (117). Ann also embraces Evelyn as an image of herself but understands her desire for Evelyn as motivated by difference and part of a masculine Oedipus complex. Ann's former lover and now married friend Silver tells her: "Love, when little boys want to marry their mothers, they have a hard enough time of it, but they manage. But when little girls want to marry their mothers . . ." (136). This exchange positions Ann as Oedipus, the boy who wants to marry his mother and who seeks difference in the place of sameness. Ann works in a Reno casino, a place filled with mirrors, one-way mirrors, two-way mirrors, metallic machine mirrors; she lives in a desert paradise of neon and slot machines, artificial light and money. The desert represents for both women the productive place of sterility, a place to celebrate divorce, a place to gamble (Evelyn wins), a place to lose a lot, a chaotic "tragic space" of uncharted desire, a place to cross but not to get to, a place of transitions and constant movement, a place of exile and loneliness, a place of the heart, but no home, no domestic place, just space. The book evokes beautifully a geography of desire in which the desert becomes a space that gives the impression of interminable sameness but, on closer inspection, reveals difference and variation at every level.

In the film *Desert Hearts* (1986), director Donna Deitch transforms the adorable butch wild child Ann from the novel into the groomed and model-like Cay. Cay is loosely compared to her brother, which is perhaps all that remains of her butch origins, and her brother comments loudly on her dating skills, wondering, "how does she get all that action without the right equipment?" The quip is humorous but loses some of its meaning in relation to masculine sibling rivalry when Ann becomes the feminine Cay. In the scene where Cay meets Evelyn, Cay passes her adoptive mother driving Evelyn home; Cay throws her car into reverse and draws alongside her mother's car and introduces herself to Evelyn. She swerves off only when a car approaches head on. This infamous driving backward scene symbolically renders Cay as the invert or perhaps the revert—she literally goes the other way. But a big car, some fancy driving, and a sassy mouth cannot do the definitional work of making Cay butch. Because Ann has become Cay, the mother-butch dynamic is also dampened and replaced by a barely butch–barely maternal dynamic in which all that remains of Ann's Oedipus complex is a vague sense of sexual aggressiveness, and all that remains of Evelyn's maternal presence is some gray hair and chronic shyness. The translation of this novel to film brings home the real stakes in 1980s lesbian cinema—the eradication of the butch and her desires.

Finally, in this section, one must consider the cinematic adaptation of Fannie Flagg's southern novel, *Fried Green Tomatoes at the Whistle Stop Cafe*.[38] This film exemplifies the tension between positive images and the compromising of lesbian representation. *Fried Green Tomatoes* (1991) won a GLAAD media award for its positive depiction of a lesbian relationship, but the erotic nature of the relationship between the two women in the film was actually so submerged that many heterosexual audiences were able to categorize what they saw as a strong friendship between two women

Figure 26. Barely butch. Mary Stuart Masterson in *Fried Green Tomatoes* (1992), directed by Jon Avnet.

rather than a dyke drama. As I have been arguing in this chapter, the lesbians are rendered invisible in this kind of film precisely because there are few traces of female masculinity. If heterosexual audiences had to watch a truly butch Idgie, there would have been little doubt as to the nature of the relationship between the two women. Furthermore, to depict Idgie in a nonthreatening way, filmmaker Jon Avnet actually diverged considerably from the novel. Avnet, curiously, depicts Idgie as a tomboy when young, but once she grows up, all traces of masculinity disappear. In an early scene, we watch an adorable cross-dressing young Idgie in suit and tie disrupt her sister's wedding by shining a mirror into the preacher's eyes. The tomboy, however, grows up to be a rumpled *Playboy* model, a kind of Madonna look-alike. In a gambling-hall scene, according to the novel, the grown-up Idgie is supposed to be one of the boys, a whore-visiting, rough-and-ready passing dyke. In one episode of the book, Idgie goes to visit Ruth while she is still married to her abusive husband. When Idgie finds out that Ruth's husband has been beating her, Idgie marches into the barbershop where Frank Bennett is getting a shave and threatens to kill Bennett if he doesn't leave Ruth alone. After Idgie leaves, Flagg writes: "The barber stood there with his mouth open. It had happened so fast. He looked at Frank in the mirror and said, 'That boy must be crazy'" (189). No hint of the "boy" or even the "crazy boy" remains in Avnet's femme-femme film.

Ultimately, an independent lesbian cinema proved to be disastrous for images of masculine women in lesbian visual contexts. Indeed, it is still quite rare to find a truly overt butch image in contemporary lesbian film. In the next section, I summarize recent attempts to put butch representation back into queer film.

## Postmodern Butches

In this section, I conclude with a quick survey of a few iconoclastic representations of lesbians in contemporary film. Indeed, some recent films have embraced queer genders, and a revitalized butch-femme dynamic has put the postmodern queer butch back into circulation. Some films, such as the cute and campy German feature *Your Heart Is All Mine* (1992), humorously view butch-femme as a clichéd but necessary form of lesbian sexual difference and as the primary locus for dyke sexiness. In *Your Heart Is All Mine*, Elke Gotz's odd and baroque lesbian comedy, the butch *is* a big cliché, and she uses totally hokey but endearing seduction tricks, such as blowing smoke rings, to get her femme. The other joke in this film is that the butch works as a butcher (perhaps this is funny only in English, however), and this gives her plenty of opportunity to wield big knives and offer slabs of choice meat to her lover.

k. d. lang turned in one of the great butch performances of all time in Percy Adlon's underrated film *Salmonberries* (1992).[39] Lesbian audiences had high hopes for this film on account of the incredible visibility of k. d. lang as a butch superstar and the cult profile of director Percy Adlon (*Baghdad Cafe*, 1988). Unfortunately, the film was not the crossover mainstream romance that many hoped it would be. *Salmonberries*, in fact, is a rather eclectic art film that pays more attention to the beauty of the Arctic landscape than it does to the beauty of two dykes thawing each other out. Seductions in this film consist of long snowmobile rides across snow-covered wastelands or furtive exchanges through fifteen layers of clothing. What this film does do, however, is tell an interesting and potentially queer tale of love in a cold climate.

*Salmonberries* tells the story of an Alaskan orphan called Kotz (k. d. lang) who goes to the library to trace back her family in the hopes of finding her real parents. At the library, she meets an older woman librarian, Roswitha (Rosel Zech), for whom Kotz develops an odd obsession. For the first thirty minutes of the film, lang is almost completely silent, and she is univer-

Figure 27. Love in a cold climate. k. d. lang in *Salmonberries* (1992), directed by Percy Adlon.

sally taken for a male owing to her butch appearance and heavy snow gear and because she passes as a boy in her work in the mines. The film finally reveals her gender when lang takes off her clothes and appears naked in front of Roswitha and then disappears into the library stacks. Roswitha, interestingly enough, continues to refer to Kotz as "he." The shot of lang's full frontal nudity is very quick, but it is an effective answer to Roswitha's gender confusion. There is also something startling in the image of nakedness in such frigid weather and in the weird juxtaposition of flesh and books. That Roswitha continues to call Kotz "he" suggests that anatomy is definitely not equivalent to gender for her; she reads Kotz's display as an odd exposure but not as a revelation of gender, and her attitude toward Kotz changes noticeably after this scene.

In ways similar to Jane Campion's *The Piano, Salmonberries* manages to open up new avenues of expression precisely by making the main character play mute. Lang's silent performance as an Eskimo boy is probably the most queer and convincing aspect of this weird film. As a silent presence, lang manages to express a range of complex emotions, and she also uses silence to bolster her masculinity: she is brooding, moody, melancholic, violent, sexy, and extremely intense. As you might imagine, things go downhill once lang begins to speak. Her interactions with Roswitha are too cheeky and upbeat given the intensity of her earlier moods, and the dynamic between the two women changes drastically once lang shifts gears from crushed-out melancholic boy dyke to mushy, sentimental, and love-stricken girl dyke. This is not to say that there are no hot moments left between the two women (despite arctic conditions), but some of the sexy tensions that are carefully developed early on evaporate all too quickly into a rather familiar tale of unrequited dyke desire for a repressed straight woman. Needless to say, there is no sex scene and only one failed seduction. Desire in this film does not play itself out between bodies but instead lies in the landscape and in relations between bodies and landscapes. Kotz and Roswitha are both as much in love with Alaska as they are in love with each other, and the camera reflects this by repeatedly giving us breathtaking shots of snow and ice. In *Salmonberries*, it is the snow-covered landscape that is sexy: the always overdressed bodies, the impossibility of anything more than brief nudity, the odd gender marking of snow clothes. *Salmonberries* makes a valuable contribution to a butch cinema because it refuses to compromise on the issue of making visible a butch desire and a butch desirability. It also plays convincingly on the connections between love and location, region and desire, sex and snow.

Butch representation within contemporary queer cinema has been at least partially replaced with a butch-femme narrative of desire. The butch-femme narrative, indeed, has become a kind of dominant code of lesbian cinema, even where efforts are made to displace it. In 1994's crossover hit *Go Fish*, by Rose Troche, the characters Max and Eli play out an elaborate ritual of dyke courtship and consummate it finally in an endearing scene of butch-femme seduction even though the film seems to mitigate against such gender codes. In *Go Fish* there is an explicit discussion of butch-femme: Eli and Max meet in a bookstore after an unsuccessful attempt at dating. Eli has chopped off her hippie hairdo and replaced it with a butch coif, and Max compliments her on it, saying it looks "very butch." They both agree, however, that butch-femme is outdated and go their separate ways. But the film works against this notion of an antiquated butch-femme system: the other couple in the film, an interracial couple, Kia and Evie are coded as butch and femme role models, and throughout the film, serious butch-femme clothing codes are in effect. Furthermore, the haircutting scene in which Eli has her hair reduced to a crew cut stands as a quintessential vision of butch self-fashioning, and the camera lovingly watches the dance of scissors on hair and the sculpting of a butch image out of the androgyny of in-betweenism. As this romance film builds to its generic conclusion—a consummation of love between the protagonists—both Max and Eli become more clearly marked as gendered. Max finally removes her baseball cap and lets her hair down, and Eli has the well-shaven head and a rather handsome shirt and seems emboldened by her new image.

Another appearance in 1990s lesbian cinema by a bona fide butch character appeared in Maria Maggenti's film *The Incredible True Adventures of Two Girls in Love* (1995). This film tells the story of young love between white tomboy Randy Dean (Laurel Holloman) and her black school friend Evie Roy (Nicole Parker). Not only is the tomboy a reasonable representation of adolescent female masculinity, but Randy's lesbian aunt, played by Kate Stafford, is also very clearly and explicitly butch. The film also handily relates butch identity to class identity but unfortunately does so at the expense of a complicated representation of racial identity. Evie is a rich black girl living with her mother in a neocolonial house in the suburbs and driving a beautiful new Range Rover. Randy is the tomboy renegade who lives with her lesbian aunt and her girlfriend in a hippy dippy household. Randy never knew her father, and her mother abandoned her for her Operation Rescue mission. In an effort to avoid stereotyping Evie as poor and underprivileged, Maggenti loads her character with wealth, security, and sophistication. She is into opera rather than hip-hop, she travels the world, and she eats sushi during quality time with her mother. Randy, on the other hand, rides roller blades, is in danger of failing to graduate, and enjoys loud and brash riot grrrl music by Team Dresch and others.

The ebony-and-ivory theme wears thin when we realize that race is nowhere referenced in the film as a significant feature of who Evie is. She faces little to no racism, and she basically articulates no real self-consciousness of race and its effects. Similarly, the girls never really have to confront the difficulties of interracial dating. In one telling scene after a dinner at Randy's house, Evie tells Randy that Randy's aunt did not seem to like her and wonders whether it is because she is black. The possibility of racism is immediately deflected by a reference to Evie's class background. "She probably has a problem with people who can fly off to Paris for a week," Randy explains. We now cut to a first kiss and effectively cut off further dialogue in this vein with the healing power of romance. Of course, the romantic diversion is a standard feature of Hollywood film in general, so we should not be surprised to find it making an appearance in

Maggenti's popular narrative. However, because *Two Girls in Love* derives humor and buoyancy from the obvious differences between the two girls, it should be capable of directly confronting the racism as well as the homophobia that the two girls will obviously face.

We have to venture away from the romance genre, however, to find some convincing images of postmodern butch. In the Austrian film *Flaming Ears* (1992), for example, Austrian avant-garde filmmakers Angela Hans Scheirl, Dietmar Schipek, and Ursula Purrer produce a cyber-butch cartoonlike character. Shot in Super 8 and blown up to 16 mm, this film manages to create a wild and glittering visual landscape. Model towns, converted cars, futuristic fashions, odd domestic interiors, and comic book–style backdrops combine to form an expressionist cartoon aesthetic that juxtaposes odd shadows and angles with saturated and vivid colors. Set in the year 2700 in the town of Asche, a peculiar band of lesbian characters—Volley, Nun, and Spy—live out a strange subcultural existence. The plot is elaborate and extravagant but can be summarized as an antiromantic horror movie. The *Women Make Movies* press packet describes the film as follows:

> The film follows the tangled lives of three women—Volley, Nun and Spy. Spy is a comic book artist whose printing presses are burned down by Volley, a sexed-up pyromaniac. Seeking revenge, Spy goes to the lesbian club where Volley performs every night. Before she can enter, Spy gets into a fight and is left wounded and lying in the street. She is found by Nun, an amoral alien in a red plastic suit with a predilection for reptiles, and who also happens to be Volley's lover. Nun takes her home and subsequently must hide her from Volley.

On the frame of this strange and rather intricate narrative trajectory hangs an exquisite visual adventure. Alternating between a kind of *Alice in Wonderland* effect of slanted, oversized rooms and a *Blade Runner* atmosphere of dilapidated urban sprawl, this film shows how easy it is to make the world look excessively different.

*Flaming Ears* really attempts to capture a queer rewriting of lesbian genders. Domestic scenes between what look like women are thoroughly sexualized in *Flaming Ears,* and whether we are watching a scene of a latex-clad gender-transitive character frying a minicrocodile in a blood-splattered kitchen, or a sex worker arranging flowers in her living room wearing a wooden cock and balls around her waist, odd genders appear in the juxtaposition of form and function. Featuring bizarre and almost unfamiliar sex scenes, the film is spliced with ritualistic violence such as vampirism and, my favorite, sex with furniture. In one extraordinary scene, we watch a particularly hot and tender encounter between Volley and a cabinet. As she rubs her crotch on the cabinet, Volley whispers to it, "don't move, dear little furniture." This encounter between woman and cabinet is perhaps the most romantic scene in the film, but there are other tender physical encounters between the cyber-butch Nun and a dead body. Nun is almost unreadable in terms of her gender, but this does not render her androgynous. Rather, she depicts an oddly masculine figure who carries her beloved, a dead girl, out of a grave and into her bed. Nun's gender is marked by her difference from Volley, who wears triangular pigtails and aprons, and by her melancholic loner image, which resonates with a whole history of butch representation from *The Well of Loneliness* to *Stone Butch Blues*. Nun's gender presentation can ultimately be summarized as "boy" even as her performance deforms and recreates boyness.

Two more recent examples of postmodern butch within mainstream film also stray far from the lesbian romance genre to work their magic. In the Wachowski brothers' film *Bound*, the butch enters the hard-boiled world of neo-noir. Jennifer Tilly plays Violet, a mob wife, prostitute, and femme with a steel-trap mind, and Gina Gershon plays Corky, Violet's ex-con lover. Gershon is quite convincing in the role of hardened thief, but she is far less convincing as a tough, handle-everything butch. The real surprise of the film, however, has to be the stunningly sexy performance by Jennifer Tilly. In the opening scenes, Tilly threatens to turn Violet into a bimbo femme with an irritating whine; however, Violet quickly develops into a shrewd and self-determined character, and she has one great speech in which she upbraids Corky for daring to suggest that her tendency to pass as heterosexual makes her less than a bona fide queer. *Bound*'s story line, in typical hard-boiled fashion, is tight and unpredictable, and its look is pure noir, with jagged camera angles and witty fades and close-ups.

Finally, an amazingly powerful representation of black butchness came from a somewhat surprising source. Queen Latifah plays Cleopatra Sims in F. Gary Gray's film *Set It Off* (1996), and she manages to handle a rough-neck butch role with verve and aplomb. Even a critic for the *New York Times* calls Cleo "a butch lesbian (with a pretty girlfriend) in whom bank-robbing brings out the latent outlaw."[40] Cleo is part of a group of four black women who decide that robbing banks is the only option society gives them to get

Figure 28. Butch noir. Jennifer Tilly and Gina Gershon in *Bound* (1996), directed by Larry and Andy Wachowski.

ahead. One woman has suffered police brutality, another has been fired from her job, another faces losing her child to the county, and Cleo faces constant discrimination, racial and sexual, at her low-paying job. To create credible butch style, Queen Latifah trades off a rap version of black masculinity and shows how quickly masculinity becomes visible as masculinity outside of white normative maleness. Certainly, as I commented earlier, the black butch fulfills certain stereotypical expectations, but ultimately the perceived inherent masculinity of blackness allows for the production of credible butchness.[41] Cleo wields a gun with power and authority, an authority that is not borrowed from men but part of her own masculine presence. Her persona resonates with similar personas developed by other rappers in black cinema—like Ice Cube in *Boyz N the Hood*, for example. And at the same time, Cleo is not at all like other black heroines played by Whitney Houston or Halle Berry.

In an interview in *Vibe* magazine appearing shortly after the release of *Set It Off*, Latifah spoke about her role in the film. She insists that she is not queer and makes a distinction between acting and being: "I'm not a dyke. . . . That's what Cleo is. Men's drawers, the whole nine—she's selling herself that way. Not me. *I did my job.* And I fear not."[42] Apart from the rather defensive denial of any personal queer identification in this declaration, Latifah does make an important point. Her own sexual identity is not the issue here; what is at stake is a credible artistic portrayal of a particular type of black lesbian, the type who watches her femme girlfriend strip, pulls her into a hard embrace, and knows guns like a gangsta. Latifah's interviewer, Danyel Smith, comments: "Cleo is not some boilerplate bulldagger. She is a full-blown human with issues that have roots in the black part, the poor part, the woman part and the provincial part of who Cleo is" (102). Indeed, the black female masculinity that Latifah portrays is convincing precisely because it is infused with racial and class dynamics that render the masculinity part and parcel of a particular form of abjected female identity. Smith names these abjected parts as "black," "poor," "woman," and "provincial," making clear the multiple markers that construct all forms of masculinity. Cleo's masculinity is as much a product of her life in the hood as it is about her lesbianism; it is a masculinity learned

Figure 29. Butch roughneck. Queen Latifah in *Set It Off* (1996), directed by F. Gary Gray.

in poverty as well as a masculinity cultivated in a female body. Cleo's masculinity is a survival skill as well as a liability, pleasure as well as danger, and ultimately she lives and dies by it.

## Conclusion

Contemporary dyke cinema is filled with sexy images of butches as tomboys, predators, perverts, and queers. Butch hardly signifies an outmoded identity or a malicious stereotype; rather, it signifies as the rough-hewn product of a tradition of unconventional females in cinema. Pre-1960s butches coded lesbianism into elaborate performances of gender deviance and social rebellion. Post-1960s butches struggled with the mandates of positive cinema and were briefly suppressed in the name of a nonstereotypical cinema. Ultimately, however, butches from the 1940s to the present have shared certain visual markers (guns, cigars, trousers, aggressive sexualities) and have often shared narrative fates (death, dishonor, disgrace). Tracing these images gives us access to one particular history of female masculinity, the history of looking butch.

*There are also women who perform as men: male impersonators ("drag butches"). They are a recognized part of the profession, but there are very few of them. I saw only one male impersonator perform during field work, but heard of several others. The relative scarcity of male impersonation presents important theoretical problems.*—Esther Newton, Mother Camp: Female Impersonators in America *(1972)*

# 7  DRAG KINGS

*Masculinity and Performance*

## What Is a Drag King?

In clubs and cabarets, theaters and private parties, in movies and on TV, the drag queen has long occupied an important place in the American drama of gender instability. Drag queens have been the subject of mainstream and independent movies,[1] and straight audiences are, and historically have been, willing to pay good money to be entertained by men in drag. And not only in performance arenas have drag queens been an important part of social negotiations over the meaning of gender. In academia, ever since Esther Newton's 1972 classic anthropological study of female impersonators in America, scholars have been vigorously debating the relation of camp to drag, of drag to embodiment, and of camp humor to gay culture.[2] But in all the articles and studies and media exposés on drag queen culture, very little time and energy has been expended on the drag queen's counterpart, the drag king. As I have argued throughout this book, the history of public recognition of female masculinity is most frequently characterized by stunning absences. And the absence of almost all curiosity about the possibilities and potentiality of drag king performance provides conclusive evidence of precisely such widespread indifference.

A drag king is a female (usually) who dresses up in recognizably male costume and performs theatrically in that costume. Historically and categorically, we can make distinctions between the drag king and the male impersonator. Male impersonation has been a theatrical genre for at least two hundred years, but the drag king is a recent phenomenon. Whereas the male impersonator attempts to produce a plausible performance of maleness as the whole of her act, the drag king performs masculinity (often parodically) and makes the exposure of the theatricality of masculinity into the mainstay of her act. Both the male impersonator and the drag king are different from the drag butch, a masculine woman who wears male attire as part of her quotidian gender expression. Furthermore, whereas the male impersonator and the drag king are not necessarily lesbian roles, the drag butch most definitely is.

In the 1990s, drag king culture has become something of a subcultural phenomenon. Queer clubs in most major American cities feature drag king acts: for example, there is a regular weekly drag king club in New York called Club Casanova whose motto is "the club where everyone is treated like a king!" There is a monthly club in London called Club Geezer and a quarterly club in San Francisco called Club Confidential. Club Confidential describes itself as "A swonderful, smarvelous, butch-femme, fag-dyke, boy-girl, retro-glam, lounge cabaret adventure" and encourages patrons to "dress to impress." This club supports lounge acts and offers lap dancing and strippers to entertain its drag clientele. In 1994 San Francisco held its first Drag King Contest, and in 1995 a Drag King calendar appeared with some of the contest's top drag kings. Mr. July, for example, is the ever dapper Stafford, co-organizer with Jordy Jones of Club Confidential; Stafford's calendar caption is a quote from Zippy the Pinhead that reads: "Gender confusion is a small price to pay for social progress." At Club Confidential and other San Francisco gender-bending nightspots such as Klubstitute, you can find drag kings and queens, contests and shows, and a crowd that gives the term "gender deviant" new meaning. At one contest, Klubstitute even featured a fake protest by fake feminists played by drag queens who disrupted the show by waving picket signs saying "Sisterhood, Not Misterhood," "Wigs Not Pigs," "Bitch Not Butch" and "Fems against Macho Butch Privilege."[3] But although drag kings seem to have become a major part of urban queer scenes, there are no indications that drag king culture is necessarily about to hit the mainstream any time soon. Nonetheless, at least one New York–based drag king, Murray Hill, has made it her goal to appear on the Rosie O'Donnell show.

I know at least three people who like to claim that *they*, and they alone, coined the name "drag king." But the truth is that as long as we have known the phrase "drag queen," the drag king has been a concept waiting to happen.[4] Some scholars have traced the use of the word "drag" in relation to men in women's costume back to the 1850s, when the term was used for both stage actors playing female roles and young men who just liked to wear skirts.[5] Male impersonation as a theatrical tradition extends back to the restoration stage, but more often than not, the trouser role was used to emphasize femininity rather than to mimic maleness. In "Glamour Drag and Male Impersonation," Laurence Senelick comments on the function of the breeches role as "a novelty" or as "a salacious turn" until the 1860s in America, when the male impersonator and the glamour drag artists brought to the stage "a plausible impression of sexes to which they did not belong."[6] Much male impersonation on the nineteenth-century stage involved a "boy" role in which a boyish woman represented an immature masculine subject; indeed, the plausible representation of mannishness by women was not encouraged. Because boys played women on the Shakespearean stage and women played boys on the nineteenth-century stage, some kind of role reversal symmetry seems to be in effect. But this role reversal actually masks the asymmetry of male and female impersonation. If boys can play girls and women, but women can play only boys, mature masculinity once again remains an authentic property of adult male bodies while all other gender roles are available for interpretation.

Male impersonation became an interesting phenomenon at the turn of the century in America with actors such as Annie Hindley developing huge female followings.[7] On and off the stage, cross-dressing women in the early twentieth century, from Annie Hindley to Radclyffe Hall, began a steady assault on the naturalness of male masculinity and began to display in public the signs and symbols of an eroticized and often (but not inevitably) politicized female masculinity. That some male impersonators carried over their cross-dressing practices into their everyday lives suggests that their relation to masculinity extended far beyond theatricality. Furthermore, the cross-dressing actress represents only the tip of the iceberg in terms of an emergent community of masculine-identified women.

The theatrical tradition of male impersonation continued and flourished for the first two decades of this century and then declined in popularity. After the passing of the 1933 Hollywood Motion Picture Production Code, which, as I discussed in my last chapter, banned all performances of so-called sexual perversion, male impersonation died out as a mainstream theatrical practice.[8] Some critics have traced the careers of one or two male impersonators such as Storme DeLaverie to show that pockets of male impersonation still existed within subcultural gay male drag culture between the 1930s and the 1960s. However, there is general agreement that no extensive drag king culture developed within lesbian bar culture to fill the void left by the disappearance of male impersonators from the mainstream theater. Indeed, Elizabeth Kennedy and Madeline Davis comment in their Buffalo oral histories that the masculinity constructed by butches in the 1940s and 1950s was accompanied by a "puzzling lack of camp."[9] Kennedy and Davis observe a notable lack of anything like drag king culture in the butch-femme bar world: "Few butches performed as male impersonators, and no cultural aesthetic seems to have developed around male impersonation" (75). Kennedy and Davis use the absence of a camp or drag aesthetic to caution against the conflation of gay and lesbian histories. The queen and the butch, they argue, do not share parallel histories. Like many other cultural commentators, Kennedy and Davis tend to attribute the lack of lesbian drag to the asymmetries of masculine and feminine performativity in a male supremacist society. Accordingly, because the business of survival as a butch woman is often predicated on one's ability to pass as male in certain situations, camp has been a luxury that the passing butch cannot afford.

While it seems very likely that the lack of a lesbian drag tradition has much to do with the need for butches to pass, at least one other reason that male impersonation did not achieve any general currency within lesbian bar culture must also be attributed to mainstream definitions of male masculinity as nonperformative. Indeed, current representations of masculinity in white men unfailingly depend on a relatively stable notion of the realness and the naturalness of both the male body and its signifying effects. Advertisements for Dockers pants and Jockey underwear, for example, appeal constantly to the no-nonsense aspect of masculinity, to the idea that masculinity "just is," whereas femininity reeks of the artificial. Indeed, there are very few places in American culture where male masculinity reveals itself to be staged or performative; when it does, however, the masculine masquerade appears quite fragile. In TV sitcoms such as

*Seinfeld,* for example, men apply comic pressure to the assumed natural-ness of maleness, and a truly messy, fragile, and delegitimized masculinity emerges. In one particularly memorable *Seinfeld* episode highlighting ab-ject male inadequacy, for example, George confesses to Jerry: "I always feel like lesbians look at me and say, 'That's the reason I am not into men!'" Such Woody Allenesque proclamations expose momentarily the instability of mainstream fictions of fortified male masculinities.

Outside of *Seinfeld,* unfortunately, white men derive enormous power from assuming and confirming the nonperformative nature of masculinity. For one thing, if masculinity adheres "naturally" and inevitably to men, then masculinity cannot be impersonated. For another, if the nonperfor-mance is part of what defines white male masculinity, then all performed masculinities stand out as suspect and open to interrogation. For example, gay male macho clones quite clearly exaggerate masculinity, and in them, masculinity tips into feminine performance. And the bad black gangsta rapper who bombastically proclaims his masculinity becomes a conve-nient symbol of male misogyny that at least temporarily exonerates less obviously misogynistic white male rock performances.[10] These clear differ-ences between majority and minority masculinities make the drag king act different for different women. For the white drag king performing conven-tional heterosexual maleness, masculinity has first to be made visible and theatrical before it can be performed. Masculinities of color and gay mascu-linities, however, have already been rendered visible and theatrical in their various relations to dominant white masculinities, and the performance of these masculinities presents a somewhat easier theatrical task. Further-more, although white masculinity seems to be readily available for parody by the drag kings, black masculinities or queer masculinities are often per-formed by drag kings in the spirit of homage or tribute rather than humor.

We call one of the most conventional forms of male neurosis "per-formance anxiety," and this term tells us everything about the strained relationship between heterosexual masculinity and performativity. Perfor-mance anxiety, of course, describes a particularly male, indeed hetero-sexual, fear of some version of impotence in the face of a demand for sexual interaction. In comic representations, performance anxiety is often depicted as "thinking about it too much" or "thinking instead of doing." Clearly, in such scenarios, the performance anxiety emerges when mascu-linity is marked as performative rather than natural, as if performativity and potency are mutually exclusive or at least psychically incompatible.

The anxiety that performance anxiety acts out, then, is not, as one might think, an anxiety about doing; it is a neurotic fear of exposing the theatricality of masculinity.[11]

"Drag" and "performance" have recently become key words within contemporary gender theory, and they are generally used to describe the theatricality of *all* gender identity. "Drag," as Esther Newton suggests, describes discontinuities between gender and sex or appearance and reality but refuses to allow this discontinuity to represent dysfunction. In a drag performance, rather, incongruence becomes the site of gender creativity. Newton also defines "camp" in relation to gay male practices and gay male humor. "Performance," of course, emerges out of Judith Butler's influential theory of gender trouble, in which she suggests that drag parodies "the notion of an original or primary gender identity" and that "the action of gender requires a performance which is repeated."[12] Butler also proposes that parodies of the notion of "true gender identities" emerge within "drag," "cross-dressing," and "butch/femme identities" (137). Butler's analysis, then, takes drag to be a gay male cultural practice and offers butch-femme as the lesbian equivalent. Because drag culture in both Butler's and Newton's analyses of gender theatricality is primarily related to gay male culture, and because it has a much more complicated relation to queer dyke cultural practices, do the very different histories of male and female impersonation produce very different notions of gender performance for male and female embodiment? If we recognize that drag has not traditionally been a part of lesbian bar culture and, furthermore, that masculinity tends to define itself as nonperformative, what are the implications for a general theory of the social production of gender? Is butch-femme really the equivalent gender parody to gay male drag? What is the impact of an emergent drag king culture on theories of gender performance?

In *Mother Camp*, Newton is quite clear on the point that gay men have "a much more elaborate subculture" than lesbians do, and she admits that the relative scarcity of male impersonators "presents important theoretical problems" (5). In a very recent essay, "Dick(less) Tracy and the Homecoming Queen," Newton returns to the scene of these "important theoretical problems" and ponders anew the problems of drag and camp in relation to a so-called butch-femme aesthetic. In "Dick(less) Tracy," Newton interrogates a renewed interest on the part of lesbian cultural critics into the practices and meanings of lesbian camp and lesbian drag, but like Kennedy and Davis, Newton cautions against easy "conflations of butch with drag (queen) and butch-femme with camp."[13] Newton is concerned that a queer formulation of camp based on contemporary butch-femme styles ignores the historical fact of a lack of camp cultures within the dyke bar culture of the fifties and sixties. "My own experience of butch-femme bar culture in the late fifties and sixties," writes Newton, "told me that butch-femme was not . . . ironic, not a camp, and certainly not, as Judith Butler had suggested, a parody, at least not then."[14] Newton, finally, calls for more attention to ethnographic and historical materials within the production of queer theories of gender and reminds us that "drag and camp are embedded in histories and power relations including when they are deployed in the theatrical venues so beloved in Cherry Grove, in the lesbian theatrical and film productions studies by performance theorists, or on the pages of academic journals" ("Dick(less) Tracy," 166). The drag performance that Newton goes on to analyze in this article is by a butch lesbian who dresses up as a drag queen and wins a drag contest in Cherry Grove. The appearance of a lesbian in a drag queen contest allows Newton to theorize the ways in which lesbians may deploy drag and camp "not to destabilize gender categories as such, but rather to destabilize male monopolies and to symbolize and constitute the power of the lesbian minority" (165–66).

For Newton, then, lesbian camp is a relatively recent phenomenon, and it is aimed at, and performed through, gay male monopolies. She resists the reading of camp back through a history of butch-femme. Lesbian scholars have vigorously debated the meanings of camp in relation to lesbian culture and while some theorize camp as readily available for lesbian appropriation,[15] others argue that it remains antithetical to lesbian representation.[16] In some accounts, camp becomes an essentially gay male aesthetic, in others it is lesbian, and more generally camp has been claimed as simply "queer." Newton specifies that she finds the conflation of butch-femme with drag and camp to be inherently problematic. Although I do not think that camp is unavailable to lesbian performers, I do think that because camp is predicated on exposing and exploiting the theatricality of gender, it tends to be the genre for an outrageous performance of femininity (by men or women) rather than outrageous performances of masculinity. Notice that when Newton extends her analysis of camp to a lesbian scene, she reads the performance of a butch performing as a drag queen, performing femininity, in other words. I think, therefore, that we can modify claims that camp cannot serve lesbians' theatrical endeavors and that it is always about male sexuality; perhaps it is more accurate to say that only lesbian performances of femininity can be inflected with camp because camp is always about femininity.

Performances of masculinity seem to demand a different genre of humor and performance. It is difficult to make masculinity the target of camp precisely because, as we have noted, masculinity tends to manifest as nonperformative. When drag king performances are campy, it is generally because the actor allows her femininity to inform and inflect the masculinity she performs. Performances of humorous masculinity demand another term, not only to distinguish them from the camp humor of femininity but also to avoid, as Newton warns, the conflation of drag and camp with butch-femme. I want to propose the term "kinging" for drag humor associated with masculinity, not because this is a word used by drag kings themselves but because I think that a new term is the only way to avoid always collapsing lesbian history and social practice associated with drag into gay male histories and practices. Accordingly, femme may well be a location for camp, but butch is not. For drag butches and drag kings who perform masculinity from a butch or masculine subject position, camp is not necessarily the dominant aesthetic. Some drag king performances, of course, may well contain a camp element, but the kinging effect, as I elaborate later, depends on several different strategies to render masculinity visible and theatrical.

The difference between men performing femininity and women performing masculinity is a crucial difference to mark out: the stakes in each are different, the performances look different, and there is a distinct difference between the relations between masculinity and performance and femininity and performance. To give one example of what I am saying about the difference between camp and kinging, I think it helps to examine an actual drag show. In a performance I saw at Club Casanova, the weekly drag king club in New York, in December 1996, the show combined both drag kings and drag queens onstage. The effect was startling. The four impersonators were performing as the B52's, and the two men in the band were played by drag kings Pencil Kase and Evil Cave Boy. The two women, with bouffant hairdos and five-inch heels, were played by drag queens: Miss Kitten played Kate, and Corvette played Cindy. While the drag queens bounced and bobbed, stumbled and slipped around the small stage, they almost blocked out the more understated drag kings. Evil Cave Boy as the lead singer, Fred, jumped up and down, but his performance was marked by restraint and containment; Pencil Kase similarly played down his role as Keith and sulked in the back with his air bass guitar.

The queens towered over the kings and barely restrained their impulses to take over the entire stage. The effect of placing drag femininity and drag masculinity side by side was positively vertiginous; on the one hand, the juxtaposition made clear the difference between a camp femininity and a very downplayed masculinity (an almost antitheatrical performance), and on the other hand, it made all gender unreadable. The kings were very convincing as men, and this made the drag queens more plausible despite the height differentials. A rather trendy bald person with shades and many visible piercings was standing next to me during the show, and after five minutes, this person called out: "I don't get it! Who are the men and who are the women?" It is a frequent event at Club Casanova for drag queens to take the stage with the drag kings, and their performances literally spill over into the drag king's careful and hilariously restrained acts, which are noticeably sincere, or, to use a Wildean term that tends to typify the very opposite of camp, "earnest." This is one part of what I call kinging: where all the emphasis is on a reluctant and withholding kind of performance.

While the spectacle of feminine and masculine drag onstage simultaneously allows for an interesting clash of gender-bending styles, the solo appearance of the drag king allows for an unusual confrontation between male and female masculinity and provides a rare opportunity for the wholesale parody of, particularly, white masculinity. The drag king performance, indeed, exposes the structure of dominant masculinity by making it theatrical and by rehearsing the repertoire of roles and types on which such masculinity depends. In the rest of this chapter, I outline the ways in which dominant forms of male masculinity manage to appear authentic and all other forms of masculinity are consequently labeled derivative. This relation is actually not reproduced within dominant femininities: as a film such as *Paris Is Burning* proved, much of what we understand to be original about female femininity already has been channeled through queer male bodies. The startling image of drag queen Willie Ninja teaching female models how to walk the catwalk in *Paris Is Burning* perhaps provides the best example of the lack of originality that we associate with female femininities. Another example of this would be recent films about young women such as *Clueless* (1995) and *Romy and Michelle's High School Reunion* (1997). In both films, the spectacle of exaggerated femininity creates a kind of heterosexual camp humor that depends totally on a prior construction of femininity by drag queens. This is particularly true in *Romy and Michelle's High School Reunion*, in which Lisa Kudrow and Mira

Sorvino, as the two women preparing for their reunion, present a spectacle of loud and outrageous femininity that is only made more camp and more evocative of a drag queen aesthetic because they are both very tall and tower over their classmates. Finally, the British TV show *Absolutely Fabulous* completely appropriates camp and drag queen motifs to portray the humorous lives of two middle-aged women in the design business. In all of these representations, humorous femininity is relayed through a gay male aesthetic. By way of comparison, it would be almost impossible to imagine a mainstream depiction of masculinity that acknowledged that it had been routed through lesbian masculinity.

The notion of female femininity as derivative, furthermore, echoes the wholesale depiction of lesbianism as epitomizing the derivative or unauthentic. According to such logic, butch lesbians are supposedly imitating men; femme lesbians are wanna-be drag queens, or else they are accused of blending seamlessly into heterosexual femininity; the androgynous lesbian has "borrowed" from both male and female; and the leather dyke or club girl parasitically draws from gay male leather culture. Drag king performances, however, provide some lesbian performers (although all drag kings are by no means lesbians) with the rare opportunity to expose the artificiality of all genders and all sexual orientations and therefore to answer the charge of inauthenticity that is usually made only about lesbian identity.

In one of the very few articles on the topic of contemporary drag kings, the notion of lesbian inauthenticity directs the author's line of inquiry. In "Dragon Ladies, Draggin' Men," an excellent introduction to the topic of lesbians and drag, Sarah Murray asks the question that lies behind most analyses of drag king culture, namely: "Why hasn't drag developed into a distinct theatrical genre among lesbians in the United States?"[17] She answers her own question by drawing on conventional notions of lesbian invisibility and by remarking on the "naturalization of the masculine." Murray states correctly, "a woman has less to grab on to when doing individual drag" (356). Obviously, my argument about the apparent stability of male masculinity concurs with Murray's analysis. I also agree with Murray that the forms of masculinity that are available for performance tend to be either working-class masculinities (the construction worker, for example), nonwhite masculinities, or explicitly performative middle-class masculinities such as the lounge lizard. However, where we diverge is on the topic of lesbian masculinities themselves. Murray, like some other cultural commentators on butch-femme, finds butch iconicity to be less about defining female masculinity and more about women appropriating male power. She reduces butchness to a historical marker of lesbian visibility that belongs to 1950s lesbian communities but not to contemporary queer dyke culture, and she suggests that lesbians, ultimately, "don't feel free to play with the masculine the way gay men play with the feminine" (360).

I would respond to these arguments by saying that it is crucial to recognize that masculinity does not belong to men, has not been produced only by men, and does not properly express male heterosexuality. A popular misunderstanding of lesbian butchness depicts it as either an appropriation of dominant male masculinity or an instance of false consciousness in which the butch simply lacks strong models of lesbian identity. I am trying to show in this chapter (and in this book in general) that what we call "masculinity" has also been produced by masculine women, gender deviants, and often lesbians. For this reason, it is inaccurate and indeed regressive to make masculinity into a general term for behavior associated with males. To argue, as Murray does, that women do not feel free to play with masculinity is to position masculinity as something separate from all lesbian women, something that they might play with or imitate, but not a quality that they may express or embody. Furthermore, butch identity has a historically complicated relation to notions of lesbian community, lesbian identity, and lesbian visibility, and, particularly, to lesbian drag. Because so little has been written about female masculinity that does not reduce it to a stereotype of the lesbian or a pathetic parody of maleness, we have yet to determine what its various relations might be to either lesbian, transgender, or masculine identification. In this book, I have argued that at times butchness is the privileged sign of lesbian identity, but at other moments, butchness represents the sign of gender inversion, which was rejected to craft a properly female and women-identified notion of lesbian identity. In recent years, furthermore, transgenderism (as I show in chapter 5) has altered the conditions for butch identification. In her article, Murray avoids any substantive discussion of transgenderism because it is really not part of her project to account for what happens when the drag is not a costume but part of an identity effect.[18] Butches, and transgender butches in particular, I propose by way of clarification, do not necessarily wear male clothing as drag; they embody masculinity.

Drag queens, it is often said, constantly walk a thin line between revering women and femininity and expressing pernicious misogyny; but what similar boundaries do drag kings traverse? Do drag kings softly tiptoe between admiring men and hating men? If so, what are the consequences? Is male impersonation more likely to be annexed to gender transgression than female impersonation? If so, what kind of transgression, what kind of gender? Following Carole-Anne Tyler's injunction to "read each instance of drag . . . symptomatically"[19] as opposed to simply asserting that each is either radical or conservative, I intend in what follows to break down drag king theater into its multiple performances and meanings, to distinguish between drag king shows and drag king contests, and to produce a taxonomy of drag king types in order to sort through the styles and performances of different women in drag.

## To Be Real: Drag King Culture, 1996

I want to proceed here from Esther Newton's suggestion that we contextualize theories of performance and queer theory in general with "ethnographically grounded social theory."[20] Newton warns against concentrating on "representational strategies" without "knowing the history of lesbian/gay male relations in the community and beyond." She queries: "How can intellectuals skip over this ethnographic step to broad abstractions and generalities without being guilty of a misleading (and reprehensible) imperialism ('Who cares what you think your representations mean, they mean what we say they do'). There is a balance to be struck between accepting the 'natives'' accounts at face value with no analysis, and discounting them completely as 'fictions' or useful only to an already determined theoretical agenda" (171). In my own research for this chapter, I have conducted interviews, talked to people in the clubs, visited many different clubs, and tried to ascertain the history and progress of each drag king space.

While I believe that this methodology is absolutely crucial to the project of charting the emergence of a nineties dyke drag king culture, I also think that interviews can be a frustrating obstacle to knowledge as much as they can produce important ethnographic information. I have no desire to force drag king representations into "an already determined theoretical agenda," but I have also become aware through the interview process that many performers are not necessarily that interested in the theoretical import of their acts or even in identifying a larger context. Many of the drag kings gave superficial answers to questions such as "Why do you like to

Figure 30. "Judith 'Jack' Halberstam," by Del Grace (1997). Photo courtesy of the artist.

dress up in drag?" They might answer, "Just for fun," or, "It seemed like a crazy thing to do," or, "I didn't really think about it." Obviously, such answers do not really convey any interesting or useful information about drag and its motivations, nor do they get to the "truth" of the drag king scene. Other methodological problems involved a level of what I can only describe as "butch-phobia" among the New York drag kings whom I interviewed. Even drag kings who wore drag on- and offstage and who had very boyish or mannish appearances would not identify as butch. The scarcity of drag kings willing to identify as butch, as Newton might say, "presents important theoretical problems." On account of the difficulties associated with the interview process, I have blended information I have obtained from the drag kings with my own observations and theoretical framings. Moreover, I do not consider myself to be completely outside the drag king culture I am depicting here. Although I have never performed as a drag king, I always attend the club in what is received as "drag" (suit and tie, for example), even though I do not wear male clothing as drag. I have been photographed and interviewed at the clubs as a drag king despite my nonappearance onstage. This blending of onstage drag and offstage masculinity suggests that the line between male drag and female masculinity in a drag king club is permeable and permanently blurred.

There are two main arenas of drag that I focus on here: first, a series of drag king contests that took place over the course of a year at Hershe Bar, and second, the regular drag king shows that take place weekly at Club Casanova. The drag king contests in New York paid cash prizes and often attracted nonwhite and non-middle-class audiences and participants. They were marked by a notable lack of theatricality and camp and depended utterly on notions of masculine authenticity rather than impersonations of maleness. As we shall see, the Hershe Bar contests and the Club Casanova shows produce very different forms of drag king culture, although there are multiple sites of intersection and overlap between the kings who participated in the contests and the kings who perform in the clubs.

### The 1995–1996 Hershe Bar Drag King Contests

On the night I attended my first drag king contest, I was asked on my way into the club whether I would like to compete. I thought long and hard about this question but said finally, "No thanks, I don't have an act." As it turned out, neither did any of the other drag kings, but this did not stop them from going onstage. I took my place in the audience and waited for the show. The club, Hershe Bar, was packed with a very diverse crowd, and the show was the center of the evening's entertainment. Finally the lights dimmed, and the evening's emcee, lesbian comic Julie Wheeler, took the stage in her own Tony Las Vegas drag and began the evening by performing an Elvis song. Soon afterward, ten drag kings filed out in various states of dress and flaunted many different brands of masculine display. Like champion bodybuilders, the drag kings flexed and posed to the now wildly cheering audience: the winner was to receive prize money of $200, and she earned the right to compete in the grand finale for a prize of $1,000. The show was a huge success in terms of producing a spectacle of alternative masculinities; however, it was ultimately a big letdown in terms of the performative. The drag kings, generally speaking, seemed to have no idea of how to perform as drag kings, and when called on to "do something," one after the other just muttered his name. When compared to the absolutely exaggerated performances featured within drag queen shows, these odd moments of drag king stage fright read as part of a puzzle around masculine performativity. While certainly part of the drag king stage fright had to do with the total lack of any prior role models for drag king performance, and while certainly this inertia has been replaced in recent months by lavish drag king acts, at least in these early contests, the stage fright was also a sign of the problem of masculine nonperformativity. The drag kings had not yet learned how to turn masculinity into theater. There were other contributing factors at work, though, including that many of the women onstage seemed to be flaunting their own masculinity rather than some theatrical imitation of maleness.

The drag king contest is a difficult scene to read because we need a taxonomy of female masculinities to distinguish carefully between the various types of identification and gender acts on display. I would like, therefore, to spend some time charting some of the masculine gender variations within the drag king contests. My models are quite particular to the contests and have not necessarily carried over into the regular performances. Drag king contests, it is worth noting, function less like traditional drag queen shows and have more in common with the various performances staged by the queens in *Paris Is Burning*. Like the Harlem balls documented in this film, these drag king contests had a cash prize and drew a largely black and Latino pool of contestants. Unlike the ball scene, the drag king events do not necessarily open out into an elaborate culture of gay houses and sex work.[21]

There are many different genres of masculine performance on display in the drag king contest, so many, in fact, that the performances tend to be incommensurable and therefore difficult to judge. For the reader to understand the kinds of performances I am describing here, this section includes photographic images of various drag kings, most of which were taken by New York–based artist Betsey Gallagher (aka drag king Murray Hill). Gallagher began an art project on drag king culture in the spring of 1996 as a development of an earlier project on drag queens. It soon became apparent to her that the drag kings she was photographing had a very different set of visual codes and gender systems than the drag queens. To capture something of the particularity of the drag king contest, Gallagher took posed, rather than action, shots of her drag king models. This creates a quiet, almost deadpan effect and emphasizes the continuities between being and performing for these drag kings. With the aid of these images, I want to outline at least five different forms of masculine performance at work in the drag king contest.

### Butch Realness

In the drag king contests, the winner would very often be a biological female who was convincing in her masculinity (sometimes convincing meant she could easily pass as male, but sometimes it meant her display of a recognizable form of female masculinity). It is not so easy to find photographic images for this category because many of the "butch realness" participants did not necessarily identify as drag kings and thus did not want to be photographed for a drag king project. To describe the "convincing" aspect of the butch realness look, then, I offer the example of the contestant who won on the first night I attended Hershe Bar. The butch who won was a very muscular black woman wearing a basketball shirt and shorts. In her "sports drag" and with her display of flexed muscles, the contestant could easily have passed as male, and this made her "convincing." This contestant won through her display of an authentic or unadorned and unperformed masculinity; she was probably a walk-on rather than someone who prepared elaborately for the contest. Interestingly enough, the category of butch realness is often occupied by nonwhite drag kings, attesting specifically to the way that masculinity becomes visible as masculinity once

Figure 31. Butch Realness. "Sean," by Betsey Gallagher (1995). Photo courtesy of the artist.

it leaves the sphere of normative white maleness. Furthermore, the relative invisibility of white female masculinity may also have to do with a history of the cultivation of an aesthetic of androgyny by white middle-class lesbians. The white drag kings in this particular contest were at something of a loss: they were not at all performative in the way some of the black and latino drag kings were (dancing and rapping) and tended to wear tuxedos as part of their drag king look. Every now and then, a white drag king would attempt a construction worker aesthetic or strike a James Dean pose.

Figure 31 shows another version of butch realness. This young Asian American drag king was utterly convincing in her masculinity, so much so that women were challenging whether she was "really a woman." This drag king had no performance and relied on some version of authenticity to win her competition: in this shot, we see her with a small fake mustache and beard, but in subsequent contests, she appeared with no facial hair and generated the same response. Because of its reliance on notions of authenticity and the real, the category of butch realness is situated on the sometimes vague boundary between transgender and butch definition. The realness of the butch masculinity can easily tip, in other words, into the desire for a more sustained realness in a recognizably male body. There is no clear way of knowing how many of the drag kings at this club had any transgender modes of identification, and because the whole show took place under the auspices of a lesbian club, one might assume that most identified at least in some way with the label of dyke or lesbian.

One way of describing the relationship between butch realness and male masculinity is in terms of what José Muñoz has called an active disidentification, or "a mode of dealing with dominant ideology, one that neither opts to assimilate within such a structure nor strictly opposes it."[22] Similarly, within butch realness, masculinity is neither assimilated into maleness nor opposed to it; rather it involves an active disidentification with dominant forms of masculinity, which are subsequently recycled into alternative masculinities.

### Femme Pretender

Butch realness is clearly opposed to femme drag king performances. These may be termed "femme pretender" performances, and they look more like drag queen shows, not simply because the disjuncture between biological sex and gender is the basis for the gender act but because irony and camp flavor the performance. In figure 32, Gallagher captures the elements of the

Figure 32. Femme Pretender. "Chico Soda," by Betsey Gallagher (1996). Photo courtesy of the artist.

femme pretender look as cultivated by Chico Soda, a New York performer who uses the drag king stage as part of her act. You can see from the photograph that the "disguise" of heavy eyebrows and a goatee are deliberately overdone, and Chico Soda's pose is deliberately, loudly theatrical and even parodic rather than quietly naturalistic like the previous shots. Another femme pretender who has garnered much attention in New York is Buster Hymen. Hymen has a song-and-dance act and often disrobes halfway through and transforms herself into a lounge kitten. Clearly, the performance is all about transformation, and it capitalizes on the idea that, as Newton puts it, "the appearance is an illusion." [23] Whereas a few male drag performers create drag drama by pulling off their wigs or dropping their voices a register or two, the femme pretender often blows her cover by exposing her breasts or ripping off her suit in a parody of classic striptease.

One or two femme pretenders would appear in every drag king contest, and their performances often revolved around a consolidation of femininity rather than a disruption of dominant masculinity. The femme pretender actually dresses up butch or male only to show how thoroughly her femininity saturates her performance—she performs the failure of her own masculinity as a convincing spectacle. These performances tend to be far more performative than butch realness ones, but possibly less interesting for the following reasons: first, the femme drag king has not really altered the structure of drag as it emerged within gay male contexts as camp; second, the femme pretender offers a reassurance that female masculinity is just an act and will not carry over into everyday life. Many femme drag kings talk about the power they enjoy in accessing masculinity through a drag act, but they return ultimately to how confirmed they feel in their femininity. Ultimately, femme drag kings tend to use drag as a way to, as Buster Hymen puts it, "walk both sides of the gender fence,"[24] and this tends to reassert a stable binary definition of gender. It is worth noting that the drag kings who have managed to garner the most publicity tend to be the femme pretenders.[25] Even some gay male writers who are conversant with the gender-bending tactics of drag tend to identify all drag kings as femme drag king. Michael Musto, in an article on drag kings for the *New York Post*, concluded his piece with a reassurance for his straight readers: he notes that very butch looking drag king Mo B. Dick "happens to love lipstick as much as any girl."[26]

### Male Mimicry

In male mimicry, the drag king takes on a clearly identifiable form of male masculinity and attempts to reproduce it, sometimes with an ironic twist and sometimes without. In one of the few performances of white masculinity at the Hershe Bar shows, for example, a drag king contestant performed a mock priest act that had the nice effect of exposing the theatricality of religion. Male mimicry is often at work in the femme pretender performances but actually can be performed by butches or femmes. It is the concept of male mimicry that props up an enterprise such as Diane Torr's Drag King Workshop. Although the workshop takes us a little off the topic of the drag king contests, the concept of male mimicry as produced by the workshops did influence some of the white contestants in the Hershe Bar contests. Indeed, many news articles attribute the origins of New York drag king culture to Diane Torr (as does Torr herself), and some drag kings such as Buster Hymen credit Torr with inspiring them to begin performing.[27] Diane Torr is a New York–based performance artist

Figure 33. Male Mimicry. "Diane Torr," by Betsey Gallagher (1996). Photo courtesy of the artist.

who, as Danny Drag King, runs a workshop in which women can become men for a day.[28] Torr's workshop advertisement tells potential participants that they can "explore another identity—you will learn the basic male behavioral patterns. How to walk, sit, talk and lie down like a man."[29] In the workshop, which has been written up in many different magazines and newspapers and filmed for the BBC, Torr instructs her students in the manly arts of taking up space, dominating conversations, nose picking, and penis wearing, and she gives them general rudeness skills. Torr's students become men for the day by binding and jockey stuffing, and then she shows them how to apply facial hair and create a credible male look. Finally, Torr takes her charges out into the mean streets of New York City and shows them how to pass. Torr herself articulates no particular masculine aspirations; she, like many of her workshop participants, avows over and over that she has no desire to *be* a man; she just wants to pass as a man within this limited space of experimentation.[30] Torr says that her reasons for cross-dressing are quite clear; she wants to experience "male authority and territory and entitlement."[31] Many workshop women discuss the feeling of power and privilege to which the masquerade gives them access, and many are titillated by the whole thing but relieved at the end of the day to return to a familiar femininity.

One account of the drag king workshop describes it as a spin on the everyday practice of gender performance. Shannon Bell claims to be what we might call "a gender queen," someone who plays butch one day and femme the next.[32] She used the Drag King Workshop to explore one of her many genders, her queer fag self. Obviously, this sense of gender as costume and voluntary performance is not at all related to the butch realness mode of female masculinity. Bell plays gender like a game precisely because her gender normativity provides a stable base for playing with alterity. Bell represents the typical workshop participant in that she understands its function as an exercise in gender fluidity and a political exposé of male privilege. Bell asks Torr why people take the workshop, and Torr provides a political justification intended to make the workshop respectable within the terms of feminist consciousness: "Part of what happens at the Drag King Workshop is that women learn certain things: we don't have to smile, we don't have to concede ground, we don't have to give away territory" (96). In this way, the workshop functions rather like a feminist consciousness-raising group but seems to have very little to do with the reconstruction of masculinity.

Diane Torr goes so far as to claim that she invented the term "drag king," and she tells interviewer Amy Linn: "It came to me in about 1989. . . . It was a day that I had done a photo shoot in male clothes, and I had an opening to go to at the Whitney. I decided to go dressed as a man."[33] When Torr found herself easily passing and receiving much attention from women, she decided to make this defamiliarizing experience available to women in the form of a workshop for assertiveness training. The workshop, obviously, has little to do with drag kings or kinging. It is a simple lesson in how the other half lives, and it usefully opens a window on male privilege for women who suffer the effects of such privilege every day. As I suggested earlier, however, it is hard to lay claim to the term "drag king," and certainly we would not want to attribute the origins of modern drag king culture to a workshop that is primarily designed for heterosexual women and unproblematically associates masculinity with maleness. For masculine women who walk around being mistaken for men every day, the workshop has no allure. The Drag King Workshop emphasizes for me the divide between a fascination in male masculinity and its prerogatives and an interest in the production of alternate masculinities.

### Fag Drag

Like other forms of minority masculinity, gay male masculinity stands apart from mainstream formulations of maleness and is very available for drag king imitation. Furthermore, some lesbians in recent years have positively fetishized gay male sex culture, and some women base their masculinity and their sex play on gay male models. This may mean copying a gay male aesthetic such as the "Castro clone." The Castro clone refers to a popular masculine aesthetic within urban gay ghettos that depends on leather and denim and a queer biker look. That the image is already identified as a clone suggests that imitation and impersonation are already part of its construction; this makes it easy for drag kings to take on fag drag. Some of the drag kings in the Hershe Bar contest cultivated a gay male look with leather or handlebar mustaches, and they often routed these looks through a Village People type of performance of hypermasculinity.

### Denaturalized Masculinity

Last in my taxonomy of female masculinities, I want to identify a category that often disappears into the other categories I have outlined. Denaturalized masculinity plays on and within both butch realness and male mimicry but differs from butch realness in its sense of theatricality and hyperbole and remains distinct from male mimicry by accessing some alternate mode of the masculine. In figure 34, we see Dred, who won the 1996 Hershe Bar contest, pulling off a tribute to blaxploitation macho with a butch twist. Dred is an interesting drag king because she plays the line between the many different versions of drag king theater. On the one hand, she appears in the bar contests heavily made up as Superfly; on the other hand, she also plays in staged drag king theatrical performances in a much more campy role in which she metamorphs from Superfly to Foxy Brown. Then again, she regularly performs with another drag king, Shon, as part of rap duo Run DMC. Dred represents the fluid boundaries between the many different drag king performances. I include her in my section on denaturalized masculinity because she combines appropriation, critique, and alternative masculinity in her presentation.

Denaturalized masculinity in many ways produces the most successful

Figure 34. Denaturalized Masculinity. "Dred," by Betsey Gallagher (1996). Photo courtesy of the artist.

drag king performances. In Julie Wheeler's act as Tony Las Vegas, the emcee for the drag king contest, for example, she wore slicked-back hair and a lounge suit. Tony made sleazy asides throughout the contest, and in the show I was at, he moved in way too close on a drag king who was clearly a femme pretender, breathing in her ear and asking what she had on under her suit. He periodically called out to the audience, "Show us yer tits," and generally made a spectacle of slimy masculinity and misogyny. Whereas the Drag King Workshop mimics maleness without necessarily parodying it, Tony makes male parody the center of his act by finding the exact mode in which male masculinity most often appears as performance: sexism and misogyny. The drag king demonstrates through her own masculinity and through the theatricalization of masculinity that there are no essential links between misogyny and masculinity: rather, masculinity seems bound to misogyny structurally in the context of patriarchy and male privilege. For masculine women who cannot access male privilege, the rewards of misogyny are few and far between, and so she is very likely to perform her masculinity without misogyny. But sexism makes for good theater, and the exposure of sexism by the drag king as the basis of masculine realness serves to unmask the ideological stakes of male nonperformativity.

While the drag king contest makes a perfect arena for the denaturalization of masculinity, assaults on natural gender and on the redundancy of the nature-nurture binary are appearing regularly in popular culture. For example, a great example of denaturalized identification was featured as a comic device in the 1995 movie *Babe*. This film tells the story of the little pig who wants to be a sheepdog partly because he realizes that pigs get eaten on the farm and dogs don't, and partly because all his primary connections and identifications are with dogs. *Babe* depicts the triumph of function over form when the pig, Babe, proves to be a better sheepdog than a sheepdog. The success of Babe's dog performance depends on assumption of the role "dog" with a difference. Babe does not merely mimic the chief sheepdog or try to look like a dog; he appropriates dogness, learns dog functions, and performs them. Whereas the master sheepdog presumes his superiority over the sheep, Babe refuses to construct a new hierarchy or to preserve natural hierarchies; instead, he proves his willingness and ability to herd and shows proper respect for the sheep and above all takes pleasure in his dogness. This film remarks on the comic disarticulation of dogness from dogs and suggests that the logic of the unnatural allows for pigs to be dogs, and in a moving subplot, it even allows ducks to be cocks or roosters.

## The Drag King Show

The drag king contests at Hershe Bar set the stage for the proliferation of drag king nightclub culture in New York City. Although performance artists such as Diane Torr remind us that drag king culture has existed on and off for the last decade or so in New York performance spaces, drag kings have never generated the subcultural life and popularity that they now enjoy. After the drag king contests, many of the contestants disappeared back into lesbian club life, but many others regrouped and took on drag king performances as a regular act. Drag king Mo B. Dick recalls that the Hershe Bar contests identified a pool of potential drag king performers, and she capitalized on this moment of exposure by holding drag king parties. Mo recalls: "I started doing parties with Michael, better known as Misstress Formika, and then we decided to host a drag king contest. It was so successful that we decided then and there, with Misstress Formika's help, knowledge, and inspiration, to start a drag king club, and Club Casanova was born."[34]

Club Casanova may well be the only weekly drag king club in the country. It is an East Village club catering to a mostly white, punk, alternative crowd that combines gay and straight, queens and kings, and it is often packed with media representatives. The women of color who competed in the Hershe Bar contests have not, for the most part, reemerged in the drag king club scene. The 1996 winner, Dred, does perform regularly at Club Casanova and other lesbian bars, and she sometimes performs alongside another black drag king, Shon, but there is definitely a muted presence of women of color on the drag king scene. In the Hershe Bar contests, many of the women of color who competed, as I suggested, were not necessarily making themselves into drag kings; they were going onstage and parading their own masculinity. This may be one reason that many of the winners of the contests have not become drag king performers.[35] Another reason may be the usual divisions of race and class that produce segregation in most urban lesbian bar scenes.[36]

Although few of the women I interviewed about drag kings had much to say directly in response to the question of why so few women of color seemed to get involved in the drag king shows, many of the women had very contrary memories and opinions about the Hershe Bar contests. Obviously, I personally found the Hershe Bar contests to be very entertaining and full of the spectacle of dyke masculinity. But many of the white women

who competed in the contests found them dissatisfying. Mo B. Dick compares them to a popularity contest or a beauty contest: "If the crowd liked
your look, you won," she notes, "if they didn't, you lost." Mo B. Dick felt
annoyed that so many of the women in the contests were not drag kings
but just "very butch women." Performance artist and occasional drag king
Shelly Mars was a judge of some of the Hershe Bar contests. Mars also felt
the contests were uninteresting: "The first one was ridiculous—no one got
dressed up to do drag. Also, it is a black and Latina place, so if you are a
white girl, you are not going to win." Indeed, few white women did win
the Hershe Bar contests, and while this may have much to do with the fact
that the club's clientele was mostly black and Latina, it also says something
about the performance of white masculinity and masculinities of color.
Much white drag king performance revolves around parody and humor,
and much black drag king performance has to do with imitation and appropriation; whereas a white drag king might parody a macho guy from
Brooklyn (as Mo B. Dick does), a black drag king tends to lip-synch to a
rap song or perform as a mackdaddy or playboy or pimp character (as Dred
does), not to parody, but to appropriate black masculine style for a dyke
performance. In the context of a contest, the genre of sexy appropriations
of male masculinity went over much better than the genre of quick parody.

Some of the best white drag king performances and shows, however, do
evolve out of a creative and hyperbolic parody. Every week, Club Casanova
becomes the scene of new and outrageous drag king performances. One
week the flyers for Club Casanova advertised an Elvis night: Elvis impersonators could get in free, and the crowd was to be treated to not one but
three performances of Elvis, all done by different drag kings. That night,
the tension built as the crowd prepared for what must be a special event in
the world of male impersonation: the kinging of the King. The first Elvis,
performed by Justin Kase, enacted the early Elvis. Kase, with slicked-back
hair and a curled lip, sang "Blue Suede Shoes." The next Elvis took on the
leather-clad, jet-black-hair look of the King's middle years. Lizerace, the
drag king deejay at Club Casanova, performed this sixties Elvis with much
hip wagging and sultry looks at the crowd. Finally, drag king Murray Hill
stepped up to capture the King in his golden years. Hill wore a tight white
jumpsuit with sequins and the requisite monster upright collar. He wore
dark shades and sweated profusely despite the towel around his neck. As
the first bars of "I Can't Help Falling in Love with You" swelled in the
background, the fat Elvis jumped back and missed his cue to start singing.

Figure 35. "Who Loves You Baby? Murray Hill as the Puffy Elvis," by Matthew Sandager (1997). Photo courtesy of the artist.

This hilariously bloated performance of Elvis at his gorgeous, puffy best captures what in drag queen culture has been called "camp" but what I am renaming here as "kinging."[37] Although earlier I identified one mode of kinging as an earnest performance of masculinity, here the kinging mode is realized through the impersonation of impersonation. This kinging effect is hilariously used by drag kings in San Francisco, where the success of Elvis Herselvis has spawned Elvis Herselvis impersonators.

It seems very important to hold on to the differences between drag kings and drag queens. Within the theater of mainstream gender roles, femininity is often presented as simply costume whereas masculinity manifests as realism or as body. In her study of female impersonators, Newton describes the way that drag queens create plausible impressions of femininity through the use of props (wigs, dresses, jewelry, makeup, hormones) and through "role playing" (*Mother Camp,* 109). Similarly, drag kings produce a plausible masculinity using suits, crotch stuffers, facial hair, and greased hair. In general, however, the theatrical performance of masculinity demands a paring down of affect and a reduction in the use of props. Drag king Maureen Fischer, for example, describes how she produces drag masculinity: "The way a woman moves is more fluid and sexy, and a man is much more tight and restrained. When I perform Mo B. Dick onstage, I have to be very conscious of my movements. Usually I move around a lot, but as a man I am much more rigid, and I hold my body a certain way, and it's much stiffer in the torso, and there's no wiggle in the hips." [38] The production of gender in the case of both the drag queen and the drag king is theatrical, but the theatrics almost move in opposite directions. Whereas the drag queen expands and becomes flamboyant, the drag king constrains and becomes quietly macho. If the drag queen gesticulates, the drag king learns to convey volumes in a shrug or a raised eyebrow. The drag king shows at Club Casanova have provided many examples of what I call "kinging," or performing nonperformativity. To "king" a role can involve a number of different modes, including understatement, hyperbole, and layering.

*Understatement.* Kinging can signify assuming a masculine mode in all its understatement, even as the performance exposes the theatricality of understatement. An example of this mode would be the drag king who performs his own reluctance to perform through an "aw shucks" shy mode that cloaks his entire act. In the B52's performance that I described earlier, understatement characterized the drag king roles as they interacted with the far more frenetic drag queens.

*Hyperbole.* Finding the exact form of masculine hyperbole can constitute another form of kinging. In the Elvis performances that I discuss, the fat Elvis played by Murray Hill clearly captured masculine hyperbole. By performing the older Elvis, Hill played Elvis playing Elvis. While femme hyperbole plays on the outrageous artificiality already embedded in social constructions of femininity, masculine hyperbole imitates itself. Murray Hill, indeed, is the master of hyperbole. His repertoire includes a range of middle-aged male icons, and Murray satirizes and parodies the forms of masculinity that these men are supposed to represent. For example, as Bela Karolyi, the Olympic women's gymnastics coach, Murray Hill parodies the image of benevolent paternalism that the coach represents. In a hyperbolic performance of Karolyi urging little Kerri Strug to make a vault despite her wounded leg, Murray yells "You can do it!" at a limping Kerri (played by Murray's drag girl sidekick Penny Tuesdae). Murray then tells Kerri that if she makes the vault, he will let her eat, and finally he gropes Kerri and then rips her gold medal off her neck and begins celebrating his own victory. Murray Hill also performs as John Travolta.

The impact of Murray Hill's hyperbolic performance is to expose the

Figure 36. "Murray Hill as Bela Karolyi and Penny Tuesdae as Kerri Strug," by Tanya Braganti (1997). Photo courtesy of the artist.

vulnerability of male midlife crisis. Murray uses very little makeup and relies mostly on clothing to convey the image of masculinity that she parodies. She does not bind her breasts and makes no attempt to create male realness. In her most recent drag king endeavor, Murray Hill ran for mayor on the slogan "A Vote for Murray Is a Vote for You." Murray campaigned with flyers of Mayor Giuliani in drag and highlighted the hypocrisy of Giuliani's trying to shut down certain queer clubs when he paraded in public in drag. Murray announces: "Mayor Giuliani has decided that only he can do drag shows." Murray pronounced himself the "nightlife candidate" and urged voters to work together to save New York's endangered nightlife.

*Layering.* When a drag king performs as a recognizable male persona (Sinatra, Elvis, Brando), she can choose to allow her femaleness to peek through, as some drag queens do in a camp act, or she can perform the role almost seamlessly. In these seamless acts, the reason that the performance looks "real" is because if the audience sees through the role at all, they catch a glimpse not of femaleness or femininity but of a butch masculinity. So the male role is layered on top of the king's own masculinity. Drag kings such as Justin Kase or San Francisco's Annie Toon and Elvis

Herselvis build their acts precisely by layering a masculine performance over a butch appearance. This form of layering often produces a very sexy drag king act that encourages lesbian audiences to applaud not the maleness they see but the dyke masculinities that peek through. Dred and Shon's rhythm and blues acts are often greeted by a crowd of screaming fans. Shon comments on this response precisely by remarking on layering: "Well, I like getting the reaction from the women, the screaming and all that. . . . They like the show, more than I would think. . . . I didn't expect them to be this into a male image. But then I don't think it's really about that, it's about the person the image is connected to, really."[39]

Layering really describes the theatricality of both drag queen and drag king acts and reveals their multiple ambiguities because in both cases the role playing reveals the permeable boundaries between acting and being; the drag actors are all performing their own queerness and simultaneously exposing the artificiality of conventional gender roles. As Newton puts it: "Female impersonators are both performing homosexuals and homosexual performers" (*Mother Camp*, 20). Most of the female impersonators interviewed by Newton were gay and made connections between gay life and drag life; in the case of male impersonators, however, the relationship between their drag acts and their sexual orientations is less clear. Many of the drag kings performing in New York, at least, are lesbians; some are straight, and others are transgendered. Obviously the drag king act, with its emphasis on costume and makeup, disguise and transformation, produces a certain amount of curiosity about what is under the suit. Although many queer king club goers indulge in fantasies of dominant masculinity layered over queer masculinity, mainstream coverage of the scene tends to evince the sincere hope that even though girls will be boys, they will eventually return to being very attractive girls. Indeed, nothing brings more satisfaction to mainstream observers of the world of gender bending than the kind of pseudo–drag king spread featuring Demi Moore in a recent issue of the men's magazine *Arena*. Demi wore a small goatee that she had made in authentic drag king style by gluing pieces of her own hair to her face, but as she glowered for the camera, she ripped open her shirt to reveal her bounteous breasts. The whole photo spread gave "redundant" new meaning: her bodice-ripping act suggested, of course, that her unveiling would dispel the mystery created by her facial hair, but truth be told, she was not so convincing anyway as a man.

Some drag kings such as Dred and Buster Hymen, for example, will also strip down to reveal the woman behind the man. Performance artist Bridge Markham tries to take this one step further by taking the stage in full female drag and then stripping all the way down to a G-string and nipple tape. Ripping off her wig to reveal an oddly androgynous bald pate, she begins a reverse strip and remakes herself onstage as a drag king now complete with eyeliner, mustache, and a dildo thrown casually into her handkerchief pocket. Bridge's act plays off the standard drag queen move in which the drag queen pulls off her wig to reveal that she is truly a man. In Bridge's act and others like it, the idea is to resist revelation and insist that each layer is as unreal as the last. In a humorous and indeed raunchy rendition of the reverse strip, London drag king Jewels performs a gyrating striptease in which he pulls off his hat, his jacket, his shirt, and finally his trousers to reveal . . . another shirt, another pair of trousers, another male costume. Jewels's antistrip parodies the notion that a true feminine self lies just beneath the masculine surface and can be accessed in a few deft moves.

Some drag performers object to the striptease as part of the drag act. The Club Confidential organizers, Stafford and Jordy, have pretty firm ideas about drag king performance, and they identify bad drag king theater as a combination of lack of planning, wearing bad shoes, and doing "butch striptease."[40] Mo B. Dick also indicates her disapproval, saying that it takes far more concentration "to stay in character" than to disrupt the drag character. She also comments that "stripping gets tired, and it also appeals to some voyeuristic tendency. . . . It's too easy to strip and be a girl, for God's sake, you're a girl every day." Mo B. Dick summarizes: "The drag king persona is quite difficult to take on and maintain, and somehow the strip act diminishes that effort." Dred explains her striptease as a way of representing the full spectrum of her gender display. Dred says that the strip lets people know "that I am a woman in drag, I think it is powerful to show that." However, Dred also acknowledges that it is not always so easy to prove this point. On an appearance that she made on the Maury Povitch show, Dred was onstage with other drag queens and kings, but s/he was dressed as a drag queen with a big wig. When she stood up and pulled the wig off to reveal her bald head, the audience thought she was revealing that she was "really" a man, and they loved it. When Povitch explained that Dred was a drag king and not a drag queen, the audience was confused and could not believe that Dred was female. Other audiences, of course, are a lot more sophisticated and can read multiple code shiftings from male to female, from one brand of masculinity to another (from superfly to soul man), from tough drag king to sexy stripper.[41]

So if the striptease in the drag king act reveals nothing about sex or gender, about real selves or authentic bodies, where do we look for the real or for something like identity? Identity proved to be a very difficult question for many drag kings to answer. Many drag kings in New York felt that drag gave them the chance to really play with gender in a way that expressed a wide range of identities. Few of the Club Casanova kings would identify themselves as butch offstage, and many talked about themselves as androgynous or even femme. Lizerace, the twenty-three-year-old drag king deejay at Club Casanova, calls herself "androgynous" and says this label gives her "more space to maneuver."[42] Dred, twenty-five, says of her offstage persona: "I'm not butch or femme, just whatever I'm feeling right then. I don't have a type of woman I go out with, either. I do have a lot of masculine energy, but I also like people knowing that I am a woman in drag." Evil Cave Boy, a twenty-seven-year-old performance artist, echoes these sentiments: "Sometimes I'm very masculine, sometimes very feminine depending on my situation; I go back and forth all the time."[43] Evil Cave Boy elaborates her gender position further by comparing herself to "a freak, a muse, a joker, a clown." Performer and actor Shelly Mars, who is thirty-six years old, also feels that she is some combination of masculine, feminine, performer, and "changer": "I change all the time—drag king is just a joke term for me. I'm a girl-boy, a tomboy, a changer, a performer." Like Evil Cave Boy, Mars articulates a very literally performative sense of her gender—it changes because she changes roles and characters constantly. To occupy a stable persona, for Mars or Evil Cave Boy, would mean renouncing their commitment to the theatricality and mobility of all roles. Fluidity, indeed, seems to define many of these drag kings' relations to gender expression, and few of them articulate a sense of feeling definitively bound to a category or a mode of expression.

It needs to be said that some of these women who refuse to have the label "butch" attached to them personally actually have quite masculine appearances. Lizerace is very boyish, and she cultivates a masculine persona offstage. When pushed on the issue of her butchness, Lizerace admits that she doesn't identify as butch because she feels she cannot "live up to the label." Another drag king who has a semimasculine appearance, Shon, aged twenty-nine, gives herself a more complicated label: "I am an aggressive femme. I am not going to say that the masculinity I perform is not a part of me, but I also have a feminine side." For Shon, the label "butch" does not adequately address the fact that she feels her femininity or femaleness is an important part of who she is. Shon, however, drives women quite wild in drag, and when she performs with Dred in their rhythm and blues show, she is a devastatingly convincing performer and male impersonator who endows her act with a smooth sexiness. "If I were a guy, I'd be a gentleman," Shon tells me. "I'd always sit with my legs crossed, I'd be very suave, very cool, a kind of quiet storm." The idiosyncratic term "quiet storm" perhaps hints at the kind of gender variance that Shon names as "aggressive femme"; what she produces here is a phrase that would express both her strong masculine appeal and her female embodiment. Shon rejects the label "butch," feeling that it doesn't describe her particular masculine blend.[44]

One New York drag king expresses an affirmative connection to the labels "butch" and "transgender." She is a twenty-eight-year-old drag king who goes by the names Retro and Uncle Louis and calls herself a "transgender Asian Pacific Islander." She comments that she often passes as a man, even at her workplace. Retro thinks that it is quite unusual to be out as a butch or transgender Asian woman, and she says that "many Asian dykes tend to identify as femme." Retro also suggests that "butch" carries a certain stigma among the New York drag kings and that few women, even those who really are butch, will identify with that term. She also notes that there is little to no transgender presence within the New York scene, and she comments on the difference in this regard between San Francisco and New York. Ultimately, however, Retro emphasizes that the New York drag scene offers a safe space for gender experimentation: "If a femme girl comes to the club femme one week, in a mustache the next, and even more in drag the next week, people will encourage that and be supportive of even straight women trying out their drag personas."[45]

The drag scenes in New York, London, and San Francisco, at least, are growing and branching out all the time. I know of at least one performer in New York, Murray Hill, who regularly performs for straight audiences at a heterosexual singles bar. But the rest of the drag king shows are confined to queer spaces and mostly take place in gay male bars on lesbian nights. Many of the drag kings talk about turning drag king performances into a career, and they wait anxiously for the breakthrough moment when a drag king will hit the jackpot and appear on prime-time TV. Murray Hill

Figure 37. "Murray Hill for Mayor—The God Bless America Show at Club Casanova," by Vivian Babuts (1997). Photo courtesy of the artist.

and Mo B. Dick speak of trying to appear on the *Rosie O'Donnell Show* or on *Late Night with David Letterman*. Dred and Shon cite the example of Ru Paul and suggest that they could do for drag kings what she has done for drag queens. Shon notes: "I think this could really fly, and whoever kicks it off could have some great opportunities." Other kings such as Retro maintain a wait-and-see approach and view the drag king claim for fame as part of a New York mind-set. In New York, Retro says, "Everyone has a blinding ambition to be a star." When drag kings do hit the mainstream, and I think they will, let us hope it is not as another supermodel in a mustache. Let us hope that it's Murray Hill doing an outrageous parody of male midlife crisis or Dred as a smooth mackdaddy or Shon as a teen idol or Mo B. Dick winking at the girlies and poking fun at male homosexual panic with his signature line: "I ain't no homo!"

## Conclusion

A theatrical tradition of male impersonation emerged at the turn of the century as a public display of cross-dressing subcultures. When male impersonation faded out as a mainstream theatrical tradition, it did not reemerge within dyke bar culture of the 1940s and 1950s. Contemporary drag king culture in queer dyke spaces manifests in two different modes: first, in the antitheater of the bar drag king contest, and second, in the elaborately produced shows at drag king clubs. In the contests, we notice a lack of performativity within drag king presentations that can be attributed to the fact that dominant male masculinities tend to present themselves in the register of the real, eschewing the performative and the artificial. For this reason, the challenge of the drag king performance is to bring to light the artifice of dominant masculinity; this is often accomplished by highlighting the tricks and gadgets of the sexism on which male masculinity depends. Minority masculinities emerge from the drag king performance as multiple articulations of various relations between racial and gendered embodiment and theater. Some drag kings display butch realness as a relay of identifications and disidentifications between masculinity and female bodies; some drag kings highlight the performative in the guise of femme pretenders; others still merely mimic maleness and leave the bond between masculinity and maleness intact. The drag king shows, however, use various techniques to parody, imitate, appropriate, and remake male masculinity. In 1997 the mayor of New York City made a prime-time public appearance in female drag, but thanks to the efflorescence of drag king culture, drag kings now have their own candidate. Murray Hill is running for mayor, and female masculinity is on the ticket.

*So gimme a stage / where this bull here can rage / and though I can fight / I'd much rather recite. / That's entertainment.* —Jake La Motta, Raging Bull

# 8 RAGING BULL (DYKE)

*New Masculinities*

When I was thirteen, I wanted a punching bag and boxing gloves for my birthday. I believe that these accoutrements of masculine competition signified for me a way to keep adult womanhood at bay. I think I also saw boxing as a way to learn how to fight back against the boys of my age, boys I used to be able to beat up easily but who now easily beat me up as they experienced their first adolescent growing spurts. I was told that boxing was not appropriate for a girl my age and that I should pick out something more feminine. This was the first time that I remember being told that I could not do something because I was a girl. Unfortunately, many more prohibitions were to follow with precisely this rationale. Soon it was soccer that was no longer appropriate for a girl "my age," and field hockey (a much more brutal game in actual fact) was offered as a suitable athletic replacement. Next came gender-appropriate clothes and all manner of social prohibitions. I personally experienced adolescence as the shrinking of my world.

Society tells girls in all kinds of ways that they must accept and take on femininity by giving up sports and active behavior in general. When I look back on the set of limitations that female adolescence bestowed on me, I feel a kind of rage, and this rage stems from the knowledge that I now have about binary gender systems and their nonsensical prescriptions. In the 1970s in England when I was a teenage girl, no explanation needed to be given for the narrowing of a girl's life once she hit puberty; indeed, adolescence produced a logic all its own, and all challenges to that logic were simply more evidence of one's irrational attachment to inappropriate behavior. Adolescent girls, according to such logic, must manage their bodies in such a way as to optimize their appearance, appeal to boys, stave off rape and sex, and display appropriate levels of femininity. Whereas this is the stuff of "Feminism 101," only rarely is female adolescence studied in terms of an expulsion of preteen female masculinity. As I argued in chapter 1, tomboyism for girls is generally tolerated until it threatens to interfere with the onset of adolescent femininity. At that point, all attachments to preadolescent freedoms and masculine activities must be dropped. Of course, ultimately, there is nothing at all irrational about girls wanting to fight or run or wear short hair; what is irrational is to deny girls access to activity because they are girls.

This book has not only been a philosophical inquiry into the whys and wherefores of female masculinity; it is also a seriously committed attempt to make masculinity safe for women and girls. Although it seems counterintuitive that such a project should be necessary in the 1990s, it has been my contention that despite at least two decades of sustained feminist and queer attacks on the notion of natural gender, we still believe that masculinity in girls and women is abhorrent and pathological. I have argued throughout this book that there is something so obvious about female masculinity and yet something so rigid about our refusal to recognize it, celebrate it, and accept it. In this, my conclusion, I would like to consolidate my sense of the new masculinities that are being produced by women in the hopes that such rewritings of masculinity can finally be recognized both as part of the history of masculinity and as its future.

While much of this book has concentrated on the masculinity in women that is most often associated with sexual variance, I also think the general concept of female masculinity has its uses for heterosexual women. After all, the excessive conventional femininity often associated with female heterosexuality can be bad for your health. Scholars have long pointed out that femininity tends to be associated with passivity and inactivity, with various forms of unhealthy body manipulations from anorexia to high-heeled shoes. It seems to me that at least early on in life, girls should avoid femininity. Perhaps femininity and its accessories should be chosen later on, like a sex toy or a hairstyle. In recent years, I believe that society has altered its conceptions of the appropriate way to raise girls; indeed, a plethora of girl problems, from eating disorders to teenage pregnancy to low intellectual ambitions, leave many parents attempting to hold femininity at bay for their young girls. Cultivating femininity in girls at a very early age also has the unfortunate effect of sexualizing them and even inducing seductive mannerisms in preteen girls. The popularity of the tomboy is one indication that many parents are willing to cultivate low levels of masculinity in their female children rather than undergo the alternatives.

If masculinity were a kind of default category for children, surely we would have more girls running around and playing sports and experimenting with chemistry sets and building things and fixing things and learning about finances and so on. I am not really arguing for such child-rearing practices in this book, but I have been struck in the last year or so by various medical reports that conclude (after months of expensive testing) that women who exercise regularly throughout their lives and maintain a proper diet and a healthy weight tend to live longer and healthier lives than women who are sedentary and inactive. This is not a startling conclusion—to me at least—but what is startling is that in the 1990s it needs to be announced as a major scientific discovery.[1] It seems to me that at least one factor that prevents parents from encouraging their young girls to engage in vigorous and healthful activity must be the fear of masculinity. This fear can be erased only by a prolonged and serious consideration of the topic of female masculinity.

To recognize how completely we have ignored female masculinity as a culture, consider the following questions: Why is there no word for the opposite of "emasculation"? Why is there no parallel concept to "effeminacy"? (In fact, these two words mean exactly the same thing!) Why shouldn't a woman get in touch with her masculinity? Why does female masculinity remain so much a stigma that many women, even lesbians, will do almost anything to avoid the label "butch"? Why are we comfortable thinking about men as mothers, but we never consider women as fathers? Gender, it seems, is reversible only in one direction, and this must surely have to do with the immense social power that accumulates around masculinity. Masculinity, one must conclude, has been reserved for people with male bodies and has been actively denied to people with female bodies. And this is not to say that all things being equal, all female-bodied people would desire masculinity, only that the protection of masculinity from women bears examination.

Even women who are involved in the most masculine of activities, such as boxing or weight lifting, attempt to turn the gaze away from their own potential masculinity. In an article on the rise of women in boxing in *Cosmopolitan*, for example, various pioneering female boxers in London are interviewed about their participation in the "manly art." The male journalist reports that women's boxing is alive and well and that indeed it lacks none of the intensity or physicality of men's boxing. At a gym in London, a group of tough female boxers are being trained by a female coach before their participation in a tournament. Although the article does focus on the positive aspects of women's boxing and takes aim at the disapproval voiced by many against the spectacle of women fighting, it also returns time and again to the fraught issue of the fighters' endangered femininity. One white woman boxer, Madeline Davies, is just fifteen years old, and as she waits for her first fight, the interviewer speaks with her father:

> Ringside, Davies's father waits. It's his daughter's first match. He believes boxing has matured her quickly and bolstered her confidence. He's quick to insist that she's lost none of her femininity. "She's never been a cuddly-toy sort of girl," he says. "But she's soft to talk to and concerned for other people. As long as she doesn't become overly aggressive, the boxing doesn't worry me.[2]

The father also mentions that he hopes his daughter will eventually lose interest in boxing. Whereas one can certainly sympathize with any parent who feels squeamish about watching his or her child become a punching bag in a boxing ring, the fear of a reduced femininity seems to come before the fear of serious physical injury.[3]

The boxers themselves, surprisingly, also voice assurances that their physical toughness is not accompanied by a depletion in femininity. A black female boxer, Fosteres Joseph, the Super-Welterweight champion in 1995, voices a common defense of the femininity of the female fighter. She says: "We're fighting a society that says women should be in the house with the children. . . . We have our father's genes as men have their mother's. Men can work on the feminine side, so why shouldn't we box? I love romance and flowery dresses, too, but I'm asserting my femininity by being true to my nature."[4] There is a missed step in Joseph's articulation of her right to fight. "Men can work on the feminine side," she argues, "so why shouldn't we box." The implication, of course, is that men can work on their feminine sides, and therefore women should be able to work on their masculinity. But masculinity is completely factored out of the equation between women and boxing, and we are left with a formulation of female boxing as an expression of a true femininity. As I have noted several times in this book, black women face far more damning accusations of masculinity than white women in our society, and one can certainly understand Joseph's desire here to protect the image of black womanhood from the usual damaging stereotypes. But there is always a subtle level of homophobia built into the defense of femininity by any female fighter. A charge of masculinity coupled with active female strength, this article presumes, must add up to lesbianism, and it is the charge of lesbianism that the women in this article and the sports writer seem anxious to avoid.[5]

Until 1977 women were not allowed to box in the United States. In that year, a state supreme court ruling from New York County decided that the prohibition against women fighters violated equal protection clauses of federal and state constitutions.[6] As Jeffrey Sammons shows, the New York Athletic Commission (NYAC) vocally objected to this decision, arguing that the spectacle of women boxers would destroy the sport and irrevocably damage its credibility. The commission went so far as to warn that boxing could damage women's breasts and reproductive organs.[7] When the ruling allowing women's boxing went into effect, licenses were granted to three women, two black women and one white woman. The white woman, Cathy "Cat" Davis, immediately became a celebrity while the black women, Marian "Lady Tyger" Trimiar and Jackie Tonawanda (who originally brought suit against the NYAC), faded into obscurity. The publicity around Cat Davis, the "Great White Hype," as Jeffrey Sammons suggests, repeats the history of black men in boxing in relation to white fighters. Because women's boxing has not so far produced any kind of financial rewards for any woman, the racial dynamics of the sport signify on a symbolic, rather than a material, level. But the continued effort to bar women from boxing and the lionization of white fighters over black fighters are the characteristics of a century-long struggle over the meaning of masculinity and the attempt to make white manhood into the only legitimate representation of true masculinity.

In her book *Manliness and Civilization*, Gail Bederman demonstrates precisely how battles over black and white manhood and masculinity were staged in turn-of-the-century prizefights. Indeed, rioting followed the victory in 1910 of black fighter Jack Johnson over white fighter Jim Jeffries, and in most cases, the rioting involved "rampaging white men" who "attacked black men who were celebrating Johnson's victory."[8] The boxing ring, obviously, has become the arena for the most public contests over the meaning of masculinity and its relation to male embodiment. "The heavy-weight's male body," writes Bederman, "was so equated with male identity and power that American whites rigidly prevented all men they deemed unable to wield political and social power from asserting any claim to the heavy-weight championship" (8). American whites also prevented all women from asserting a claim to the heavyweight championship, and it is this double exclusion of nonwhite men and nonmale masculinity that must properly be accounted for to produce the history of relations between manliness and civilization. Women were allowed to compete at boxing as recently as the eighteenth century in Britain and as late as the 1860s in America.[9] Presumably, the disappearance of women's boxing in both England and America by the turn of the century had everything to do with Victorian notions of womanhood and an emergent conception of middle-class masculinity. The withering of differences between the sexes, indeed, became a source of great cultural anxiety at the turn of the century.

Sports for women is still afflicted by a Victorian concern over the fate of femininity in modern times. In her excellent book on gender, sexuality, and women's sports, Susan Cahn reaches the conclusion that although women in America today can find many competitive opportunities, there are still many obstacles. She insists: "Women's athletic freedom requires that certain attributes long defined as masculine—skill, strength, speed, physical dominance, uninhibited use of space and motion—become human qualities and not those of a particular gender."[10] The only way to extend such attributes to women, I argue, is not simply to make them "human" but to allow them to extend to women as masculinity. I do not believe that we are moving steadily toward a genderless society or even that this is a utopia to be desired, but I do believe that a major step toward gender parity, and one that has been grossly overlooked, is the cultivation of female masculinity.

Boxing, at long last however, has become a hot topic in lesbian circles, and it is there that the association between alternative masculinities and boxing are cultivated—*Curve* magazine, for example, recently featured an article on super butch Gina "Boom Boom" Guidi, North American Women's Welter Weight Champion.[11] Boxing also played a role in Peggy Shaw's one-man show "Just Like My Father," in which Shaw shadowboxes onstage while telling her story of growing up as a masculine woman. And in an article by Jenni Olson called "What's Dirty about Boxing" in the popular zine *Girljock,* Olson writes about what happens to her masculinity when she boxes: "It inspires a maleness in me that's not just plain old butchness. When I box I forget the difference between being a girl and doing something that men do, and just being my own unique kind of man—I'm a different kind of man than my father was, I'm a different kind of man than my twin brother is. . . . But when I recreate myself in my father's image, I am what I wanted him to be—and I am the man of my dreams."[12] Just like my father . . . I am a different kind of man than my father was . . . these butch meditations on boxing engage a butch or transgender fantasy of maleness that is not simply confusion or castration as the mainstream accounts would have us believe, it is precisely the re-creation of maleness in the image of the butch.

Obviously, the entry of women into boxing or the appearance on mainstream TV of a drag king or the release of a film starring a butch woman will not in and of themselves overturn the cultural, social, and political prohibitions against female masculinity. But in each case—boxing, drag acts, lesbian film—the exclusion of butch women signals a widespread cultural anxiety about the potential effects of femaleness and masculinity. Presumably, female masculinity threatens the institution of motherhood: I suppose people think that if female masculinity is widely approved, then no one will want to take responsibility for the trials and pains of reproduction. We seem to assume that no one really wants to be a girl or a woman, and therefore some people, say female-bodied people, must be forced into these abject genders. Of course, femininity holds its own appeal even within compulsory heterosexuality, and we should perhaps double our efforts to make femininity a safe haven for boys and girls even as we attempt to make masculinity extend to women. This book has spent little time on female femininity and male femininity, but this is not to say that these forms of gender are not also important locations for the struggle against binary gender. They are, however, accorded far more attention today than female masculinity.

Some people have asked me during the writing of this book also to consider the toll that masculinity takes on boys and men and to recognize that masculinity is not simply a privilege, but that sometimes it may also be a burden. I think compulsory masculinity is a burden on many different kinds of men and boys, and it takes its toll in a variety of ways

Figure 38. Raging Bull. Robert De Niro as Jake La Motta in *Raging Bull* (1980), directed by Martin Scorsese.

from extreme physical damage to the self within sports to extreme violence directed at others. It is hard to be very concerned about the burden of masculinity on males, however, if only because it so often expresses itself through the desire to destroy others, often women. Indeed, this dual mechanism of a lack of care for the self and a callous disregard for the care of others seems to characterize much that we take for granted about white male masculinity. For me, no representation captures better the burden of masculinity than the male boxing film. In films such as *Raging Bull* and *Rocky* (I, II, and III), the masculinity of the boxer is determined not by how quickly he can knock the other guy out but by how many punches the boxer can take without going down himself. In these films, boxing is a trial in which the male body withstands physical assault. "Punch me," Jake La Motta (Robert De Niro) urges his brother, and he offers up his chin. He continues to taunt his brother until the fists start flying. Taking a punch is everything to La Motta, fighting back is just the final flourish demanded to win the fight. Typical psychoanalytic descriptions of masochism seem to depict it as a female perversion, but in fact, as the boxing film shows, masochism is built into male masculinity, and the most macho of spectacles is the battered male body, a bloody hunk of ruined flesh, stumbling out of the corner for yet another round.[13] The winner is always the one who has been beaten to a pulp but remains standing long enough to deliver the knockout punch. (This tactic was called "rope a dope" in Mohammed Ali's famous upset of George Foreman in Zaire in 1975 and consisted of Ali allowing himself to be beaten by Foreman until Foreman was completely worn out.) At the moment that his opponent tires, the prizefighter steps up and delivers a quick, almost anticlimactic blow to the chin.

The boxing ring, finally, provides a nice metaphor for the power of dominant masculinities and their relations to subordinate masculinities. Although the battered white male boxer takes massive amounts of abuse in the ring, he also manages to emerge triumphant every time. He absorbs the blows, weathers the storm, and in boxing films, he inevitably wins the decisions. This is not unlike the structure of white male masculinity, which seems impervious to criticism or attack and maintains hegemonic sway despite all challenges to its power. In one boxing film, however, *Raging Bull*, Martin Scorsese bravely captures the decline of the great white hope. Jake La Motta declines from a fighting stud to a lonely, overweight, impotent abuser reduced to reciting little poems as a stand-up comic in a nightclub. "I coulda been a contender," La Motta mugs, quoting Marlon Brando from *On the Waterfront*. The spectacle of the fallen fighter citing another icon of failed masculinity, and of De Niro quoting Brando, produces a drag king effect in which we see for once the costume of masculinity as it slips off the form of the male body. De Niro rambles on: "So gimme a stage / where this bull here can rage / and though I can fight / I'd much rather recite. / That's entertainment." The raging bull has been reduced to insipid rhymes. The power of the punch has been replaced by the power of the punch line, and for the male fighter, that is no power at all. Very few mainstream films really take apart male masculinity in a way that allows us to see both its structure and its weaknesses. But *Raging Bull* gives us an exact account in slow motion and in excruciating black-and-white detail of every vulnerable point on the male body. The film is ultimately one of the best records we have of white male masculinity in the balance.

My chapter on cinematic images of butch women suggested that when women lack powerful images of masculine women, they cross-identify. The results of such cross-identifications are fertile productions of lesbian James Deans, butch Marlon Brandos, and dyke renditions of male masculinity: the tactic of cross-identification can even turn a raging bull into a raging bull dyke. My drag king chapter also showed how the parodies, ironic interpretations, and even faithful renditions of male performers both exposed the methods and tactics of male masculinity and produced new masculinities that depended on a complex relay of gender effects through the drag performance. Indeed, male and female masculinities are constantly involved in an ever-shifting pattern of influences. We tend to identify the pattern as moving only in one direction, however, rather than seeing the possibilities of an active matrix of exchange between male and female masculinities. Exchanges between male and female masculinities, I suggest, have the potential to go both ways. The question, then, might be not what do female masculinities borrow from male masculinities, but rather what do men borrow from butches? If we shift the flow of power and influence, we can easily imagine a plethora of new masculinities that do not simply feed back into the static loop that makes maleness plus power into the formula for abuse but that re-create masculinity on the model of female masculinity.

The boxing strategy of "taking it like a man" is not a favored strategy for the masculine woman; she is much more likely to transform the mechanisms of masculinity and produce new constellations of embodiment, power, and desire. She is more likely, furthermore, to give than to take. The stone butch, we saw, was the partner who wanted to be "doing all the doing." Radclyffe Hall told her lover Souline: "If I am the 'giver' then take what I give . . . and take it without misgiving." She describes her hero Stephen Gordon's desire, furthermore, as "a bitter loving." In each formulation, the butch counters the power of her masculinity with her own abjection, her own loss, her own vulnerability, and the butch-femme couple in particular create a complex exchange between their different modes of loving. Cut off from the most obvious rewards of masculinity—political power and representation—many masculine women have had to create elaborate rationales for their ways of lovings, their desire to provide for and protect a loved one, their decisions to live explicitly masculine lives. They have had to imaginatively recreate masculinity through writing and other forms of cultural production.

Throughout this book, I have cataloged and accounted for the multiple ways in which women produce and name new masculinities. Sometimes these new masculinities are produced as new renditions of male masculinities; sometimes they are produced as original forms of a growing sub-culture. The painting on the cover of this book, for example, "Raging Bull," by British artist Sadie Lee, generates a connection between the spectacle of boxing and the spectacle of the fighting butch. The painting confronts us with the hard stare of a bull dyke, a powerful and built body that is not obviously female but that is obviously not male. The face has no facial hair, and the chest gives a hint of bound breasts. The bull dyke's arms are folded in defiance, and they are disproportionately large for the body. The raging bull wears butch drag, the white T-shirt, blue jeans, and black belt, and the red backdrop reflects the rage in the bull dyke's eyes. Like the portraits of alternately gendered bodies by Del Grace and Cathy Opie, this image challenges the viewer by staring straight out from the canvas and fixing the viewer within the butch's gaze. The butch resists the position of becoming an object of scrutiny and returns the stare with hard resolve. In my introduction, I talked about the relay of looks between artist, viewer, and subject in the photographs of Grace and Opie, and in my chapter on queer cinema, I discussed the possibility of a butch gaze. This look, the look of a raging bull, the stare down, the challenge, lets the viewer know that this is the stage where this bull can rage, and though she can fight . . . she'd rather recite. That's entertainment.

## 1  An Introduction to Female Masculinity

1  For an extension of this discussion of tomboys see my article "Oh Bondage Up Yours: Female Masculinity and the Tomboy," in *Sissies and Tomboys: A CLAGS Reader* (New York: New York University Press, forthcoming).

2  For more on the punishment of tomboys see Phyllis Burke, *Gender Shock: Exploding the Myths of Male and Female* (New York: Anchor Books, 1996). Burke analyzes some recent case histories of so-called GID or Gender Identity Disorder, in which little girls are carefully conditioned out of male behavior and into exceedingly constrictive forms of femininity.

3  Carson McCullers, *The Member of the Wedding* (1946; reprint, New York: Bantam, 1973), 1.

4  R. C. Lewontin, "Sex, Lies, and Social Science," *New York Review of Books* 42, no. 7 (20 April 1995): 24.

5  Thanks to Esther Newton for making this point and suggesting when and how survey methods are useful. For an example of the kinds of questions used in sex surveys see John Gagnon et al., *Sex in America* (Boston: Little Brown, 1994). This particular volume is remarkable because the explicit questions

it asks about the kinds of sex people were having focus obsessively on the couple, and the study links certain activities definitively to certain identities. So, for example, questions about anal sex are directed only at male/female and male/male couples because anal sex is defined as "when a man's penis is inside his partner's anus or rectum" (260). There are no questions directed specifically at female/female couples and no questions about sex toys or use of dildos or hands in this section.

6 Steven Epstein, "A Queer Encounter: Sociology and the Study of Sexuality," *Sociological Theory* 12, no. 2 (July 1994): 189.

7 Arlene Stein and Ken Plummer, "I Can't Even Think Straight": Queer Theory and the Missing Revolution in Sociology," *Sociological Theory* 12, no. 2 (July 1994): 184.

8 Cindy Patton, "Tremble Hetero Swine," in *Fear of a Queer Planet: Queer Politics and Social Theory*, ed. Michael Warner (Minneapolis: University of Minnesota Press, 1993), 165.

9 The conference papers were collected in a volume called *Constructing Masculinity*, ed. Maurice Berger, Brian Wallis, and Simon Watson (New York: Routledge, 1996), and the one intervention on behalf of nonmale masculinities was made by Eve Kosofsky Sedgwick.

10 I am using the terms "female born" and "male born" to indicate a social practice of assigning one of two genders to babies at birth. My terminology suggests that these assignations may not hold for the lifetime of the individual, and it suggests from the outset that binary gender continues to dominate our cultural and scientific notions of gender but that individuals inevitably fail to find themselves in only one of two options.

11 Berger, Wallis, and Watson, introduction to *Constructing Masculinity*, 7.

12 More and more journals are putting together special issues on masculinity, but I have yet to locate a single special issue with a single essay about female masculinity. The latest journal announcement that found its way to me was from *The Velvet Light Trap: A Critical Journal of Film and Television*. They announced an issue on "New Masculinities" that featured essays titled "The 'New Masculinity' in *Tootsie*," "On Fathers and Sons, Sex and Death," "Male Melodrama and the Feeling Man," and so forth. This is not to say that such topics are not interesting, only that the "new masculinities" sound remarkably like the old ones. See *The Velvet Light Trap*, "New Masculinities," no. 38 (fall 1996).

13 Berger, Wallis, and Watson, *Constructing Masculinity*.

14 Paul Smith, ed., *Boys: Masculinities in Contemporary Culture* (Boulder, Colo.: Westview Press, 1996), 3.

15 Paul Smith, introduction to *Boys: Masculinities in Contemporary Culture*, 4–5.

16 See Monique Wittig, "The Straight Mind," in *The Straight Mind and Other*

*Essays* (Boston: Beacon Press, 1992); Judith Butler, "Imitation and Gender In-subordination," in *Inside/Out: Lesbian Theories, Gay Theories,* ed. Diana Fuss (New York: Routledge, 1991), 13–31; Jacob Hale, "Are Lesbians Women?" *Hypatia* 11, no. 2 (spring 1996): 94–121.

17   Indeed, one such ethnography has been carried out, but significantly it took English soccer hooligans as its topic. See Bill Buford's remarkable *Among the Thugs* (New York: Norton, 1992). A similar work on American male fans would be extremely useful.

18   For verification of such topics of concern just check out the men's sections that are popping up in your local bookstores. More specifically see the work of Michael Kimmel and Victor Seidler: Michael Kimmel, *Manhood in America: A Cultural History* (New York: Free Press, 1996); Victor J. Seidler, *Unreasonable Men: Masculinity and Social Theory* (New York: Routledge, 1994).

19   The continued viability of the category "woman" has been challenged in a variety of academic locations already: Monique Wittig, most notably, argued that "lesbians are not women" in her essay "The Straight Mind," 121. Wittig claims that because lesbians are refusing primary relations to men, they cannot occupy the position "woman." In another philosophical challenge to the category "woman," transgender philosopher Jacob Hale uses Monique Wittig's radical claim to theorize the possibility of gendered embodiments that exceed male and female (see Jacob Hale, "Are Lesbians Women?" *Hypatia* 11, no. 2 [spring 1996]). Elsewhere, Cheshire Calhoun suggests that the category "woman" may actually "operate as a lesbian closet" (see Cheshire Calhoun, "The Gender Closet: Lesbian Disappearance under the Sign 'Women,'" *Feminist Studies* 21, no. 1 [spring 1995]: 7–34).

20   Leslie Feinberg, *Stone Butch Blues: A Novel* (Ithaca, N.Y.: Firebrand, 1993), 59.

21   Nice Rodriguez, *Throw It to the River* (Toronto, Canada: Women's Press, 1993), 25–26.

22   Lee Edelman, "Tearooms and Sympathy, or The Epistemology of the Water Closet," in *Homographesis: Essays in Gay Literary and Cultural Theory* (New York: Routledge, 1994), 158.

23   Marjorie Garber, *Vested Interests: Cross-Dressing and Cultural Anxiety* (New York: Routledge, 1992), 47. Obviously Garber's use of the term "waterloo" makes a pun out of the drama of bathroom surveillance. Although the pun is clever and even amusing, it is also troubling to see how often Garber turns to punning in her analyses. The constant use of puns throughout the book has the overall effect of making gender crossing sound like a game or at least trivializes the often life-or-death processes involved in cross-identification. This is not to say gender can never be a "laughing matter" and must always be treated seriously but only to question the use of the pun here as a theoretical method.

24 See Jacques Lacan, "The Agency of the Letter in the Unconscious," in *Ecrits: A Selection*, trans. Alan Sheridan (New York: Norton, 1977), 151.

25 Susan Bordo argues this in "Reading the Male Body," *Michigan Quarterly Review* 32, no. 4 (fall 1993). She writes: "When masculinity gets 'undone' in this culture, the deconstruction nearly always lands us in the territory of the degraded; when femininity gets symbolically undone, the result is an immense elevation of status" (721).

26 Richard Fung, "Looking for My Penis: The Eroticized Asian in Gay Video Porn," in *How Do I Look? Queer Video and Film*, ed. Bad Object Choices (Seattle, Wash.: Bay Press, 1991), 145–68. Fung, writing about gay male porn, suggests that pornographic narrative structures assume a white male viewer who embodies a normative standard of male beauty and male desirability. Within this scopic field, porn characterizes black men as excessively sexual and as wholly phallic and Asian men as passive and asexual.

27 For an essay on the politics of visibility in relation to black women's sexuality, see Evelynn Hammons, "Toward a Genealogy of Black Female Sexuality: The Problematic of Silence," in *Feminist Genealogies, Colonial Legacies, Democratic Futures*, ed. M. Jacqui Alexander and Chandra Talpade Mohanty (New York: Routledge, 1997), 170–82. Hammons notes that "black women's sexuality . . . is rendered simultaneously invisible, visible (exposed), hypervisible, and pathologized in dominant discourses" (170). I examine this claim more closely in chapter 4.

28 David Pagel, "Catherine Opie," *Art Issues* (September/October 1994): 45.

29 Anna Marie Smith, "The Feminine Gaze: Photographer Catherine Opie Documents a Lesbian Daddy/Boy Subculture," *The Advocate*, 19 November 1991, 83. This is a great early review of Opie's work, although the title "The Feminine Gaze" seems to insist on the femininity of all things produced by women. Let's face it, there is nothing feminine about Opie's work.

30 Catherine Opie, "Catherine Opie with Russell Ferguson," interview by Russell Ferguson, *Index* (April 1996): 29.

31 Michael Cohen, "Catherine Opie—Regen Projects," *Flash Art* (December 1994): 98.

32 Opie, "Catherine Opie with Russell Ferguson," 30.

33 Transgenderism is the name for the general category of cross-identification. Very often transgenderism does not directly feed into transsexual definition and often is used as an umbrella term for gender variance.

## 2 Perverse Presentism

1 Eve Kosofsky Sedgwick, *Epistemology of the Closet* (Berkeley and Los Angeles: University of California Press, 1990), 23. Sedgwick defines her "nonce taxonomy" as "the making and unmaking and remaking and redissolution of

hundreds of old and new categorical imaginings concerning all the kinds it may take to make up a world."

2   George Chauncey, "Christian Brotherhood or Sexual Perversion? Homosexual Identities and the Construction of Sexual Boundaries in the World War I Era," in *Hidden from History: Reclaiming the Gay and Lesbian Past,* ed. Martin Duberman, Martha Vicinus, and George Chauncey Jr. (New York: Penguin, 1989), 312.

3   In *Gay New York,* George Chauncey Jr. elaborates this position, and he argues: "The invert and the normal man, the homosexual and the heterosexual, were not inventions of the elite but were popular discursive categories before they became elite discursive practices" (*Gay New York: Gender, Urban Culture, and the Making of the Gay Male World, 1890–1940* [New York: Basic Books, 1994], 27).

4   Lisa Duggan, "The Trials of Alice Mitchell: Sensationalism, Sexology, and the Lesbian Subject in Turn-of-the-Century America," *Signs* 18, no. 4 (summer): 791–814.

5   George L. Mosse, *The Image of Man: The Creation of Modern Masculinity* (Oxford: Oxford University Press, 1995), 3.

6   To give just one example of male masculinity emulating female masculinity, recent research by Laura Doan shows that both women's and men's fashions of the 1920s were influenced by the preponderance and the visibility of masculine women in and around Paris and London. Women's fashions became very "boy," and men were shown in popular cartoons comparing their masculinity to a much more virile form displayed by women (Manuscript, "Fashioning Sappho in the 1920's: The Origins of a Modern English Lesbian Culture").

7   Gail Bederman, *Manliness and Civilization: A Cultural History of Gender and Race in the United States, 1880–1917* (Chicago: University of Chicago Press, 1995), 7.

8   See, for example, Lillian Faderman, *Surpassing the Love of Men: Romantic Friendship and Love between Women from the Renaissance to the Present* (New York: William Morrow, 1981).

9   Michel Foucault, *The History of Sexuality, Volume 1: An Introduction,* trans. Robert Hurley (1978; reprint, New York: Vintage, 1990), 42–43.

10  Emma Donoghue, *Passions between Women: British Lesbian Culture, 1668–1801* (New York: HarperCollins, 1993), 7.

11  Randolph Trumbach, "London's Sapphists: From Three Sexes to Four Genders in the Making of Modern Culture," in *Third Sex, Third Gender: Beyond Sexual Dimorphism in Culture and History,* ed. Gilbert Herdt (New York: Zone, 1994), 112. Trumbach claims that in the eighteenth century, "tommy" was a slang word for "sapphist" and that the two terms were used in much the same way that "sodomite" and "molly" were for men (112).

12 There are books specifically dedicated to the histories of such women. See, for example, Dianne Dugaw, *Warrior Women and Popular Balladry, 1650–1850* (Chicago: University of Chicago Press, 1989).

13 Michel Foucault, *Discipline and Punish: The Birth of the Prison*, trans. Alan Sheridan (1977; reprint, New York: Vintage, 1979), 31.

14 Mitchell Dean, *Critical and Effective Histories: Foucault's Methods and Historical Sociology* (New York: Routledge, 1994), 33.

15 Sedgwick, *Epistemology of the Closet*, 44. This line is actually the title of axiom 5.

16 Terry Castle, *The Apparitional Lesbian: Female Homosexuality and Modern Culture* (New York: Columbia University Press, 1993), 14.

17 Judith Butler, "Imitation and Gender Insubordination," in *Inside/Out: Lesbian Theories, Gay Theories* (New York: Routledge, 1991), 14.

18 Martha Vicinus, "'They Wonder to Which Sex I Belong': The Historical Roots of the Modern Lesbian Identity," *Feminist Studies* 18, no. 3 (fall 1992): 471.

19 In "They Wonder to Which Sex I Belong," Vicinus opens with a discussion of the gender confusion produced by painter Rosa Bonheur. Vicinus cites a passage in which Bonheur recalls being mistaken for a man when wearing a painter's smock and trousers. Vicinus comments: "Bonheur's bemused description of the impact her androgynous appearance had upon the general public pinpoints many of the major difficulties historians face in reconstructing the history of the lesbian" (467). A woman who is mistaken for a man is not "androgynous"; I think it is crucial to recognize Bonheur as masculine, not androgynous, especially because Bonheur is clearly embracing her masculinity. Furthermore, the easy union of "androgynous" and "lesbian" here makes both terms into unproblematic signifiers of phenomena that we presumably already know and recognize.

20 Alice Greenough, *Physical Culture* magazine (1937), as quoted in Candace Savage, *Cowgirls* (London: Bloomsbury Publishing, 1996), 67.

21 Thomas Laqueur, *Making Sex: Body and Gender from the Greeks to Freud* (Cambridge: Harvard University Press, 1990).

22 Valerie Traub, "The Psychomorphology of the Clitoris," *GLQ* 2 (1996): 81–113.

23 Ibid., 104 n. 9.

24 Obviously, a woman can tribadically rub on a male body, but we do not have evidence that the sexual threat the tribade represented extended to the sexual aggression represented by female domination of a male partner.

25 Lillian Faderman, *Scotch Verdict* (New York: Columbia University Press, 1993).

26 For the original text of the case see *Miss Marianne Woods and Miss Jane Pirie against Dame Helen Cumming Gordon* (New York: Arno Press, 1975).

27 Lisa Moore, "'Something More Tender Still than Friendship': Romantic

Friendship in Early-Nineteenth-Century England," *Feminist Studies* 18, no. 3 (fall 1992): 516–17.

28 "Lord Meadowbank's Notes on the Testimony of Miss Jane Cumming, March 27, 1811," in Faderman, *Scotch Verdict*, 153.

29 Moore, "Something More Tender Still than Friendship," 512.

30 Anna Clarke, "Anne Lister's Construction of Lesbian Desire," *Journal of the History of Sexuality* 7, no. 11 (1996): 23.

31 Whitbread, *No Priest but Love*, and *I Know My Own Heart: The Diaries of Anne Lister* (New York: New York University Press, 1992).

32 Terry Castle, "Matters Not Fit to Be Mentioned: Fielding's *The Female Husband*," *ELH* 49 (1991): 612.

33 Castle, *The Apparitional Lesbian*, 9.

34 See chapter 4 on the "stone butch" for one example of such a sexual identity.

35 This is Carole Smith Rosenberg's description of romantic friendship systems between women in the nineteenth century. See Carole Smith Rosenberg, "The Female World of Love and Ritual: Relations between Women in Nineteenth Century America," *Signs* 1, no. 1 (autumn 1975): 1–29.

### 3 "A Writer of Misfits"

1 Michel Foucault, *The History of Sexuality, Volume 1: An Introduction*, trans. Robert Hurley (New York: Vintage, 1980).

2 Richard von Krafft-Ebing, *Psychopathia Sexualis*, trans. Franklin S. Klaf (1886; reprint, New York: Bell Publishing, 1965).

3 Havelock Ellis, "Sexual Inversion in Women," in *Studies in the Psychology of Sex* (New York: Random House, 1900), 222.

4 It is worth observing that Freud's theory of female homosexuality never took on the legitimacy of earlier sexological explanations. His argument that the homosexual woman labors under a mother complex has failed to impact a general understanding of lesbianism, and his notion of "penis envy" is really just another way of saying "female inversion."

5 Esther Newton, "The Mythic Mannish Lesbian: Radclyffe Hall and the New Woman," *Signs* 9, no. 4 (1984): 567.

6 As an example of such criminality, Ellis footnotes two cases. The first was the case of Alice Mitchell in Memphis, and the second was the case of the "Tiller Sisters," "two quintoons," as he calls them, who were both actresses and were romantically involved. In each case, one of the women kills the other after jealous rages. For an excellent analysis of cases of "sapphic slashers" see Lisa Duggan, "The Trials of Alice Mitchell," and her forthcoming book *Sapphic Slashers* (Berkeley and Los Angeles: University of California Press, 1998).

7 For information on gender-variant working-class women during this period

see the San Francisco Lesbian and Gay History Project, "'She Even Chewed Tobacco': A Pictorial History of Passing Women in America," in *Hidden from History: Reclaiming the Gay and Lesbian Past*, ed. Martin Duberman, Martha Vicinus, and George Chauncey Jr. (New York: Penguin, 1989), 183–94. See also Jonathan Katz, *Gay American History: Lesbians and Gay Men in the USA: A Documentary Anthology* (New York: Cromwell, 1973).

8 Radclyffe Hall, *Miss Ogilvy Finds Herself* (New York: Harcourt, Brace, 1934), 11.

9 Toupie Lowther in correspondence with Miss Conway in 1920 about "The Hackett-Lowther Unit 1918–1919," Women in War Special Collection, London Imperial War Museum.

10 Toupie Lowther correspondence, Imperial War Museum.

11 Michael Baker, *Our Three Selves: The Life of Radclyffe Hall* (New York: William Morrow, 1985), 125–26. Baker provides some interesting details about Lowther but is also invested in depicting Lowther as "deeply insecure," "tiresomely clinging and chronically self-absorbed" (126). Although my discussion of Hall and her circle is indebted to Baker's research, I find many of his observations about the masculine women who surrounded Hall and Troubridge to be suspect. It is not clear that he really understands the community he studies.

12 "Englishwomen with the French Army," *London Times*, 5 August 1919, n.p. This article was included in a file on Toupie Lowther's ambulance corps held at the London Imperial War Museum in the Women in War Special Collection.

13 Bernice Hausman, *Changing Sex: Transsexualism, Technology, and the Idea of Gender* (Durham, N.C.: Duke University Press, 1995), 117.

14 George Chauncey Jr., "From Sexual Inversion to Homosexuality: The Changing Medical Conceptualization of Female 'Deviance,'" in *Passion and Power: Sexuality in History*, ed. Kathy Peiss and Christina Simmons with Robert Padgug (Philadelphia: Temple University Press, 1990), 104.

15 Glasgow, *Your John*, 165. What John does not mention here is that Mickie hated Souline on account of Souline's rabid anti-Semitism.

16 Emily Hamer, *Britannia's Glory: A History of Twentieth-Century Lesbians* (London: Cassell, 1996), 40–53.

17 Baker, *Our Three Selves*, 170.

18 Terry Castle, *Noel Coward and Radclyffe Hall: Kindred Spirits* (New York: Columbia University Press, 1996), 31.

19 Glasgow, introduction to *Your John*, 9.

20 Baker, *Our Three Selves*, 151. Baker claims to have found all of this in Una's diaries, which are in a private collection owned by Nacelle Rossi-Lemeni in Fregene, Italy. Baker also consulted the Lovat Dickson Collection at the National Archive in Ottawa.

21 Julie Wheelwright, *Amazons and Military Maids: Women Who Dressed as Men in Pursuit of Life, Liberty, and Happiness* (London: Pandora, 1989), 1–6. Wheel-

wright gives a quick account of this case, but Laura Doan is working on a longer discussion based on her research of London newspapers that reported on the trial.

22  Valerie Arkell Smith, "I Posed as a Man for 30 Years," *Empire News and Sunday Chronicle,* 19 February 1956, 2. This article is the first of a series of reports over a period of three months in which Smith confesses to her "amazing masquerade."

23  Ibid.

24  Valerie Arkell Smith, "A Bride but My Love Ended," *Empire News and Sunday Chronicle,* 26 February 1956, 2.

25  Valerie Arkell Smith, "Why I Became a 'Man.'" *Empire News and Sunday Chronicle,* 4 March 1956, 2.

26  Smith, "I Posed as a Man," 2.

27  Smith, "Why I Became a 'Man,'" 2.

28  Radclyffe Hall to Audrey Heath, 19 March 1929, Ottawa. Cited in Baker, *Our Three Selves.*

29  Laura Doan, "Passing Fashions: Reading Female Masculinities in the 1920's," in *Fashioning Sappho in the 1920's: The Origins of Modern English Lesbian Culture* (New York: Columbia University Press, forthcoming), 3.

30  Wheelwright, *Amazons and Military Maids,* 3.

31  Ibid., 10–11. Wheelwright cites two newspaper articles: "Woman's Strange Life as a Man," *Daily Express,* 6 March 1929, and "How the Colonel's Secret Was Revealed," *Daily Sketch,* 6 March 1929.

32  For another example refer to the life of French anti-Semitic cross-dressing author Gyp. See Willa Z. Silverman, *The Notorious Life of Gyp: Right-Wing Anarchist in Fin-de-Siecle France* (New York: Oxford University Press, 1995).

33  Valerie Arkell Smith, "Exposed!" *Empire News and Sunday Chronicle,* 25 March 1956, 11.

34  *The Sunday Dispatch,* 31 March 1929.

35  Smith, "I Posed as a Man," 2.

36  Smith, "I Shocked a Court" *Empire News and Sunday Chronicle* 1 April 1956, 1.

37  For more on the history of female-to-male transsexuals in the twentieth century and their distinct narratives see Jay Prosser, *Second Skins: Body Narratives of Transsexuals* (New York: Columbia University Press, 1998).

38  Newton, "The Mythic Mannish Lesbian," 559.

39  Toni McNaron, "A Journey into Otherness: Teaching *The Well of Loneliness,*" in *Lesbian Studies: Present and Future,* ed. Margaret Cruikshank (New York: Feminist Press, 1982), 88–92.

40  The Ladies of Llangollen were two unmarried women (at least one of whom was noticeably mannish), Lady Eleanor Butler and Sarah Ponsonby, who lived together openly and became celebrities in the early nineteenth century. Anne

Lister knew of them and wrote about wanting to visit their house. For more on them see Elizabeth Mavor, *The Ladies of Llangollen: A Study in Romantic Friendship* (Harmondsworth: Penguin, 1973). Whereas this book positions the women as romantic friends, other accounts render them as a butch-femme couple.

41   For an account of the trial see Vera Brittain, *Radclyffe Hall: A Case of Obscenity?* (New York: A. S. Barnes, 1968).

42   For more on Oscar Wilde and gay male identity formation see Ed Cohen, *Talk on the Wilde Side* (New York: Routledge, 1993).

43   *The Picture of Dorian Gray* was described as "poisonous," as "filled with the odors of moral and spiritual putrefaction," and as obsessed with "disgusting sins and abominable crimes." As quoted in Isobel Murray's introduction to *The Picture of Dorian Gray* (Oxford: Oxford University Press, 1981). One of these reviews was an unsigned piece in the *Daily Chronicle*.

The first and best-known attack on the obscenity of *The Well of Loneliness* was made by James Douglas, editor of the *Sunday Express*. He called the novel "outrageous," and referencing the fear of contagion to which the novel gave rise, he wrote: "I would rather give a healthy boy or a healthy girl a phial of prussic acid than this novel" (*Sunday Express*, 19 August 1928).

44   See, for example, Ed Cohen, "Writing Gone Wilde: Homoerotic Desire in the Closet of Representation," *PMLA* 102 (1987): 801–13.

45   See, for example, Sonja Ruehl, "Inverts and Experts: Radclyffe Hall and the Lesbian Identity," in *Feminism, Culture, and Politics*, ed. Rosalind Brunt and Carolyn Rowan (London: Lawrence and Wishart, 1982), 15–36; Jean Radford, "An Inverted Romance: *The Well of Loneliness* and Sexual Ideology," in *The Progress of Romance: The Politics of Popular Fiction*, ed. Jean Radford (London: Routledge, 1986), 97–111.

46   Michel Foucault, *The History of Sexuality, Volume 1: An Introduction*, trans. Robert Hurley (New York: Vintage, 1980).

47   Eve Kosofsky Sedgwick, *Epistemology of the Closet* (Berkeley and Los Angeles: University of California Press, 1990).

48   Marjorie Garber has commented on the overlap of sartorial and erotic style in the cross-dressing of some women in the 1920s. However, Garber's account of transvestism relies too much on the transvestite as a "third" term between male and female, and she makes transvestism the repository for all sexual and gender variance. See *Vested Interests: Cross-Dressing and Cultural Anxiety* (New York: Routledge, 1992), 153–55.

49   Histories of modern dress that trace the evolution of gender through the vicissitudes of fashion tend to neglect the history of the cross-dressing woman. Anne Hollander, for example, sees female cross-dressing at the end of the nineteenth century as a sad imitation of male costume, but not as part of

any kind of developing aesthetic. Hollander writes: "But women who adopted male clothes or heavily masculinized clothes could not strike the right note that way: they might look serious but they couldn't be taken seriously if they looked somehow falsified or too wilfully unappetizing." The oddly conservative resonance of this observation is made emphatic in her last sentence: "Perversely negative effects may startle but they always fail to persuade" (*Sex and Suits: The Evolution of Modern Dress* [New York: Kodansha, 1995], 123).

50  Radclyffe Hall, *The Well of Loneliness* (1928; reprint, New York: Anchor Books, 1990), 35.

51  Hall's letters to Souline also mention her obsessive and even erotic relation to clothes. There are many accounts of clothes shopping, and her outfits are sometimes described in loving detail: "I have ordered a new over-coat, same as the shabby faun one but dark blue this time, it should be very smart. I have ordered two flannel suits, a grey and a blue. And a pair of faun colored trowsers for St. Maxime" (5 April 1935, p. 114).

52  Elizabeth Lapovsky Kennedy and Madeline Davis, *Boots of Leather, Slippers of Gold: The History of a Lesbian Community* (New York: Routledge, 1993).

53  Teresa de Lauretis, "The Lure of the Mannish Lesbian: The Fantasy of Castration and the Signification of Desire," in *The Practice of Love: Lesbian Sexuality and Perverse Desire* (Bloomington: Indiana University Press, 1994), 203.

54  Sigmund Freud, "The Psychogenesis of a Case of Homosexuality in a Woman," in *Sexuality and the Psychology of Love,* ed. Philip Rieff (1920; reprint, New York: Collier Books, 1963), 133–59.

55  De Lauretis juxtaposes her negative reading of Hall's novel in this chapter on "The Lure of the Mannish Lesbian" with an affirmative reading of Cherríe Moraga's *Giving Up the Ghost.* She makes no attempt to account for the historical and cultural differences between these texts, and her reading of Moraga is brief and, to use her word, fetishistic.

56  Glasgow, *Your John,* 129–30.

57  Ibid., 52.

58  Laura Doan is writing about the historical significance of the emergence of the Women's Police Service. She claims that this group was attacked mercilessly by the commissioner of the metropolitan police because he was concerned about the predominance of masculine women in their ranks. See Laura Doan, "Legislating the Lesbian in a Culture of Inversion," in *Fashioning Sapphism in the 1920's: The Origins of a Modern English Lesbian Culture* (New York: Columbia University Press, forthcoming).

59  Joan Lock, *The British Policewoman: Her Story* (London: Robert Hale, 1979), 150. Lock reports this fact, however, as evidence of Allen's "silliness."

60  Baker, *Our Three Selves,* 267.

61  Una Troubridge's diary, 9 January 1931.

62  Hamer, *Britannia's Glory*, 46.

63  Mary S. Allen, *The Pioneer Policewoman*, edited and arranged by Julie Helen Honeymoon (London: Chatto and Windus, 1925), 240–41. The photo appears on p. 241. This book is dedicated to her former lover as follows: "Dedicated to the Memory of the 'Chief' Mary Damer Dawson."

## 4  Lesbian Masculinity

1  Elizabeth Lapovsky Kennedy and Madeline D. Davis, *Boots of Leather, Slippers of Gold: The History of a Lesbian Community* (New York: Penguin, 1993), 204.

2  Robert Reid-Pharr, "Dinge," in the "Queer Acts" special issue of *Women and Performance* 8:2, no. 16 (1996): 76.

3  Anna Marie Smith, "The Regulation of Lesbian Sexuality through Erasure: The Case of Jennifer Saunders," in *Lesbian Erotics*, ed. Karla Jay (New York: New York University Press, 1995), 175.

4  Evelynn Hammonds, "Toward a Genealogy of Black Female Sexuality: The Problematic of Silence," in *Feminist Genealogies, Colonial Legacies, Democratic Futures*, ed. M. Jacqui Alexander and Chandra Talpade Mohanty (New York: Routledge, 1997), 170.

5  Marilyn Frye, "Lesbian Sex," in *An Intimate Wilderness: Lesbian Writers on Sexuality*, ed. Judith Barrington (Portland, Oreg.: Eighth Mountain, 1991), 6.

6  Joan Nestle, *A Restricted Country* (Ithaca, N.Y.: Firebrand, 1987); Kennedy and Davis, *Boots of Leather, Slippers of Gold*.

7  Gayle Rubin, "Thinking Sex: Notes for a Radical Theory of the Politics of Sexuality," in *Pleasure and Danger: Exploring Female Sexuality*, ed. Carole Vance (Boston: Routledge, Kegan and Paul, 1984), 267–319.

8  Ibid., 267.

9  Leo Bersani also cautions against the notion that sexual transgression may easily be aligned with radical politics in "Is the Rectum a Grave?" in *AIDS: Cultural Analysis, Cultural Activism*, ed. Douglas Crimp (Cambridge: MIT Press, 1988).

10  In "Street Talk/Straight Talk," Samuel R. Delany continues the call—an urgent call in the age of AIDS—for a sexual discourse rather than simply a discourse about sex: "What I am asking is that all of us begin to put forward the monumental effort needed not to interpret what we say, but to say what we do" Delany, "Street Talk/Straight Talk," in "Queer Theory" issue of *Differences* 3, no. 2 [summer 1991]: 38).

11  Esther Newton and Shirley Walton, "The Misunderstanding: Toward a More Precise Sexual Vocabulary," in *Pleasure and Danger*, ed. Carole Vance (Boston: Routledge, Kegan and Paul, 1984), 250.

12  "Posttranssexual" is Sandy Stone's term from her essay "The Empire Strikes

Back: A Posttranssexual Manifesto," in *Body Guards: The Cultural Politics of Gender Ambiguity*, ed. Julia Epstein and Kristina Straub (New York: Routledge, 1993), 280–304. I discuss the significance of the transsexual to contemporary late-capitalist discourses of masculinity in chapter 5. The body with multiple organs refers to Gilles Deleuze and Felix Guattari's term from *Anti-Oedipus: Capitalism and Schizophrenia*, trans. Robert Hurley, Mark Seem, and Helen R. Lane (Minneapolis: University of Minnesota Press, 1983). "Posthuman" is a term that Ira Livingston and I use in an anthology called *Posthuman Bodies* to describe one particular configuration of the body in relation to a blasted notion of the human in the late twentieth century (see Judith Halberstam and Ira Livingston, eds., introduction to *Posthuman Bodies* [Bloomington: Indiana University Press, 1995], 1–22).

13   Kate Bornstein, *Gender Outlaw: Men, Women, and the Rest of Us* (New York: Routledge, 1993).

14   Leslie Feinberg, *Transgender Warriors* (Boston, Mass.: Beacon Press, 1996). Unfortunately, in this book, Feinberg makes sweeping generalizations about the history of transgender people in many different cultural contexts, and s/he unilaterally assigns gender tolerance to economically cooperative societies and gender oppression to capitalism. Flows of power between gender systems and economic systems are unfortunately never so predictable.

15   There are numerous works on the denaturalization of gender. Most important for our purposes would be Judith Butler, *Gender Trouble* (New York: Routledge, 1990); Ann Fausto-Sterling, *Myths of Gender: Biological Theories about Women and Men*, rev. ed. (New York: Basic Books, 1992); Gayle Rubin, "The Traffic in Women: Notes on the 'Political Economy' of Sex," in *Toward an Anthropology of Women*, ed. Rayna R. Reiter (New York: Monthly Review Press, 1975), 157–210.

16   Suzanne J. Kessler and Wendy McKenna, *Gender: An Ethnomethodological Approach* (1978; reprint, Chicago: University of Chicago Press, 1985). Kessler and McKenna explain: "We will use gender, rather than sex, even when referring to those aspects of being a woman (girl) or man (boy) that have traditionally been viewed as biological. This will serve to emphasize our position that the element of social construction is primary in all aspects of being female or male" (7).

17   Judith Butler, *Bodies That Matter: On the Discursive Limits of "Sex"* (London: Routledge, 1993), 7.

18   Holly Devor makes a similar point about the applicability of "gender dysphoria" to other forms of uncomfortable embodiment in an excellent article. Devor creates a multitiered model of gender dysphoria that takes into account "the depth of dissatisfactions felt by females toward the various aspects of the social meanings attached to the configurations of their bodies." See Holly

Devor, "Female Gender Dysphoria in Context: Social Problem or Personal Problem?" *Annual Review of Sex Research* 7: 44–89.

19  Esther Newton, "The Mythic Mannish Lesbian: Radclyffe Hall and the New Woman," *Signs* 9, no. 4 (1984): 557–75.

20  Gayle Rubin, "Of Catamites and Kings: Reflections on Butch, Gender, and Boundaries," in *The Persistent Desire: A Femme-Butch Reader*, ed. Joan Nestle (Boston: Alyson Publications, 1992), 467.

21  See, for example, Sheila Jeffreys, "Butch and Femme: Now and Then," in *Not a Passing Phase: Reclaiming Lesbians in History, 1840–1985*, ed. Lesbian History Group (London: Women's Press, 1989), 158–87.

22  Mabel Hampton, interview by Joan Nestle, in *The Persistent Desire: A Femme-Butch Reader*, ed. Joan Nestle (Boston: Alyson Publications, 1992), 42–44.

23  Merril Mushroom, "Confessions of a Butch Dyke," *Common Lives, Lesbian Lives* 9 (fall 1983): 39.

24  For a graphic reproduction of multiple butch-femme names, see the cover of *Swagger and Sway: A Quarterly Newsletter for the Lesbian Butch/Femme Community* 2, no. 2 (spring 1994).

25  Cherríe Moraga, *Loving in the War Years* (Boston: South End Press, 1983).

26  Ibid., 125.

27  Rita Laporte, "The Butch/Femme Question," *The Ladder* 15, nos. 9–10 (June/July 1971): 4.

28  In chapter 3, I also talked about the "parsimony of science." I had not read Laporte's essay when I wrote this, and I am delighted to find a similar phrase in her excellent essay.

29  Leslie Feinberg, *Stone Butch Blues* (Ithaca, N.Y.: Firebrand Books, 1993), 213–14. This novel is the obvious counterpart to Radclyffe Hall's *The Well of Loneliness*. Both novels are thinly disguised autobiographical confessions of the dangers and pleasures of butch survival.

30  For a fascinating article on lesbian receptivity, see Ann Cvetkovich, "Recasting Receptivity," in *The Lesbian Erotic*, ed. Karla Jay (New York: New York University Press, 1995), 125–46.

31  Kennedy and Davis, *Boots of Leather, Slippers of Gold*, 192.

32  Judith Butler, "Imitation and Gender Insubordination," in *Inside/Out: Lesbian Theories, Gay Theories*, ed. Diana Fuss (New York: Routledge, 1991), 24.

33  Jeffreys, "Butch and Femme: Now and Then," 169.

34  Julia Penelope, "Whose Past Are We Reclaiming?" *Common Lives, Lesbian Lives* 9 (fall 1983): 18.

35  Victoria Brownworth, "Butch/Femme, Myth/Reality or More of the Same?" *WICCE: A Lesbian/Feminist Newspaper* 4 (summer 1975): 7–10.

36  Audre Lorde, *Zami: A New Spelling of My Name* (Freedom, Calif.: Crossing Press, 1982), 169.

37  Audre Lorde, "Eye to Eye: Black Women, Hatred, and Anger," in *Sister Out-sider* (Trumansburg, N.Y.: 1984), 160. Thanks to Liz Hines for bringing this line to my attention.

38  Biddy Martin, "Sexualities without Genders and Other Queer Utopias," *Dia-critics* 24, nos. 2–3 (summer/fall 1994): 104.

39  For a more extended discussion of Martin's essay and the problem of femme visibility see my "Between Butches," in *Theorizing Butch-Fem*, ed. Sally Munt (London: Cassell, 1998). For an excellent and ironic discussion of the tangled associations between femininity and femmeness see Lisa Duggan and Kath-leen McHugh, "A Fem(me)inist Manifesto," *Women and Performance*, special issue, "Queer Acts," ed. José Muñoz and Amanda Barrett, 8:2, no. 16 (1996): 150–60.

40  Alice Echols, "The Taming of the Id: Feminist Sexual Politics, 1968–1983," in *Pleasure and Danger: Exploring Female Sexuality*, ed. Carole Vance (New York: Routledge, Kegan and Paul, 1984), 50–72.

41  Valerie Solanas, *S.C.U.M. Manifesto* (New York: Olympia Press, 1970).

42  Laura Lederer, *Take Back the Night: Women on Pornography* (New York: Mor-row, 1980).

43  Andrea Dworkin, *Pornography: Men Possessing Women* (New York: Dutton, 1989).

44  Carole Vance, "Negotiating Sex and Gender in the Attorney General's Com-mission on Pornography," in *Sex Exposed: Sexuality and the Pornography De-bate*, ed. Lynne Segal and Mary McIntosh (London: Virago, 1992), 29–49.

45  For more on radical lesbian sex culture see Caught Looking, Inc., *Caught Look-ing: Feminism, Pornography, Censorship* (East Haven, Conn.: Long River, 1992).

46  Teresa Lilliandaughter, "Making Adjustments," *Common Lives, Lesbian Lives: A Lesbian Quarterly* 7 (spring): 35.

47  Susie Bright in conversation with Shar Rednour, "The Joys of Butch," in *Dag-ger: On Butch Women*, ed. Lily Burana, Roxxie and Linea Due (San Francisco: Cleis Press, 1994), 144.

48  Pat Califia, "Butch Desire," in *Dagger: On Butch Women*, 222.

### 5  Transgender Butch

1  For more on this see Phyllis Burke, *Gender Shock: Exploding the Myths of Male and Female* (New York: Doubleday, 1996), 60–66.

2  Judith Halberstam, "F2M: The Making of Female Masculinity," in *The Lesbian Postmodern*, ed. Laura Doan (New York: Columbia University Press, 1994), 210–28.

3  Sandy Stone, "The 'Empire' Strikes Back: A Posttranssexual Manifesto," in *Body Guards: The Cultural Politics of Gender Ambiguity*, ed. Julia Epstein and Kristina Straub (New York: Routledge, 1993), 280–304.

4   See *FTM International Newsletter* 29 (January 1995).

5   Isabella, "Review Essay," *FTM Newsletter* 29 (January 1995): 13–14.

6   Janice Raymond, *The Transsexual Empire: The Making of the She-Male* (Boston: Beacon Press, 1979).

7   The tendency to equate lesbian desire with fluidity is too general to trace in all its specificity, but it surfaces most clearly in the so-called sex debates documented by critics such as Alice Echols and Lisa Duggan and Nan Hunter (see Alice Echols, "The Taming of the Id: Feminist Sexual Politics, 1968–1983," in *Pleasure and Danger: Exploring Female Sexuality,* ed. Carole Vance [New York: Routledge, Kegan and Paul, 1984], 50–72; Lisa Duggan and Nan D. Hunter, *Sex Wars: Sexual Dissent and Political Culture* [New York: Routledge, 1995]). The idea that lesbian sex should be autonomous from male sexuality and from butch-femme roles has also been articulated by sex-negative feminists such as Sheila Jeffreys (see chapter 3). My point here, however, is that the belief in the sexual fluidity of lesbian desire cannot be limited to the puritanical impulses of a few feminists. Rather, in magazines, zines, and all manner of popular lesbian representation, androgyny or the movement back and forth between femininity and masculinity has been held up as a virtue.

8   Jay Prosser, "No Place like Home: The Transgendered Narrative of Leslie Feinberg's *Stone Butch Blues," Modern Fiction Studies* 41, nos. 3–4 (1995). I should say here that I find Prosser's work challenging and provocative, and I believe that his book on transsexual body narratives will be a crucial intervention into transgender discourse. My disagreements with Prosser are particular to this article. See Prosser, *Second Skins: The Body Narratives of Transsexuals* (New York: Columbia University Press, 1998).

9   Leslie Feinberg, *Transgender Liberation: A Movement Whose Time Has Come* (New York: World View Forum, 1992), 5.

10  Jordy Jones, "Another View of F2M," *FTM Newsletter* 29 (January 1995): 14–15.

11  See Stone, "Empire Strikes Back."

12  An example of an article that represented this kind of hostile attitude toward FTMs by lesbians appeared in the *Village Voice* in response to the horrifying murders of transgender man Brando Teena, his girlfriend Lisa Lewis, and another friend, Philip DeVine (see Donna Minkowitz, "Gender Outlaw," *Village Voice,* 19 April 1994, 24–30). Many people wrote to the *Village Voice* charging Minkowitz with insensitivity to the chosen gender of Teena.

13  See Elaine K. Ginsberg, "Introduction: The Politics of Passing," in *Passing and the Fictions of Identity,* ed. Elaine K. Ginsberg (Durham, N.C.: Duke University Press, 1996), 3. Ginsberg also blurs the lines between racial and gendered passing in this essay and makes the two analogous, thereby losing the very different social and political structures of gender and race.

14 Deva, "FTM/Female-to-Male: An Interview with Mike, Eric, Billy, Sky, and Shadow," in *Dagger: On Butch Women,* ed. Lily Burana, Roxxie, and Linnea Due (Pittsburgh and San Francisco: Cleis Press, 1994), 154–67.

15 For an example of this tendency see Henry Rubin, *Female to Male Transsexuals: A Phenomenological Study* (Chicago: University of Chicago Press, forthcoming).

16 See chapter 4 for more on this history. See also Elizabeth Lapovsky Kennedy and Madeline Davis, *Boots of Leather, Slippers of Gold: The History of a Lesbian Community* (New York: Routledge, 1993).

17 Heather Findlay, "Stone Butch Now," *Girlfriends Magazine,* March/April, 1995, 45.

18 I have maintained the female gender pronouns used in the article here until I refer to Jay as FTM, and then I use male pronouns.

19 Leslie Feinberg, *Stone Butch Blues: A Novel* (New York: Firebrand, 1993), 147.

20 Mario Martino, with harriett, *Emergence: A Transsexual Autobiography* (New York: Crown Publishers, 1977), 132.

21 Mark Rees, *Dear Sir or Madam: The Autobiography of a Female-to-Male Transsexual* (London: Cassell, 1996), 59.

22 "Guys" is an insider term used between FTMs and within transsexual circles.

23 Unfortunately, I cannot provide a citation for such a list because the lists are often anonymous and circulate only within a limited list with no intention of becoming public.

24 Amy Bloom, "The Body Lies," *New Yorker* 70, no. 21 (18 July 1994): 38–49.

25 Michel Foucault, *The History of Sexuality, Volume 1: An Introduction,* trans. Robert Hurley (New York: Vintage, 1980), 96.

26 Again, this is difficult to document, if only because transsexual discourse is still in the making. I am thinking of one particular conference I attended on transsexual and transgender issues in which a group of transsexual panelists insistently defined their political strategies in opposition to gay and lesbian political aims, which they considered to be mainstream and transsexual insensitive: "Transformations" Conference, CLAGS, Thursday, 2 May 1996.

27 For example, one critic comments on the effect of immigration on the Filipino third gender category of *bakla* (see Martin Manalansan, "Under the Shadows of Stonewall: Gay Transnational Politics and the Diasporic Dilemma," in *Worlds Aligned: Politics and Culture in the Shadow of Capital,* ed. David Lloyd and Lisa Lowe [Durham, N.C.: Duke University Press, 1997].

28 Bernice Hausman, *Changing Sex: Transsexualism, Technology, and the Idea of Gender* (Durham, N.C.: Duke University Press, 1995), 110.

29 Hausman, to her credit, does look at this shared history in a section on early-twentieth-century sexology. She studies the language of inversion and claims:

" 'Transsexual' is not a term that can accurately be used to describe subjects exhibiting cross-sex behaviors prior to the technical capacity for sex reassignment . . . there is no transsexuality without the surgeon" (117).

30  Holly Devor, "Female Gender Dysphoria in Context: Social Problem or Personal Problem?" *Annual Review of Sex Research* 7 (1997): 44–89.

31  Raymond, *Transsexual Empire.*

32  Hausman, *Changing Sex,* 140.

33  Prosser, "No Place like Home," 489.

34  Henry S. Rubin, "Do You Believe in Gender?" *Sojourner* 21, no. 6 (February 1996): 7–8.

35  Rita Felski, "Fin de Siecle, Fin de Sexe: Transsexuality, Postmodernism, and the Death of History," *New Literary History* 27, no. 2 (spring 1996): 337.

36  See Jean Baudrillard's comments on transsexualism in *The Transparency of Evil* (New York: Verso, 1993); see also Arthur Kroker and Marilouise Kroker, *Body Invaders: Panic Sex in America* (New York: St. Martin's Press, 1987), and their *The Last Sex* (New York: St. Martin's Press, 1993).

37  Radclyffe Hall, *The Well of Loneliness* (1928; reprint, New York: Anchor, 1990), 79.

38  Feinberg, *Stone Butch Blues.*

39  Rose Tremain, *Sacred Country* (New York: Washington Square Press, 1992), 179.

40  In an essay on one such passing woman, Loreta Velazquez, Elizabeth Young comments on the complex of meanings that arise from the history of women who engage in the so-called scandal of cross-dressing but do so often for patriotic or nationalist purposes. Velazquez commemorated her cross-dressed adventures in a mammoth first-person narrative called *The Woman in Battle,* in which she recorded her adventures as a man, her marriages as a woman, the battles she fights as a Confederate soldier, romances she carries on with women as a man, childbirth, her experiences as a Confederate spy in the Union army, and other multiply contradictory experiences. Young carefully and assiduously sorts through the details of *The Woman in Battle* and concludes: "Confederate cross-dressing is simultaneously and inseparably a question of gender, sexuality, race, region and nation, and the constitutive presence of metaphor in each of these realms can have both reactionary and radical consequences" (Young, "Confederate Counterfeit: The Case of the Cross-Dressed Civil War Soldier," in *Passing and the Fictions of Identity,* ed. Elaine K. Ginsberg [Durham, N.C.: Duke University Press, 1996], 213).

41  Jan Morris, *Conundrum: An Extraordinary Narrative of Transsexualism* (New York: Henry Holt, 1986), 99.

42  Stone, "Empire Strikes Back"; Marjorie Garber, "The Chic of Araby: Transvestism, Transsexualism, and the Erotics of Cultural Appropriation," in *Body*

Guards: The Cultural Politics of Gender Ambiguity, ed. Julia Epstein and Kristina Straub (New York: Routledge, 1994), 223–47.

43  Dorinne Kondo, "The Narrative Production of 'Home,' Community, and Political Identity in Asian American Theater," in *Displacement, Diaspora, and Geographies of Identity*, ed. Smadar Lavie and Ted Swedenburg (Durham, N.C.: Duke University Press, 1996), 97.

44  Gloria Anzaldúa, *Borderlands/La Frontera: The New Mestiza* (San Francisco: Spinsters/Aunt Lute Foundation, 1987), 13.

## 6  Looking Butch

This chapter began as a video lecture that Jenni Olson and I collaborated on. I could not have put this survey of butches on film together without her and her amazing archiving skills and talents.

1  See Esther Newton, "The Mythic Mannish Lesbian: Radclyffe Hall and the New Woman," *Signs* 9, no. 4 (summer 1984): 557–75.

2  Gloria Anzaldúa, "To(o) Queer the Writer—Loca, escritora y chicana," in *In-Versions: Writing by Dykes, Queers, and Lesbians*, ed. Betsy Warland (Vancouver, Canada: Press Gang Publishers, 1991), 252.

3  Judith Butler, "Imitation and Gender Insubordination," in *Inside/Out: Lesbian Theories, Gay Theories*, ed. Diana Fuss (New York: Routledge, 1991), 14.

4  "The Motion Picture Production Code," reprinted in Gerald C. Gardner, *The Censorship Papers: Movie Censorship Letters from the Hays Office, 1934–1968* (New York: Dodd Mead, 1987), 207–12. For an excellent article on the relations between audiences, critics, and producers of queer images during the Production Code see Chon Noriega, "SOMETHING'S MISSING HERE! Homosexuality and Film Reviews during the Production Code Era, 1934–1962," *Cinema Journal* 30, no. 1 (fall 1990): 20–39.

5  See Noriega, "SOMETHING'S MISSING HERE!"

6  Valerie Traub, "The Ambiguities of 'Lesbian' Viewing Pleasure: The (Dis)-Articulations of *Black Widow*," in *Body Guards: The Cultural Politics of Gender Ambiguity*, ed. Julia Epstein and Kristina Straub (New York: Routledge, 1991), 309.

7  Laura Mulvey, "Visual Pleasure and Narrative Cinema," in *Issues in Feminist Film Criticism*, ed. Patricia Erens (Bloomington: Indiana University Press, 1990), 57–68.

8  Some of the most interesting rewritings of Mulvey include Teresa de Lauretis, *Alice Doesn't: Feminism, Semiotics, Cinema* (Bloomington: Indiana University Press, 1984); Mary Ann Doane, "Film and the Masquerade: Theorizing the Female Spectator," *Screen* 23, nos. 3–4 (September/October 1982): 74–87; see also Laura Mulvey, "Afterthoughts on 'Visual Pleasure and Narrative Cinema' Inspired by *Duel in the Sun*," in *Framework* 15–17 (summer 1981): 12–15.

9   Judith Mayne, *Cinema and Spectatorship* (New York: Routledge, 1993), 80.
10  Traub obviously creates a "queer" gaze by suggesting that the male gaze is easily appropriated by a lesbian gaze. Judith Mayne conceptualizes the female gaze in terms of "a woman at the keyhole" where "the keyhole represents something of both the vision of the camera and the vision onto the screen" (see Judith Mayne, *The Woman at the Keyhole: Women's Cinema and Feminist Criticism* [Bloomington: Indiana University Press, 1990], 62).
11  See Linda Artel and Susan Wengraf, "Positive Images: Screening Women's Films," in *Issues in Feminist Film Criticism,* ed. Patricia Erens (Bloomington: Indiana University Press, 1990).
12  The best of these is Vito Russo, *The Celluloid Closet: Homosexuality in the Movies* (New York: Harper and Row, 1981).
13  Richard Dyer, "Stereotyping," in *Gays and Film* (New York: Zoetrope, 1984), 31.
14  "My Failure to Assimilate" is the ironic title of a Cecilia Dougherty video in which talking heads sort through the dangers and pleasures of real and imagined sexual and psychological roles.
15  The most influential articulation of the productive power of racial stereotyping is Homi Bhabha, "The Other Question: Stereotype, Discrimination, and the Discourse on Colonialism," in *The Location of Culture* (New York: Routledge, 1994).
16  For the gay media response to negative images see Christopher Sharrett, "Hollywood Homophobia," *USA Today* 121, no. 25, 66 (July 1992): 93; Janice C. Simpson, "Out of the Celluloid Closet," *Time* 139, no. 14 (6 April 1992): 65; Michaelangelo Signorile, "Hollywood Homophobia," *The Advocate,* 5 April 1992, 37; and David Ehrenstein, "Basic Instinct," *The Advocate,* 21 March 1992, 87.
17  In *Hollywood Androgyny* (New York: Columbia University Press, 1993), Rebecca Bell-Metereau covers some similar ground on the subject of cinematic butches and also tries to locate the "male impersonator" generically and historically. She uses categories such as "The Career Woman," "Tomboy, Pal, Companion," and "The Western Heroine" to locate the masculine woman and her function within particular genres. My categories are formed less by generic considerations and more by the function of the butch or her role in each set of films. I would argue for greater specificity than Bell-Metereau allows for. Also, "androgyny" seems like an inadequate term for the project of identifying the visual pleasure associated with masculine women because it implies some kind of ungendered essence.
18  It is important to carefully bracket the tomboy film off from other lesbian and butch narratives because this genre does not explicitly announce itself as lesbian. However, the preadult tomboy characters who populate these narratives

represent a powerful early form of female masculinity. What is more, they threaten not to be contained by a chronological framework within which the character passes through a tomboy phase and emerges at the other end as a properly feminine woman.

Barbara Creed has pointed to the existence of the tomboy movie, but she erases the category by allowing it to mesh with other cinematic genres of female masculinity. As I try to show in this chapter, these genres of butch representation are quite distinct (see Barbara Creed, "Lesbian Bodies: Tribades, Tomboys, and Tarts," in *Sexy Bodies: The Strange Carnalities of Feminism,* ed. Elizabeth Grosz and Elspeth Probyn [London: Routledge, 1995]). In *Hollywood Androgyny,* Rebecca Bell-Metereau also creates a tomboy category, but she does so within a chapter on "male impersonation," and she links the tomboy to the "female cross-dresser who acts as a buddy" (95). I do not see the tomboy as either a male impersonator or a cross-dresser but as a preadolescent gender within which the adult imperatives of binary gender have not yet taken hold. Bell-Metereau also stopped her summary of tomboy movies with *The Member of the Wedding* (1953), and many tomboy films were yet to come after this film was made.

19 See John D'Emilio and Estelle Freeman, *Intimate Matters: A History of Sexuality in America* (New York: Harper and Row, 1988), 319.

20 Virginia Spencer Carr, *The Lonely Hunter: A Biography of Carson McCullers* (New York: Doubleday, 1975), 29–31.

21 This film was also released as *Willie/Millie* and *I Was a Teenage Boy.*

22 In *Hollywood Androgyny,* Rebecca Bell-Metereau devotes a whole section of her study of "male impersonation" films to "The Western Heroine" and describes this character as an interesting role reversal within a genre "dominated by masculine virtues" (80). In a sense, Bell-Metereau suggests, the genre demands a masculine heroine when and where the woman is forced into action: "A woman in dire circumstances is forced to become a man to survive" (81). Bell-Metereau provides a fascinating historical context for transitions within the genre from glam cowgirl to tough cowgirl and back again. She discusses *Johnny Guitar* and *Calamity Jane* in this section, and some of my analysis draws from hers.

23 For more on the production history and reception of *The Killing of Sister George* see Russo, "Frightening the Horses," in *The Celluloid Closet,* 170–74.

24 Mel Gussow, "Beryl Reid, Actress, 76, Dies; Gave Life to Varied Eccentrics," *New York Times,* Obituaries, 15 October 1996, B10.

25 Juanita Diaz-Cotto, *Gender, Ethnicity, and the State: Latina and Latino Prison Politics* (Albany: State University of New York Press, 1996), 299.

26 For an excellent analysis of Agnes Moorehead's queer career, see Patricia

White, "Supporting Character: The Queer Career of Agnes Moorehead," in *Out in Culture: Gay, Lesbian, and Queer Essays on Popular Culture,* ed. Corey K. Creekmur and Alexander Doty (Durham, N.C.: Duke University Press, 1995), 91–114.

27 James Robert Parish, *Prison Pictures from Hollywood: Plots, Critiques, Casts, and Credits for 293 Theatrical and Made-for-Television Releases* (Jefferson, N.C.: McFarland, 1991), 73.

28 Carol Clover, *Men, Women, and Chain Saws: Gender and the Horror Film* (Princeton, N.J.: Princeton University Press, 1992), 35.

29 Bell-Metereau, *Hollywood Androgyny,* chap. 3.

30 Chris Straayer, "Redressing the 'Natural': The Temporary Transvestite Film," in *Deviant Eyes, Deviant Bodies: Sexual Re-orientations in Film and Video* (New York: Columbia University Press, 1996), 42–78.

31 Bell-Metereau includes her discussion of *Homicidal* in a chapter on post–Production Code films. She situates the film as follows: "William Castle's *Homicidal* (1961) was one of the first films after *Psycho* to employ gender disguise to create suspense and a surprise ending" (*Hollywood Androgyny,* 133).

32 For more on the Takarazuka Review see the film *Dream Girls* (1993) by Kim Longinotto and Jano Williams. For more on this tradition in Japanese theater, see Jennifer Robertson, "Butch and Femme on and off the Takarazuka Stage: Gender, Sexuality, and Social Organization in Japan," Working Paper Series, (East Lansing: Michigan State University, 1989).

33 I discuss this film at length in my article "F2M: The Making of Female Masculinity," in *The Lesbian Postmodern,* ed. Laura Doan (New York: Columbia University Press, 1994), 210–28.

34 Indeed, the notion that lesbian desire works by setting up sameness between women and produces intimacy through commonality still characterizes mainstream depictions of lesbianism. In the 1997 "outing" of Ellen on the sitcom of the same name, Ellen Degeneres's character was depicted as someone who found another woman attractive because they had so much in common. Audiences were treated to a very comforting image of lesbianism as blond lipstick lesbians who desire other blond lipstick lesbians.

35 For a consideration of *Personal Best*'s audience, see Chris Straayer, "*Personal Best:* Lesbian Feminist Audience," *Jump Cut* 29 (February 1984): 40–44.

36 For an excellent account of the fear of lesbianism in women's sports see Susan Cahn, *Coming On Strong: Gender and Sexuality in Twentieth Century Women's Sport* (Cambridge: Harvard University Press, 1994).

37 Jane Rule, *Desert of the Heart* (New York: Arno Press, 1975), 157.

38 Fannie Flagg, *Fried Green Tomatoes at the Whistle Stop Cafe* (New York: Random House, 1987).

39 k. d. lang has had a playful relation to drag and butchness throughout her

career. The latest manifestation of her playful attitude is her CD *Drag* (1997), which is all about forbidden pleasures such as smoking.

40 Stephen Holden, "Trying to Get Even While They Get Rich: *Set It Off*," *New York Times*, 6 November 1996, C11, C14.

41 Because of the intense visibility of black female masculinity, it is interesting to note the absence of any representations of black female masculinity in the art show "Black Masculinity" that appeared first in New York at the Whitney and then moved to Los Angeles.

42 Queen Latifah, "Heads Ain't Ready for Queen Latifah's Next Move," interview by Danyel Smith, *Vibe*, December 1996/January 1997, 98–102.

## 7  Drag Kings

1 To just name a few mainstream and independent films that have been about, or have prominently featured, drag queens: *Some Like It Hot* (1959, dir. Billy Wilder), *Tootsie* (1982, dir. Sydney Pollack), *Wigstock* (1993, dir. Tom Rubnitz), *Priscilla: Queen of the Desert* (1994, dir. Stephan Elliot), *The Crying Game* (1992, dir. Neil Jordan), *Mrs. Doubtfire* (1993, dir. Chris Columbus). Drag queen Ru Paul also currently has his own talk show. By comparison, there is not a single mainstream film that features a drag king or a male impersonator who produces anything like credible masculinity. *Victor/Victoria* (1982, dir. Blake Edwards), for example, is really still about drag queens, and Julie Andrews totally fails to pass.

2 See two anthologies for examples of such academic work on drag: David Bergman, ed., *Camp Grounds: Style and Homosexuality* (Amherst: University of Massachusetts Press, 1993); Moe Meyer, ed., *The Politics and Poetics of Camp* (New York: Routledge, 1994).

3 See Amy Linn, "Drag Kings," *San Francisco Weekly*, 27 September–3 October 1995, 10–11, 13–16, 18.

4 Esther Newton had the following to say about the history of the term "drag king": "As one segment of a drag queen context I witnessed in the late sixties in Chicago, there was a 'drag king' competition (and although I wrote earlier that this term was never used then, I seem to remember that in this one context, on stage, it was), and I do have slides of it. I agree that the concept was always available but, as Sarah Murray has noted, it never developed into a continuously generating tradition the way drag queen has." Newton, in personal correspondence with the author (July 1997).

5 See Elizabeth Drorbaugh, "Sliding Scales: Notes on Storme DeLaverie and the Jewel Box Revue, the Cross-Dressed Woman on the Contemporary Stage, and the Invert," in *Crossing the Stage: Controversies on Cross-Dressing*, ed. Lesley Ferris (London: Routledge, 1993), 120–43.

6 Laurence Senelick, "Boys and Girls Together: Subcultural Origins of Glamour

Drag and Male Impersonation on the Nineteenth-Century Stage," in *Crossing the Stage: Controversies on Cross-Dressing,* ed. Lesley Ferris (London: Routledge, 1993), 82.

7  Lisa Duggan reads female-to-male cross-dressing practices of this period as "the seeds of a new identity" and as a practice far more complex than "temporary or superficial disguise" (Duggan, "The Trials of Alice Mitchell: Sensationalism, Sexology, and the Lesbian Subject in Turn-of-the-Century America," *Signs* 18, no. 4 [summer 1993]: 809).

8  Drorbaugh, "Sliding Scales," 124.

9  Elizabeth Lapovsky Kennedy and Madeline Davis, *Boots of Leather and Slippers of Gold: The History of a Lesbian Community* (New York: Routledge, 1993), 62.

10  See my article on drag kings and rap for an elaboration on this point: "Mackdaddy, Superfly, Rapper: Gender, Race, and Masculinity in the Drag King Scene," *Social Text* (fall 1997), Special Issue on Race and Sexuality, edited by José Muñoz and Ann McClintock.

11  For an extended consideration of the permutations of "performance anxiety," see Ann Pellegrini, *Performance Anxiety* (New York: Routledge, 1996).

12  Judith Butler, *Gender Trouble: Feminism and the Subversion of Identity* (New York: Routledge, 1990), 140.

13  Esther Newton, "Dick(less) Tracy and the Homecoming Queen: Lesbian Power and Representation in Gay Male Cherry Grove," in *Inventing Lesbian Cultures in America,* ed. Ellen Lewin (Boston: Beacon Press, 1996), 164.

14  Newton, "Dick(less) Tracy," 163–64.

15  Sue Ellen Case, "Toward a Butch/Femme Aesthetic," in *The Lesbian and Gay Studies Reader,* ed. Henry Abelove, Michele Aina Barale, and David Halperin (New York: Routledge, 1993), 294–306. Case identifies camp as an ironic and queer rejection of realism which can as easily be deployed by lesbians as by gay men.

16  Kate Davy, "Fe/Male Impersonation: The Discourse of Camp," in *The Politics and Poetics of Camp,* ed. Moe Meyer (New York: Routledge, 1994), 133, 134. Davy disputes Sue Ellen Case's theory of lesbian camp and argues that camp is always only about male sexuality and that it is ultimately unable "to serve lesbian women engaged in theatrical endeavors in the same way it serves gay men." (133–134).

17  Sarah Murray, "Dragon Ladies, Draggin' Men: Some Reflections on Gender, Drag, and Homosexual Communities," *Public Culture* 6, no. 2 (winter 1994): 344.

18  When Murray does briefly mention transgender figures such as Billy Tipton, furthermore, she imprecisely and incorrectly characterizes them as "female" and uses feminine pronouns to talk about their performed identities.

19  Carole-Anne Tyler, "Boys Will Be Girls: The Politics of Gay Drag," in *In-*

*side/Out: Lesbian Theories, Gay Theories,* ed. Diana Fuss (New York: Routledge, 1991), 33.

20   Newton, "Dick(less) Tracy," 171.

21   Although I do not have any specific information about the relationship between these drag king performers and their involvement or lack of involvement in sex work, I am trying to establish here the lack of an organized "house" system as the productive matrix for these contests. The contests featured random women, mostly butch women who went up on stage mostly to try to win $200. That most of the contestants were butch should also suggest that sex work is not the obvious backdrop for the contests.

22   José Muñoz, "Famous and Dandy like B. 'n' Andy: Race, Pop, and Basquiat," in *Pop Out: Queer Warhol* (Durham, N.C.: Duke University Press, 1996), 147. Muñoz articulates the complex relations between minority subjects and mainstream culture, and he finds that very often the forms of cultural resistances produced by such subjects are constructed out of contradictory relations between dominant and minority identifications. Disidentification, Muñoz writes, "is a strategy that tries to transform a cultural logic from within" (148).

23   Newton, *Mother Camp,* 101.

24   Kimberly Pittman, "Walk like a Man: Inside the Booming Drag King Scene," *Manhattan Pride,* June 1996, 4.

25   The femme drag kings, it must be said, garner both the good and the bad publicity. In a truly offensive article for *Penthouse,* Ralph Gardner Jr. went in search of a "beautiful lesbian" by exploring the drag king scene and spent time hanging out with Buster Hymen and villain. This did not save them from becoming the objects of Gardner's lascivious attention in print. He also made racist remarks about Dred ("Drag Kings," *Penthouse,* February 1997, 85, 86, 128).

26   Michael Musto, *New York Post,* Arts Section, 20 February 1997, 43–44.

27   Buster Hymen is described as a "graduate of Torr's testosterone training" by Kimberly Pittman ("Drag Kingdom Come," *Manhattan Pride,* June 1996, 3).

28   Torr has been running the workshop since about 1989, and she charges $100 a session. Torr is a performance artist and has performed as a go-go dancer and in cross-dressing performances for many years in New York City.

29   Copy from a flyer advertising the workshop in March 1997. On the flyer, Torr describes herself as "a performance artist" and states that "she lives and works in New York where as a cross-dresser, she is a member of the F2M (female-to-male) fraternity." Because Torr is not an FTM transsexual and not an "out" lesbian, it is not altogether clear what this self-positioning statement means.

30   See, for example, Julie Wheelwright, "Out of My Way, I'm Man for a Day," *Independent,* 11 November 1994, 27–28; Anna Burnside, "Walk like a Man," *Scotland on Sunday,* 24 May 1995, 5.

31  As quoted in Phyllis Burke, "Diane Torr's Drag King Workshop," in *Gender Shock: Exploding the Myths of Male and Female* (New York: Anchor Books, 1996), 147.

32  Shannon Bell, "Finding the Male Within and Taking Him Cruising," in *The Last Sex*, ed. Arthur Kroker and Marilouise Kroker (New York: St. Martin's Press, 1993), 91–97.

33  Linn, "Drag Kings," 12.

34  Mo B. Dick [Maureen Fischer], interview by the author, 10 November 1996.

35  See my essay on gender, race, and masculinity for more on women of color and the drag king scene in New York City: "Mackdaddy, Superfly, Rapper: Gender, Race, and Masculinity in the Drag King Scene," in a special issue, "Queer Transexions of Race, Nation, and Gender," edited by Phillip Brian Harper, Ann McClintock, José Estaban Muñoz, and Trish Rosen, in *Social Text* 15, nos. 3–4 (fall-winter 1997): 104–31.

36  See Rochella Thorpe, "A House Where Queers Go": African-American Lesbian Nightlife in Detroit, 1940–1975," in *Inventing Lesbian Cultures in America*, ed. Ellen Lewin (Boston: Beacon Press, 1996), 40–61.

37  In 1996 female Elvis impersonation hit the news in a big way. San Francisco drag king Elvis Herselvis found herselvis at the center of considerable controversy. She had been hired by an Elvis Presley conference to perform as part of their cultural festivities. However, Graceland officials promptly pulled their funding of this cultural studies conference when they learned that it would feature a drag king act. The irony of this incident is hard to miss—the conference focuses on, and contributes to, the posthumous legacy of the King; part of this legacy involves the almost fanatical practice of Elvis impersonation. Graceland officials recognize Elvis impersonation as part of Elvis's legend, and they are comfortable sponsoring a conference that may feature any number of different Elvis impersonation acts.

38  Mo B. Dick, interview by the author, 16 November 1996.

39  Shon, interview by the author, 30 December 1996.

40  Linn, "Drag Kings," 15.

41  Dred, interview by the author, 13 November 1996.

42  Lizerace, interview by the author, 10 November 1996.

43  Evil Cave Boy, interview by the author, 13 November 1996.

44  Shon, interview by the author, 30 December 1996.

45  Retro, interview by the author, 10 November 1996.

## 8  Raging Bull (Dyke)

1  For a plethora of such articles, see the *New York Times* in 1997 between February and April. One example comes with the following headline: "Study Bolsters Idea That Exercise Cuts Breast Cancer Risk," *New York Times*, 1 May

1997, A1, B14. This article makes the shocking discovery that "regular exercise protects against breast cancer." Only a few months earlier there was an article in the *Times* announcing that young girls who exercise during their youth live longer and healthier lives. The article concluded that parents should encourage their girl children to exercise. Such pronouncements produce in this reader an excessively unscholarly response: duh!

2   Seth Linder, "Women in the Ring," *Cosmopolitan*, October 1995, 31.

3   Another way that boxing is being made safe for women is the transformation of it into a form of aerobics. "Boxercise" is the name given to the activity of women's boxing in many trendy gyms; boxercise involves a choreographed routine performed by women in front of punching bags and using both their fists and kicking action. A humorous rendition of boxercise appears in the camp film *Michelle and Romy's High School Reunion* (1996), in which Michelle and Romy, in a desperate effort to get in shape for their reunion, try every exercise the gym has to offer. In matching Day-Glo boxing outfits, they try to keep pace with an extremely regimented group of women who are punching and kicking in time to aerobics music.

4   Linder, "Women in the Ring," 32.

5   Obviously lesbianism is the specter that has haunted women's sports throughout the century. But even the emergence of visible lesbian communities has not dispelled the effect of homophobia on women's sports. A new women's version of *Sports Illustrated*, for example, features prominently an article on Olympic softball star Dot Richardson, who complains about being mistaken for a lesbian; a photograph of Dot at her prom accompanies the article (reported in Robert Lipsyte, "Magazine Explores Its Feminine Side," *New York Times*, 13 April 1997, sec. 8, p. 2).

6   *Garrett v. New York State Athletic Commission*, 286 NYS 2d 795 (1975). Most of my information on the history of women in boxing comes from Jeffrey Sammons, who supplied me with articles and gave me a chapter on women and boxing from his dissertation (Sammons, "Women and Boxing," in "America in the Ring: The Relationship of Boxing to American Society" [Ph.D. diss., University of North Carolina, 1982]).

7   Sammons, "Women and Boxing," 69.

8   Gail Bederman, *Manliness and Civilization: A Cultural History of Gender and Race in the United States, 1880–1917* (Chicago: University of Chicago Press, 1995), 3.

9   Sammons notes that "ironically, the first reported case, *People v. Floss*, interpreting the original New York statute of 1956 outlawing prize-fighting, came in a bout between women boxers" (52) (*People v. Floss*, 7 NYS 504 [1889]).

10  Susan Cahn, *Coming On Strong: Gender and Sexuality in Twentieth-Century Women's Sport* (Cambridge: Harvard University Press, 1994), 279.

11  Nancy L. Warren, "With This Ring: Gina 'Boom-Boom' Guidi Is Fighting Hard
    to Put Women's Boxing on the Map," *Curve* 7, no. 1 (March 1997): 28–29.
12  Jenni Olson, "What's Dirty about Boxing?" *Girljock* (summer 1992): 22–24.
13  For an interesting appraisal of male masochism see Kaja Silverman, *Male
    Subjectivity: Masculinity in the Margins* (New York: Routledge, 1994). Although
    Silverman makes male masochism into a marginal masculinity, I am suggest-
    ing here that masochism is central to dominant masculinity.

# BIBLIOGRAPHY

Alexander, Jacqui, and Chandra Talpade Mohanty, eds. *Feminist Genealogies, Colonial Legacies, Democratic Futures.* New York: Routledge, 1997.

Allen, Mary S. *The Pioneer Policewoman.* Edited and arranged by Julie Helen Heyneman. London: Chatto and Windus, 1925.

Anzaldúa, Gloria. *Borderlands/La Frontera: The New Mestiza.* San Francisco: Spinsters/Aunt Lute Foundation, 1987.

———. "To(o) Queer the Writer—Loca, escritora y chicana." In *InVersions: Writing by Dykes, Queers, and Lesbians,* edited by Betsy Warland. Vancouver, Canada: Press Gang Publishers, 1991.

Bad Object Choices, eds. *How Do I Look? Queer Film and Video.* Seattle: Bay Press, 1991.

Baker, Michael. *Our Three Selves: The Life of Radclyffe Hall.* New York: William Morrow, 1985.

Bederman, Gail. *Manliness and Civilization: A Cultural History of Gender and Race in the United States, 1880–1917.* Chicago: University of Chicago Press, 1995.

Bell, Shannon. "Finding the Male Within and Taking Him Crusing: Drag King for a Day." In *The Last Sex,* edited by Arthur and Marilouise Kroker, 91–97. New York: St. Martin's Press, 1993.

Bell-Metereau, Rebecca. *Hollywood Androgyny.* New York: Columbia University Press, 1993.

Berger, Maurice, Brian Wallis, and Simon Watson, eds. *Constructing Masculinity.* New York: Routledge, 1996.

Bergman, David, ed. *Camp Grounds: Style and Homosexuality.* Amherst: University of Massachusetts Press, 1993.

Bersani, Leo. "Is the Rectum a Grave?" In *AIDS: Cultural Analysis, Cultural Activism,* edited by Douglas Crimp. Cambridge: MIT Press, 1988.

Bornstein, Kate. *Gender Outlaw: Men, Women, and the Rest of Us.* New York: Routledge, 1993.

Brittain, Vera. *Radclyffe Hall: A Case of Obscenity?* New York: A. S. Barnes, 1968.

Brittan, Arthur. *Masculinity and Power.* New York: Basil Blackwell, 1989.

Buford, Bill. *Among the Thugs.* New York: Vintage, 1991.

Burana, Lily Roxxie, and Linea Due, eds. *Dagger: On Butch Women.* San Francisco: Cleis Press, 1994.

Burke, Phyllis. *Gender Shock: Exploding the Myths of Male and Female.* New York: Doubleday, 1996.

Butler, Judith. *Gender Trouble: Feminism and the Subversion of Identity.* New York: Routledge, 1990.

———. "Imitation and Gender Insubordination." In *Inside/Out: Lesbian Theories, Gay Theories,* edited by Diana Fuss, 13–31. New York: Routledge, 1991.

———. *Bodies That Matter: On the Discursive Limits of "Sex."* New York: Routledge, 1993.

Cahn, Susan. *Coming On Strong: Gender and Sexuality in Twentieth Century Women's Sport.* Cambridge: Harvard University Press, 1994.

Carr, Virginia Spencer. *The Lonely Hunter: A Biography of Carson McCullers.* New York: Doubleday, 1975.

Case, Sue-Ellen. "Toward a Butch-Femme Aesthetic." In *The Lesbian and Gay Studies Reader,* edited by Henry Abelove, Michele Aina Barale, and David Halperin, 294–306. New York: Routledge, 1993.

Castle, Terry. *The Apparitional Lesbian: Female Homosexuality and Modern Culture.* New York: Columbia University Press, 1993.

———. *Noel Coward and Radclyffe Hall: Kindred Spirits.* New York: Columbia University Press, 1996.

Caught Looking, Inc. *Caught Looking: Feminism, Pornography, Censorship.* East Haven, Conn.: Long River, 1992.

Chapman, Rowena, and Jonathan Rutherford. *Male Order: Unwrapping Masculinity.* London: Lawrence and Wishart, 1988.

Chauncey, George, Jr. "Christian Brotherhood or Sexual Perversion? Homosexual Identities and the Construction of Sexual Boundaries in the World War I Era." In *Hidden from History: Reclaiming the Gay and Lesbian Past,* edited by Martin Duberman, Martha Vicinus, and George Chauncey Jr., 294–317. New York: Penguin, 1989.

———. "From Sexual Inversion to Homosexuality: The Changing Medical Conceptualization of Female 'Deviance.'" In *Passion and Power: Sexuality in History,* edited by Kathy Piess and Christina Simmons, 87–117. Philadelphia: Temple University Press, 1989.

———. *Gay New York: Gender, Urban Culture, and the Making of the Gay Male World, 1890–1940.* New York: Basic Books, 1994.

Clarke, Anna. "Anne Lister's Construction of Lesbian Desire." *Journal of the History of Sexuality* 7, no. 11 (summer 1996): 23–50.

Clover, Carol. *Men, Women, and Chain Saws: Gender and the Horror Film.* Princeton: Princeton University Press, 1992.

Cohen, Ed. "Writing Gone Wilde: Homoerotic Desire in the Closet of Representation." *PMLA* 102 (1987): 801–13.

———. *Talk on the Wilde Side.* New York: Routledge, 1993.

Cook, Blanche Wiesen. "The Historical Denial of Lesbianism." *Radical History Review* 20 (spring/summer 1979): 60–65.

Cornwell, Anita. *Black Lesbians in White America.* Tallahassee, Fla.: Naiad Press, 1983.

Creed, Barbara. "Lesbian Bodies: Tribades, Tomboys, and Tarts." In *Sexy Bodies: The Strange Carnalities of Feminism,* edited by Elizabeth Grosz and Elspeth Probyn, 86–103. London: Routledge, 1995.

Cvetkovich, Ann. "Recasting Receptivity: Femme Sexualities." In *The Lesbian Erotic,* edited by Karla Jay, 125–46. New York: New York University Press, 1995.

Davy, Kate. "Fe/Male Impersonation: The Discourse of Camp." In *The Politics and Poetics of Camp,* edited by Moe Meyer, 130–48. New York: Routledge, 1994.

Delany, Samuel R. *The Motion of Light in Water.* New York: Plume, 1992.

De Lauretis, Teresa. *Technologies of Gender: Essays on Theory, Film, and Fiction.* Bloomington: Indiana University Press, 1987.

———. "The Lure of the Mannish Lesbian." In *The Practice of Love: Lesbian Sexuality and Perverse Desire,* 203–56. Bloomington: Indiana University Press, 1994.

Dellamora, Richard. *Masculine Desire: The Sexual Politics of Victorian Aestheticism.* Chapel Hill: University of North Carolina Press, 1990.

Delueze, Gilles, and Felix Guattari. *Anti-Oedipus: Capitalism and Schizophrenia.* Translated by Robert Hurley, Mark Seem, and Helen R. Lane. Minneapolis: University of Minnesota Press, 1983.

D'Emilio, John. *Sexual Politics, Sexual Communities: The Making of a Homosexual Minority in the United States, 1940–1970.* Chicago: University of Chicago Press, 1983.

D'Emilio, John, and Estelle Freeman. *Intimate Matters: A History of Sexuality in America.* New York: Harper and Row, 1988.

Deva. "FTM/Female-to-Male: An Interview with Mike, Eric, Billy, Sky, and Shadow." In *Dagger: On Butch Women,* edited by Lily Burana, Roxxie, and Linnea Due, 154–67. San Francisco: Cleis Press, 1994.

Diaz-Cotto, Juanita. *Gender, Ethnicity, and the State: Latina and Latino Prison Politics.* Albany: State University of New York Press, 1996.

Doan, Laura. *Fashioning Sappho in the 1920's: The Origins of Modern English Lesbian Culture.* New York: Columbia University Press, forthcoming.

Doane, Mary Ann. "Film and the Masquerade: Theorizing the Female Spectator." *Screen* 23, nos. 3–4 (September/October 1982): 74–88.

Donoghue, Emma. *Passions between Women: British Lesbian Culture, 1668–1801.* New York: HarperCollins, 1993.

Drorbaugh, Elizabeth. "Sliding Scales: Notes on Storme DeLaverie and the Jewel Box Revue, the Cross-Dressed Woman on the Contemporary Stage, and the Invert." In *Crossing the Stage: Controversies on Cross-Dressing,* edited by Lesley Ferris, 120–43. London: Routledge, 1993.

Duberman, Martin Bauml, Martha Vicinus, and George Chauncey Jr., eds. *Hidden from History: Reclaiming the Gay and Lesbian Past.* New York: New American Library, 1989.

Dugaw, Dianne. *Warrior Women and Popular Balladry, 1650–1850.* Chicago: University of Chicago Press, 1989.

Duggan, Lisa. "The Trials of Alice Mitchell: Sensationalism, Sexology, and the Lesbian Subject in Turn-of-the-Century America." *Signs* 18, no. 4 (summer 1993): 791–814.

Duggan, Lisa, and Nan D. Hunter. *Sex Wars: Sexual Dissent and Political Culture.* New York: Routledge, 1995.

Duggan, Lisa, and Kathleen McHugh. "A Fem(me)inist Manifesto." *Women and Performance* 8:2, no. 16 (1996): 150–60. Special issue "Queer Acts," edited by José Muñoz and Amanda Barrett.

Dyer, Richard. *Gays and Film.* London: BFI, 1977.

Echols, Alice. "The Taming of the Id: Feminist Sexual Politics, 1968–1983." In *Pleasure and Danger: Exploring Female Sexuality,* edited by Carole Vance, 50–72. New York: Routledge, Kegan and Paul, 1984.

Edelman, Lee. *Homographesis: Essays in Gay Literary and Cultural Theory.* New York: Routledge, 1994.

Ekins, Richard, and Dave King, eds. *Blending Genders: Social Aspects of Cross-Dressing and Sex-Changing.* New York: Routledge, 1996.

Ellis, Havelock. "Sexual Inversion in Women." In *Studies in the Psychology of Sex.* New York: Random House, 1900.

Epstein, Julia. "Either/Or—Neither/Both: Sexual Ambiguity and the Ideology of Gender." *Genders* 7 (spring 1990): 99–142.

Epstein, Julia, and Kristina Straub. *Body Guards: The Cultural Politics of Gender Ambiguity.* New York: Routledge, 1991.

Faderman, Lillian. *Surpassing the Love of Men: Romantic Friendship and Love between Women from the Renaissance to the Present.* New York: William Morrow, 1981.

——. *Scotch Verdict.* New York: Columbia University Press, 1993.

Fausto-Sterling, Ann. *Myths of Gender: Biological Theories about Women and Men.* Rev. Ed. New York: Basic Books, 1992.

Feinberg, Leslie. *Transgender Liberation: A Movement Whose Time Has Come.* New York: World View Forum, 1992.

——. *Stone Butch Blues: A Novel.* New York: Firebrand, 1993.

——. *Transgender Warriors.* Boston: Beacon Press, 1996.

Felski, Rita. "Fin de Siecle, Fin de Sexe: Transsexuality, Postmodernism, and the Death of History. *New Literary History* 27, no. 2 (spring 1996): 337–49.

Ferris, Lesley, ed. *Crossing the Stage: Controversies on Cross-Dressing.* New York: Routledge, 1993.

Flagg, Fannie. *Fried Green Tomatoes at the Whistle Stop Cafe.* New York: Random House, 1987.

Foster, Jeannette H. *Sex Variant Women in Literature.* Tallahassee, Fla.: Naiad Press, 1985.

Foucault, Michel. *Herculine Barbin: Being the Recently Discovered Memoirs of a Nineteenth Century French Hermaphrodite.* Translated by Richard McDougall. New York: Pantheon Books, 1980.

——. *The History of Sexuality, Volume 1: An Introduction.* Translated by Robert Hurley. New York: Vintage Books, 1980.

Freud, Sigmund. "The Psychogenesis of a Case of Homosexuality in a Woman." In *Sexuality and the Psychology of Love,* 133–59. 1920. Reprint, New York: Collier, 1963.

Frye, Marilyn. "Lesbian Sex." In *An Intimate Wilderness: Lesbian Writers on Sexuality,* edited by Judith Barrington, 1–8. Portland, Oreg.: Eighth Mountain, 1991.

Fuss, Diana, ed. *Inside/Out: Lesbian Theories, Gay Theories.* New York: Routledge, 1991.

Garber, Eric. "Gladys Bentley: The Bulldagger Who Sang the Blues." *Out/Look* 1, no. 1 (spring 1988): 52–61.

Garber, Marjorie. *Vested Interests: Cross-Dressing and Cultural Anxiety.* New York: Routledge, 1992.

Ginsberg, Elaine K., ed. *Passing and the Fictions of Identity.* Durham, N.C.: Duke University Press, 1996.

Glasgow, Joanne, ed. *Your John: The Love Letters of Radclyffe Hall*. New York: New York University Press, 1997.

Hacker, Marilyn. *Love, Death, and the Changing of the Seasons*. New York: Norton, 1986.

Halberstam, Judith. "Between Butches." In *Dagger: On Butch Women*, edited by Sally Munt. London: Cassell, 1998.

———. "F2M: The Making of Female Masculinity." In *The Lesbian Postmodern*, edited by Laura Doan, 210–28. New York: Columbia University Press, 1994.

———. "Mackdaddy, Superfly, Rapper: Gender, Race, and Masculinity in the Drag King Scene." *Social Text* (fall 1997): 104–31. Special issue, "Queer Transexions of Race, Nation, and Gender, edited by Phillip Brian Harper, Ann McClintock, José Esteban Muñoz, and Trish Rosen.

Halberstam, Judith, and Ira Livingston, eds. *Posthuman Bodies*. Bloomington: Indiana University Press, 1995.

Hale, Jacob. "Are Lesbians Women?" *Hypatia* 11, no. 2 (spring 1996): 94–121.

Hall, Radclyffe. *The Well of Loneliness*. 1928. Reprint, New York: Anchor Books, 1990.

———. *Miss Ogilvy Finds Herself*. New York: Harcourt, Brace, 1934.

Hamer, Emily. *Britannia's Glory: A History of Twentieth-Century Lesbians*. London: Cassell, 1996.

Hammonds, Evelynn. "Toward a Genealogy of Black Female Sexuality: The Problematic of Silence." In *Feminist Genealogies, Colonial Legacies, Democratic Futures*, edited by M. Jacqui Alexander and Chandra Talpade Mohanty, 170–82. New York: Routledge, 1997.

Hausman, Bernice. *Changing Sex: Transsexualism, Technology, and the Idea of Gender*. Durham, N.C.: Duke University Press, 1995.

Herdt, Gil, ed. *Third Sex, Third Gender: Beyond Sexual Dimorphism in Culture and History*. New York: Zone Books, 1994.

Hollander, Anne. *Sex and Suits: The Evolution of Modern Dress*. New York: Kodansha Globe Books, 1994.

Isabella. Review Essay. *FTM Newsletter* 29 (January 1995): 13–14.

Jay, Karla, ed. *Lesbian Erotics*. New York: New York University Press, 1995.

Jeffreys, Sheila. "Butch and Femme: Now and Then." In *Not a Passing Phase: Reclaiming Lesbians in History, 1840–1985*, edited by the Lesbian History Group, 158–87. London: Women's Press, 1989.

Jones, Jordy. "Another View of F2M." *FTM Newsletter* 29 (January 1995): 14–15.

Kennedy, Elizabeth Lapovsky, and Madelaine Davis. *Boots of Leather and Slippers of Gold: The History of a Lesbian Community*. New York: Routledge, 1993.

Kessler, Suzanne J., and Wendy McKenna. *Gender: An Ethnomethodological Approach*. Chicago and London: University of Chicago Press, 1990.

Kimmel, Michael. *Manhood in America: A Cultural History.* New York: Free Press, 1996.

Kondo, Dorinne. "The Narrative Production of 'Home,' Community, and Political Identity in Asian American Theater." In *Displacement, Diaspora, and Geographies of Identity,* edited by Smadar Lavie and Ted Sedenburg, 97–118. Durham, N.C.: Duke University Press, 1996.

Krafft-Ebing, Richard von. *Psychopathia Sexualis.* Translated by Franklin S. Klaf. 1886. Reprint, New York: Bell Publishing, 1965.

Kroker, Arthur, and Marilouise Kroker. *Body Invaders: Panic Sex in America.* New York: St. Martin's Press, 1987.

———, eds. *The Last Sex.* New York: St. Martin's Press, 1993.

Laqueur, Thomas. *Making Sex: Body and Gender from the Greeks to Freud.* Cambridge: Harvard University Press, 1990.

Lock, Joan. *The British Policewoman: Her Story.* London: Robert Hale, 1979.

Lorde, Audre. *Zami: A New Spelling of My Name.* Trumansburg, N.Y.: Crossing Press, 1982.

———. *Sister Outsider.* Trumansburg, N.Y.: Crossing Press, 1984.

Manalansan, Martin. "Under the Shadows of Stonewall: Gay Transnational Politics and the Diasporic Dilemma." In *Worlds Aligned: Politics and Culture in the Shadow of Capital,* edited by David Lloyd and Lisa Lowe. Durham, N.C.: Duke University Press, 1997.

Martin, Biddy. "Sexualities without Genders and Other Queer Utopias." *Diacritics* 24, nos. 2–3 (summer/fall 1994): 104–21.

Martino, Mario, with harriett. *Emergence: A Transsexual Autobiography.* New York: Crown Publishers, 1977.

Mayne, Judith. *The Woman at the Keyhole: Women's Cinema and Feminist Criticism.* Bloomington: Indiana University Press, 1990.

———. *Cinema and Spectatorship.* New York: Routledge, 1993.

McCullers, Carson. *The Member of the Wedding.* 1946. Reprint, New York: Bantam Books, 1958.

Meyer, Moe, ed. *The Politics and Poetics of Camp.* New York: Routledge, 1994.

Middleton, Peter. *The Inward Gaze: Masculinity and Subjectivity in Modern Culture.* London: Routledge, 1992.

Minkowitz, Donna. "Gender Outlaw." *Village Voice,* 19 April 1994, 24–30.

Moore, Lisa, " 'Something More Tender Still than Friendship': Romantic Friendship in Early-Nineteenth-Century England." *Feminist Studies* 18, no. 3 (fall 1992): 499–520.

Moraga, Cherríe. *Loving in the War Years.* Boston: South End Press, 1983.

Moraga, Cherríe, and Gloria Anzaldúa. *This Bridge Called My Back: Writings by Radical Women of Color.* New York: Women of Color Press, 1981.

Morris, Jan. *Conundrum: An Extraordinary Narrative of Transsexualism.* New York: Henry Holt, 1986.

Mosse, George L. *The Image of Man: The Creation of Modern Masculinity.* New York and Oxford: Oxford University Press, 1996.

Mulvey, Laura. "Visual Pleasure and Narrative Cinema." In *Issues in Feminist Film Criticism,* edited by Patricia Erens, 57–68. Bloomington: Indiana University Press, 1990.

Muñoz, José. "Famous and Dandy like B. 'n' Andy: Race, Pop, and Basquiat." In *Pop Out: Queer Warhol,* edited by José Muñoz et al., 144–79. Durham, N.C.: Duke University Press, 1996.

Murray, Sarah. "Dragon Ladies, Draggin' Men: Some Reflections on Gender, Drag, and Homosexual Communities." *Public Culture* 6, no. 2 (winter 1994): 343–63.

Nestle, Joan. *A Restricted Country.* Ithaca, N.Y.: Firebrand Books, 1987.

———. *A Persistent Desire: The Femme-Butch Reader.* Boston: Alyson Publications, 1992.

Newton, Esther. *Mother Camp: Female Impersonators in America.* Chicago: University of Chicago Press, 1972; reprint, 1979.

———. "The Mythic Mannish Lesbian: Radclyffe Hall and the New Woman." *Signs* 9, no. 4 (summer 1984): 557–75.

———. "Dick(less) Tracy and the Homecoming Queen: Lesbian Power and Representation in Gay Male Cherry Grove." In *Inventing Lesbian Cultures,* edited by Ellen Lewin, 162–93. Boston: Beacon Press, 1996.

Newton, Esther, and Shirley Walton. "The Misunderstanding: Toward a More Precise Sexual Vocabulary." In *Pleasure and Danger,* edited by Carole Vance, 244–50. Boston: Routledge, Kegan and Paul, 1984.

Noriega, Chon. "SOMETHING'S MISSING HERE! Homosexuality and Film Reviews during the Production Code Era, 1934–1962." *Cinema Journal* 30, no. 1 (fall 1990): 20–39.

Olson, Jenni. "Butch Icons of the Silver Screen." In *Dagger: On Butch Women,* edited by Lily Burana, Roxxie, and Linnea Due, 58–76. San Francisco: Cleis Press, 1994.

———. "What's Dirty about Boxing?" *Girljock* (summer 1992): 22–24.

Penley, Constance, and Sharon Willis, eds. *Male Trouble.* Minneapolis: University of Minnesota Press, 1993.

Phelan, Shane. *Identity Politics: Lesbian Feminism and the Limits of Community.* Philadelphia: Temple University Press, 1989.

Prosser, Jay. "No Place like Home: The Transgendered Narrative of Leslie Feinberg's *Stone Butch Blues.*" *Modern Fiction Studies* 41, nos. 3–4 (1995): 483–514.

Radford, Jean. "An Inverted Romance: *The Well of Loneliness* and Sexual Ideology." In *The Progress of Romance: The Politics of Popular Fiction,* edited by Jean Radford. London: Routledge, 1986.

Raymond, Janice. *The Transsexual Empire: The Making of the She-Male.* Boston: Beacon Press, 1979.

Rechy, John. *Sexual Outlaw.* New York: Grove Press, 1975.

Rees, Mark. *Dear Sir or Madam: The Autobiography of a Female-to-Male Transsexual.* London: Cassell, 1996.

Reid-Pharr, Robert. "Dinge." *Women and Performance* 8:2, no. 16 (1996): 75–86. Special issue, "Queer Acts."

Rodriguez, Nice. *Throw It to the River.* Toronto, Canada: Women's Press, 1993.

Roper, Michael, and John Tosh. *Manful Assertions: Masculinities in Britain since 1800.* London: Routledge, 1991.

Rubin, Gayle. "The Traffic in Women: Notes on the 'Political Economy' of Sex." In *Toward an Anthropology of Women,* edited by Rayna R. Reiter, 157–210. New York: Monthly Review Press, 1975.

———. "Thinking Sex: Notes for a Radical Theory of the Politics of Sexuality." In *Pleasure and Danger: Exploring Female Sexuality,* edited by Carole Vance, 267–319. Boston: Routledge, Kegan and Paul, 1984.

———. "Of Catamites and Kings: Reflections on Butch, Gender, and Boundaries." In *The Persistent Desire: A Femme-Butch Reader,* edited by Joan Nestle, 466–83. Boston: Alyson Publications, 1992.

Rubin, Henry. "Do You Believe in Gender?" *Sojourner* 21, no. 6 (February 1996): 7–8.

Ruehl, Sonia. "Inverts and Experts: Radclyffe Hall and the Lesbian Identity." In *Feminism, Culture, and Politics,* edited by Rosalind Brunt and Carolyn Rowan. London: Lawrence and Wishart, 1982.

Rule, Jane. *Desert of the Heart.* New York: Arno Press, 1975.

Russo, Vito. *The Celluloid Closet: Homosexuality in the Movies.* New York: Harper and Row, 1981.

Samois, ed. *Coming to Power.* Boston: Alyson Publications, 1981.

Savage, Candace. *Cowgirls.* London: Bloomsbury Publishing, 1996.

Sedgwick, Eve K. *Between Men: English Literature and Male Homosocial Desire.* New York: Columbia University Press, 1985.

———. *Epistemology of the Closet.* Berkeley: University of California Press, 1990.

———. *Tendencies.* Durham, N.C.: Duke University Press, 1993.

Seidler, Victor. *Unreasonable Men: Masculinity and Social Theory.* New York: Routledge, 1994.

Senelick, Laurence. "Boys and Girls Together: Subcultural Origins of Glamour Drag and Male Impersonation on the Nineteenth-Century Stage." In *Crossing the Stage: Controversies on Cross-Dressing,* edited by Lesley Ferris, 80–95. London: Routledge, 1993.

Silverman, Kaja. *Male Subjectivity at the Margins.* New York: Routledge, 1992.

Silverman, Willa Z. *The Notorious Life of Gyp, Right-Wing Anarchist in Fin-de-Siecle France*. New York: Oxford University Press, 1995.

Smith, Anna Marie. "The Regulation of Lesbian Sexuality through Erasure: The Case of Jennifer Saunders." In *Lesbian Erotics*, edited by Karla Jay, 164–82. New York: New York University Press, 1995.

Smith, Paul, ed. *Boys: Masculinities in Contemporary Culture*. Boulder, Colo.: Westview Press, 1996.

Snitow, Ann, Christine Stansell, and Sharon Thompson, eds. *Powers of Desire: The Politics of Sexuality*. New York: Monthly Review Press, 1983.

Solanas, Valerie. *S.C.U.M. Manifesto*. New York: Olympia Press, 1970.

Stone, Sandy. "The 'Empire' Strikes Back: A Posttranssexual Manifesto." In *Body Guards: The Cultural Politics of Gender Ambiguity*, edited by Julia Epstein and Kristina Straub, 280–304. New York: Routledge, 1993.

Straayer, Chris. *Deviant Eyes, Deviant Bodies: Sexual Re-orientations in Film and Video*. New York: Columbia University Press, 1996.

Stryker, Susan. "My Words to Victor Frankenstein above the Village of Chamounix: Performing Transgender Rage." *GLQ* 1 (1994): 237–54.

Sullivan, Louis. *From Female to Male: The Life of Jack Bee Garland*. Boston: Alyson Publications, 1990.

Traub, Valerie. "The Ambiguities of 'Lesbian' Viewing Pleasure: The (Dis) Articulations of *Black Widow*." In *Body Guards: The Cultural Politics of Gender Ambiguity*, edited by Julia Epstein and Kristina Straub. New York: Routledge, 1993.

———. "The Psychomorphology of the Clitoris." *GLQ* 2 (1996): 81–113.

Tremain, Rose. *Sacred Country*. New York: Washington Square Press, 1992.

Trumbach, Randolph. "London's Sapphists: From Three Sexes to Four Genders in the Making of Modern Culture." In *Third Sex, Third Gender: Beyond Sexual Dimorphism in Culture and History*, edited by Gilbert Herdt. New York: Zone Books, 1994.

Tyler, Carole-Anne. "The Supreme Sacrifice? TV, 'TV,' and the Renee Richards Story." *Differences* 1, no. 3 (fall 1989): 160–86.

Vance, Carole. "Negotiating Sex and Gender in the Attorney General's Commission on Pornography." In *Sex Exposed: Sexuality and the Pornography Debate*, edited by Lynne Segal and Mary McIntosh, 29–49. London: Virago, 1992.

———, ed. *Pleasure and Danger: Exploring Female Sexuality*. Boston: Routledge, 1984.

Vicinus, Martha. "'They Wonder to Which Sex I Belong': The Historical Roots of the Modern Lesbian Identity." *Feminist Studies* 18, no. 3 (fall 1992): 467–98.

Wallis, Brian, ed. *Constructing Masculinities*. New York: Routledge, 1996.

Warner, Michael, ed. *Fear of a Queer Planet: Queer Politics and Social Theory*. Minneapolis: University of Minnesota Press, 1993.

Warren, Nancy L. "With This Ring: Gina 'Boom-Boom' (Guidi Is Fighting Hard to Put Women's Boxing on the Map," *Curve* 7, no. 1 (March 1997): 28–29.

Wheelwright, Julie. *Amazons and Military Maids: Women Who Dressed as Men in Pursuit of Life, Liberty, and Happiness*. London: Pandora, 1989.

Whitbread, Helena, ed. *I Know My Own Heart: The Diaries of Ann Lister*. New York: New York University Press, 1992.

———, ed. *No Priest but Love: The Diaries of Anne Lister from 1824–1826*. New York: New York University Press, 1992.

Wilde, Oscar. *The Picture of Dorian Gray*. 1892. Reprint, Oxford: Oxford University Press, 1981.

Wittig, Monique. "The Straight Mind." In *The Straight Mind: Collected Essays*, 21–33. New York: Routledge, 1990.

Young, Elizabeth. "Confederate Counterfeit: The Case of the Cross-Dressed Civil War Soldier." In *Passing and the Fictions of Identity*, edited by Elaine Ginsberg, 181–217. Durham, N.C.: Duke University Press, 1996.

## FILMOGRAPHY

*Alice Doesn't Live Here Anymore* (1974), directed by Martin Scorsese.
*Aliens* (1986), directed by James Cameron.
*Babe* (1995)
*Bad Girls' Dormitory* (1984), directed by Tim Kincaid.
*Basic Instinct* (1992), directed by Paul Verhoeven.
*Bound* (1996), directed by Larry and Andy Wachowski.
*Cabaret* (1972), directed by Bob Fosse.
*Caged* (1950), directed by John Cromwell.
*Caged Heat* (1974), directed by Jonathan Demme.
*Calamity Jane* (1953), directed by David Butler.
*The Children's Hour* (1961), directed by William Wyler.
*Chopper Chicks in Zombietown* (1990), directed by Dan Hoskins.
*Cruising* (1980), directed by William Friedkin.
*The Crying Game* (1992), directed by Neil Jordan.
*Desert Hearts* (1986), directed by Donna Deitch.
*Desperate Living* (1977), directed by John Waters.

*Easy Rider* (1969)

*Flaming Ears* (1992), directed by Angela Hans Scheirl, Dietmar Schipek, and Ursula Purrer.

*Foxes* (1980), directed by Adrian Lyne.

*Fried Green Tomatoes* (1991), directed by Jon Avnet.

*Go Fish* (1994), directed by Rose Troche.

*Goldeneye* (1995), directed by Martin Campbell.

*Homicidal* (1961), directed by William Castle.

*The Incredible True Adventures of Two Girls in Love* (1995), directed by Maria Maggenti.

*Johnny Guitar* (1954), directed by Nicholas Ray.

*The Killing of Sister George* (1968), directed by Robert Aldrich.

*The King* (1968), directed by Looney Bear.

*Lianna* (1982), directed by John Sayles.

*The Living End* (1992), directed by Gregg Araki.

*Little Darlings* (1980), directed by Ronald F. Maxwell.

*Looking for Langston* (1988), directed by Isaac Julien.

*The Member of the Wedding* (1953), directed by Fred Zinneman.

*Mrs. Doubtfire* (1993), directed by Chris Columbus.

*Orlando* (1993), directed by Sally Potter.

*Paper Moon* (1973), directed by Peter Bogdanovitch.

*Personal Best* (1982), directed by Robert Towne.

*Poison* (1991), directed by Todd Haynes.

*Priscilla: Queen of the Desert* (1994), directed by Stephan Elliot.

*Queen Christina* (1933), directed by Rouben Mamoulian.

*Raging Bull* (1980), directed by Martin Scorsese.

*Salmonberries* (1992), directed by Percy Adlon.

*Scorpio Rising* (1964), directed by Kenneth Anger.

*Set It Off* (1996), directed by F. Gary Gray.

*The Silence of the Lambs* (1991), directed by Jonathan Demme.

*Some Like It Hot* (1959), directed by Billy Wilder.

*Something Special* (1986), directed by Paul Schneider.

*Summer Vacation 1999* (1988), directed by Shusuke Kaneko.

*Swoon* (1992), directed by Tom Kalin.

*Terminator* (1984), directed by James Cameron.

*Terminator 2: Judgment Day* (1991), directed by James Cameron.

*Thelma and Louise* (1990), directed by Ridley Scott.

*Times Square* (1980), directed by Alan Moyle.

*Tongues Untied* (1989), directed by Marlon Riggs.

*Tootsie* (1982), directed by Sydney Pollack.

*A Touch of Evil* (1958), directed by Orson Welles.

*Vera* (1986), directed by Sergio Toledo.
*Victor/Victoria* (1982), directed by Blake Edwards.
*The Wild One* (1954), directed by Laslo Beneder.
*Your Heart Is All Mine* (1992), directed by Elke Gotz.

# INDEX

**Judith Halberstam** is Associate Profes-
sor in the Department of Literature at
the University of California, San Diego.
She is the author of *Skin Shows: Gothic
Horror and the Technology of Monsters*
(Duke University Press, 1995).

---

Library of Congress Cataloging-in-
Publication Data
Halberstam, Judith.
Female masculinity / Judith Halberstam.
p.   cm.
Includes bibliographical references and
index.
ISBN 0-8223-2226-9 (alk. paper). —
ISBN 0-8223-2243-9 (pbk. : alk. paper)
1. Lesbians—Identity.  2. Gender identity.
3. Sex role.  4. Transsexualism.
5. Lesbianism in literature.
6. Lesbianism in motion pictures.
7. Gender identity in literature.
I. Title.
HQ75.5.H33   1998
305.48'9664—dc21   98-19527   CIP